Acrylic Flower Decorat

Table of Contents

Painting with Acrylics	2
Synthetic Brushes	3
Surface Preparation	5
Varnishing	6
Shear and Halftone	8
Painting a Rose- Basic Technique	10
Negative Painting	12
Tint and Wash	14
Creating Movement	15
Color Theory and Mixing	18

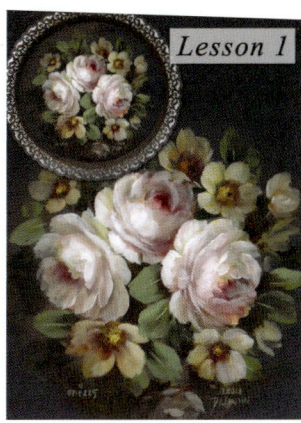

Lesson 1- 23

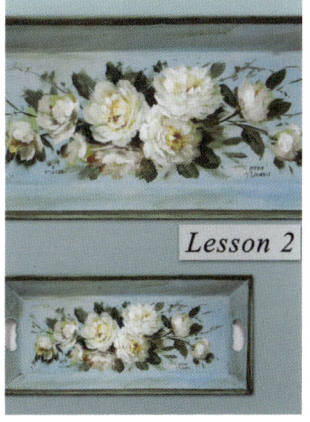

Lesson 2- 41

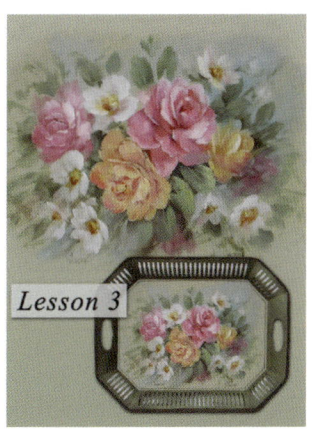

Lesson 3- 56

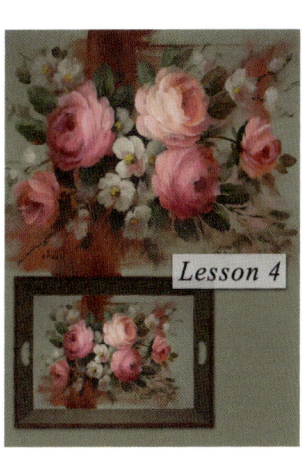

Lesson 4- 74

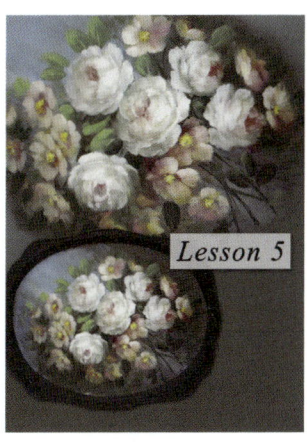

Lesson 5- 92

Published by
Jansen Art Studio Inc.
Elizabethtown, PA USA
David and Martha Jansen

Multimedia Content
Jansen Studio Productions
Ironville, PA USA
Jessica Jansen & Dave Parmer

Copyright Notice

No mechanical reproduction of any form may be used to reproduce the contents in this book. Those who lawfully purchase this book may print the designs and lessons for personal use only. Copies for any other reason are prohibited without written permission from Jansen Art Studio Inc. Teacher can not teach the material in this book without the written permission of Jansen Art Studio Inc. Copying this book or any of its contents without permission violates both US and International law. Those who wish to teach the content of this book must contact Jansen Art Studio Inc. for written permission. Failure to do so constitutes a violation of the copyright. U.S. Title 17 reserved.

Painting With Acrylics for More Life

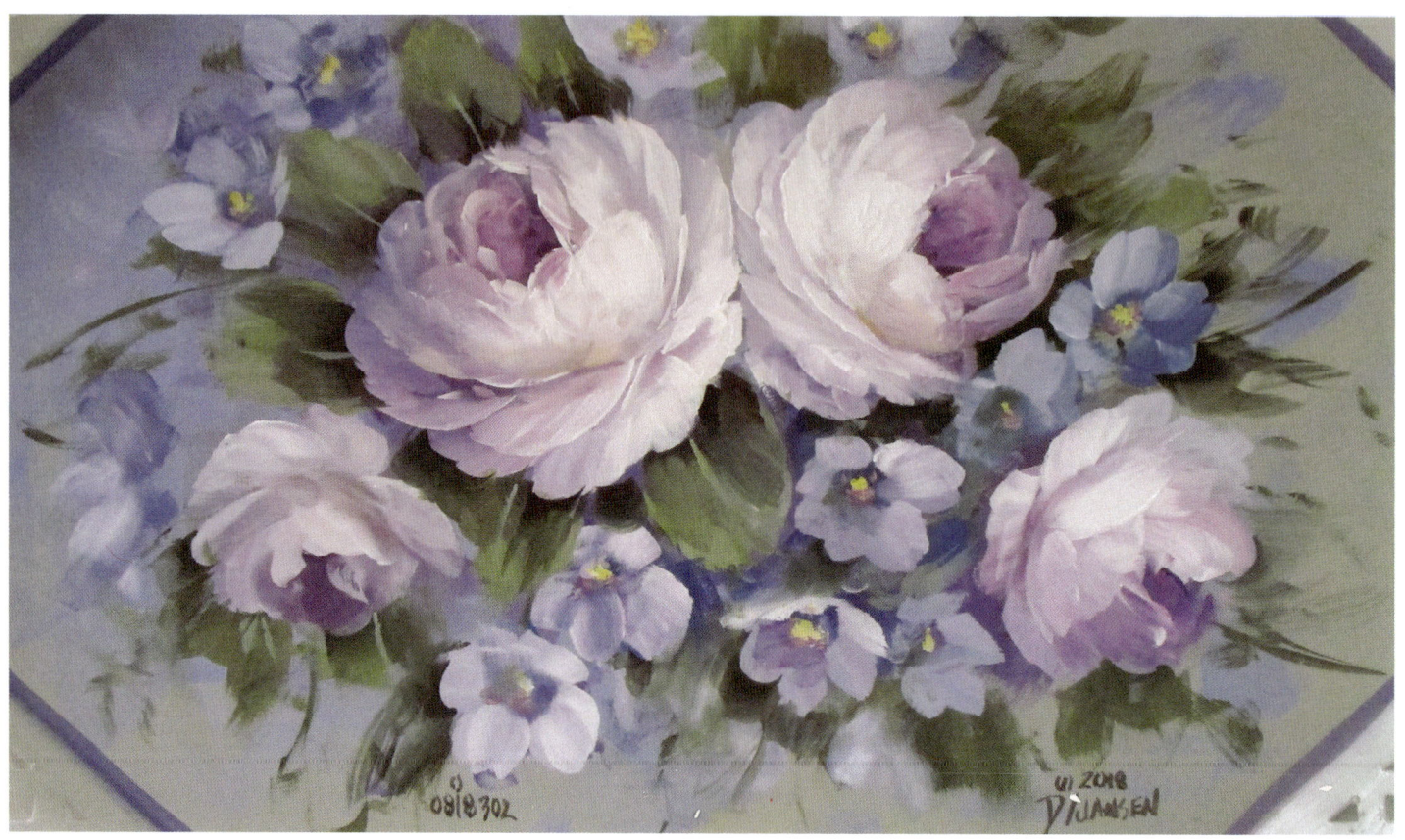

Painted Pure Acrylic. No Extender. Looks Like Oils!

I have been painting now for almost 40 years. I started in the mid 1970's with oil paints. After switching to acrylics for health reasons, I spent years trying to emulate oil techniques. I created a method of "globalizing acrylic colors" to extend the blending time. Then, while studying Alla Prima techniques, it hit me like a brick wall: the artists of old did not blend. Part of this beautiful technique is painting for the "optical blending" properties of the human eye. Thus the expansion of more casual techniques.

By looking closely at John Singer Sargent master paintings, I realized that he is not blending. He is making very controlled tonal marks applied next to one another. The human eye blends them together and that gives life to the painting. It is the controlled tones and use of color that create realism and harmony, not the blending abilities of oils. So why was I trying to make my acrylics blend like oils when the Alla Prima masters did not blend? Artists like Sargent and Cauchois did not have acrylics paints; this medium wouldn't be developed for another 100 years. Rather, they used the materials of their time. They didn't use oils to blend their colors. They applied unblended optical tones.

So if I mix my tones correctly, I don't need to blend. I concentrate on my tones, like an Alla Prima painter, so I don't need to use extended blending techniques. If I feel the need to blend, I mixed the wrong color! I work on mixing the correct color on my palette so that I don't need to blend. What an eye opening realization! I am changing the way I paint. Yes, I use global paints occasionally, but most of the time I am working pure acrylic! With a faster trying time, acrylics do these quick techniques even better!

Global Art Supply Synthetic Brushes

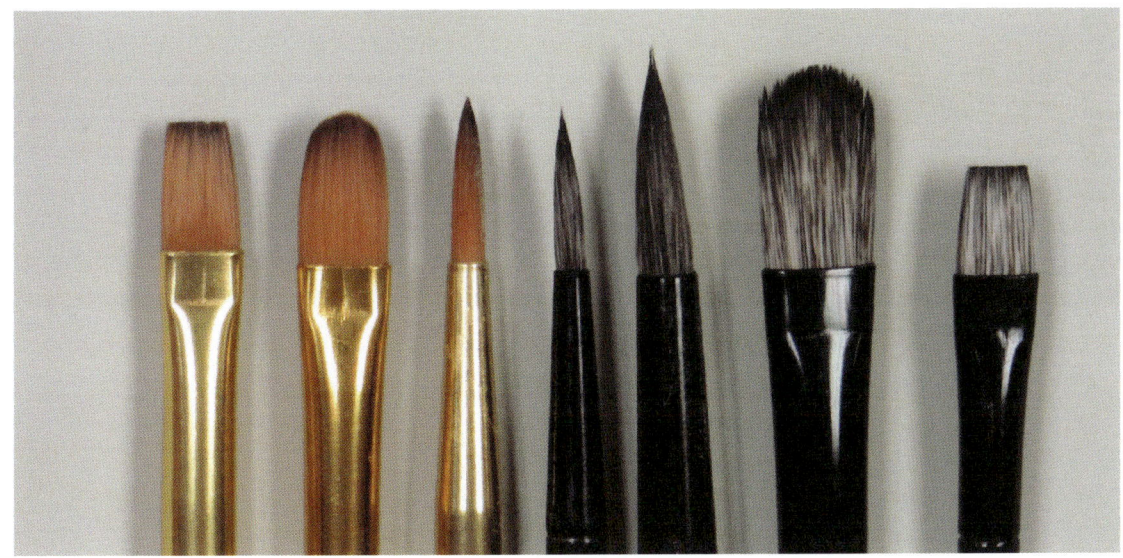

Modern Synthetic Brushes

Synthetic Brushes   **Fusion Brushes**
Flat   Filbert   Round   Rounds   Filbert   Flat

Paint brushes have a rich history, and a little knowledge can help you with the painting techniques. Your choice between brush type, shape, and hair vary with technique and paint. For example, squirrel and sable hair brushes are wonderful brushes for watercolor. The natural hair absorbs a little of the water and keeps the brush wet. This creates better natural flow to the watercolor paint. In general, soft haired brushes are called sables and stiff brushes are called bristles.

Early artists made their own brushes. The most popular hair was from the ear of a cow or ox. Various lengths of hair were combined to soften the movement of the brush. The quantity of hair helped control the "stiffness" of the brush. The brush needed to be soft enough to make a gradual C curve and yet stiff enough to push the paint around. When I first started painting, we had a few bristle brushes but mainly used Red Sables and, if you could afford it, a Kolinsky for detail work.

Throughout history, flat and round brush shapes were the most popular. Both types were used for scroll painting with preference shifting with location. Telemark Rosemalers used flat brushes while Hindeloopen artists used round ones. Then, with the introduction of acrylic paints and the American Rogaland Style of Rosemaling, came the invention of the filbert brush. This was my teacher's favorite brush. He told me that, with a little practice, it would become my favorite brush too because it is the most versatile of the brush shapes. But, at the time, I loved the round brush and would sneak it into his classes. I was sure that someone took a round brush and ran over it with a car to create a filbert shape. But, he was correct! For many years, the filbert was my favorite brush- until Heritage Acrylics and the Fusion Flats.

When developing Heritage Acrylics we expanded our search for high performance brushes. With the help of the FM Brush Company, we tested brush shapes and hairs and designed the Fusion hair. Fusion brushes are acrylic fibers that act like squirrel hair to create a soft look. They don't have the same "snap" as the synthetics but the soft hair makes a beautiful lost and found edges. These brushes are perfect tools for casual Rosemaling and, because of their versatility, are a vital part of the "Paint It Simply" techniques.

Brushes and paint work hand in hand. The brush is made to move the paint around. As acrylic paint technology advanced and became more popular, new types of synthetic hairs were developed to work with the new paints. Softer synthetics were created in the 1990's that allowed for better blending and finer details. The goal was to find fibers that would emulate the 3 main classes of brushes: the sable (kolinsky), the bristle (hog's hair) and the squirrel hair.

Kolinsky Sable

These hairs do not come from a sable but rather from the tail of a type of mink from Siberia and northeastern China. The hair has "spring" and "snap" and follows the hand very well. It is excellent for fine liner details. However, it is quite expensive.

Red Sable
This brush is made from a member of the weasel family. The hair is softer than most other hairs. The brush is soft, has a relatively good "snap", and is considered a good alternative to the more expensive Kolinsky.

Squirrel
This brush is perfect for watercolors and thin washes of paint. It works well for liner details, but the paint needs to be thin because the brush doesn't have as much "snap" or "spring" when responding to the movement of the hand. It is an excellent alternative to the more expensive Kolinsky.

Hog Bristle
Today most high quality hog bristle brushes come from China. However, during the 1800's they came from Germany and many crossed over into the Norwegian schools. Hog's hair has excellent resilience and is used to push thick paint around the surface.

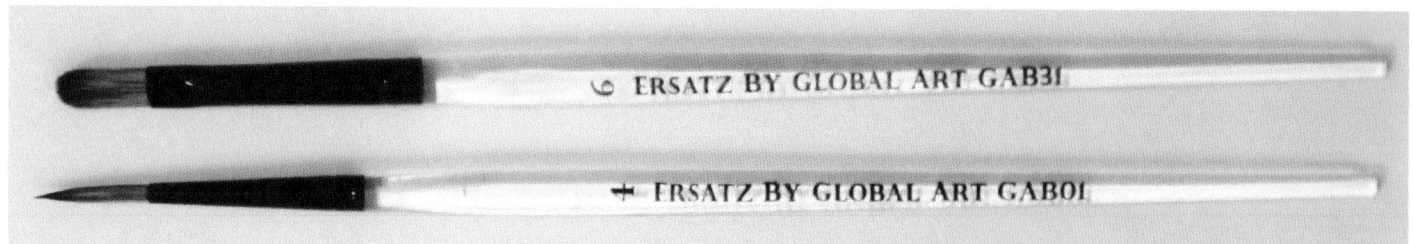

Global Art Supply Fusion Filbert and Round- Casual Painting

As you approach these lessons, think about the shape of the brush and how you will use it. Synthetic and fusion hairs are available in flat, round, and filbert shapes. Each shape will give a different look to the flowers. Finding your favorite one is part of creating your own style. Overall, flats can be used to paint every style of flowers you can imagine. I tend to use the filbert brush when I want to paint roses and blossoms that have a more "stroked" look to them. This comes from many years of folk art and Rosemaling with a filbert brush. I perceive the filbert brush for "strokes' more than I do the flat.

There is large connection between the development of paints, hairs of the brushes and painting techniques. If you want to expand your style and create new looks, we need to look at what brushes do and how they do it. Maybe you will use your brush differently. There are so many things to try!

Preparation of Metal and Metal Trays for This Book.

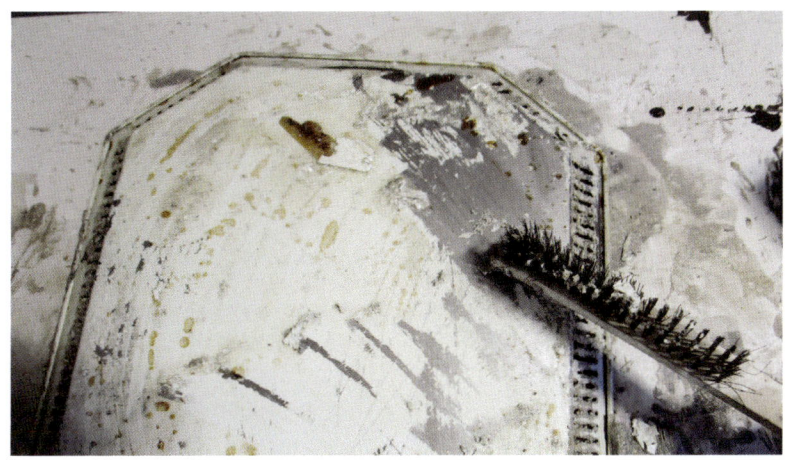

There are many ways to recondition old metal trays and I prefer having them sand-blasted by a professional.

Another method is using a chemical paint stripper from a local hardware store. **Follow the label instructions and ALWAYS wear protective gear.** This method works well but it is very messy and requires careful clean up. Wire brushes and paint scrapers help remove soften paint layers.

Next, wash the tray with soap and water. I also use a cleanser such as Comet. Dry and sand with 180 emery cloth. Emery cloth is for sanding metal surfaces prior to painting. It is not expensive.

Treat rust spots with a rust neutralizer such as Naval Jelly or Rustoleum's Rust Neutralizer. I also like Ospho which you can get from your auto parts store.

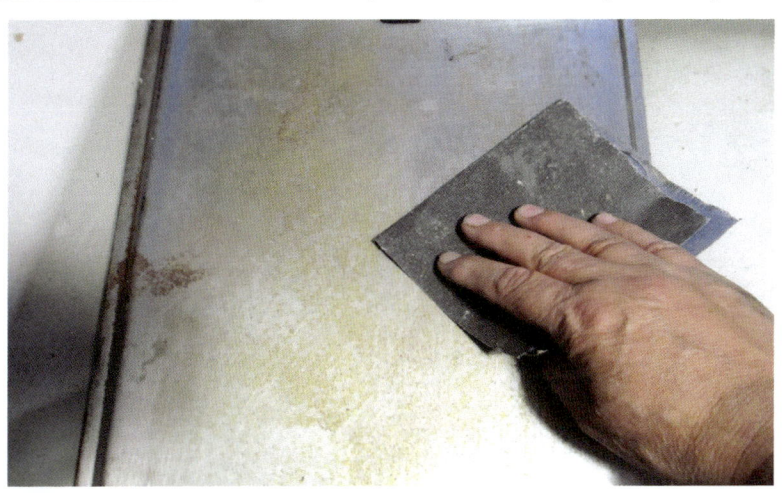

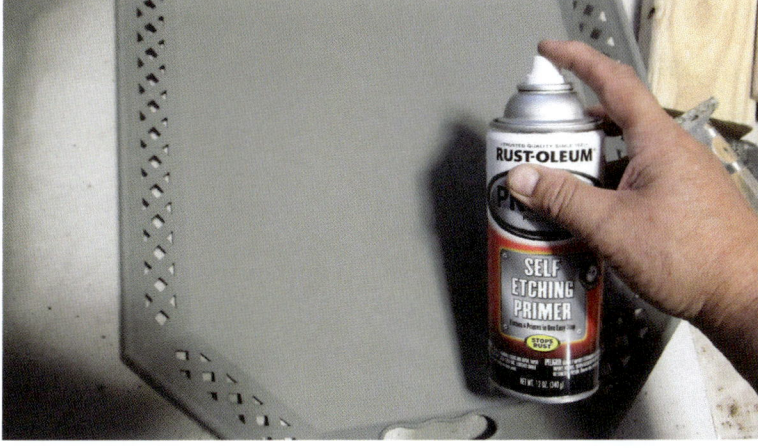

Prime the surface prior to base coating. I use two methods:
First is Rustoleum's Self Etching Primer. This product should be sprayed outside. **Please follow the label precautions.** I am very careful when I use it. This primer stops rust and chemically etches into the metal. Let it dry 24 hours before base coating. Paint directly on the primer with Heritage Acrylics. They make a strong bond.

Another way is using MultiSurface Sealer. Heritage MultiSurface Sealer is a great way to prep for painting. If you have any rust, neutralize it. Then give 1 or 2 coats of Heritage MultiSurface Sealer. Let dry 24 hours and base coat. No mess, no chemical smell, and very safe to use. Make sure you coat all surfaces before base coating.

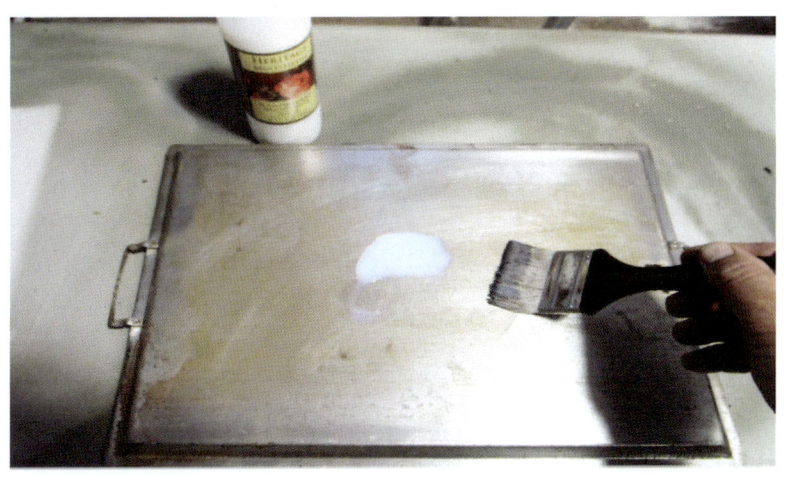

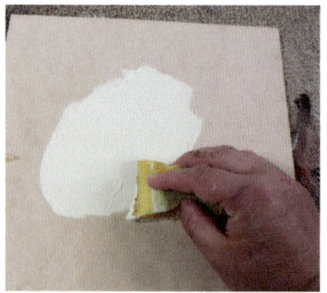

Preparing Wood Panels

If you are going to use wood panels for these lessons, please follow the instructions below. If your using metal trays, please see the previous page for special preparation instructions.

Step 1

Mix desired color as shown in each lesson. Add an equal amount of Multi-Surface Sealer and mix. Apply with soft brush or sponge.

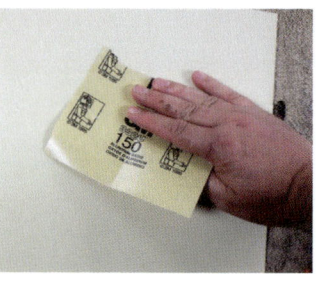

Step 2

Sand the surface with 150 to 220 grit sand paper to smooth. Do not use too fine a paper (such as 400) because you will make the surface too slick. You can work directly on the surface now, or you can give a second coat.

Step 3

Transfer design or sketch with pencil. Follow next direction for each lesson. Give the surface a light transparent coat of paint and Extender.

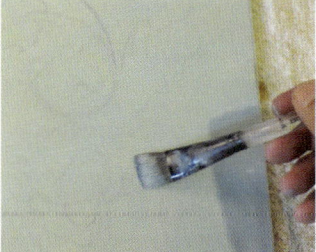

Step 4

When coating the surface do not have too much paint or too thin (watery) paint. This will make painting the design difficult.

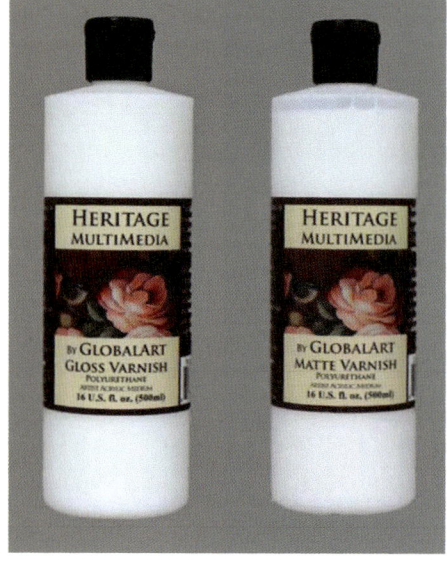

Varnishing Your Finished Painting

Heritage Varnishes are a clear, non-yellowing, resin-based polyurethane varnish. They brush on smoothly and are self-leveling so that the artist doesn't have to stroke and stroke to smooth it out. It gives the quality protection of a Polyurethane varnish with the ease of application of an acrylic.

Heritage Varnish is excellent for both interior and exterior use. When dry, it creates a hard, durable satin, gloss or matte finish that is ideal for artwork on a variety of surfaces. It dries quickly in 5 to 10 minutes, depending on weather conditions. You can slow the drying time by adding Extender Medium to the Varnish. For best results, thin the varnish with a little to equal amount of water. This makes application easier. Mix varnishes to create desired sheen. To make a Satin finish mix the Gloss and Matte Varnishes 1 to 1.

Heritage Varnish is compatible with all Heritage paints and mediums. It is non-toxic and cleans up with soap and water. Because it is an acrylic product, it should not be used over oil based products.

Directions: Surface should be dust free and completely dry. Shake well then let the bottle stand for a few minutes. Apply with a brush or sponge. Varnish is easier to apply if thinned with water. Apply with a wet brush. Mist the surface with water if varnish begins to dry before you have finished the surface. You can lengthen the drying time by adding Extender Medium. Additional coats can be applied as soon as the last coat is dry. Rinse brush thoroughly after use. Clean up with soap and water. Two coats are sufficient for indoor use, three coats for exterior use.

How to Use Heritage MultiMedia Polyurethane Varnish

Apply Heritage varnish with a large soft brush. Dampen brush with water. You can thin the varnish with a little water before using if desired.

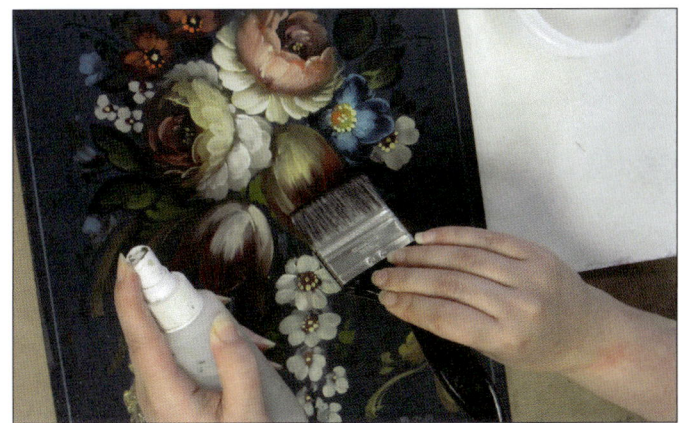

If the varnish start to dry or drag too much as you are applying it, you can lightly mist the surface with clean water and keep varnishing.

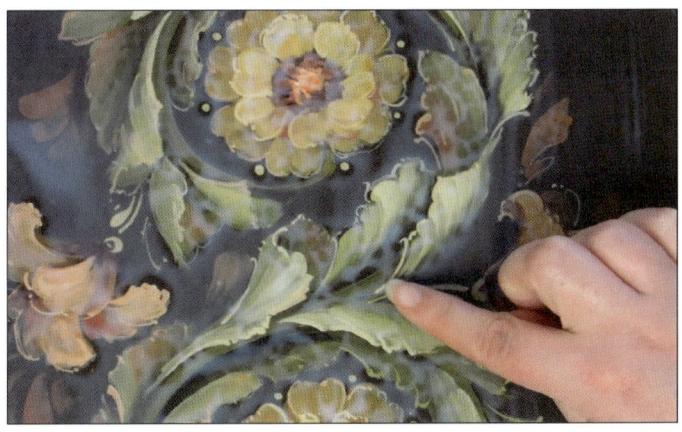

If you apply too much varnish the surface will "alligator". This is where the varnish pulls away from the surface. Too much varnish is the cause.

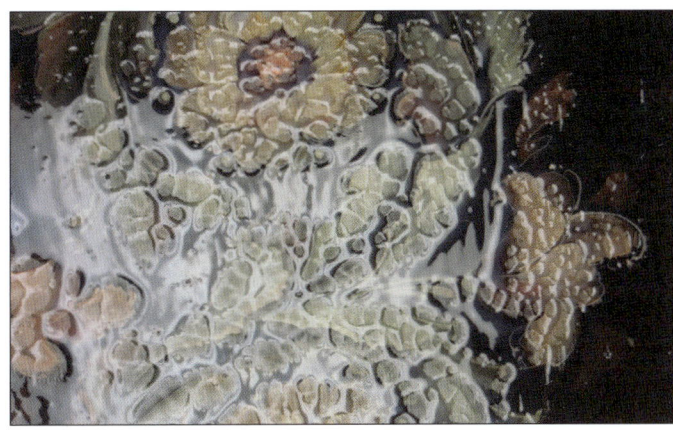

Holding the piece at an angle you can clearly see the "alligatoring". The best way to apply varnish is with 2 to 4 thin coats. Not too much all at once.

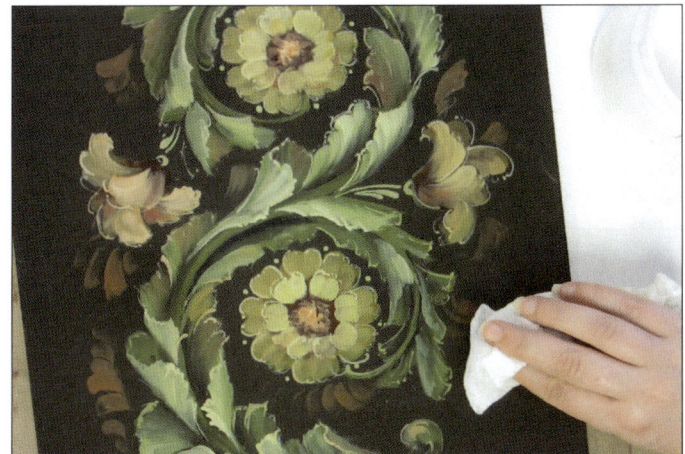

To correct the "alligator" surface, wipe off the excess while the varnish is wet. You can use a moist paper towel for this.

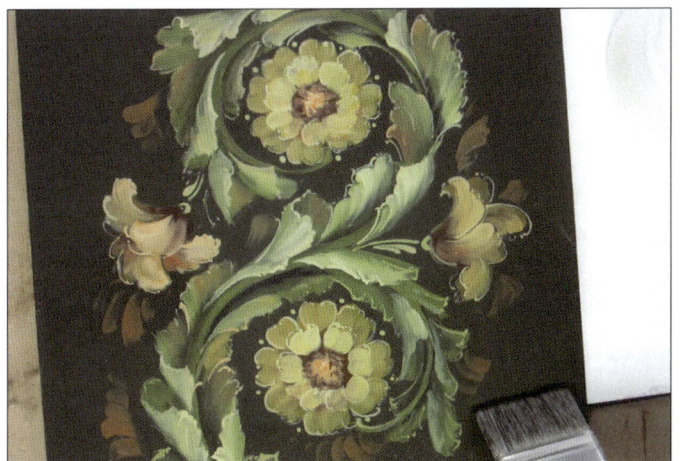

Using the soft brush, smooth out the remaining vanish. You can mist lightly with water if it starts to dry before you smooth. Use thin coats.

Value Shear Technique- Halftone Technique

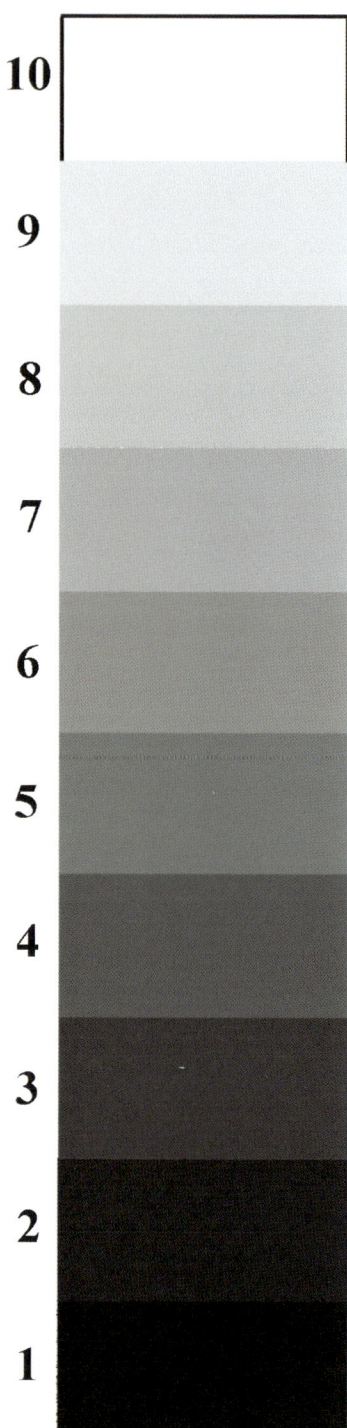

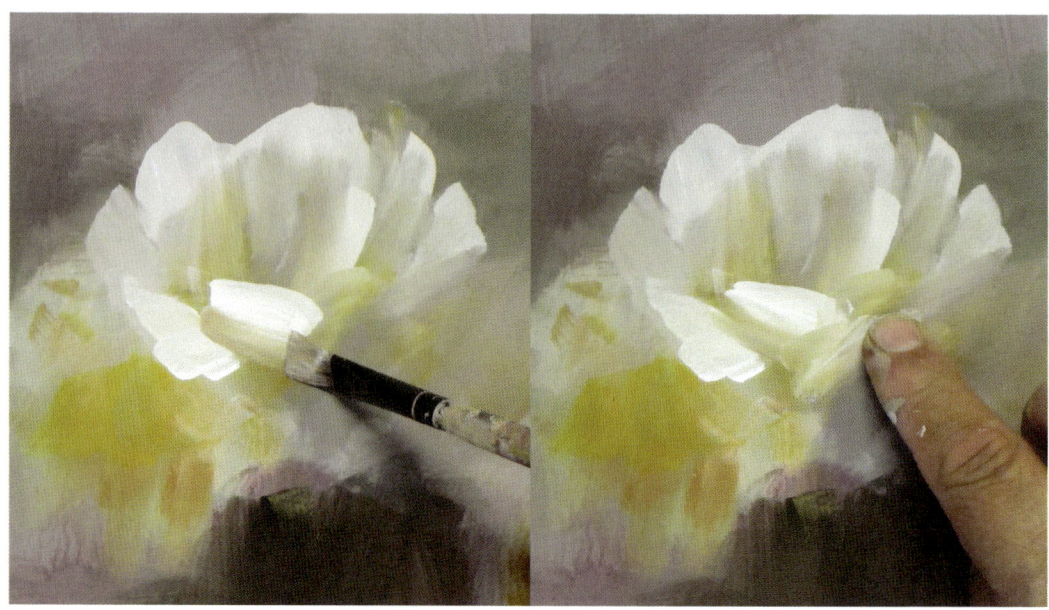

This is an amazing technique. I want to utilize the advantages of acrylics in historic oil techniques. Many artists didn't blend! Where did all this blending come from? For this technique follows along the lines of Alla Prima color marks and the broken color techniques that were done with oils. Colors were applied to "optically blend" but not physically blended on the surface. The viewers eye blends the colors when looked at from the appropriate distance. To accomplish this effect, we must understand value progression and the eye's ability to optically blend.

Looking closely at a great alla prima artist's brush calligraphy shows us distinct application of color tones. Many applied the color passages in quick, but careful, "marks." Stepping back from the painting, softens the effect of the individual strokes. Blend the tones together too much the object loses interest. Color passages tend to flatten out as you step back. By adjusting and fixing a stroke, the energy and power of the initial statement diminishes. Plan your color marks so that they sit in the right place when viewing the painting at a slight distance. Step away from a painting regularly to check your progress. If the painting was on a wall, how far away would you stand to look at it?

A vital part of this technique is awareness of the value scale. In this book, I never apply colors that are more than 2 values apart. Look at the images above. In this example, on a white rose, I base the shape a value 8. Then I strike a highlight mark as a value 10. Then I push the color with my finger to make a middle value (9). Because the applied tones are close together, it is easy to push them and make the 9. If the values are too far apart, the middle value is impossible to make. The goal in these painting is to control the value scale. A rose is a value scale. Always work 2 values apart. Base an object with a value 6, highlight with a value 8, and use your finger to make a value 7. If you have difficulties- check your value scale!

Value Shear Technique - Halftone Technique

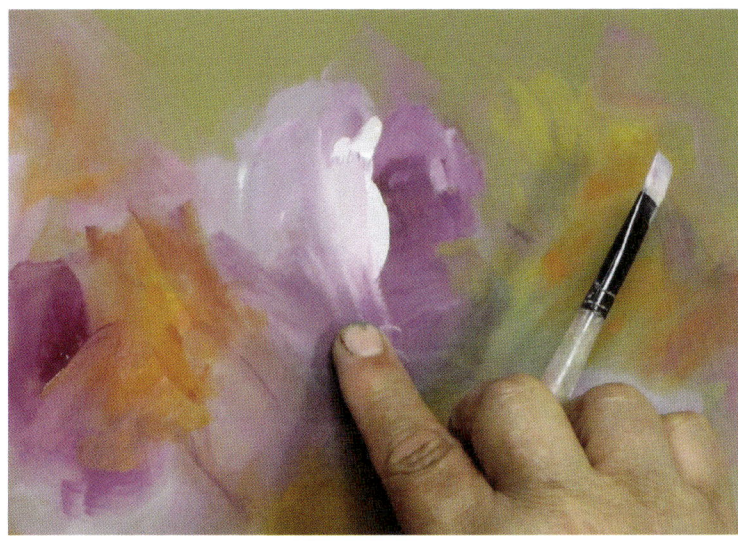

Shearing the Paint

Halftone Used to Reduce Value Contrast

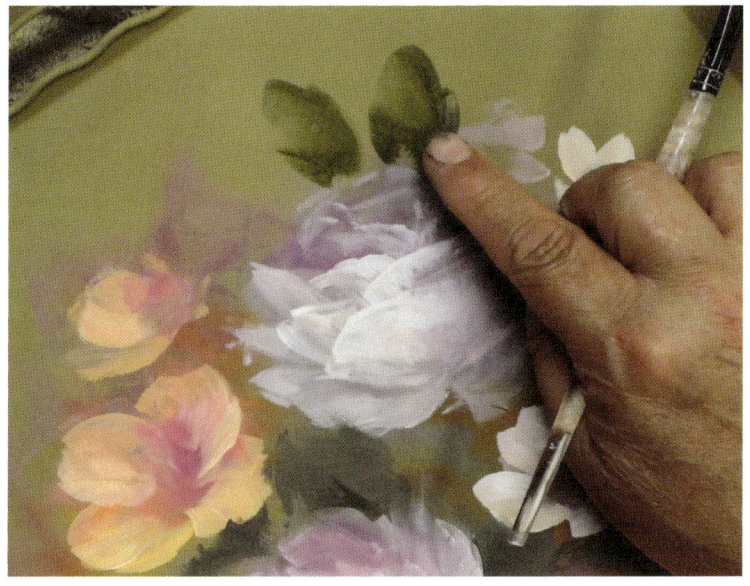

One Color Shear. Pushing Hard

As you paint a flower, work up and down the value scale. That is the secret. Never work more than 2 values apart and painting flows naturally. Mix the values on your palette. If you feel the need to blend, you are using values that are too far apart or out of place.

The **shear** of the paint is its ability to move across a surface. For the value shear technique, we push/pull color across the surface, removing some, and allowing the color underneath to show through. For example, apply the light color on top of the base color (2 values apart). Then push your finger along the paint's bottom edge. Removing some of the light color allows the base color to show through. This creates a softened, blended look without blending. How much you push off depends on how much tonal contrast you need. You never need to blend if you are within 2 values of each other. The eye optically blends them.

The **halftone** is used when colors are more than 2 values apart. You mix a tone that is 1/2 between the light and dark ones that you applied. In the second photo, I stroked the top light petals on the base coat of the rose. There are more than 2 values between the base coat and highlight. So, I apply a value that is 1/2 between the light and dark tones. Then I push the colors with my finger to soften the effect. Always watch your value scale!

Many times, often in the leaves, I intentionally apply a tone that is more than a value difference and push REALLY HARD to remove some of the paint. (Left Photo). Control the effect by watching how long you let the color dry before you shear off the paint. For this example, I used a green that is darker than the base coat of the tray. I push (shear) off the paint on the light side (left) to create the highlight. Push hard to make more values.

Painting A Rose- Basic Technique- Establishing Structure

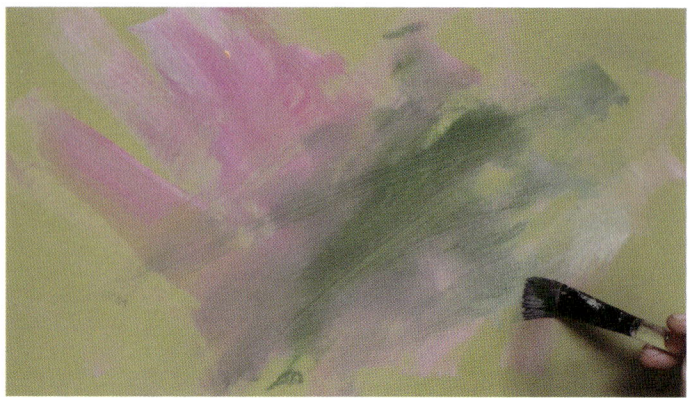

Step 1- Determine the Type of Rose.
Casually base in the area the rose will occupy. You should have an idea of the type of rose. Open or closed. Casual or stroke. Move the color in a circular motion for a round rose.

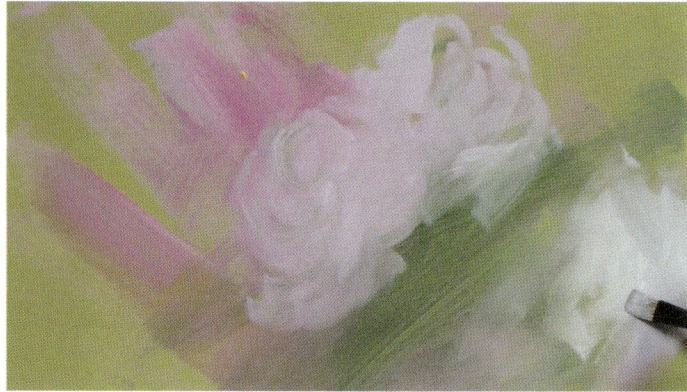

Step 2- Determine the Size and Placement.
Next determine the size and gaze of the rose. I usually do this by starting the 3 circles: the inside throat, the bowl, and the area for the reaching petals. Keep this soft using my finger.

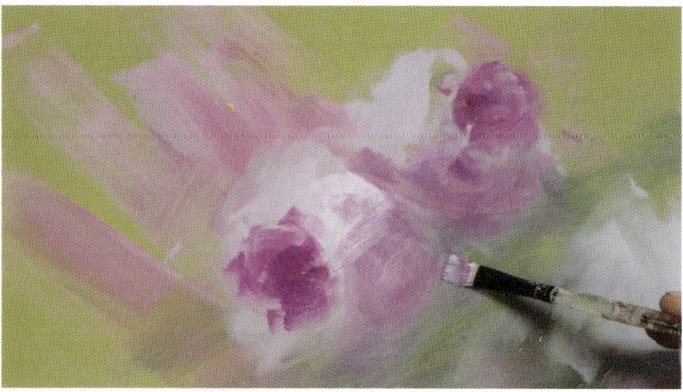

Step 3- Determine Light Source and Shadow.
I next refine or determine the shadow side of the rose. This indicates the light source. Cool and darken one side of the rose so you can see the shadows. Soften the shadows and incorporate them into the rose.

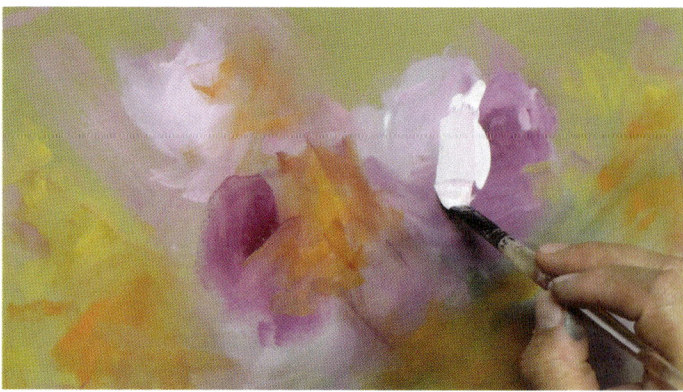

Step 4- Determine Warm and Cool Areas.
Warm the color and lighten it so you can begin to apply the light colored areas. This usually is the most forward part of the rose. Soften the color as you go around the rose to the back side.

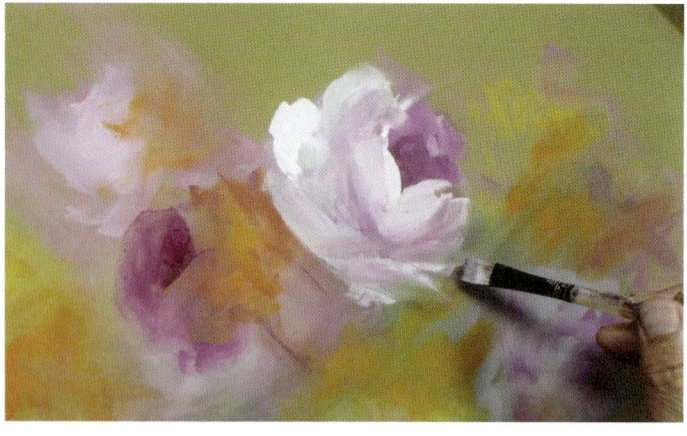

Step 5- Define the 3 Circles with Color.
Add the area for the reaching petals. This now clearly defines the 3 circles of the rose. Throat, bowl and reaching petals. Keep soft.

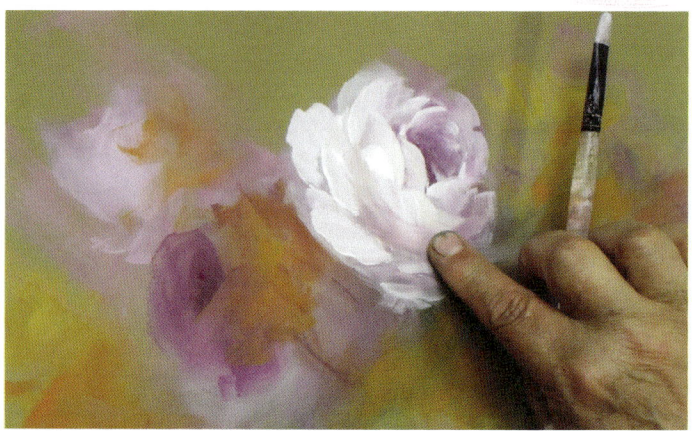

Step 6- Establish the Movement and Petals.
Use finger or a soft brush to move the color in the circular motion for the bowl and in and out for the reaching petals. The rose is now ready to decorate with desired petals.

Casual Rose Shapes with Acrylic

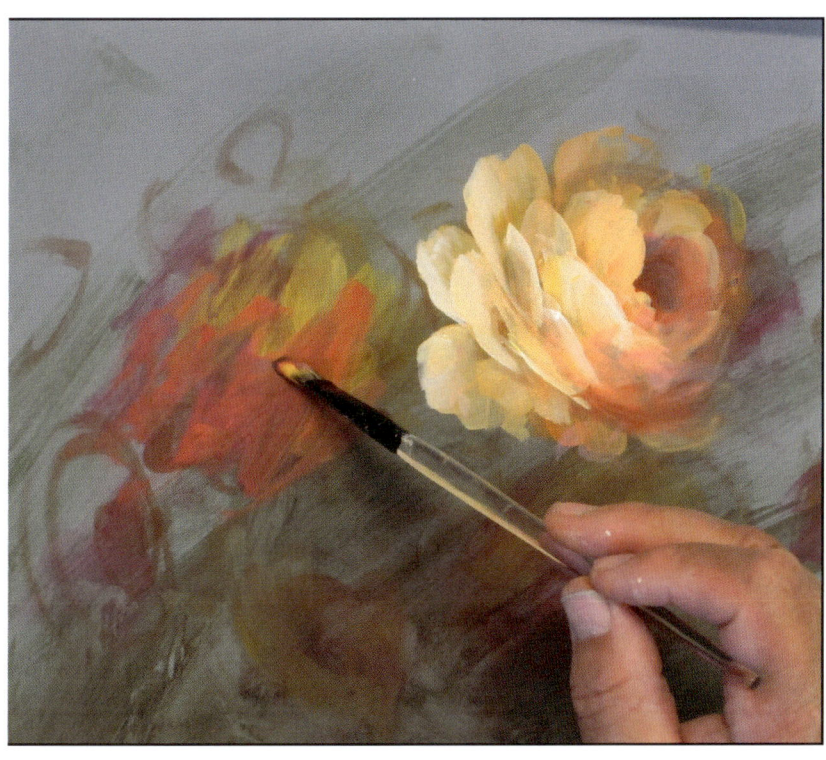

I love this technique! It allows me to see the basic rose and to set the light source for the composition. By keeping the colors soft and casual, you can change the shapes and light later on without too much trouble. Start with simple colors to shape the roses and help you see the composition.

Do not begin with a lot of contrast. Start with gentle shadows. Gradually build toward the desired contrast level.

When I start the rose, I mottle a color that is just a little lighter or darker than the basecoat color of the surface. Then, mottle a soft, cool shadow color that is a couple values darker than the first rose color. I keep the darkest part of the center just a little darker than the shadow color of the rose bowl. This keeps the contrast inside of the rose and directs the eye into the rose and toward the bowl shadow. Contrast directs the eye. We need to add it slowly.

Ghost Flowers and Shapes for More Color Movement

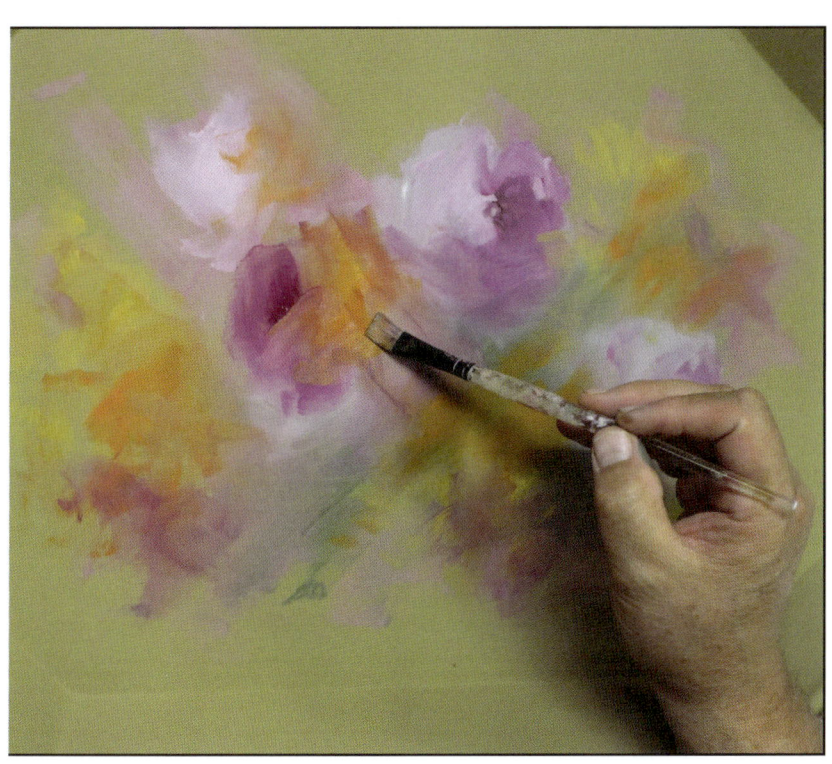

"Ghost flowers" are colorful flowers without a lot of form or shape. They add a tremendous amount of interest to your design. Not only do they move color throughout the design for greater harmony, they also add visual interest in areas of the composition without distracting from your center of interest.

Start by casual movements of the brush. If you are painting small flowers, keep the movements small. Vary the colors and the pressure on the brush to make various shapes. Try to paint the forms of the flowers without the details. Try squinting down your eyes to see the forms without the edges. I imagine the movement of flowers forms without the petal details. Focus on color movement and the flow of design forms.

Negative Painting the Edges of a Petal

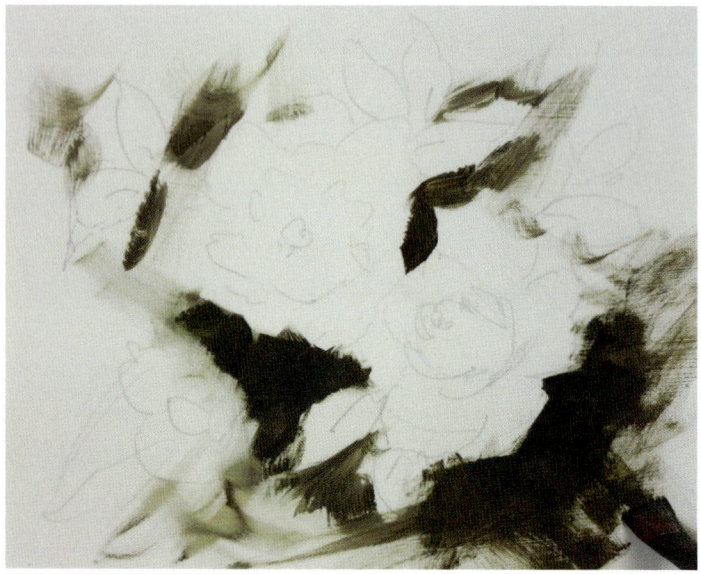

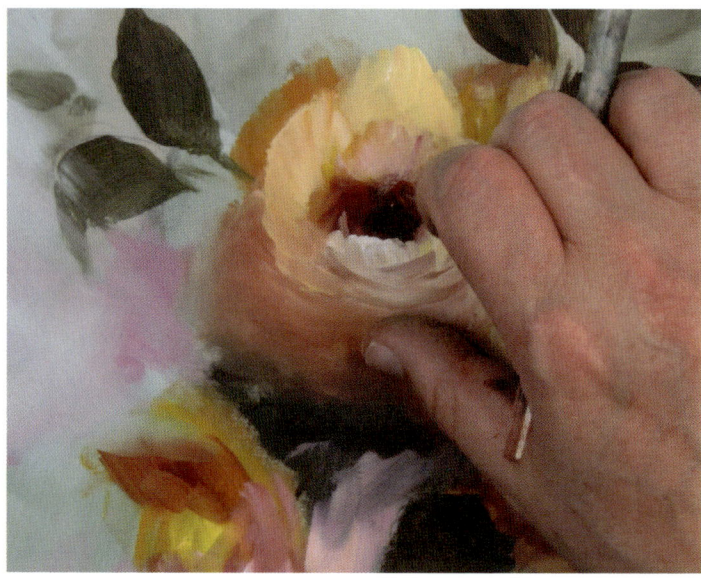

Negative painting is painting around an object with the background color. You can also remove paint layers to reveal the color underneath. For these lessons, we use the background to shape the roses and give them form. This technique is used by many china painters but works well with these acrylics.

The most important part about the technique is to create an in/out movement to the petals as shown in this photo. This give the softness and movement to the flower. By using your finger to push color, you take a little background color into the petals and create a transparent effect.

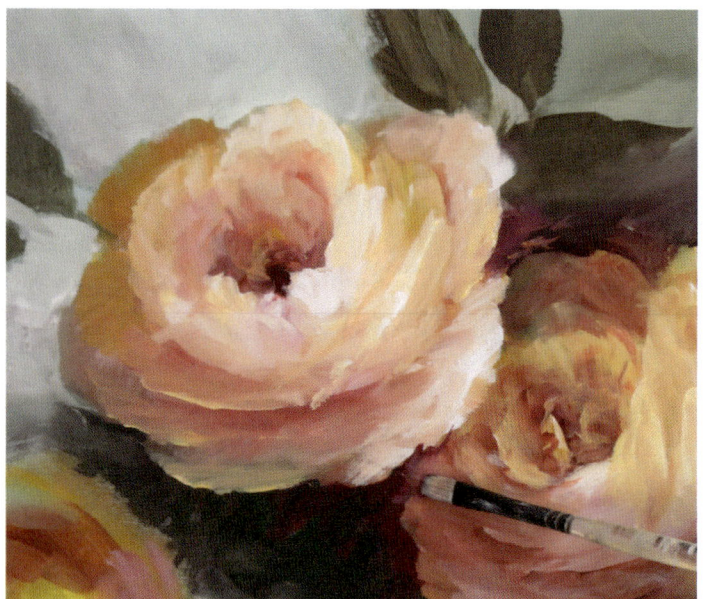

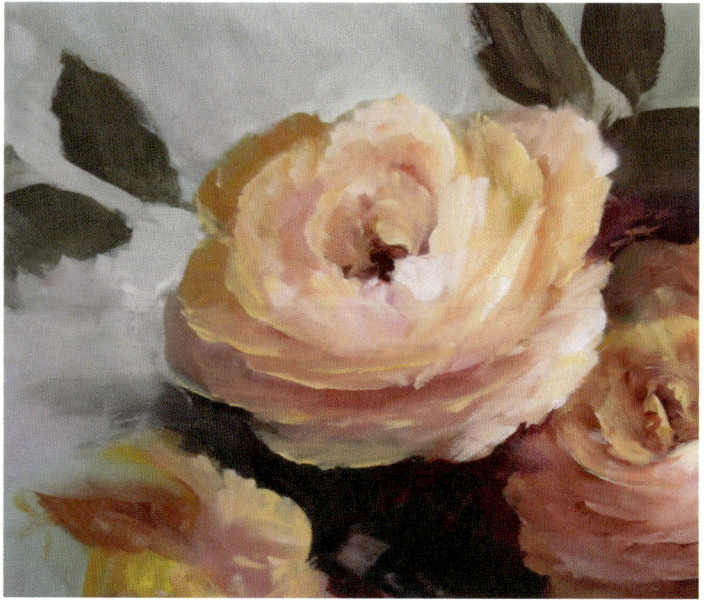

Start with soft edges or create a "blurry" look to the roses. Then slowly define the edges. Smaller touches of other colors can be used in the background to begin the shapes. Remember to subtly vary the color tones. Color movement is key to a beautiful composition of roses. When you negative paint the edges of the petals don't just use one color.

The difference between the background color and floral tones controls the contrast. In some lessons, I use a light background and darker rose petals. Here I am painting dark leaf greens around the lighter petals. Both options work well. As a rose painter, you have a wide variety of techniques. Use them all!

Negative Painting to Create Refined Edges

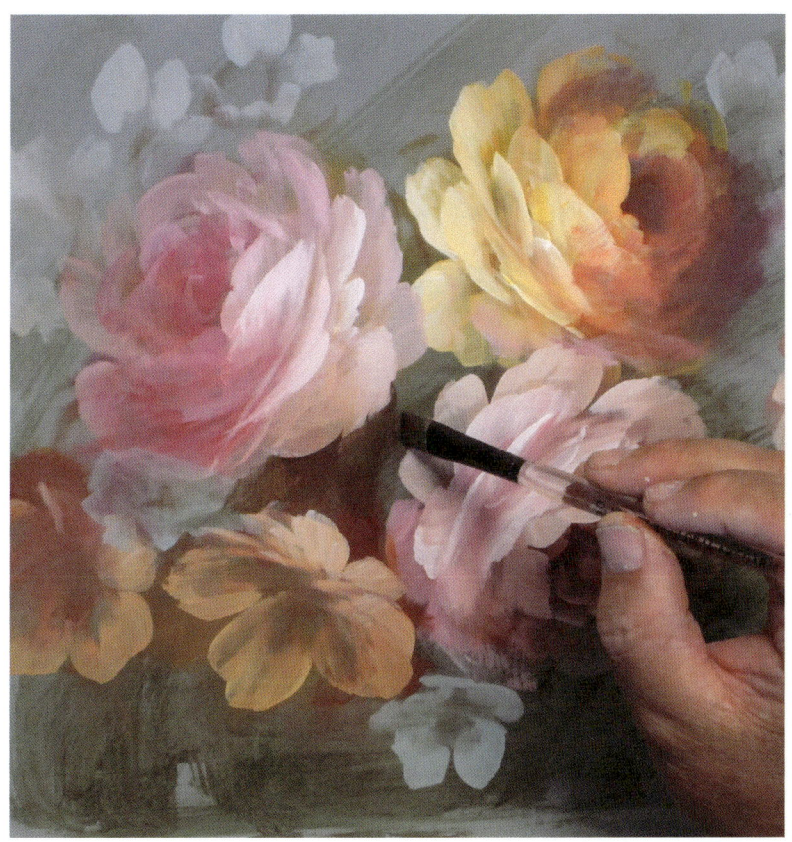

I use a lot of negative Painting. I paint for a casual feeling and use Negative Painting at near the end to refine the edges. Small touches quickly create contrast and petal variations. Often, I paint a flower very casually and loose. I capture a feeling and then refine the details with negative painting. So I intentionally paint the petals more loose and without form. I refine it later with the negative technique.

This works well when you want to make transparent rose petals on a rose. Don't paint the edge of the petal. Let the color run off into the background. After you have finished most of the painting, come back with a slightly darker and cooler version of the background and refine the petal edge. This give a little transparency to the petal. I like it!

Creating a Petal with the Petal Stroke

For most of the florals in this book, I use the petal stroke to build form. Relax the technique and use it casually for different situations. Here is the basic premise:

Each petal is made with 3 strokes of the brush. I start on the petal's light side. With thick paint, apply the first stroke. Curve slightly to make the outside edge of the petal. The second stroke is in the middle and straight down. The third stroke makes the other side of the petal and is slightly curve out to make the edge of the petal.

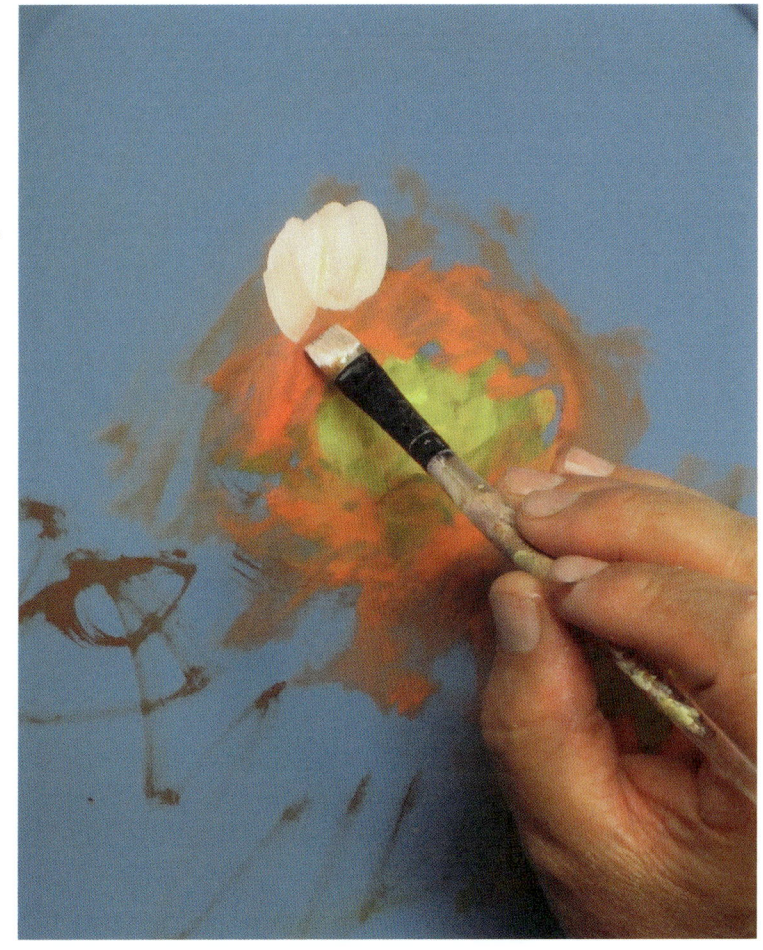

Vary this basic technique as needed. Sometimes, I reload the brush with more paint between strokes. Sometimes, I run out of paint on one side to create a lost edge. I use more pressure on large outside petals and light pressure on smaller petals. Try stroking one side with the chisel of the brush. Try stroking with the brush's corner. Practice variations of the same stroke progression.

Tint Wash Technique to Hue Shift or Restate Colors

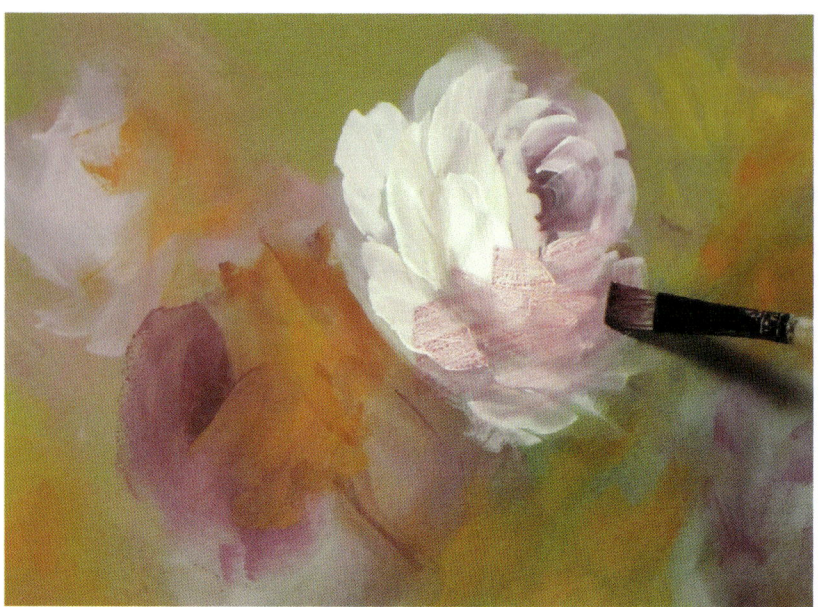

Another great variation is the tint wash technique. It is extremely easy with acrylics if you use the shear technique or incorporate the colors like I do here.

On a dry flower, apply a thin wash of the desired color. Use water to thin the color. Here I am cooling one side of the rose with very thin wash of Quinacridone Violet. Lightly brush over the cool side but don't try to make the color smooth.
That will happen later.

Next, wipe the brush and pick up a light value color from the light side of the rose. Remember to stay within 2 values. Use very thin light color because light colors can be more opaque because they contain more white. Lightly go over the tint of Quinacridone Violet. You do not need to go over all of it, just a little on the light side. Wipe your brush and drag though the color. It incorporates the color into the rose. Place the light color on top of the tint.

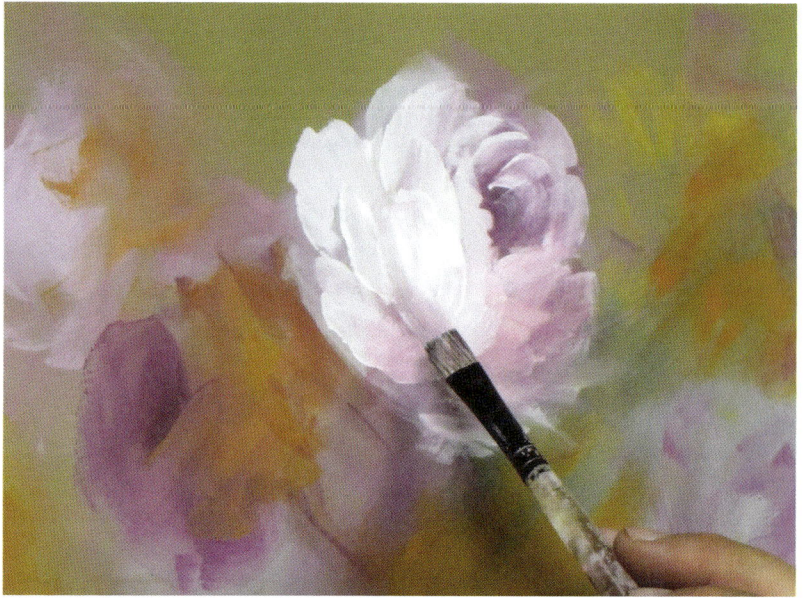

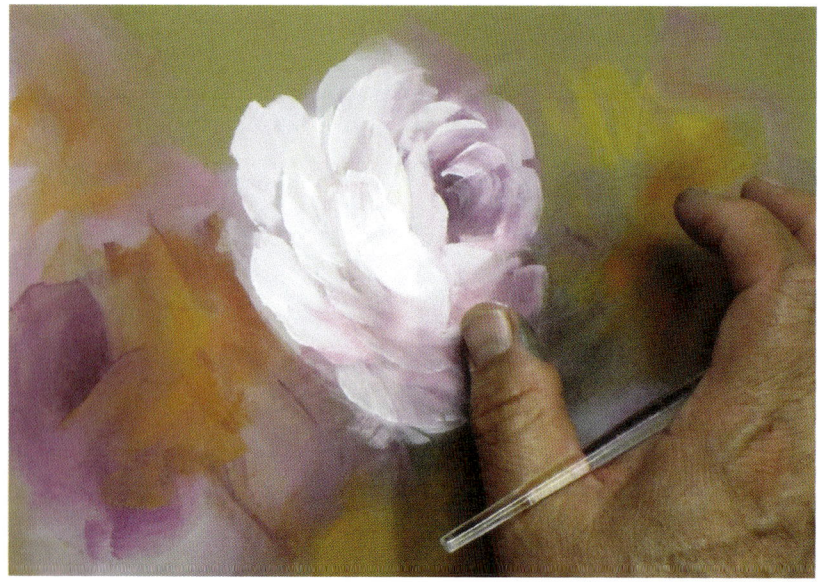

I don't always do this step, but many times I will in order to keep the rose casual. I soften the movement of the tint with my finger. Your finger softens in a completely different way than the brush. Usually without the defined edges that the brush can give. Move your finger with the rounding of the bowl or the reaching of the petals. Soften for movement. Do not look at this as blending. I am "incorporating" the tint. I am moving color to push the tint into the flower. I do not blend.

Movement of the Bowl to Make a Beautiful Rose

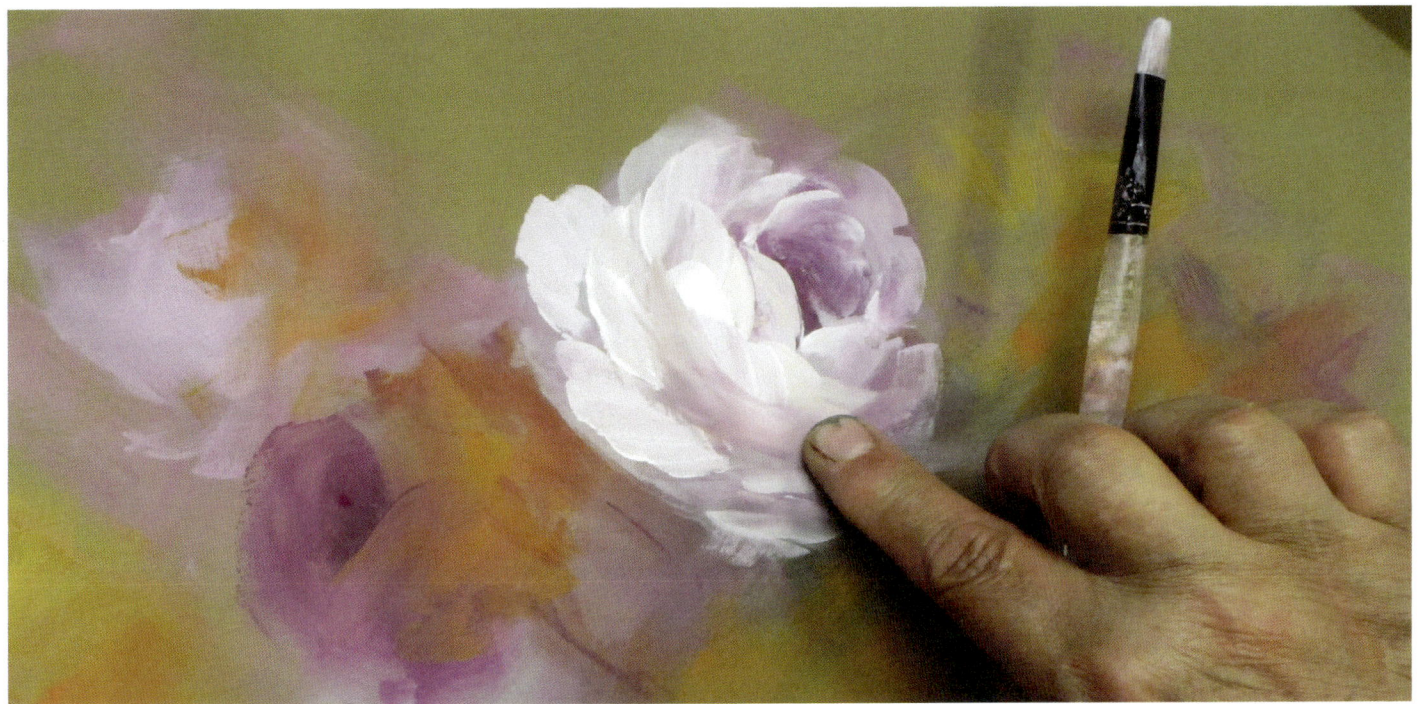

The one thing in all the painting concepts that completely changed my roses is the "movement of the bowl". For many years, I stroked petals on roses and they always looked a little stiff to me. Why? Because I painted over painted them. Many times, in trying to make the perfect petal, I was actually making the rose worse. I was making it stiff. The worse thing you can do on a casual rose is to over paint the darn thing. And, it happens a lot as we practice.

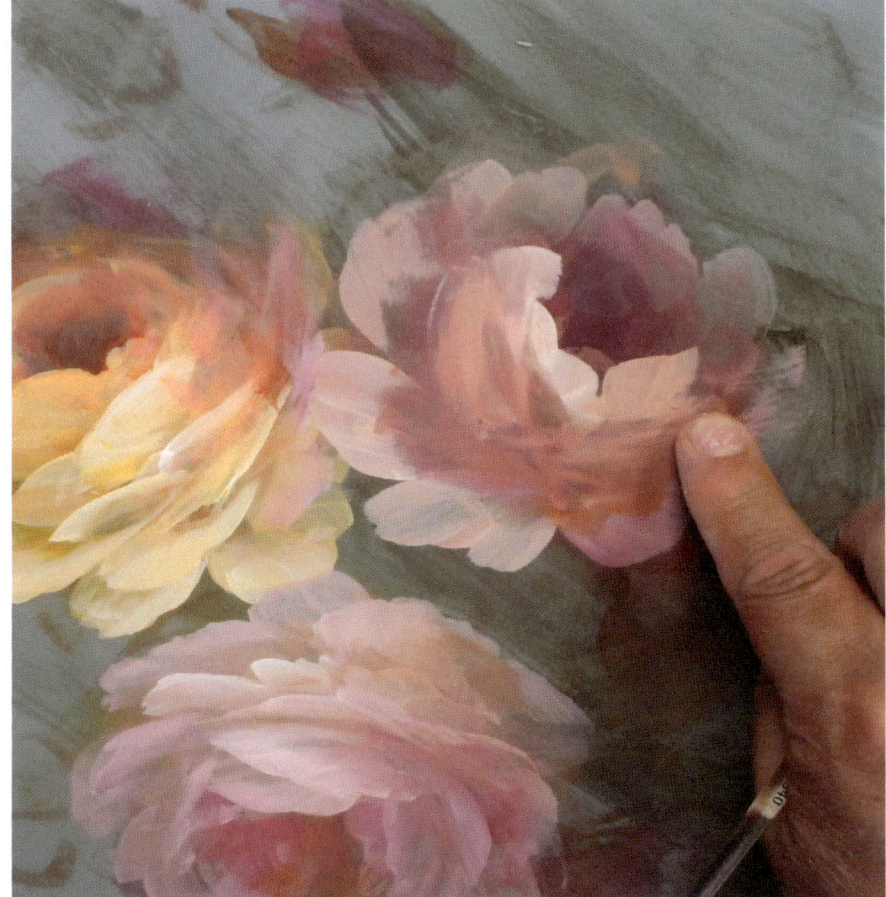

The best thing you can do on a casual rose is to paint the suggestion of movement. I don't really paint petals on my roses anymore. I paint movement and use the edge of a brush to suggest the petals.

The more casual I want a rose, the more casual I need to make the movement. Instead of the brush, I will use my finger so I have movement within definite petal edges.

The bowl of the rose is the most important part and should always rounded on the bottom. A round bowl makes a round rose. The petals reach out from the bowl and move in and out. Keep it that simple. Push round on the bottom of the bowl and in and out to make the petals. Movement!

Creating Edges with Interest

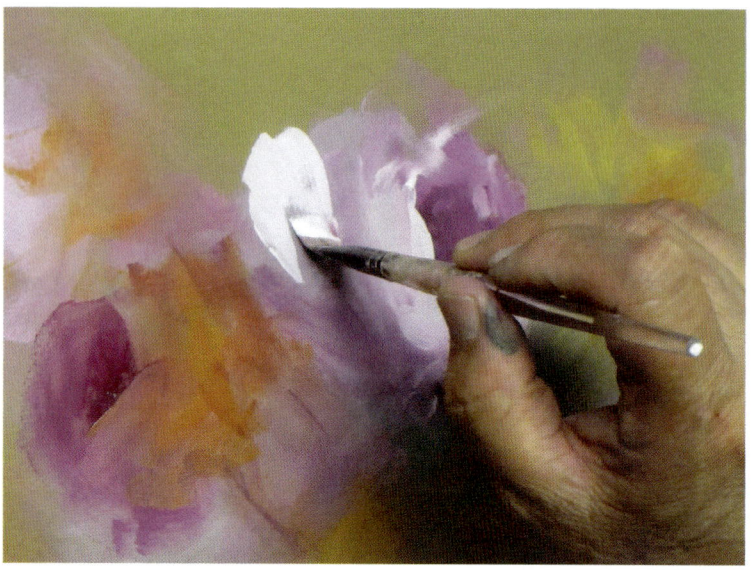
Lightly hold brush like you do your pencil.

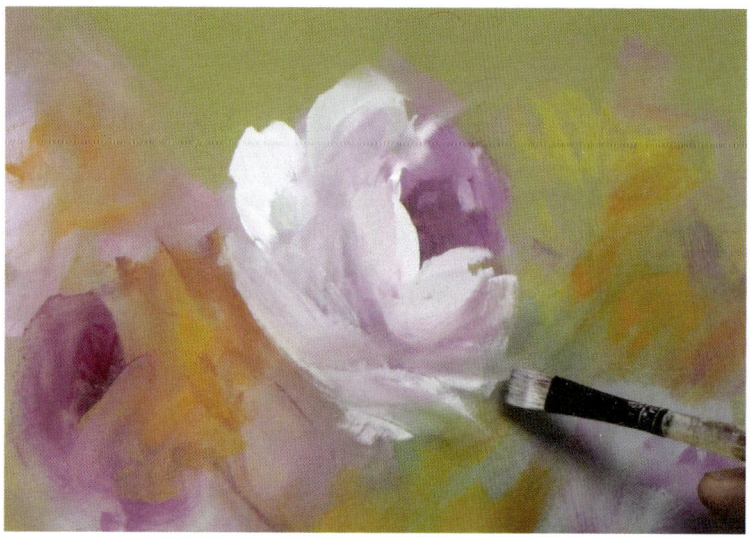
Hold back on handle pull out for soft petals

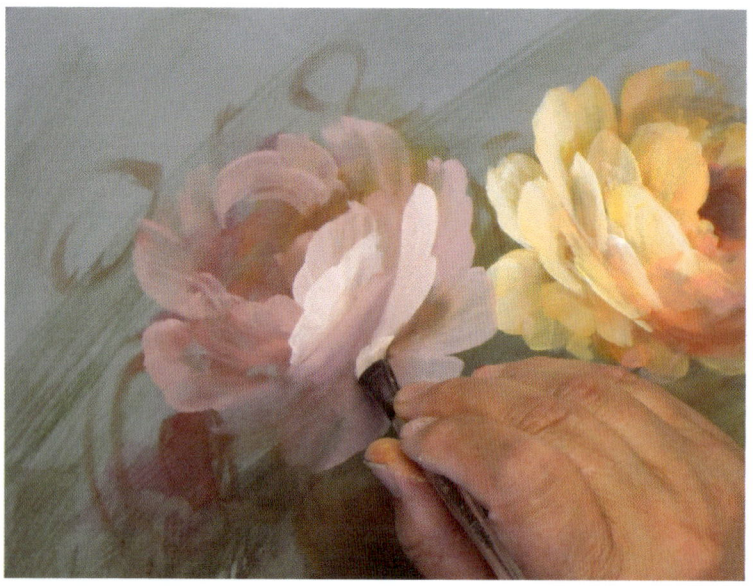
Use chisel of the brush for detail petals

Almost all of the flowers in these lessons were painted with the # 10 Fusion Flat brush. I use this one brush because I can control it very easily. The secret is in the edges. Look at the flat brush: you have corners, chisel, and the flat side. Different edges of the brush create different edges on your flowers.

As I have said before: "Edges create interest." If you only stroke in one way throughout the painting, you never really add all the potential interest for the design. Variation of edges create more interest. Not always changing to a different brush.

I used to always change brushes, change brushes, and change brushes to paint the flowers. I was looking for a brush that made the flower easier to paint. John Singer Sargent said that an artist should use as large a brush as possible to create a color passage. This changed the way I painted forever.

We don't need a different brush to make it easier to paint. We need to use a brush that allows us to paint the object with variation. I practiced painting small flowers with a large brush. This made me use the corner or chisel of the brush to make a petal. What a difference it made!

I realized the corners, edges and chisels of the brush made different marks for detailed petals as well as soft receding edges. I could use the same brush, but by expanding the way I hold the brush, stroke the brush and use different parts of the brush, I created flowers with more interest and life.

Try painting with as large a brush as possible. Try to use the different parts of the brush to make the color marks. Try to hold the brush differently from time to time to see what it does to the petal and flowers. Don't paint to make it easy. Making something difficult can also make it different.

Establishing a Mottled and Interesting Background

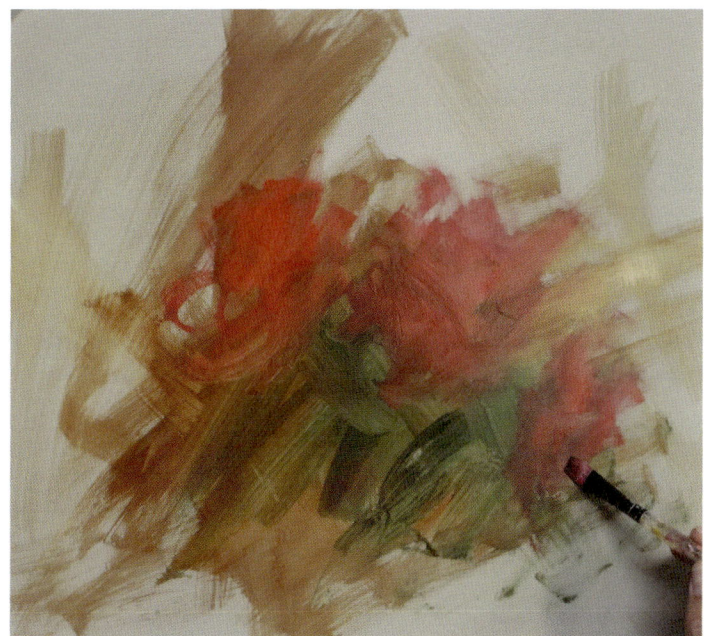

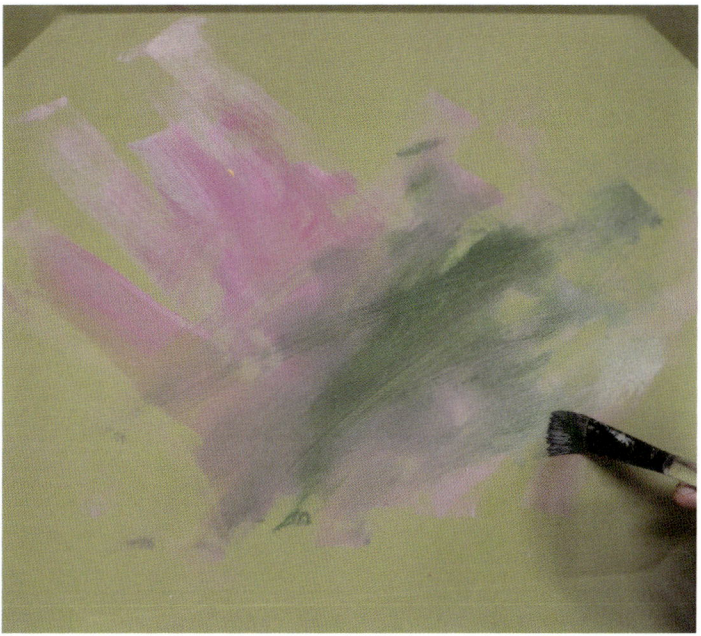

A casual background can add interest to your painting but needs to support and enhance the design elements. In this book, I mottle the backgrounds with the brush and other painting tools such as my fingers and paper towel. I vary the colors and temperatures to contrast the flowers and push them forward.

I start with a simple brush sketch to place the flowers. Then, I add colors to the background that will contrast those flowers. For example, yellow roses contrast with violets in the background. A warm green can be used to contrast the cool violet so that the background has additional interest.

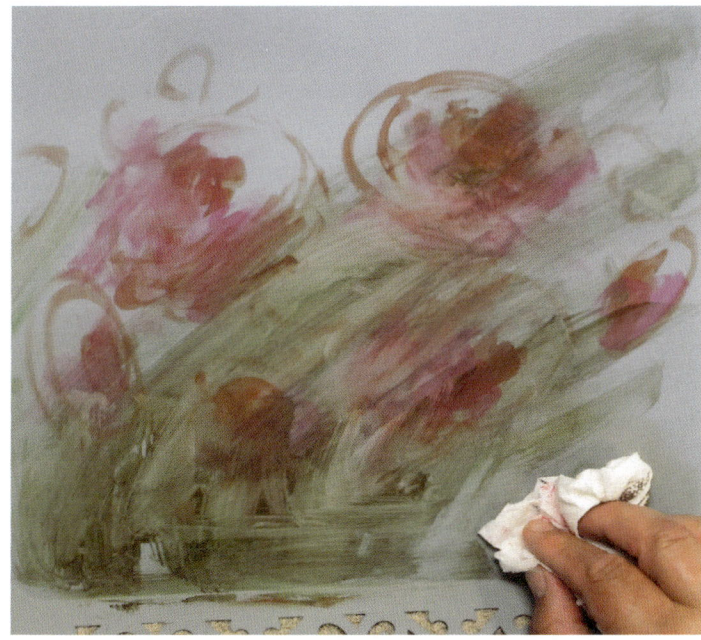

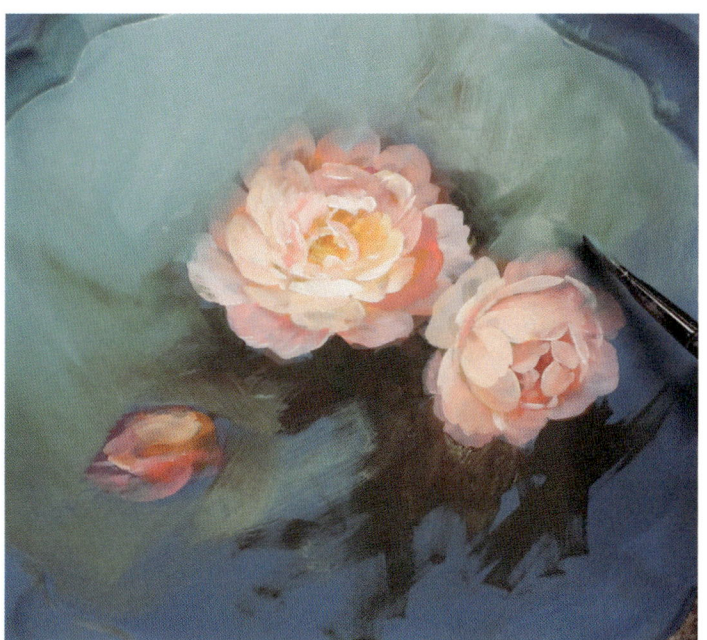

You also need to develop the path of light and dark in the painting. Usually, I cool and darken the background colors on the opposite side of the light source. After I set the main colors for the background, I continue to refine and develop additional colors.

For example, I might add a light cool blue to an upper right corner. Dragging touches of this color through the background creates harmony and interest through temperature variation. Movement adds interest. You can always revisit your background to soften the movement or add additional color. Experiment!

Color Theory and Mixing Techniques

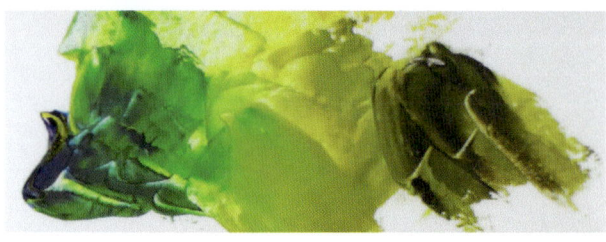

Greens- Leaves, Scrolls
Hansa Yellow will make a wide variety of greens. On the left you can see Hansa mixed with Phthalo Blue. On the right, it is mixed with a tiny touch of Carbon Black. Combine both for more greens!

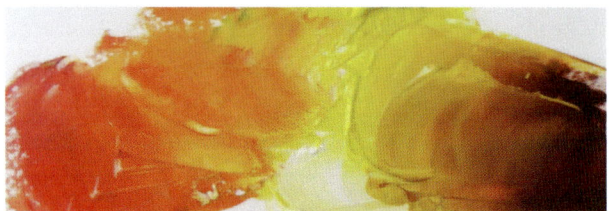

Yellows- Flowers, Leaves, Scrolls
Hansa is a bright yellow. I like to use it soft. Add browns or touches of Red Violet and Red add more variety. White lightens and opaques the yellow.

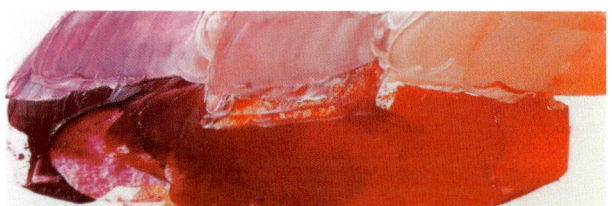

Reds- Flowers, Leaves
Naphthol Red Light is a warm red orange. Red Violet is a cool red violet. Mix together to make a wide range of reds and lighten with white to make soft pinks.

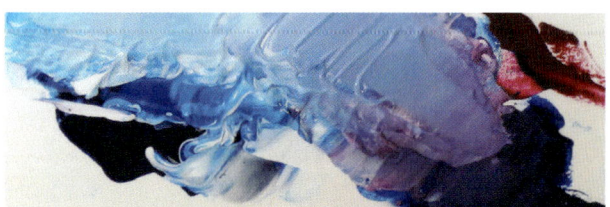

Blues- Flowers, Leaves, Scrolls
Phthalo Blue is a dark blue that leans to the green side. If you add a tiny touch of Red Violet, then lighten with white, you will make a wide variety of blues and blue violets.

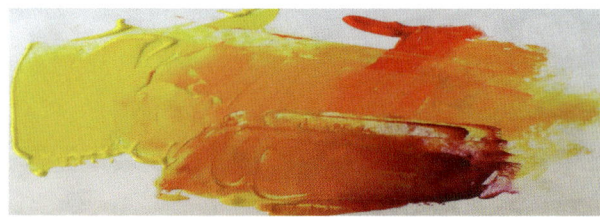

Oranges- Flowers, Leaves
Hansa Yellow can be used as a base for a wide variety of oranges. Tiny touches of Naphthol Red Light make warm oranges and touches of Red Violet make cooler oranges.

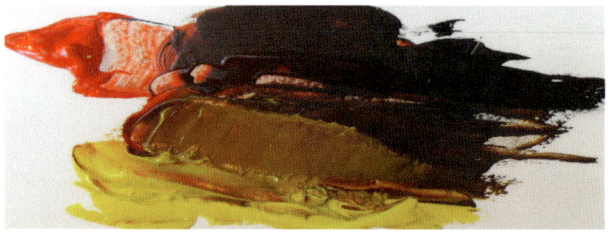

Browns- Flowers, Leaves
Base Brown is 2 parts Naphthol Red Light and 1 part Carbon Black. I vary this color in many brush mixes with additions of Hansa Yellow which lightens and make more sienna colors.

What happens to Yellow? (See Right Photo) The red warms, but the black cools. Increasing the black makes the color greener and cooler. Increasing the red makes the color more orange and warmer. The second mix shows Red Violet and Carbon Black. Here the color becomes cooler because Red Violet and Black are cool. There are many ways to cool a color. Hansa Yellow and Black make green. The green cools from left to right because Black is cooler than Hansa Yellow. Add Red Violet and the color cools even further.

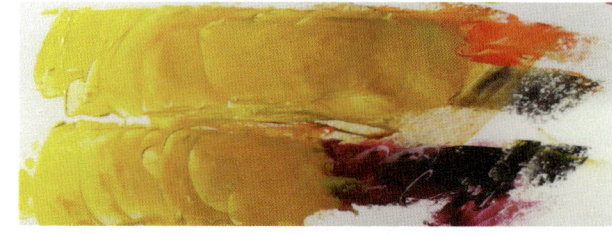
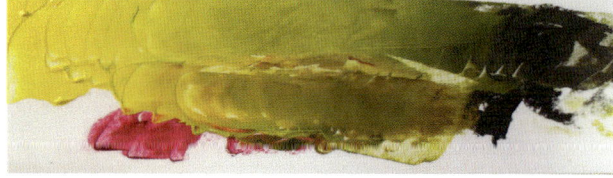

Tonal Qualities of Color

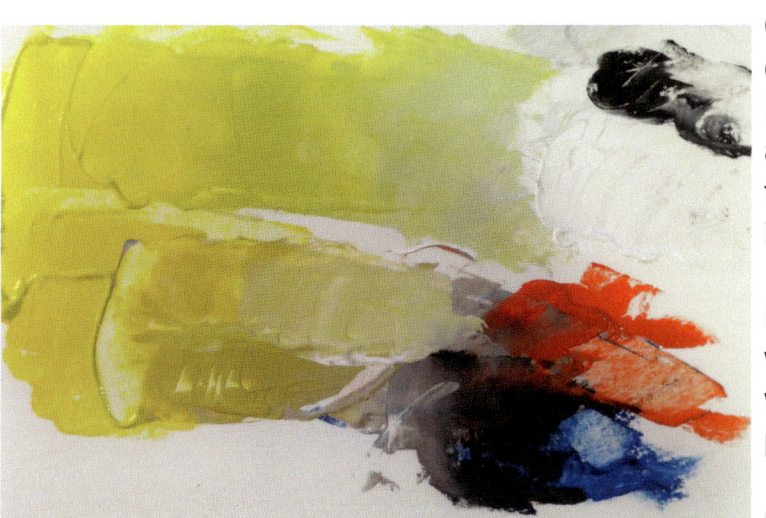

Color tone refers to the mixing of a neutral color with a pure color. For example, if I take Hansa Yellow, a bright, slightly warm yellow, and add a touch of light grey, I have made a tone of Hansa or a tonal color of Yellow. This is a broad definition of the term.

In this book we will not use the grey tonal values of color. We will not mix black and white to make grey and then add that to a pure color.

In this book, we mix complimentary colors to make greys that have more life and better harmony with the other colors in the palette. Lets look at some examples and how we can add "tonal harmony" to our colors.

Above, I have mixed Hansa Yellow with the tonal range of white and black. This is a broad definition of tonal color-making: a tone that is less intense tone of Hansa Yellow. This is a Tone of Yellow. The second example uses Phthalo Blue, Naphthol Red Light, and Titanium White. This makes a "tertiary color." Tertiary means 3. The three primary colors are red, yellow, and blue. When these 3 colors are combined in any variation, they make a "tone" of a color because they make a "tertiary" grey. Adding white to lighten the color to the same value of Hansa Yellow, is making a grey tone or Tonal Yellow.

Temperature of Your Colors

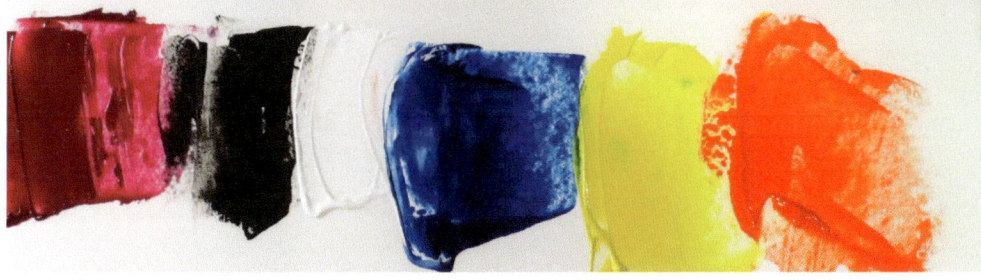

Cool Color | Neutral | Warm Temperature
Red Violet - Carbon Black- T.White- Phthalo Blue- Hansa Yellow- Nap. Red Light

Red Violet is the coolest color in the Paint It Simply palette. Carbon Black is a neutral that leans cool. Not all black pigments are cool, some are warm. Temperature varies with the pigment's source. Heritage Titanium White is also a neutral color.

Phthalo Blue and Ultramarine Blue are warm pigments. However, blues appear cool when used in association with warmer colors. This is due to **Simultaneous Contrast**.

For example, look above. The Phthalo Blue is slightly warm of neutral. According to the scale, it is cooler than the Naphthol Red Light. So, if both are used in a painting, the Phthalo Blue will look cool and the Naphthol Red Light will look warm. The human eye is constantly balancing colors. You may see the blue as cool in a painting, but it only appears that way based on the colors that surround it. Trust the scale above and you can paint temperature in any Paint It Simply lesson.

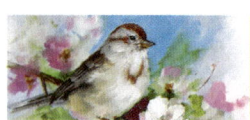 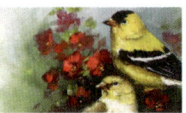

Adjusting Brightness or Intensity

Brightness or Intensity in a color is also referred to as **Saturation**. In the tonal lesson we learned that any tertiary color (or grey) will tone a color. Also, we want to create harmony within our painting. **Harmony** is when all the colors go together. When we use a common toner to adjust the brightness of a color, we also increase the harmony between the colors. This is a benefit of using a limited palette.

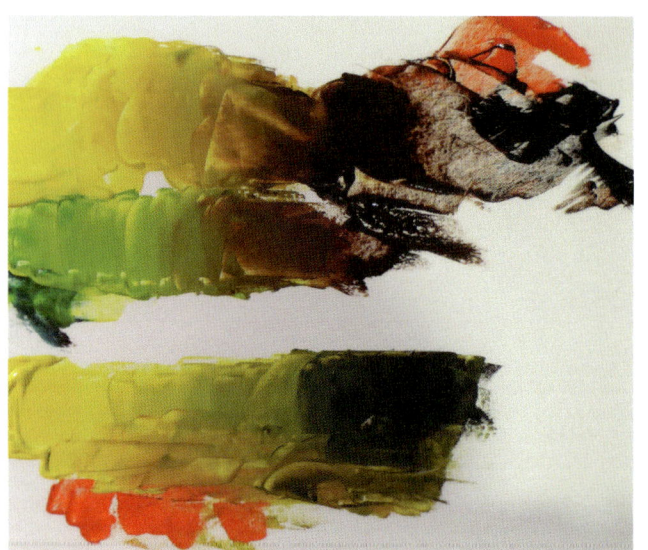

Let's look at some color. In this example, I mixed Brown (2 parts red to 1 part black). The top line is Hansa Yellow mixed with Brown. The intensity (or saturation) of the yellow reduces from left to right. Next, I made green with Hansa Yellow and a touch of Phthalo Blue. By slowly adding Brown, the intensity reduces from left to right. Both colors have harmony because I am toning with the same color so they "go" together. In this case, Brown is our common toner.

The next example shows the "grey" method of toning. Greys and blacks are added to Hansa Yellow to lower the intensity. However, you can see that Yellow turns green with the addition of Black. Adding small touches of Red will bring the Yellow back to a Toned Yellow. Blacks are wonderful to tone with and do add harmony. However, sometimes, they change the "hue" or color, as in this case, yellow becomes green. Using tertiary colors can lower the intensity while maintaining the same hue.

The Colors of Burnt Sienna and Pine Green

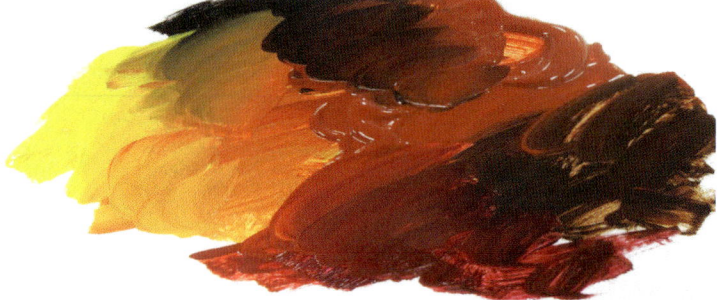 

Burnt Sienna is a pure pigment and is an the earth color. A burnt orange color, it is extremely warm in temperature. Think of it as a toned orange and you can predict mixing results with ease. Mixing Burnt Sienna with Hansa Yellow (shown on the left) yields a wide range of toned yellows. At the top, the yellow mixes are cooled with a tiny touch of Black or a little Red Violet as shown at the bottom. Adding a touch of Black to the Burnt Sienna alone will give you beautiful umbers. Add a touch of Blue for soft greys when lightened with White. You can make endless color combinations!

Pine Green is not a pure color but rather mixed from several pigments. It is a great, vibrant shortcut. Pine Green is a warm color. (See the example above from left to right.) Add Hansa Yellow for bright yellow greens. Add a touch of Phthalo Blue for intense teal and blue greens. Tone with Burnt Sienna to make brown greens. Mix with Red Violet for cool darks. Add Black for deep dark greens. It is a powerful benchmark green for your limited palette.

Additional Techniques Used In Paint It Simply Techniques

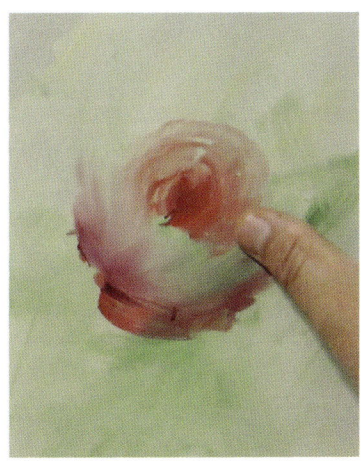

Transparent Color Washes- Sketching Shapes
Artists for hundreds of years have concentrated on paint consistencies to enhance the designs. With these lesson you will see several times where you add various colors into the background and also within the petals. This is called a "mosaic" of color. When you apply this mosaic of color, vary the consistency by thinning some colors with additional Extender Medium. Varying the consistency of the colors will increase the variation within the blossoms. The soft blending that occurs as you move the brush around the surface is controlled by the paint consistency. If a certain lesson is not working, I highly suggest changing the consistency of the paint for a better result.

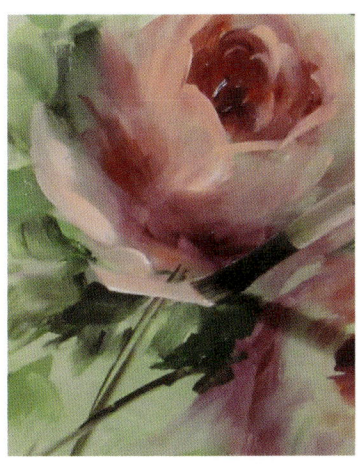

Light Color Petal Edging
The Fusion brush excels in applying white edges then softening them with other strokes. Tap one edge of the brush into the White or light color. Sometimes I use the chisel edge, flat edge or at an angle. Wiggle the brush as you draw the outside edge of the petal. Varying the amount of paint will create different petal effect. Once I have drawn the outside edge of the petal, I then stroke the brush back and forth to fill in the petal with color. If anything gets too harsh or too much, I soften with my finger.

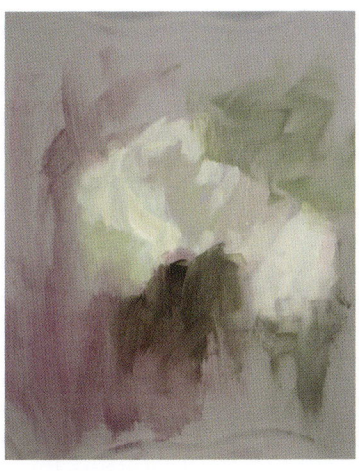

Optical Blending
This is a concept made famous by the Impressionist painters of the late 19th century. With this, the artist leaves portions of the painting "un-blended" allowing the viewers eye to blend the tones from a short distance. Usually the artists take a step back of about 3 feet to view the painting. This softens the effect. The photographic cameras usually soften the effects of a photo. When artists paint from that photo, the result is an over blended painting. To combat this, we leave more areas of color exchanges. Try not to stroke more than 3 times in any area. Do not stroke many times! Leave streaks.

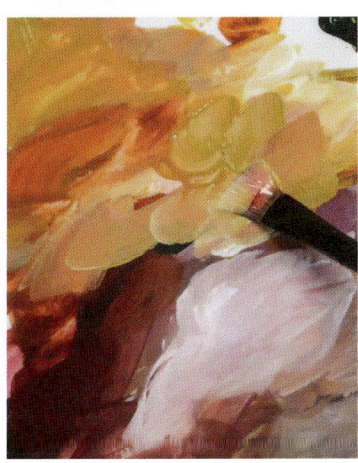

Flow Texture
The secret to a successful painting is paint. We say in the Program: "It is easier to paint with paint!" This is so true. When painting the lessons you need to use a lot of paint and use if fast.
One of the greatest painters during the 19th century said that the artist should use paint so thick that is flows together, rather than mixing. This is the technique! Do not mix, let the color "swirl" and flow together, then optical blending will soften the colors when view from a short distance.

Additional Techniques Used In Paint It Simply Techniques

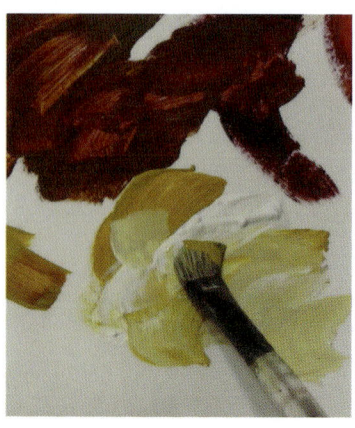

Brush Mottling
To create a mottled brush you need to have colors about the same consistency. Place the colors right next to each other on the palette. Tap the brush up and down on the palette to load into the brush. Do not stroke the brush on the surface of the palette because this will cause them to blend and soften. Tap the colors on the palette just enough to cause them to load into the tip of the brush. Apply the colors to the flower or blossom with a light tapping motion. Use a very light pressure on the brush so that the tapping doesn't continue to blend the colors. A great technique for interest in the flowers.

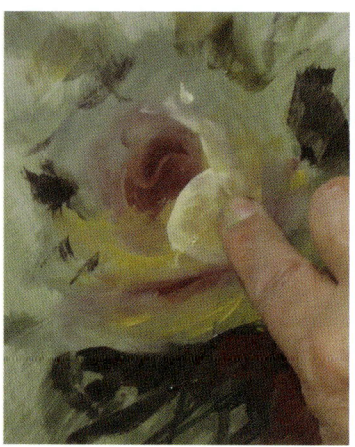

Pushing Color
I love the casual look that is created with the fingers. Apply color to the surface. Mottle several colors. Pushing color works the best if the background is wet with thick paint. Most techniques require thicker paint so make sure you have it on the surface. Apply the paint with the fusion brush. Then, using good pressure with your finger, push the paint around into the shape of the object you are painting. I love to do this technique on the fronts of roses, where you want the colors to mottle and swirl, but not to blend. Too much brushwork can blend the color where pushing them around with your finger preserves the color.

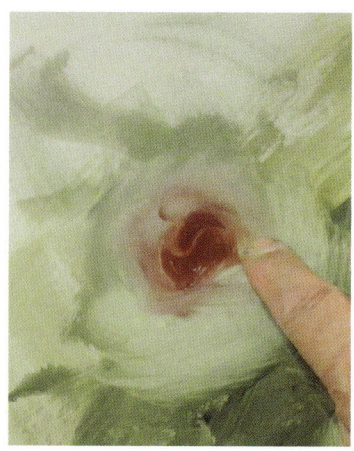

Blur Objects for Depth
This is a technique that is very important to the lessons in this book. Here we will start large areas of color. Do not paint each object perfectly. We leave edges undefined. I describe this to students in this way.... We start the painting like we are looking through a camera that has not focused on the subject. Do not find the edges.... Move colors and strokes around without finding perfect shapes. Think of it as slowly turning the focus ring on your camera, bringing it into focus. This will help develop tremendous depth in your painting. Start soft and undefined. Slowly add more edges to object.

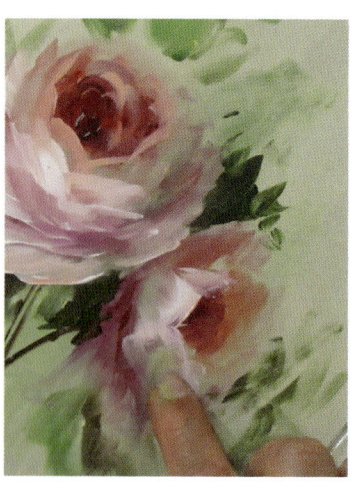

Lost Edge of the Petal
Artists are painters of edges. We fill in pattern lines or paint objects with edges that give them form and structure. The edges though are very important for dimension within the painting.
In real life, the human eye can not see all the details in objects that are far away. Edges of the objects "blur" as you get farther away from them. Our eyes are used to seeing this concept everyday. To capture this visual depth, the artist will paint a very clear edge to objects that they want to come forward such as the front petal of a flower. They will soften or blur the back ones so they recede. I use my finger for this. Softening the edges of objects that are not important brings forward the others.

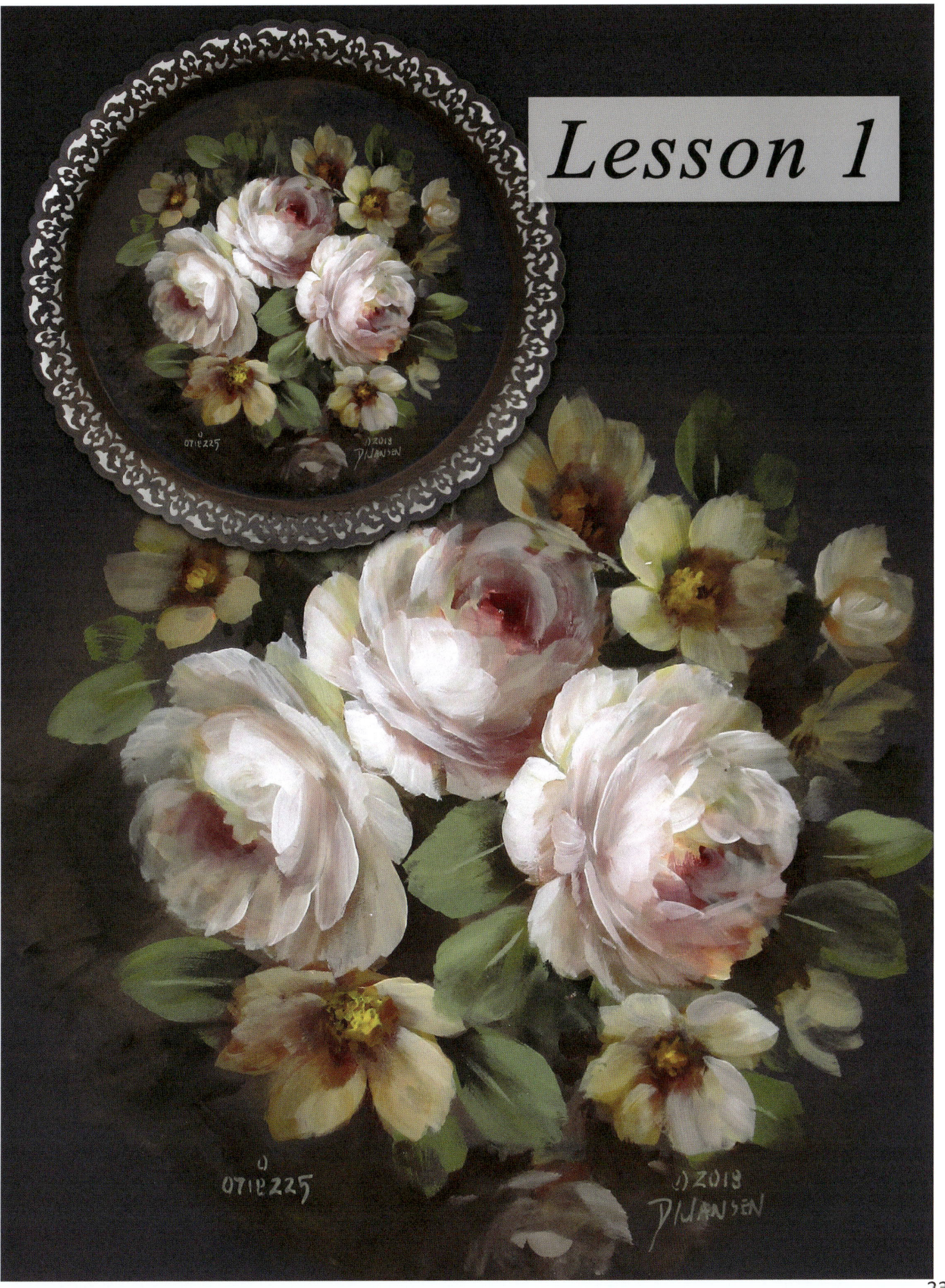

Lesson 1

White Lace- Tinting Acrylics

For years I tried to make acrylics act like oils. Today, I realize that while I can slow down the acrylics to work like oil paint, it is not necessary. Acrylic techniques allow for more options because the paint dries faster! This drying time make layering techniques so much easier.

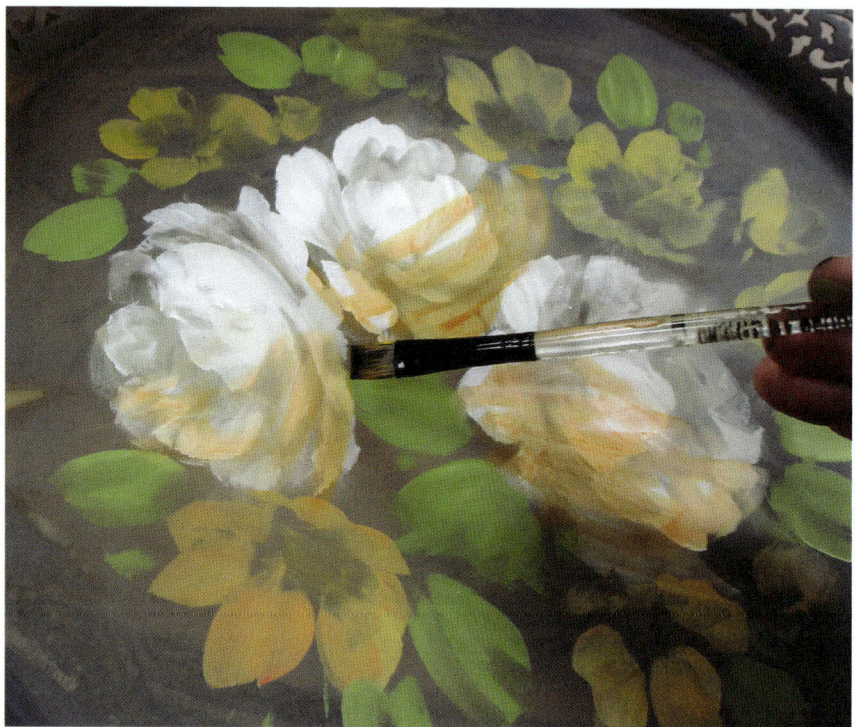

For this lesson with will do our first tinting of colors. This is an older technique that dates back 400 years to the Dutch Masters of the Golden Age. However, the Dutch had to wait for their oil paintings to dry before they could tint colors. This could take weeks! With acrylics, we only have to wait 30 minutes or use a hair dryer.

Tinting can add so much life to a design. Techniques like this were created by the Dutch Masters who painted in layers rather than blend the colors.

Today many artists think about working the colors together wet into wet and blending. I don't. I have developed several techniques in the past couple of years specifically for Heritage Acrylics. I love the results and many people think I paint in oils! Let's give it a try!

Paint It Simply Palette
Base Color- Toned Warm Grey
Medium Grey + Touch
Yellow Oxide or Hansa Yellow. Gold for the edge of tray.

Palette Colors

PAINT IT SIMPLY COLORS	OPTIONAL COLORS
Naphthol Red Light	Yellow Oxide
Red Violet	Diarylide Yellow
Titanium White	Pine Green
Carbon Black	Quinacridone Violet
Phthalo Blue	Burnt Sienna
Hansa Yellow	

Painting Surface
Metal Tray

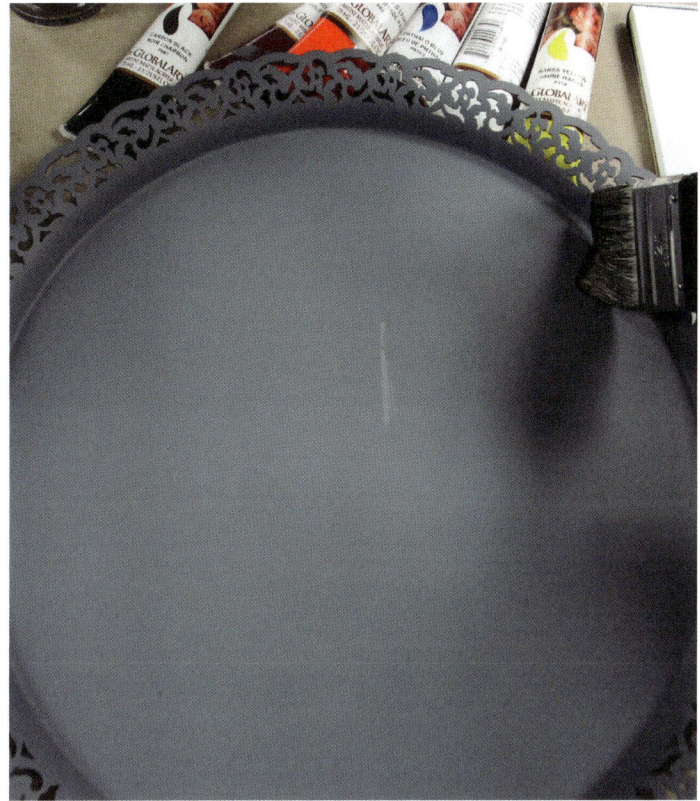

Step 1 I love the primer color from the metal etching Rustoleum. If you don't have it, mix a base color with medium grey and then warm with touch Yellow Oxide.

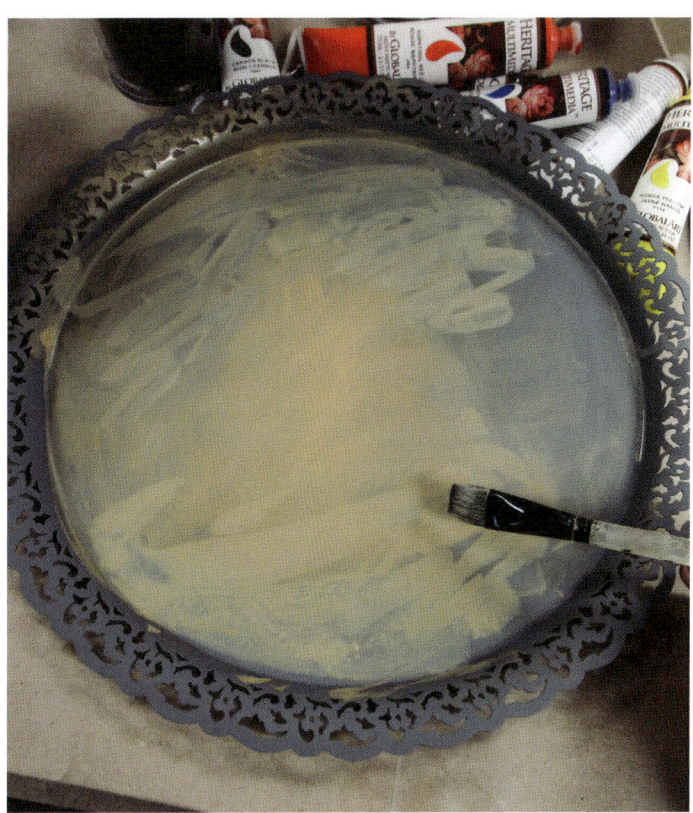

Step 2 Using 3/4 inch brush and medium beige, brush over the surface using just water. Work fast and casual. Do not cover completely. Allow some background to show through.

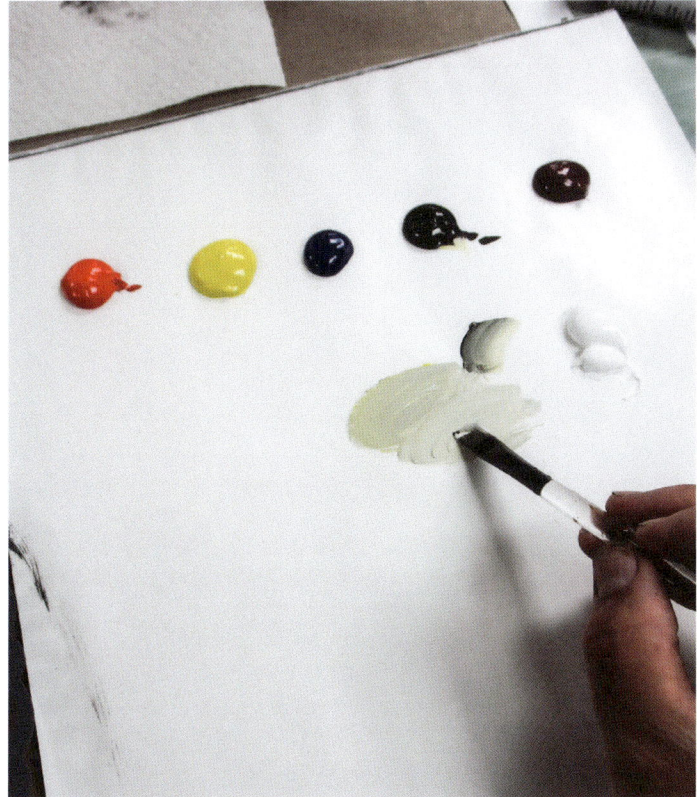

Step 3 Here is my basic palette for this painting. The Paint It Simply 6 color set. Mottle a medium white color about value 6 or 7 with white, black and touch Hansa Yellow.

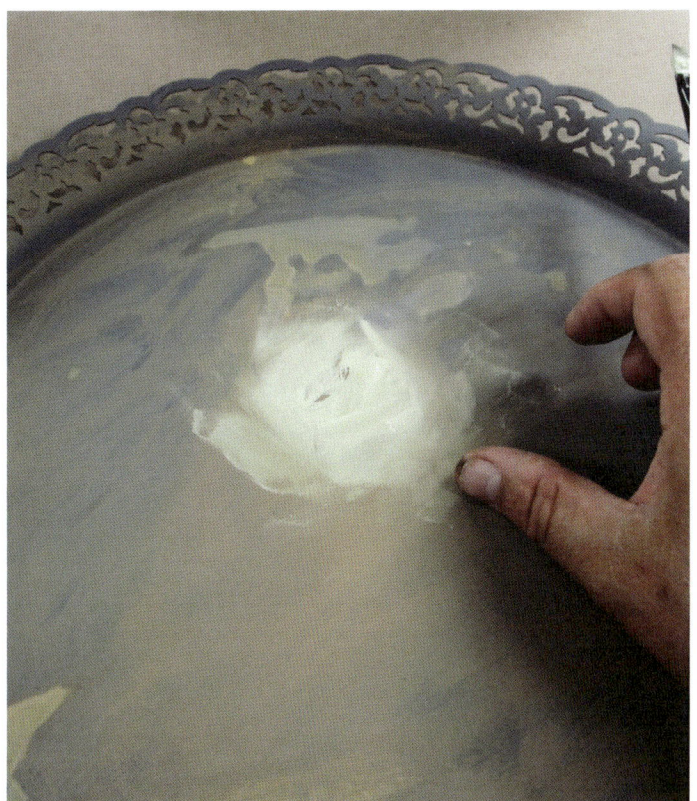

Step 4 Base in the round shape of the first rose and shear off the edges into the background with your fingers. Keep soft edges.

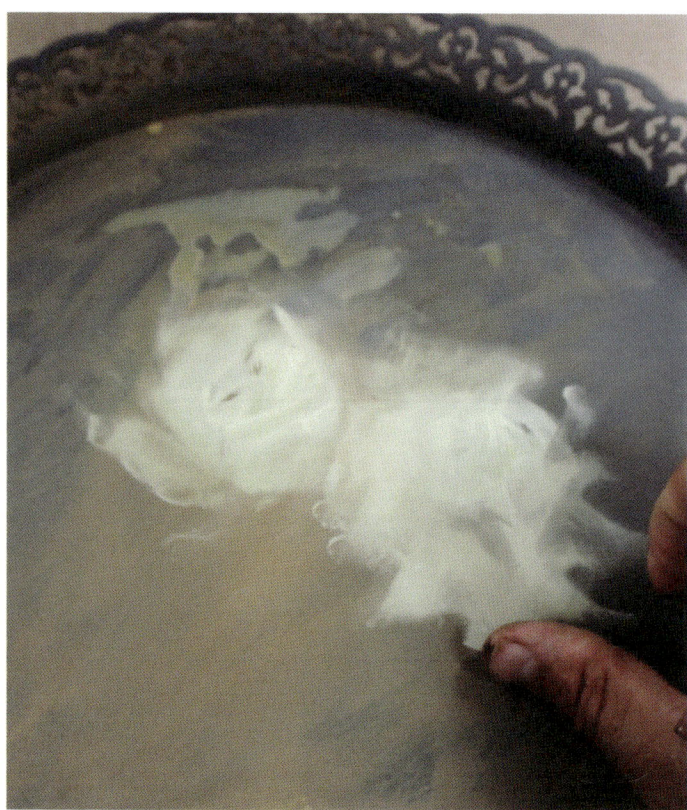

Step 5 Add the round shape of the next rose and shear off the edges into the background like we did with the first rose.

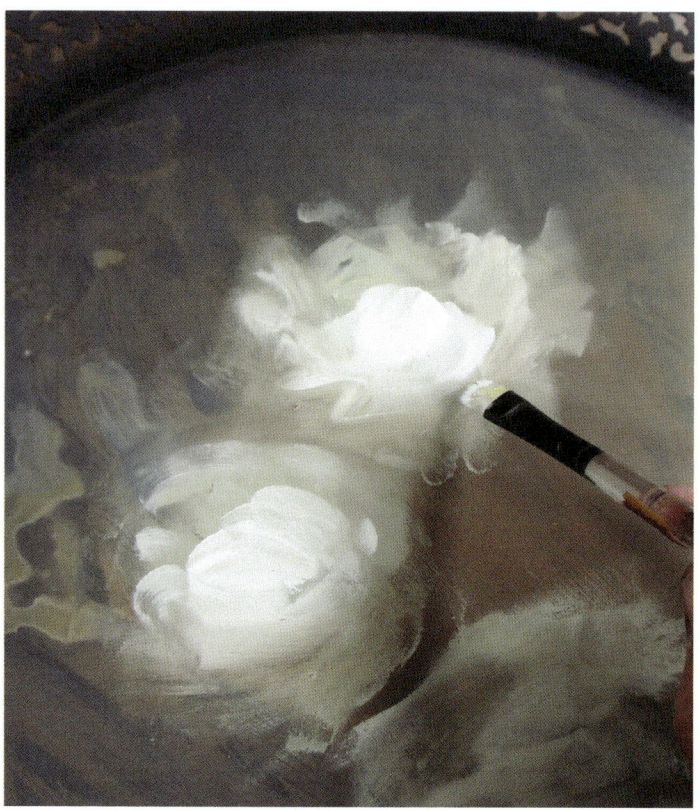

Step 6 Mottle the brush with more white and then add to the front area of the rose. This builds the front of the bowl and will make it advance in the painting.

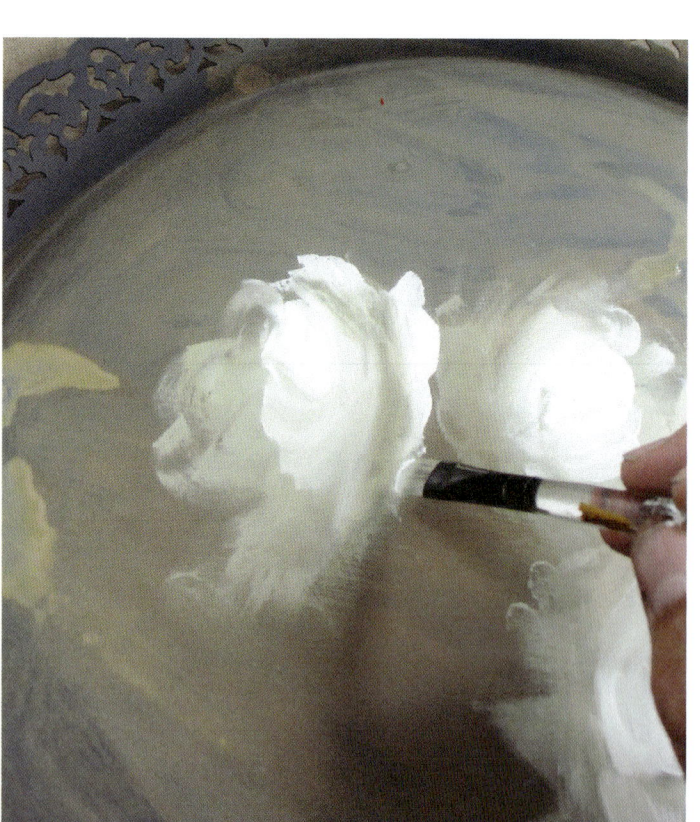

Step 7 Using the chisel of the flat brush begin the shapes of the reaching petals. Mostly white in the front and shear off the sides so they stay soft.

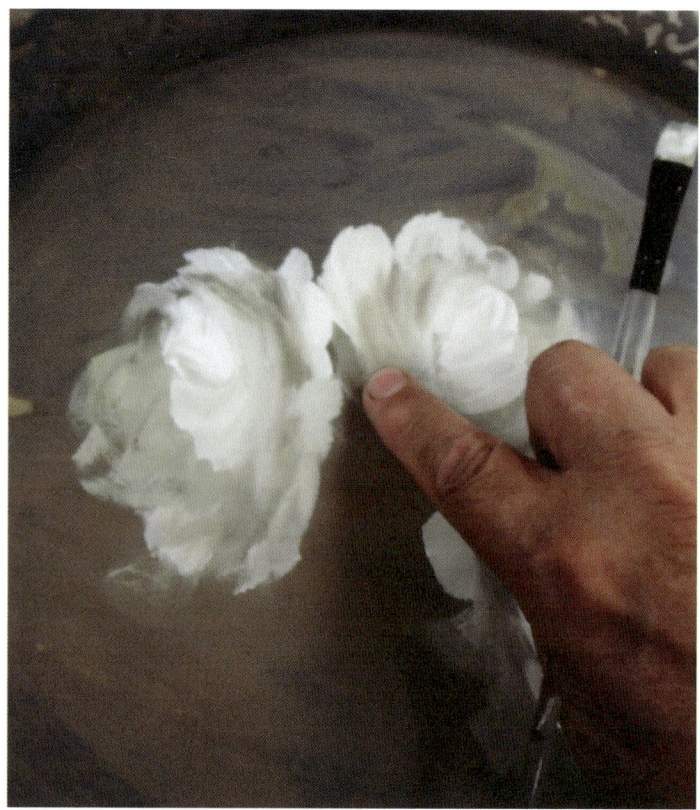

Step 8 Use your finger to push the round shape to the bottom of the bowl. Like with all roses, we don't want to lose the bottom of the bowl. Keep the shapes.

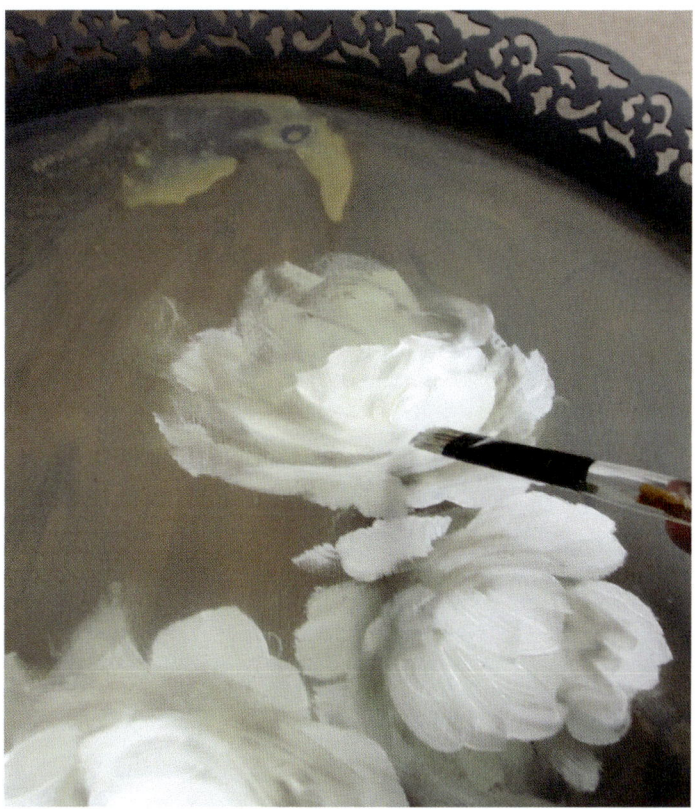

Step 9 Continue to build the white in the front of the roses. This will make them advance when we tint with color.

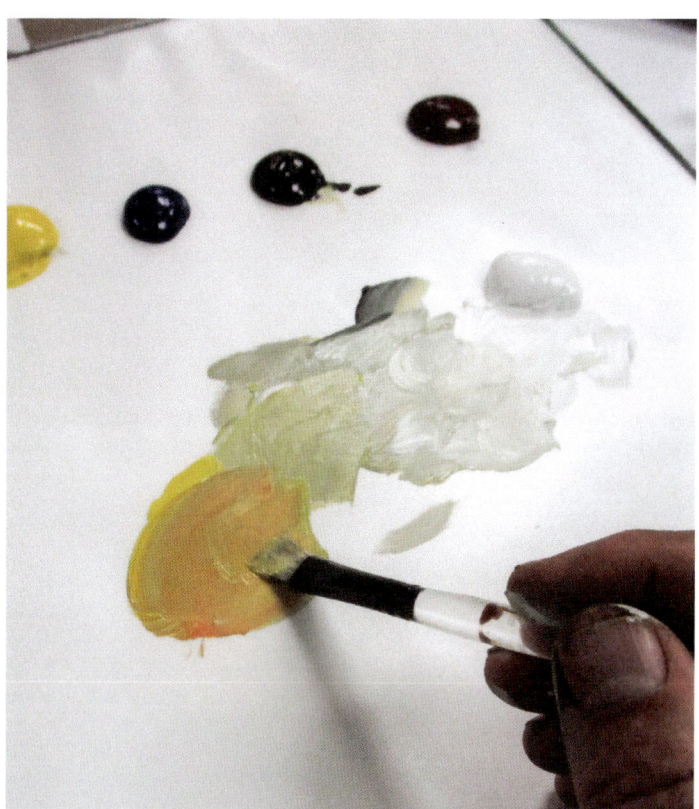

Step 10   Mottle a soft yellow orange with the greys, Hansa and touch Naphthol Red Light. Keep the color soft and not too bright.

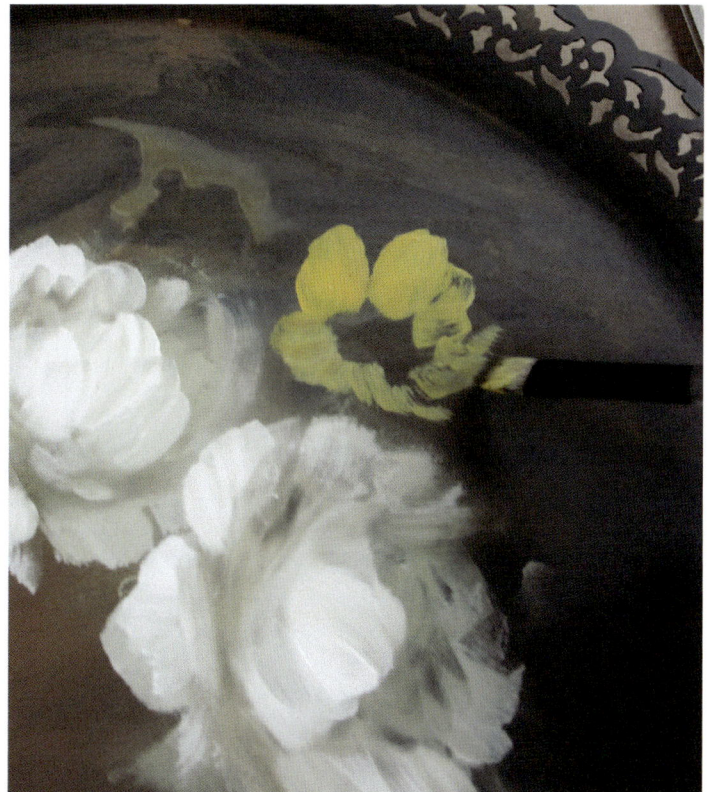

Step 11 Using the # 8 flat fusion brush begin shaping the blossoms petals. Notice how the blossom petals vary in size and shape. Pull some in and some out of the center.

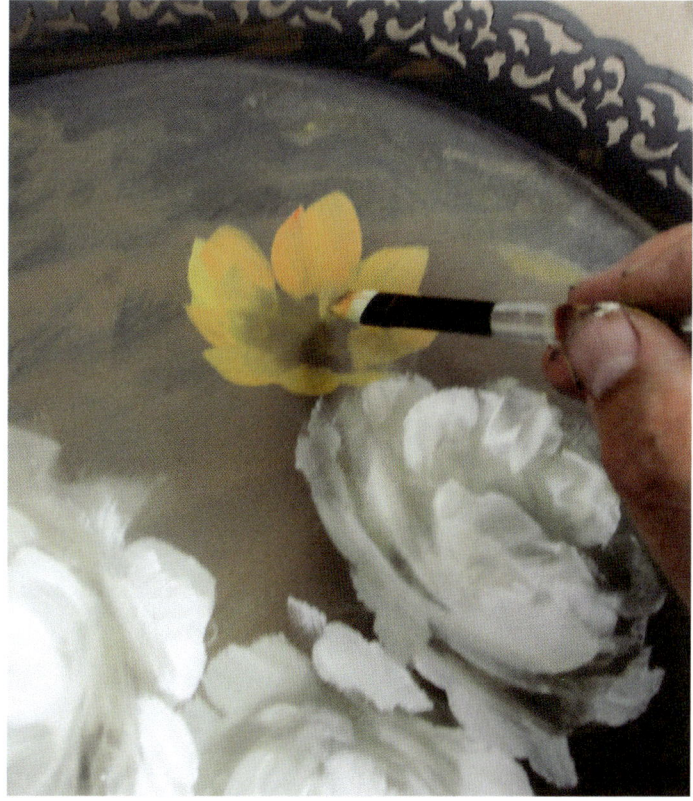

Step 12 Mottle the color with a touch more red and add some color variation to the petals.

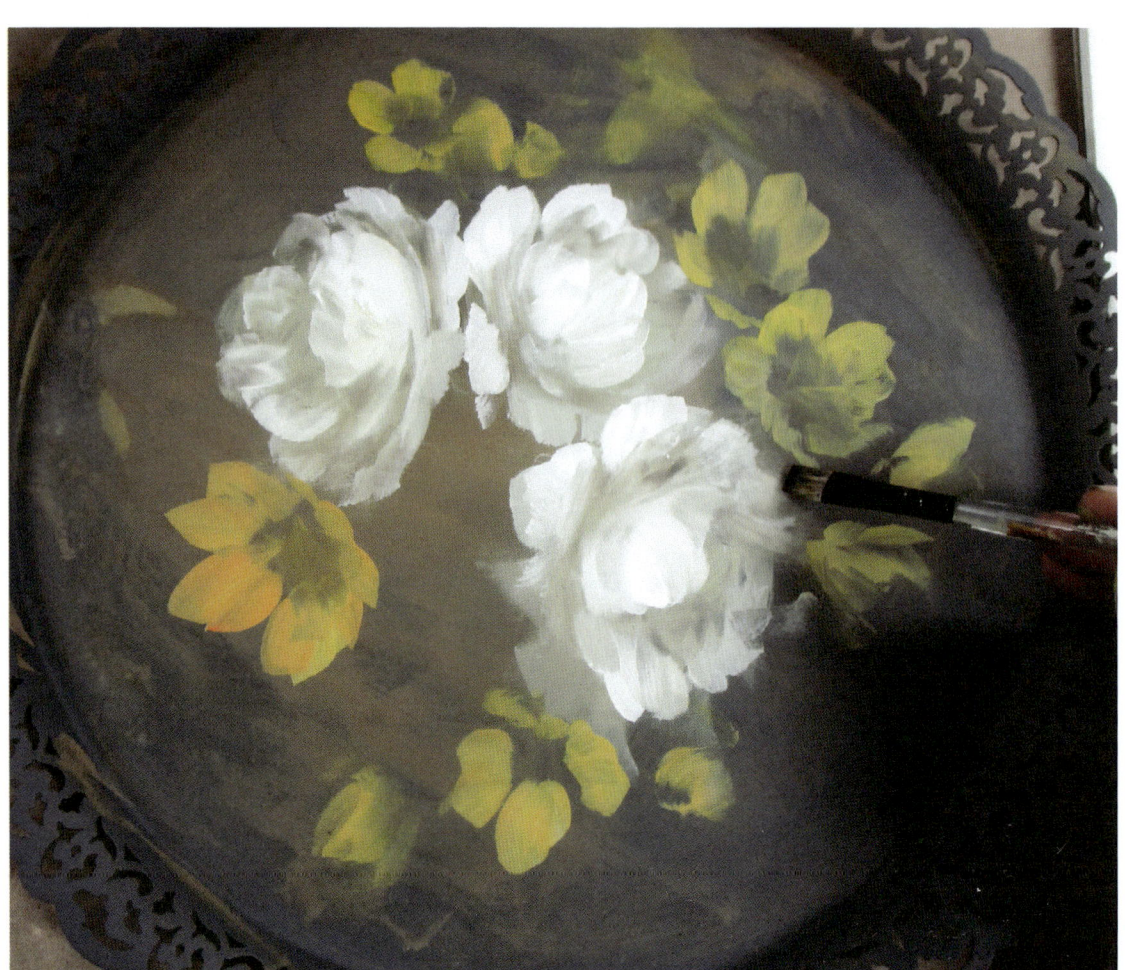

Step 13
Here you can see the blossoms added to the design. I try to make them each a little different. Vary the size, shape and turn in different directions to give them more interest. Make oval shapes to indicate buds of the blossoms. Not all flowers should be open. Vary the age of the blossom making some closed and some partially open. This adds interest.

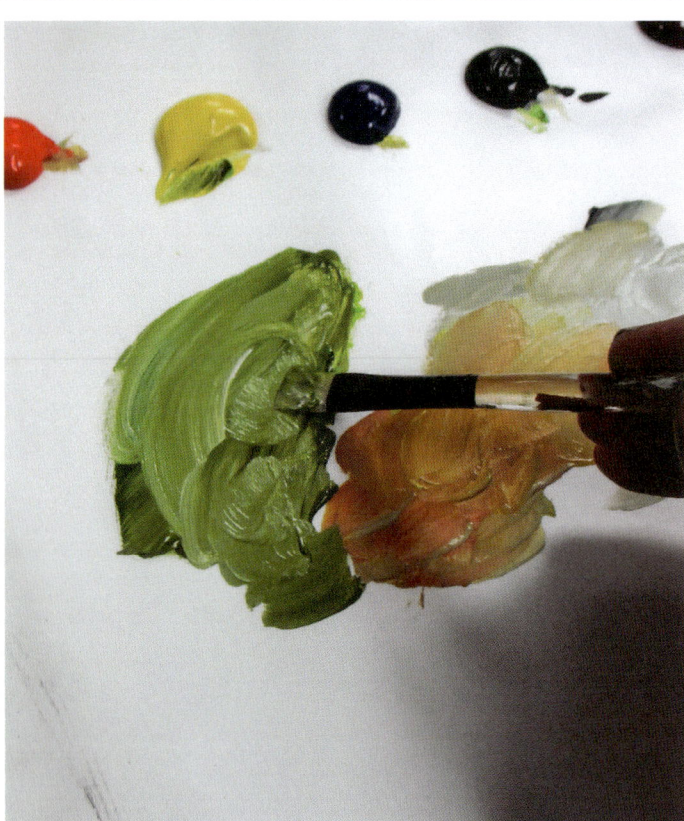

Step 14 Mottle a yellow green with Hansa and touch blue. You can very the color with a touch of black. Do not over mix the color. Let some streaks stay in the mix.

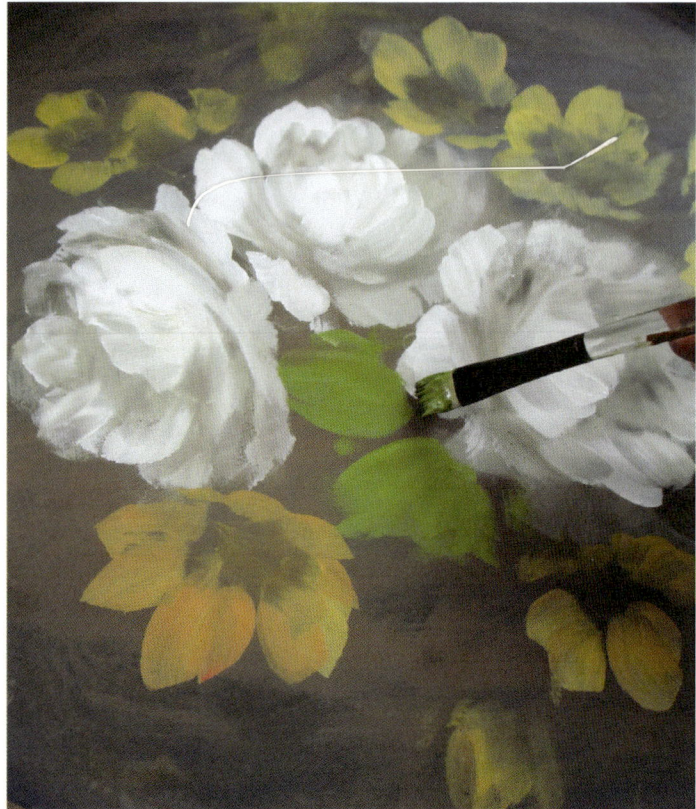

Step 15 Begin shaping the oval leaves in the composition. Leave some of the edges broken and soft. Do not make them too perfect. This is about the roses.

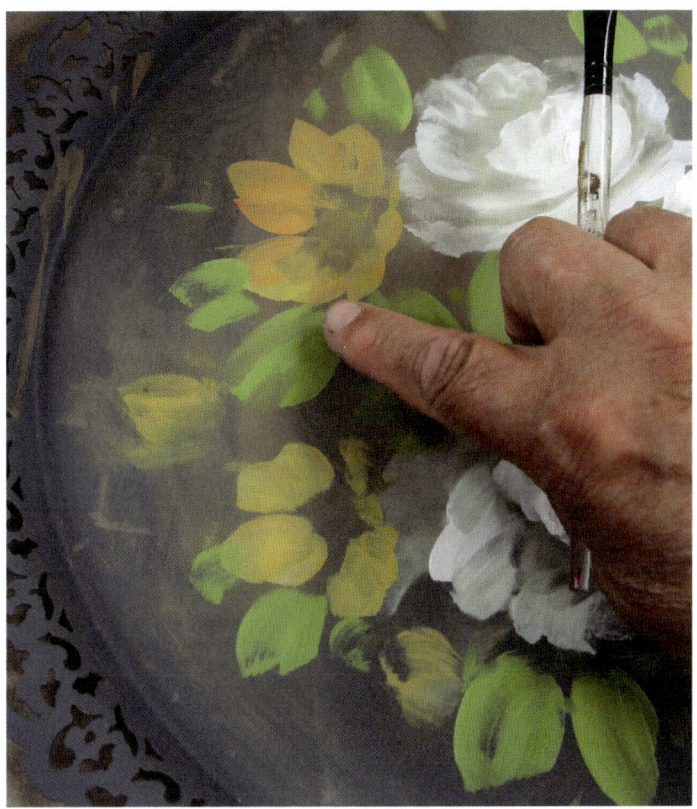

Step 16 Here I am using my finger to push the color in and out of the leaves. Allow some background to show through and create streaks. Again, this adds interest.

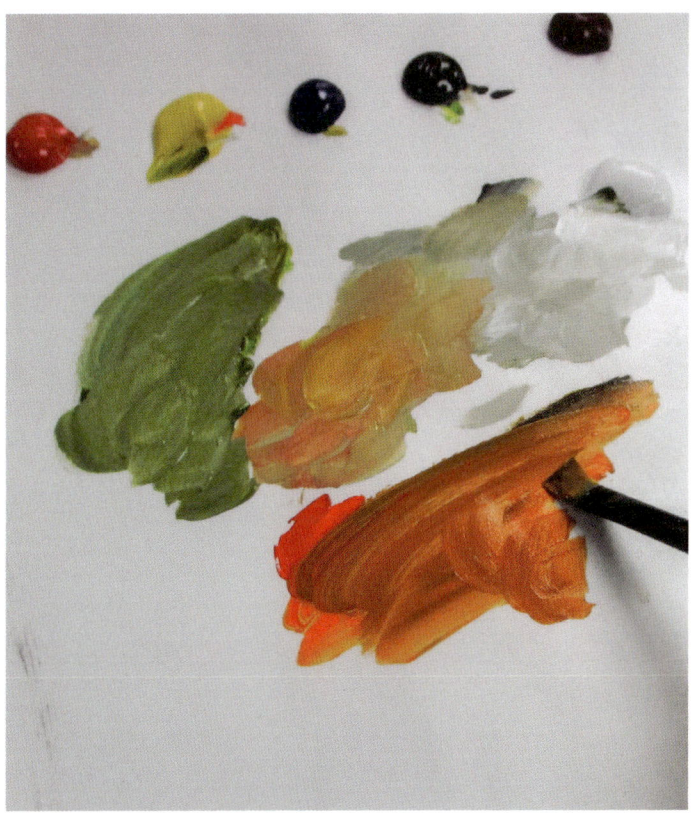

Step 17 Mottle red with yellow and touch greys to soften. Thin with some water or you could use a small amount of Extender if desired. Do not over mix.

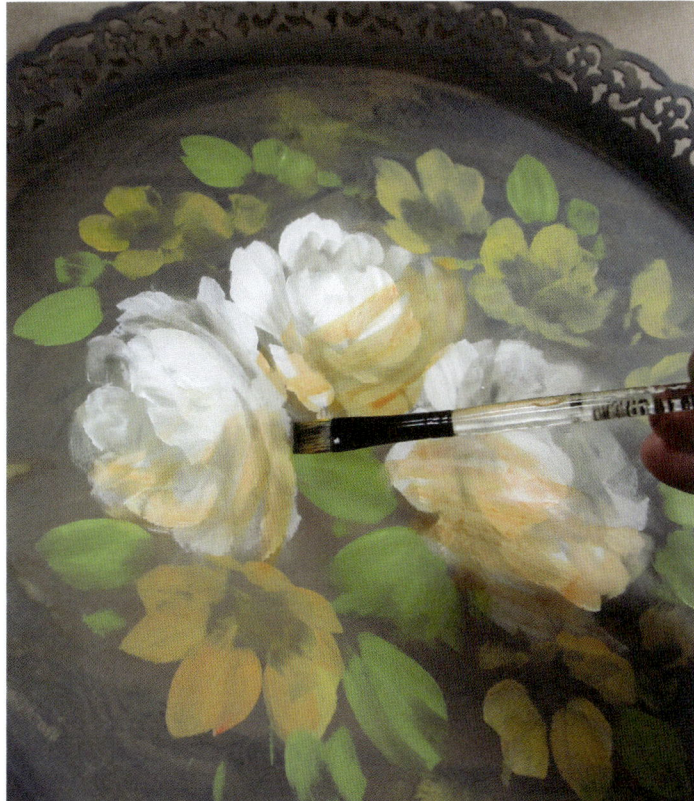

Step 18 Using thin color wash over the bottom sides of the roses. This starts the first tints of the roses.

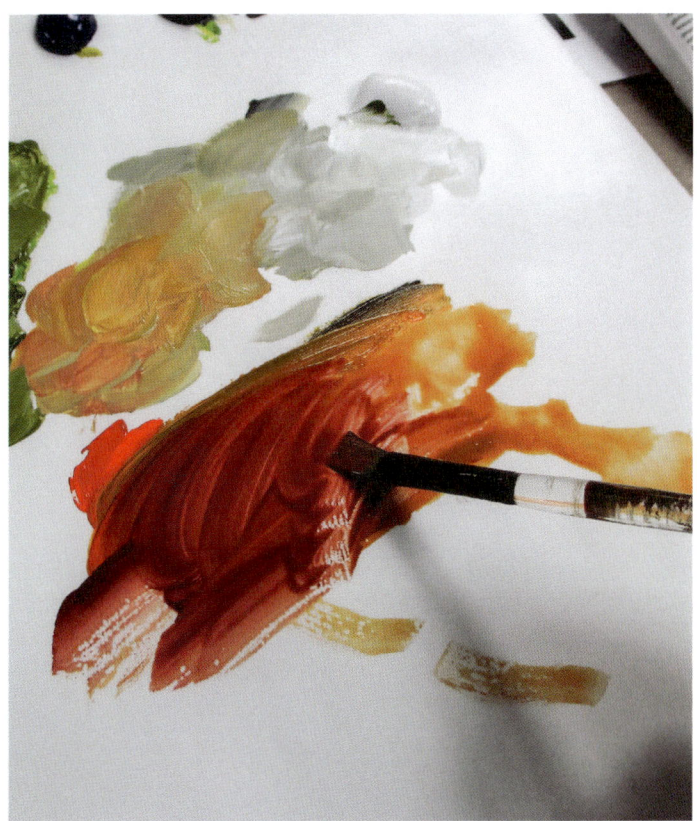

Step 19 Mottle the soft orange yellow we just used with Red Violet to darken and cool.

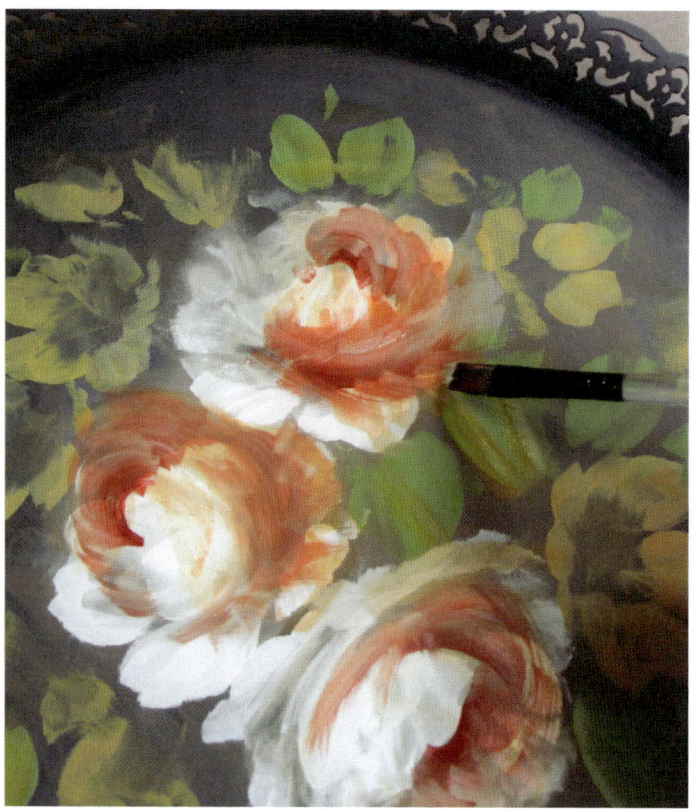

Step 20 Following the good shadow technique for roses establish the center shadow and the bowl shadow. Wash out and soften the edges with your finger.

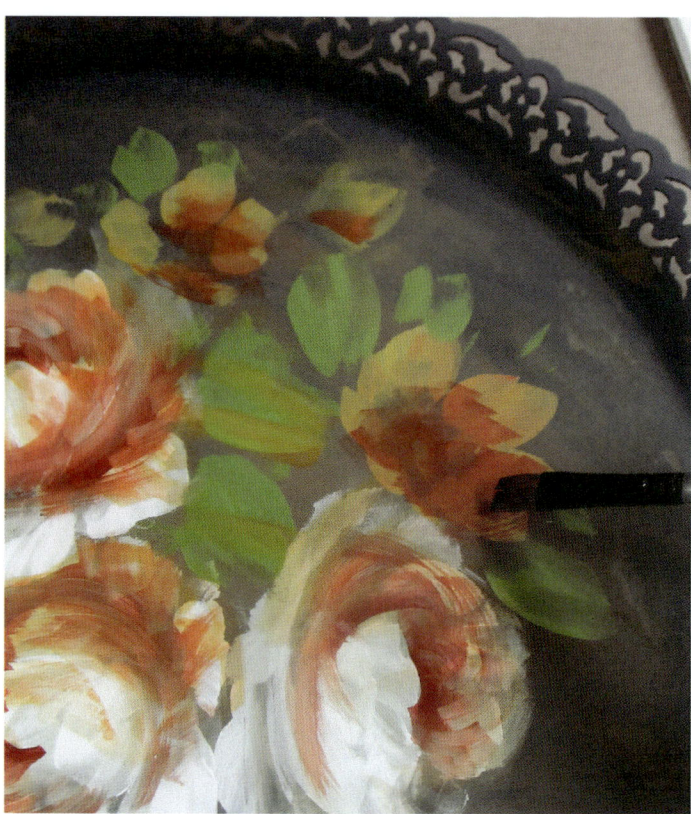

Step 21 Wash the cooler red color over the centers of the blossoms. This will form the cool centers for contrast later on.

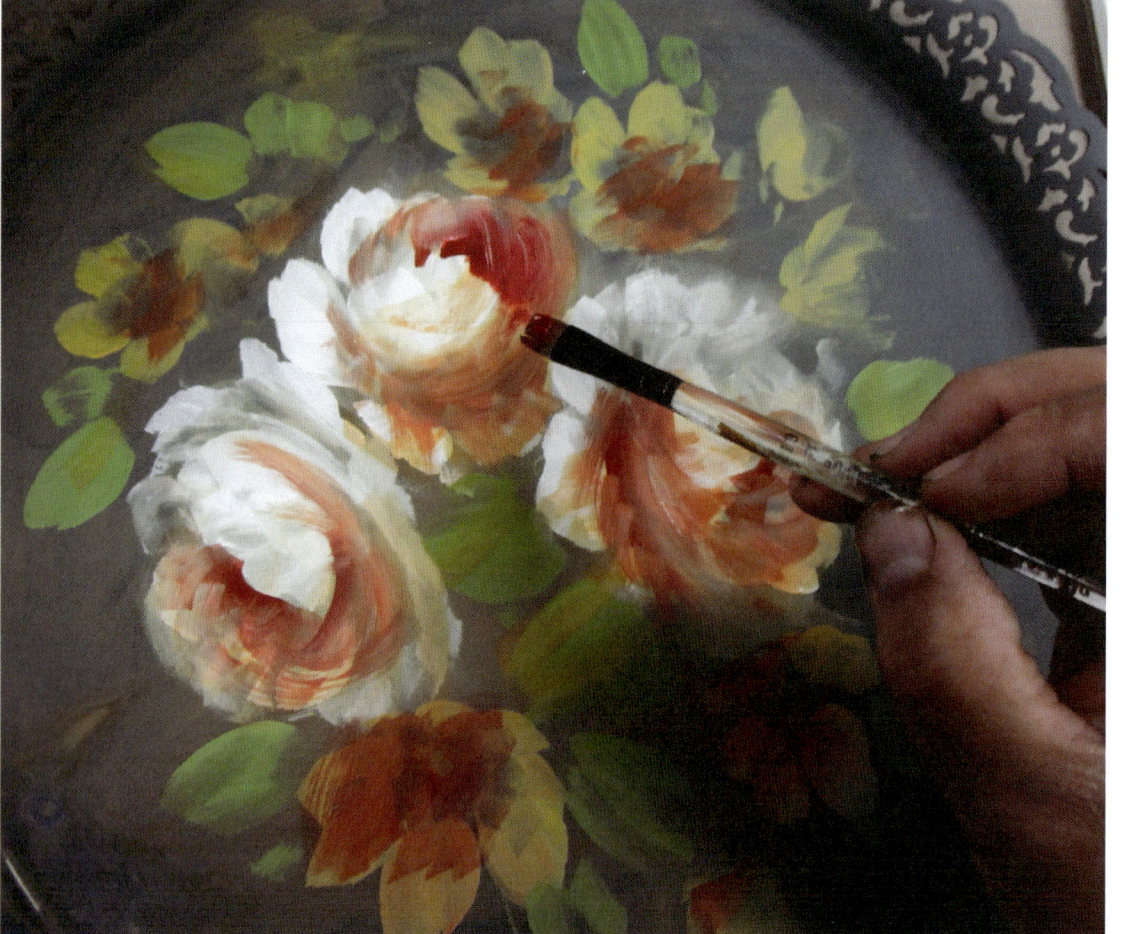

Step 22 Darken the color with more Red Violet. Add the deeper darker, cool color to the center of the roses. Try to keep the color a little darker in the deep center part of the rose. This will give more contrast with the front of the rose. Thin the color slightly and then add darker shadows to the bowl of the rose. Keep the shadows to the bottom side and not as dark as the center of the rose.

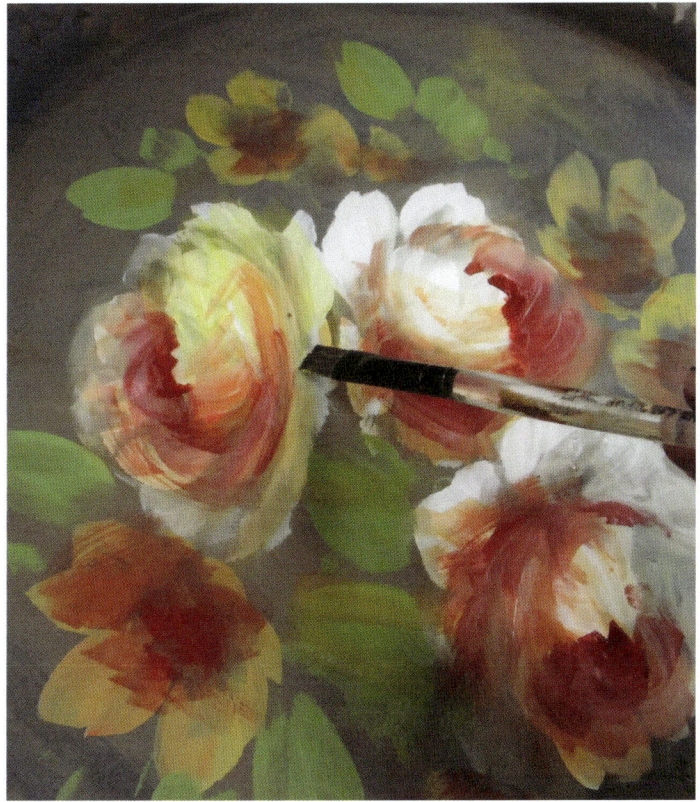

Step 23 Thin Hansa Yellow with some water or small amount of Extender and wash over the top light or warmer side of the roses. This will give them a yellow tint.

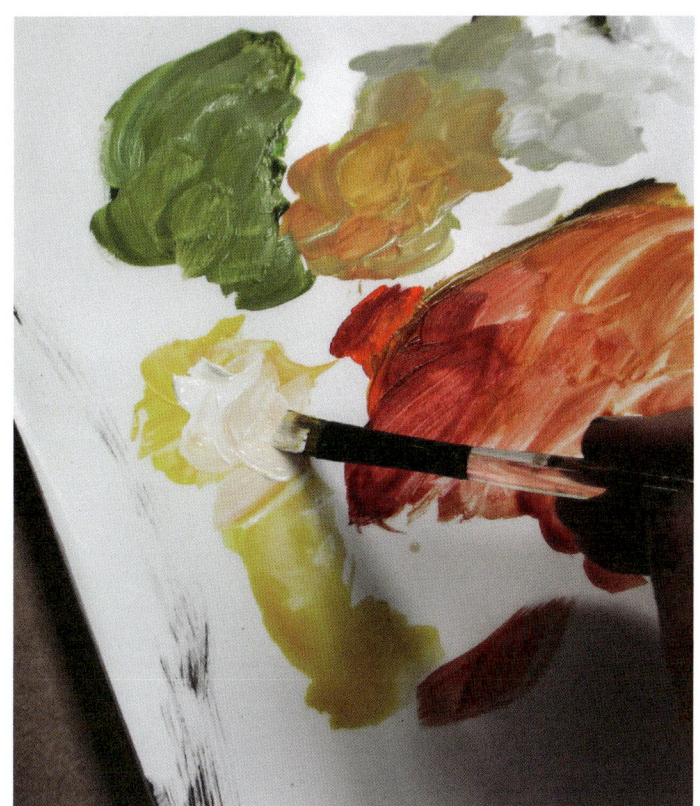

Step 24 Mottle the Hansa Yellow with thick white to lighten and thick the paint. You can also vary the color with a touch of red.

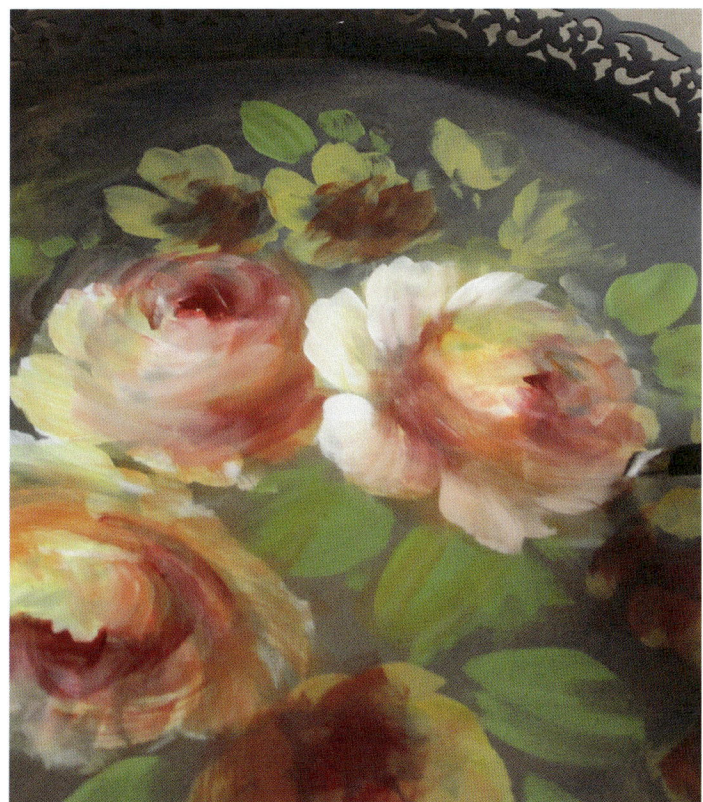

Step 25 Using the light thicker color, stroke on the reaching petals to the roses pulling towards the center bowl. Do not cover completely. Let some of the other colors show through.

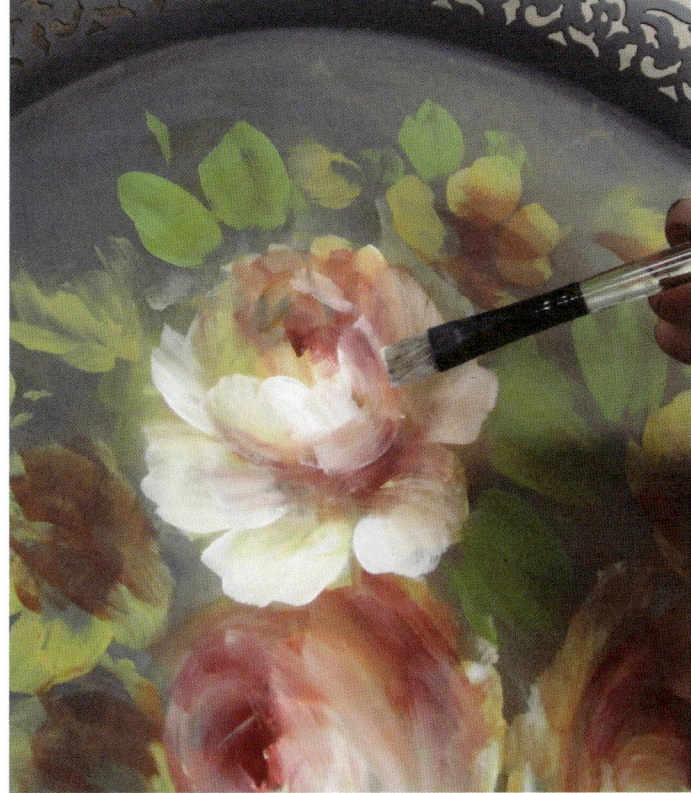

Step 26 Using the corner of the flat and the thicker light color, add indications of front petals to the roses. Pull down to incorporate into the roundness of the bowl.

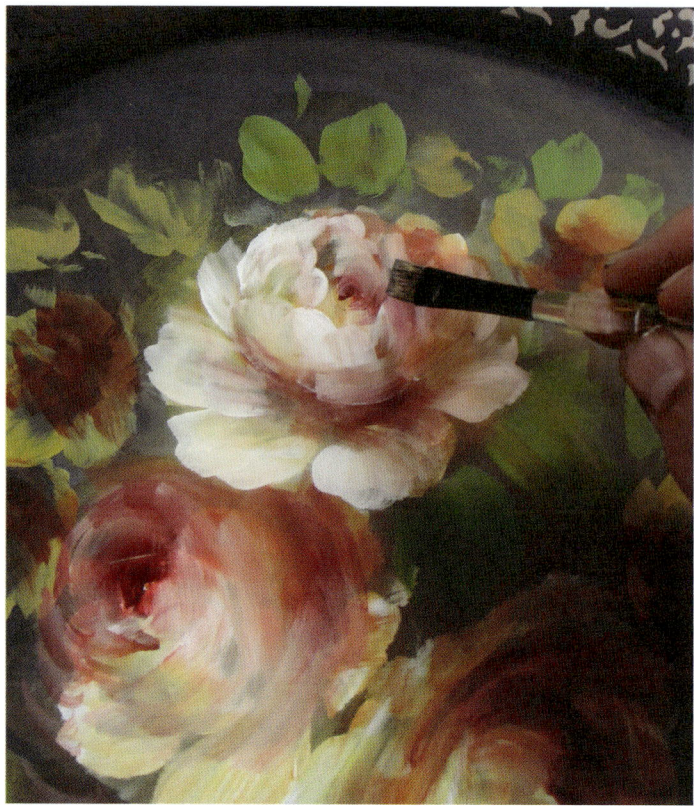

Step 27 Use the tip of the corner of the brush and work very small to add white movement petals in the center of the rose. Not too much because you you don't want them too opaque.

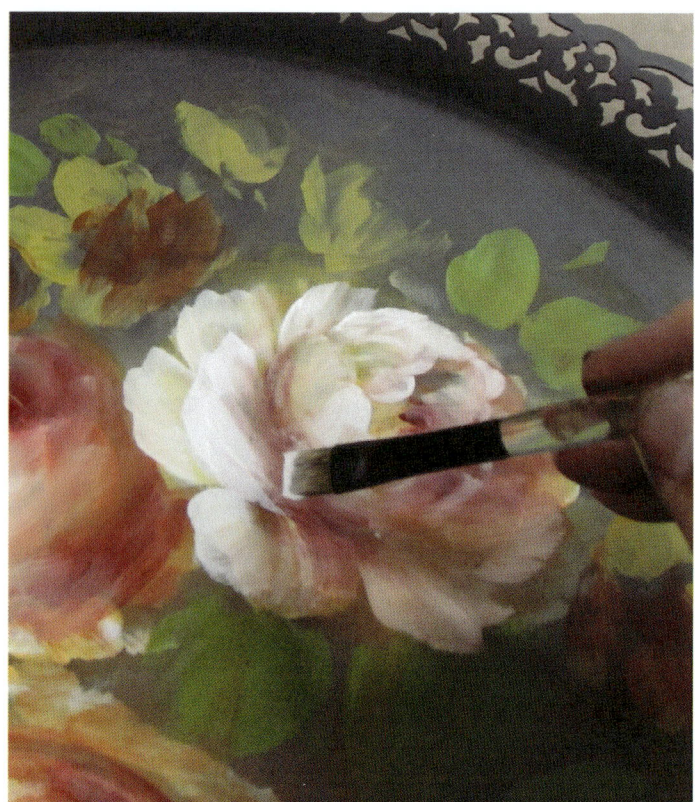

Step 28 Mottle the brush with more white and add the second layer of light petals pulling in towards the bowl of the rose.

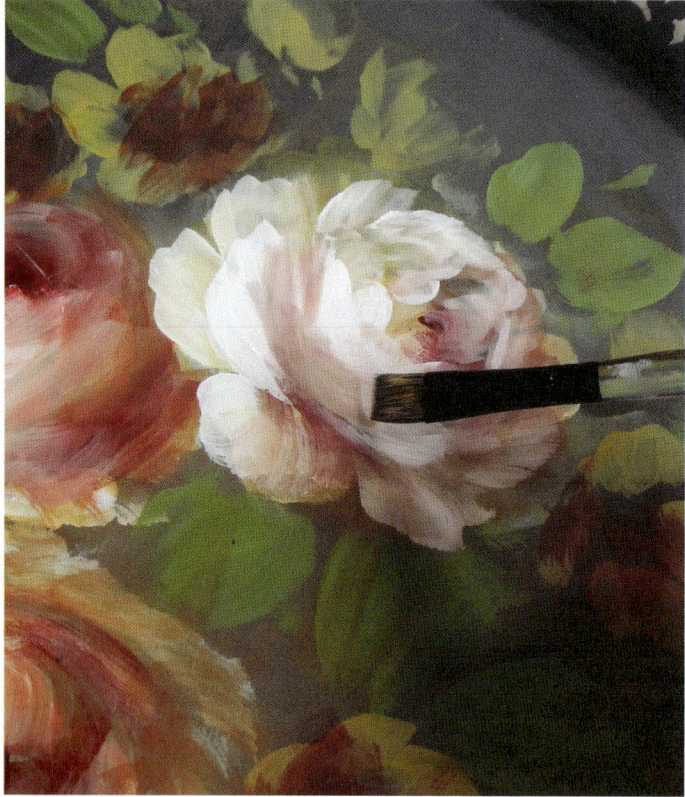

Step 29 Here I stroked on the white fronts of the rose. Then I wiped the brush and lifted off the excess moving up from the bottom of the bowl. This preserves the shadow on the bowl.

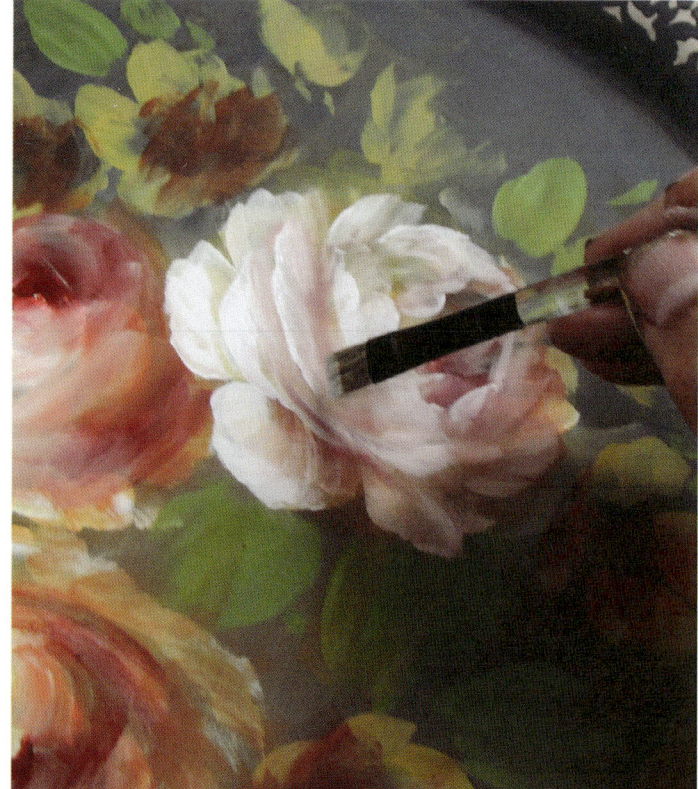

Step 30 Use the chisel of the brush to make the petal edges between the bowl of the rose and the reaching petals.

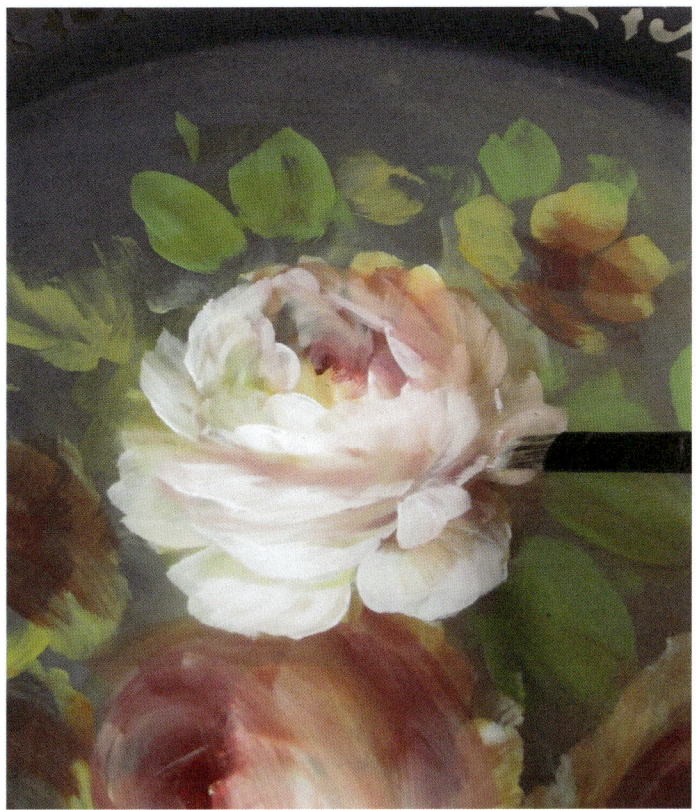

Step 31 Use the chisel and the tip of the brush to add smaller movements to the front of the rose to suggest front angled petals.

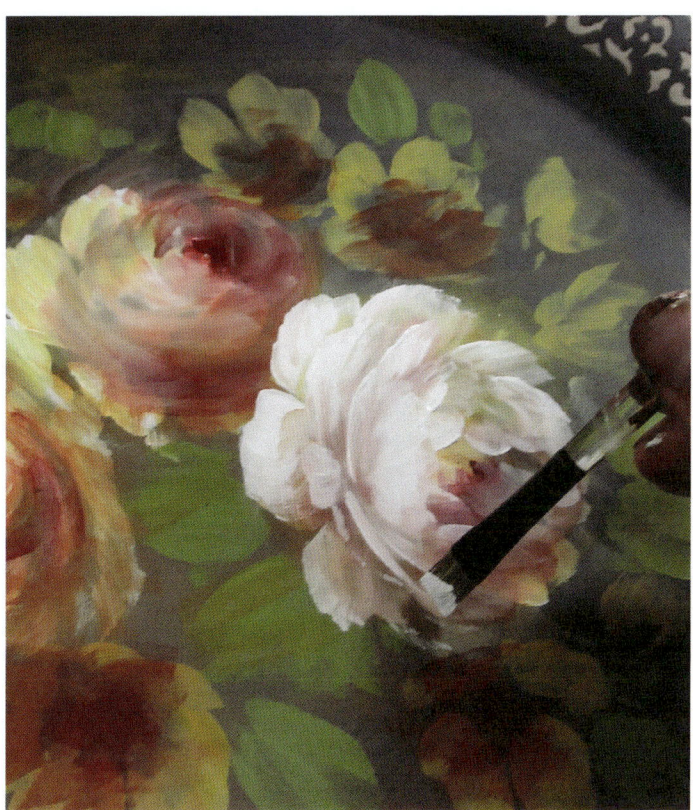

Step 32 Here I am using the chisel of the brush to make edges of petals. Since this is on the shadow side of the rose, I pull out lifting the brush to let it have a softer edge.

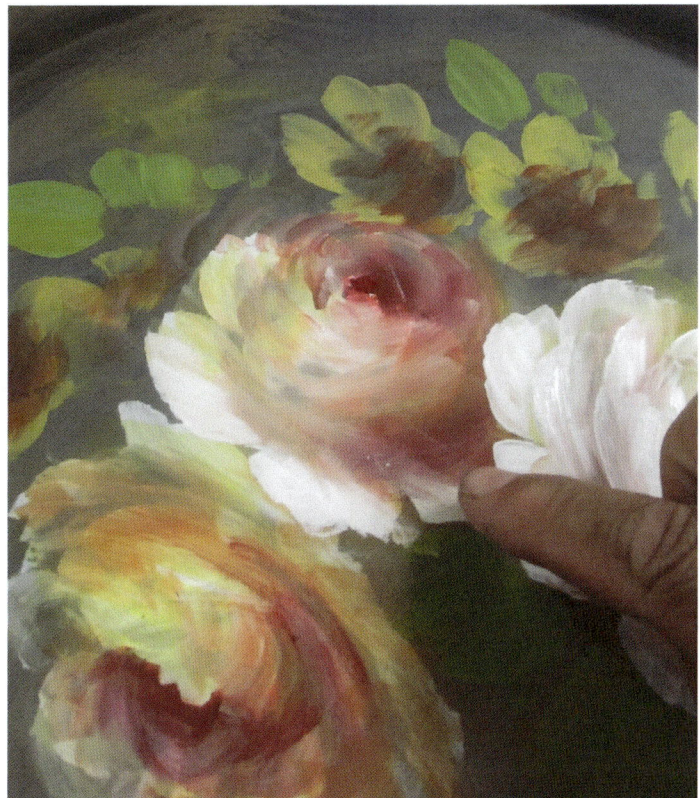

Step 33 Here I am starting the next row of petals using my finger to push in and out of the bowl to create movement. I paint mostly for movement.

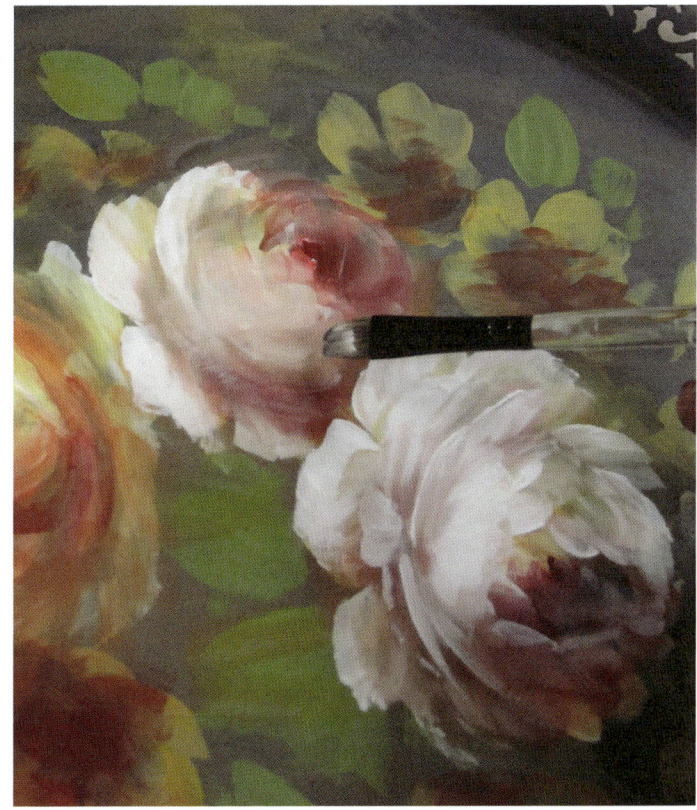

Step 34 Softly begin lighter colors on the bowl of the rose moving the brush in the round shape of the bowl. Movement is key. Don't think petals, think round bowl movement.

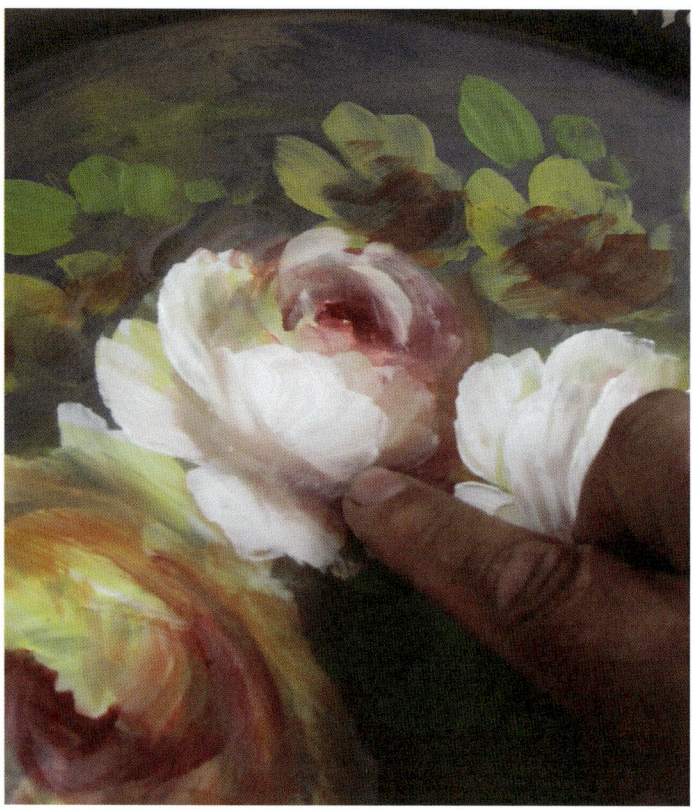

Step 35 Lighten front of the rose with more white. Then soften the edges into the shadow by pushing with your finger. This is the shear technique.

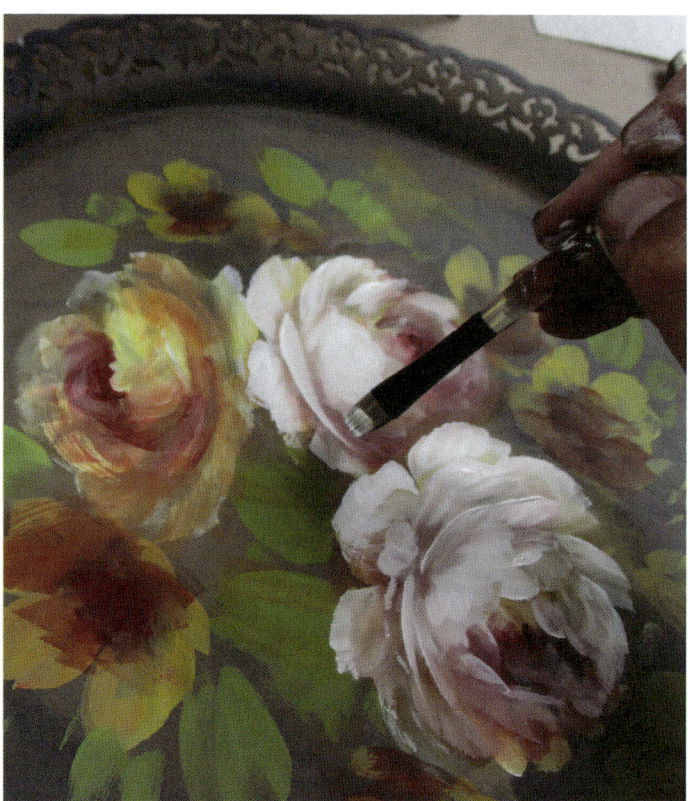

Step 36 Here I use the chisel to make the edge of the front petal. Use different petal shapes to make the rose look different from each other.

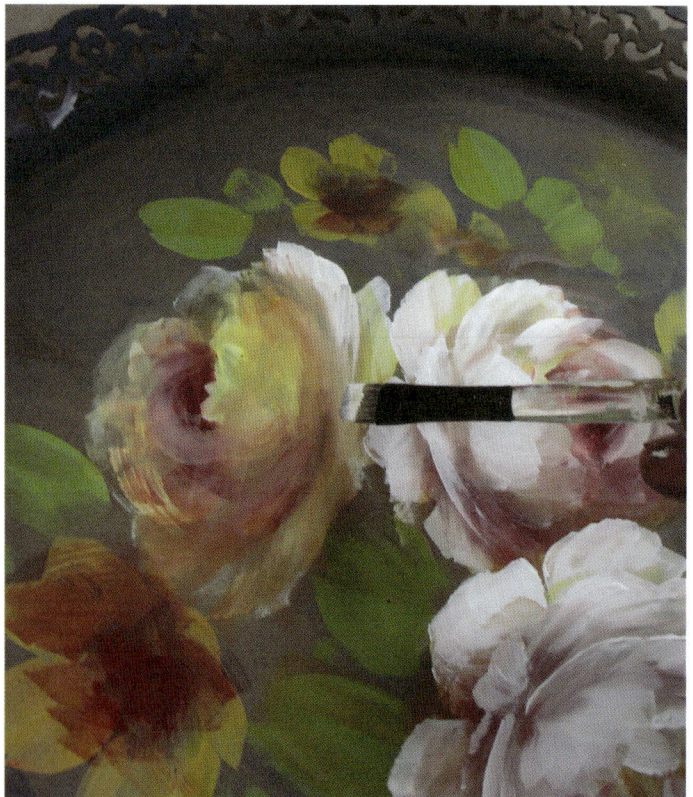

Step 37 Here I am adding reaching petals to the next rose. Lift the brush off as you approach the bowl of the rose. Use your finger to shear the color if you need.

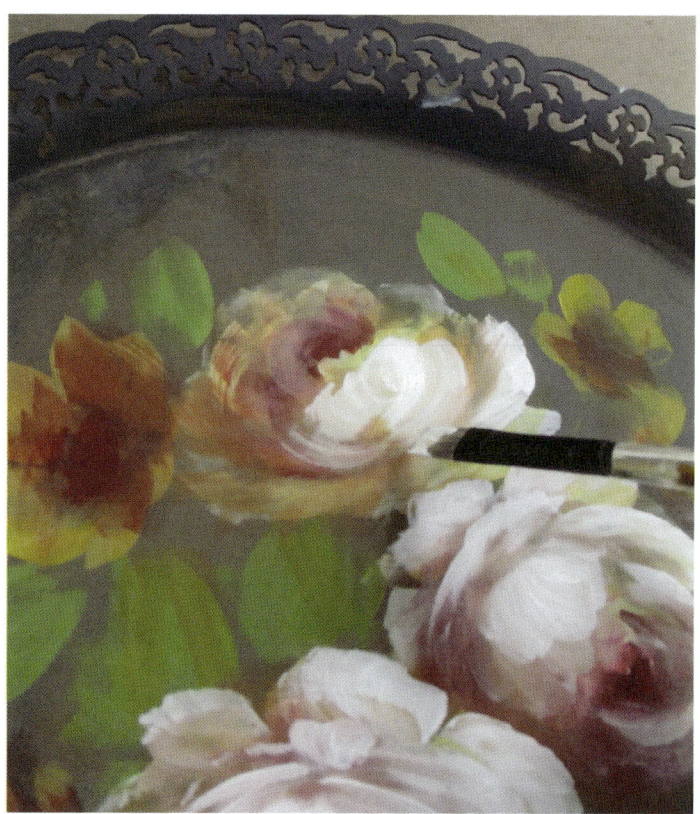

Step 38 Here I am building more white in the front of the rose. This will make the front advance. Do not do too much; you might lose the shadow on the bowl.

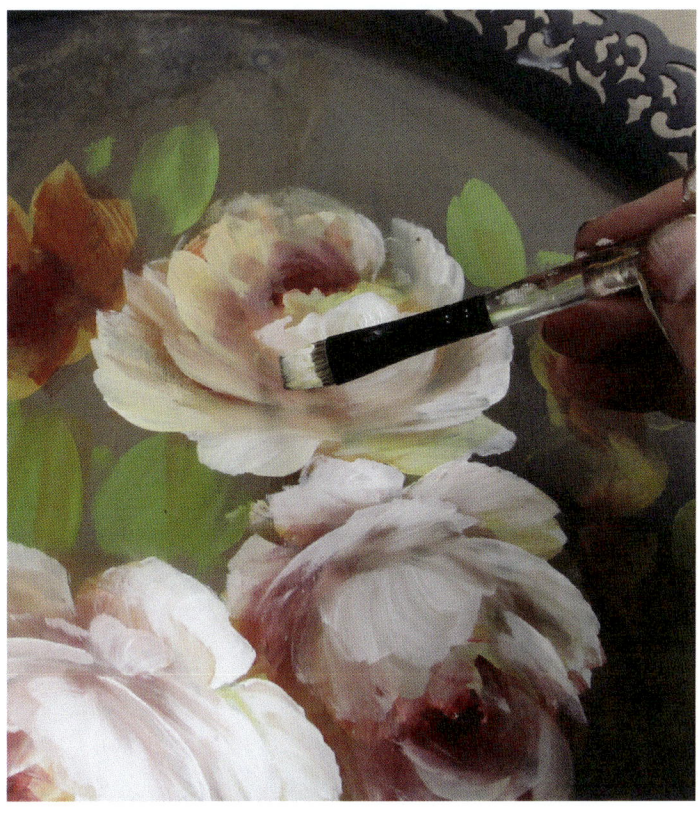

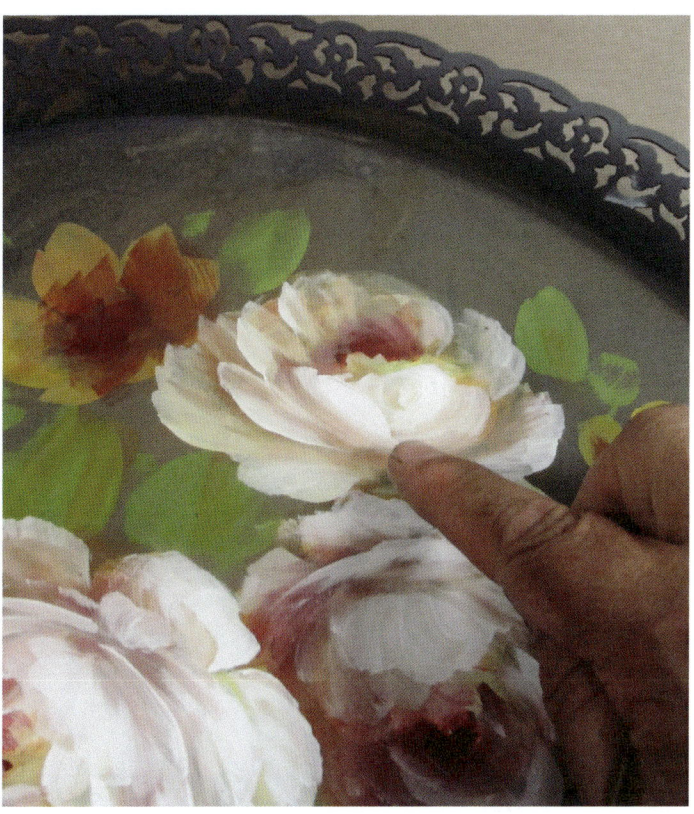

Step 39 Mottle the color a little darker with yellows and reds. Add the petals to the shadow side of the rose. These should be darker than the front petals.

Step 40 Here I am using my finger to preserve the roundness at the bottom of the bowl. This is very important. Save the shadow and the roundness by pushing color.

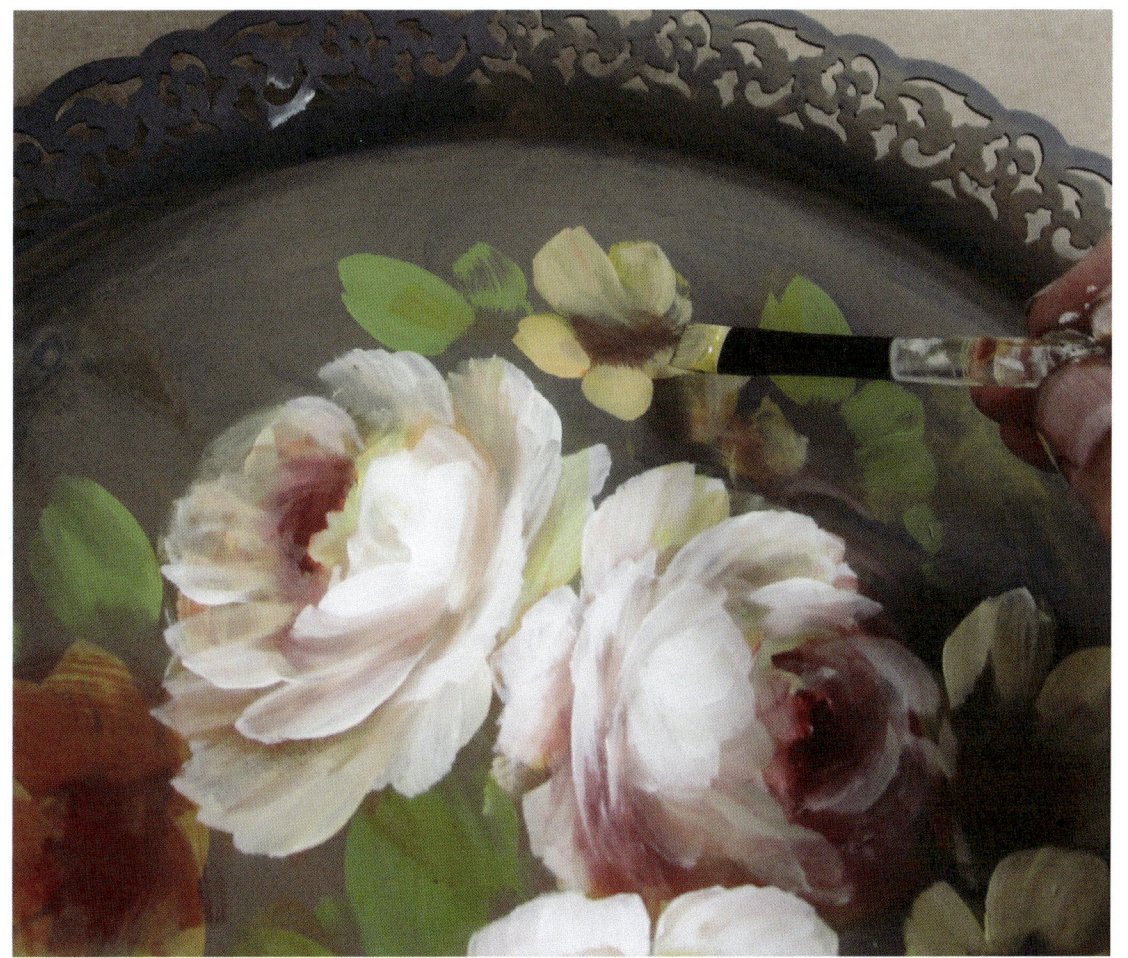

Step 41 Lighten the yellows and yellow oranges we used on the blossoms with additional white. Then add highlights to the blossoms. Lift off as you get to the center to preserve the cool shadow in the center with applied earlier. Again, vary the sizes, shapes, and colors for more interest. Refer to the final photo for ideas.

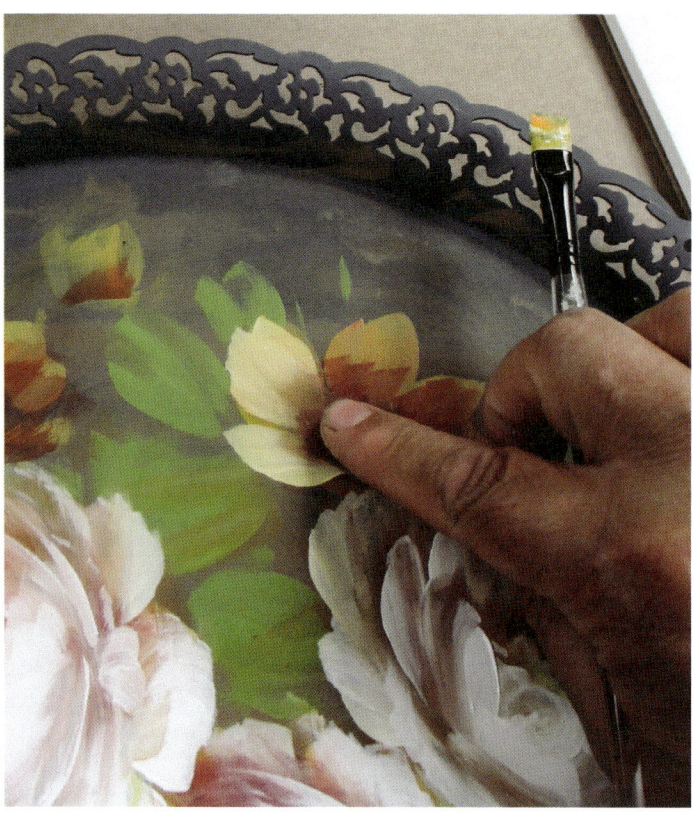

Step 42 Push in and out of the center with your finger. This will give movement to the petals. I like the natural movement of the finger on many flowers rather than the brush.

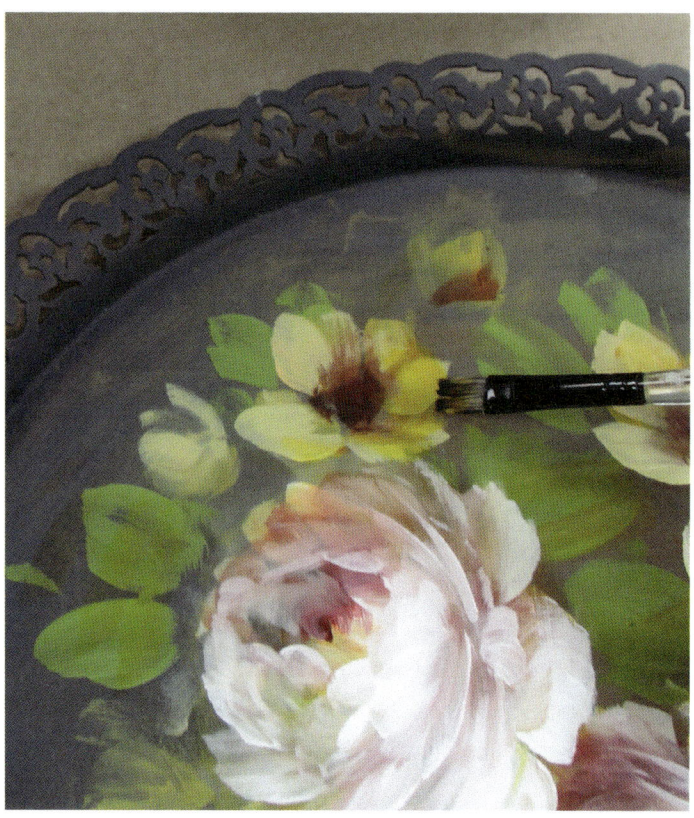

Step 43 Here I am washing transparent Hansa yellow over the blossoms to vary the colors. Don't wash over equally. Vary the amount for interest.

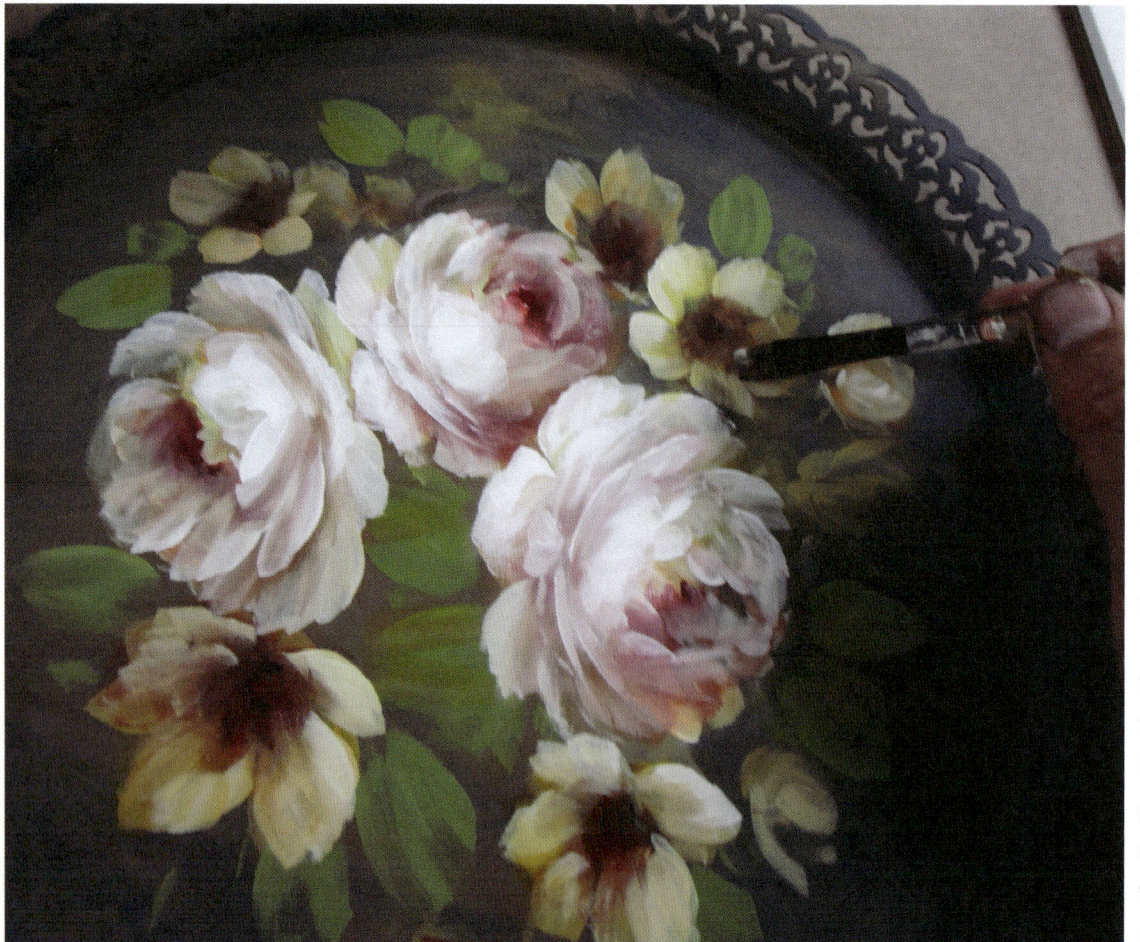

Step 44 After I wash some transparent Hansa I reset the light petals. Vary the amounts of light and the strokes for interest. On the 2 large blossoms, notice how I lightened the petals on the bottom a little more. I felt this pulled the viewers eye down from the roses and helped the eye move through the painting. Since our background is dark, pay close attention to the lights and their placement.

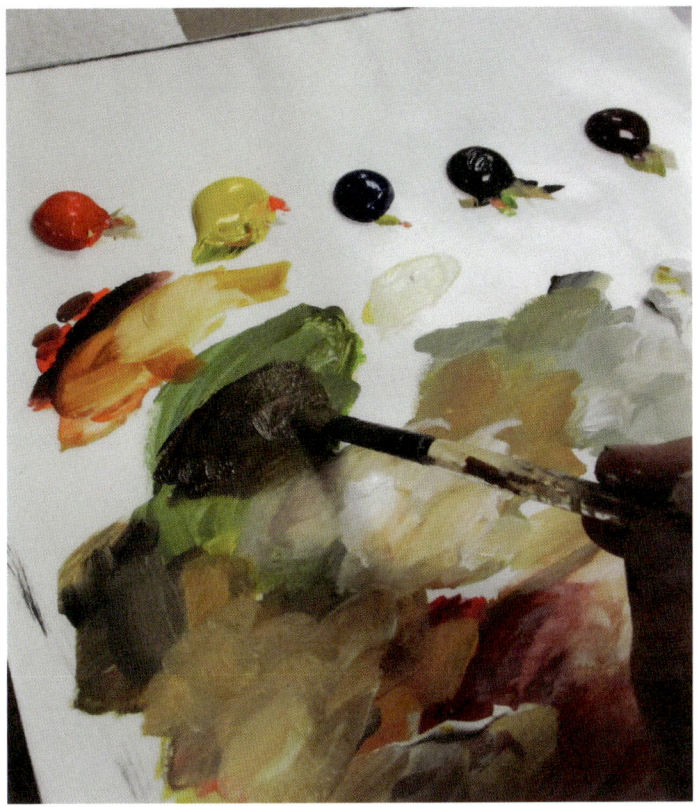

Step 45 Mottle the greens with a touch of black to darken. Cool with a touch Red Violet. Do not over mix the color.

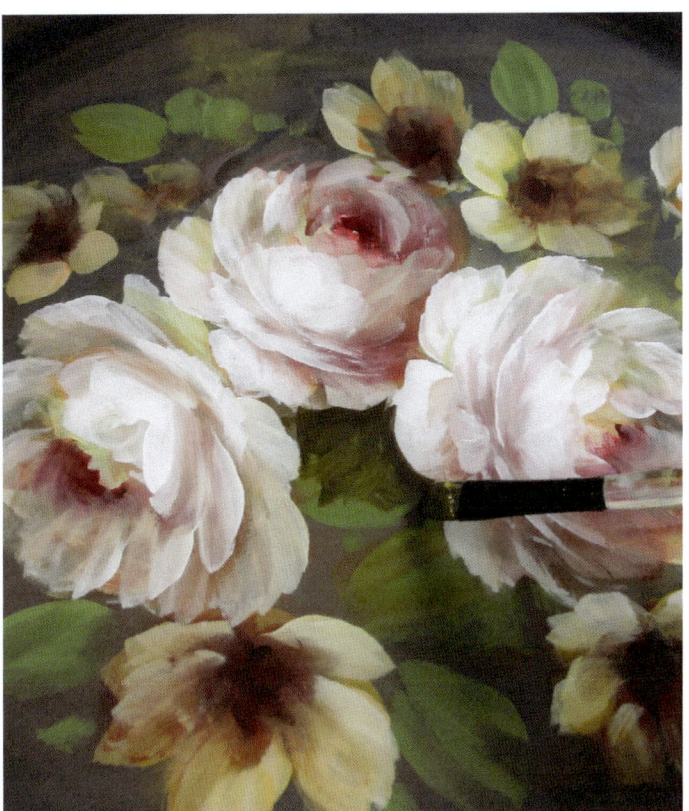

Step 46 Add the cooler dark color to the shadow sides of the leaves. This is also where you can do some negative painting on the roses to correct and clean up the edges for contrast.

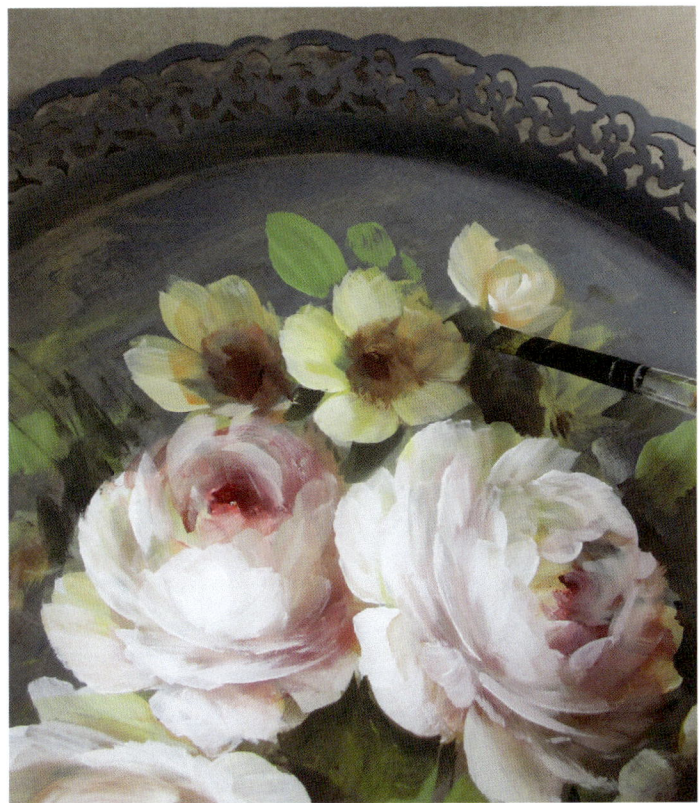

Step 47 Here I am using some darker cooler greens to shadow the back of the roses between the blossoms. Negative painting can be used for interest.

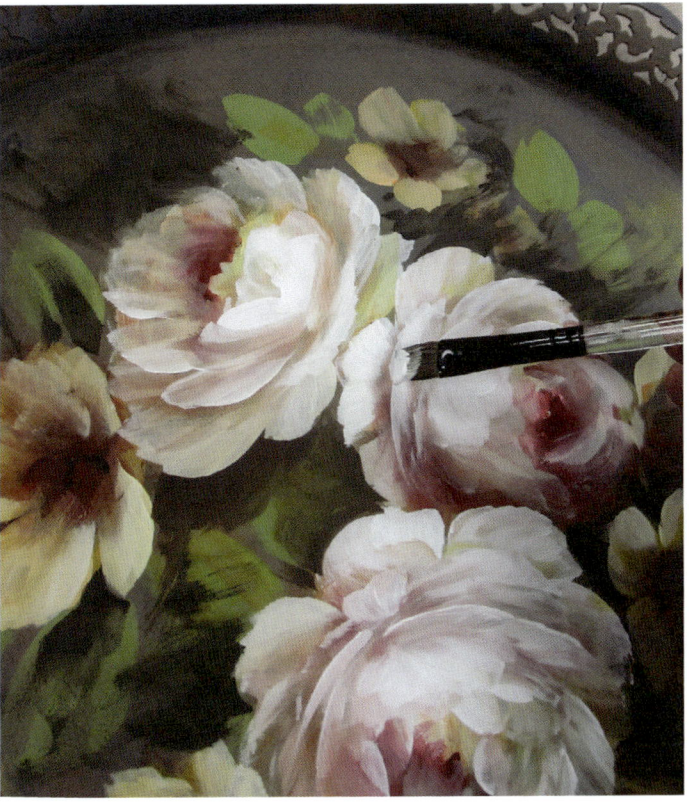

Step 48 After I have added some shadows, I revisit the highlights on the center of interest flowers. Here I am adding more white to the front roses.

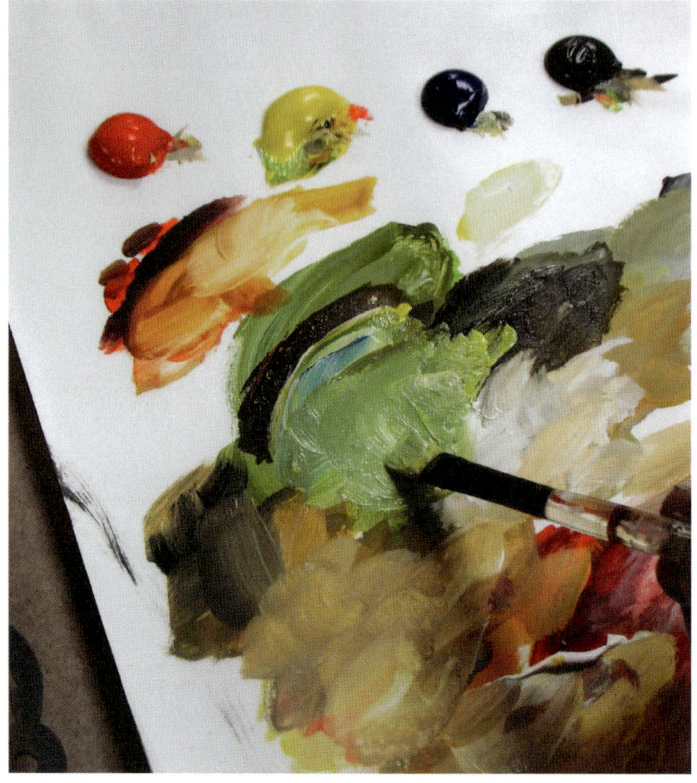

Step 49 Mottle a lighter green with more Hansa Yellow. I add a touch of Phthalo Blue and White to vary the color. Do not over mix.

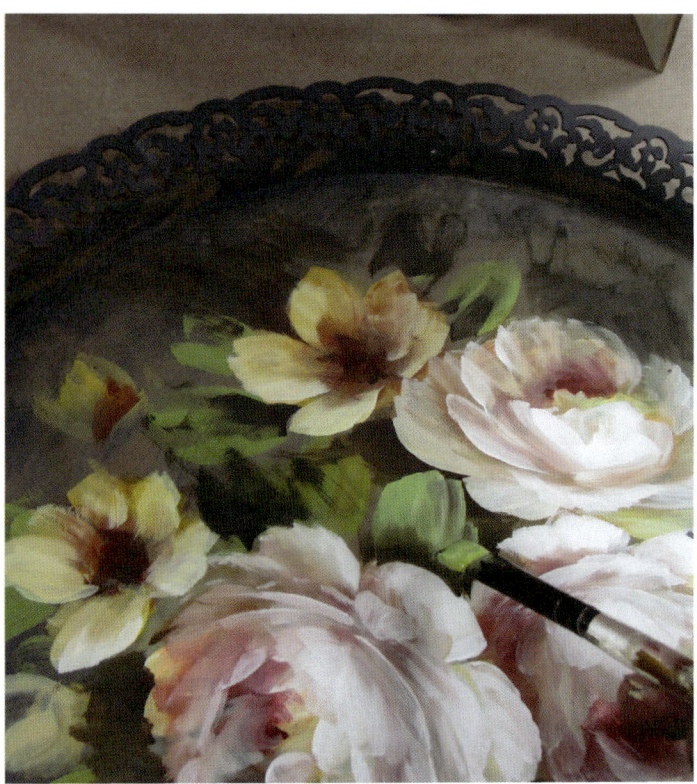

Step 50 Add strokes of the light green highlight to the leaves starting in the center. Lift off as you get to the shadows so you preserve them.

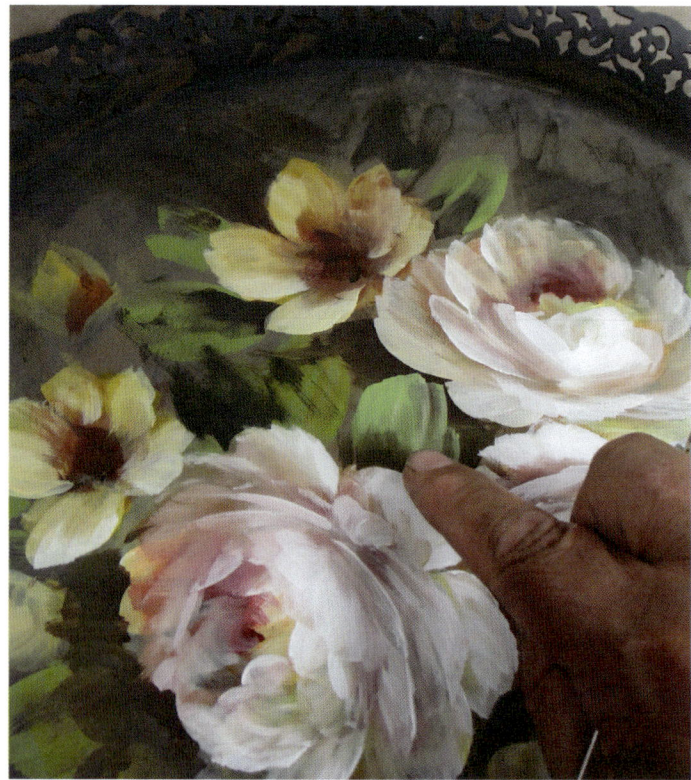

Step 51 Here again I use my finger to create movement in and out of the shadow. I paint for movement more than anything else.

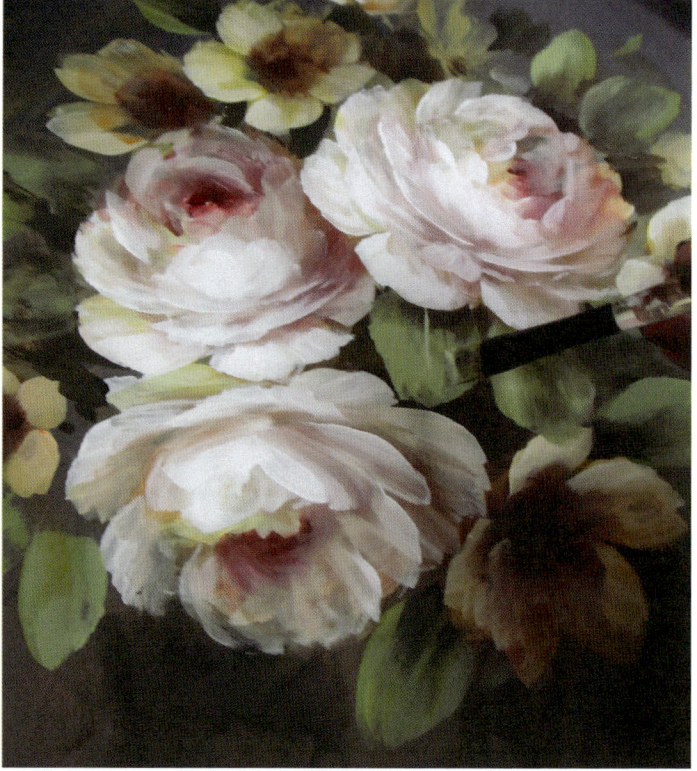

Step 52 Restate more lights and then use the chisel of the flat to simulate a vein line in the center of the leaf.

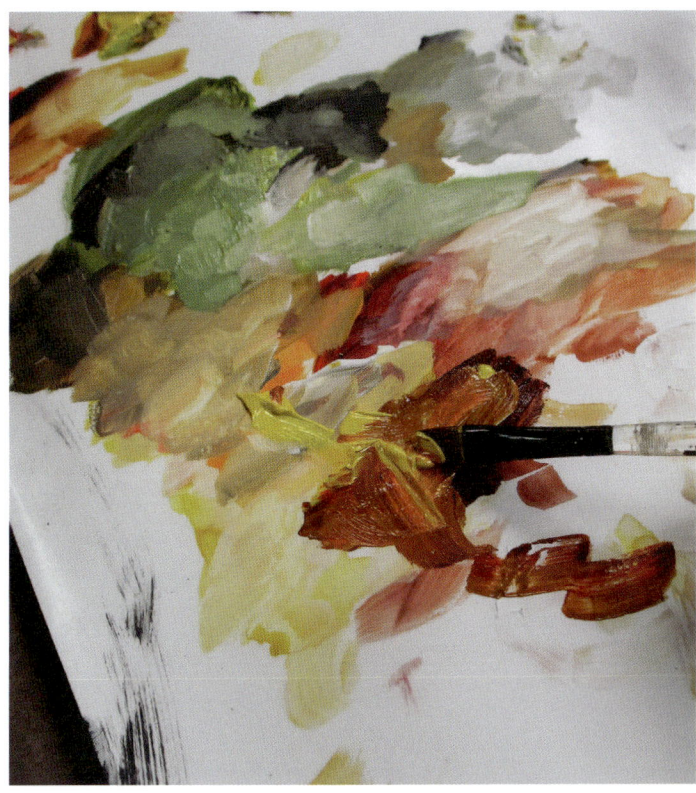

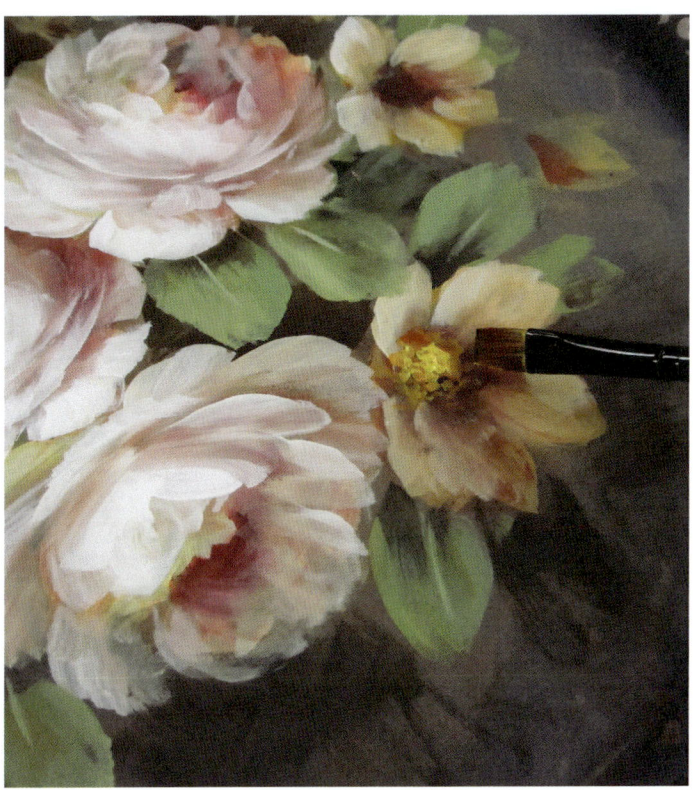

Step 53 Mottle the brush with reds and yellows. I tone this with a touch of green and black. Mottle the color on the brush, then corner the brush with a touch of Hansa Yellow for contrast.

Step 54 Start in the center of the blossom with the Hansa Yellow corner and then work out towards the petals letting the color get softer and darker. Use a light touch on the outside.

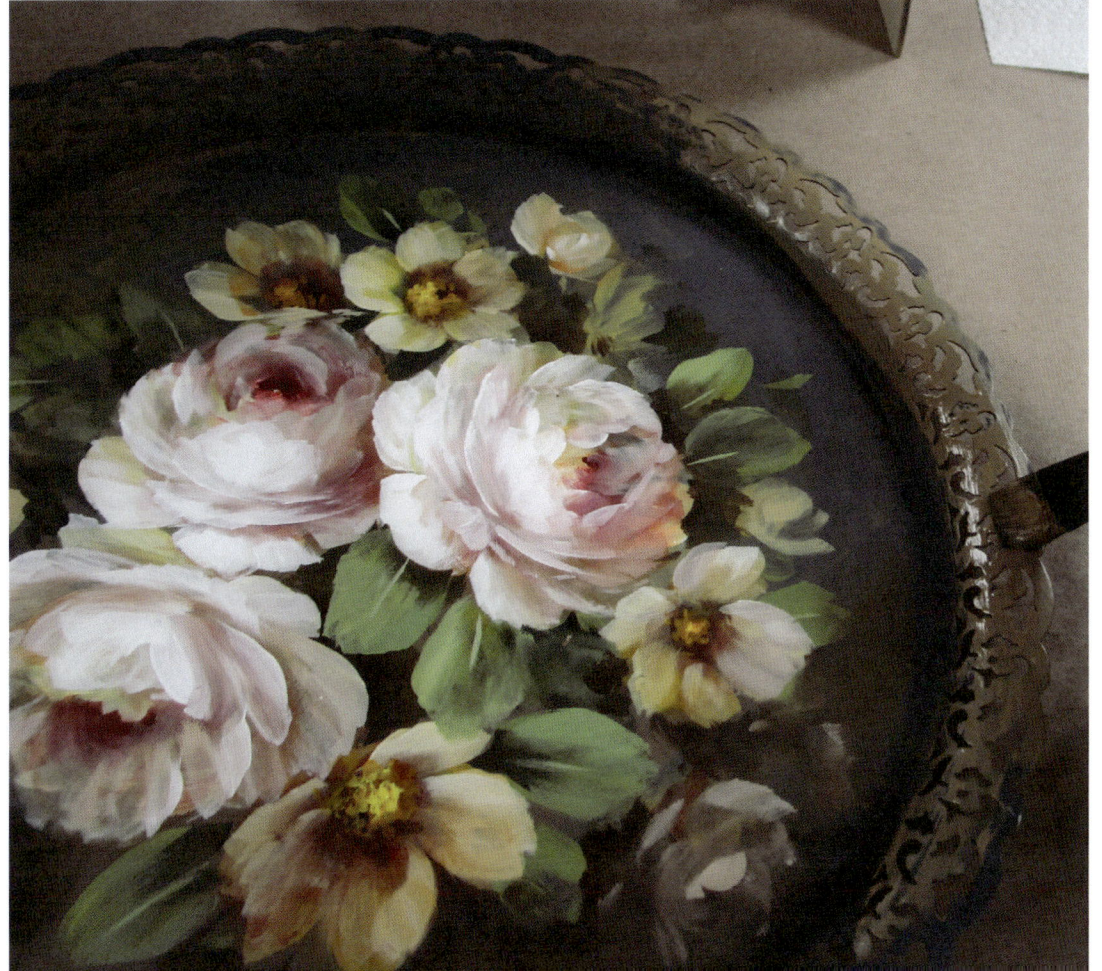

Step 55 Overall I enjoy this technique. By letting the white flowers dry and washing them with the yellows, the colors do not mix and the yellows stay lighter and brighter. By working the whites in slowly, you can build the amount of contrast you like. For the rim of this tray I love gold. First I used the light browns from the second step. I then went over with gold to brighten. Enjoy!

Lesson 1
Pattern

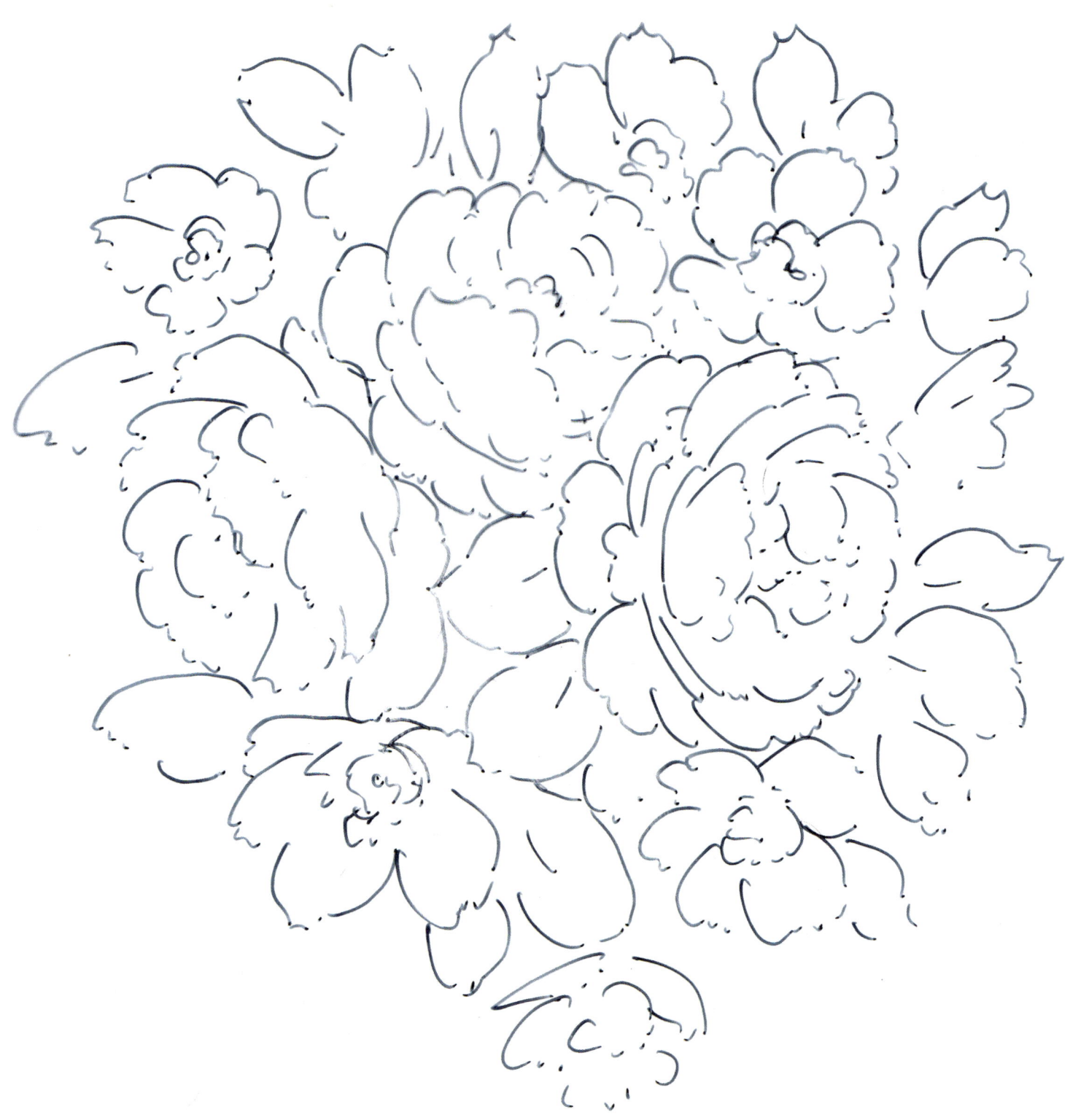

Copyright © 2018 David Jansen

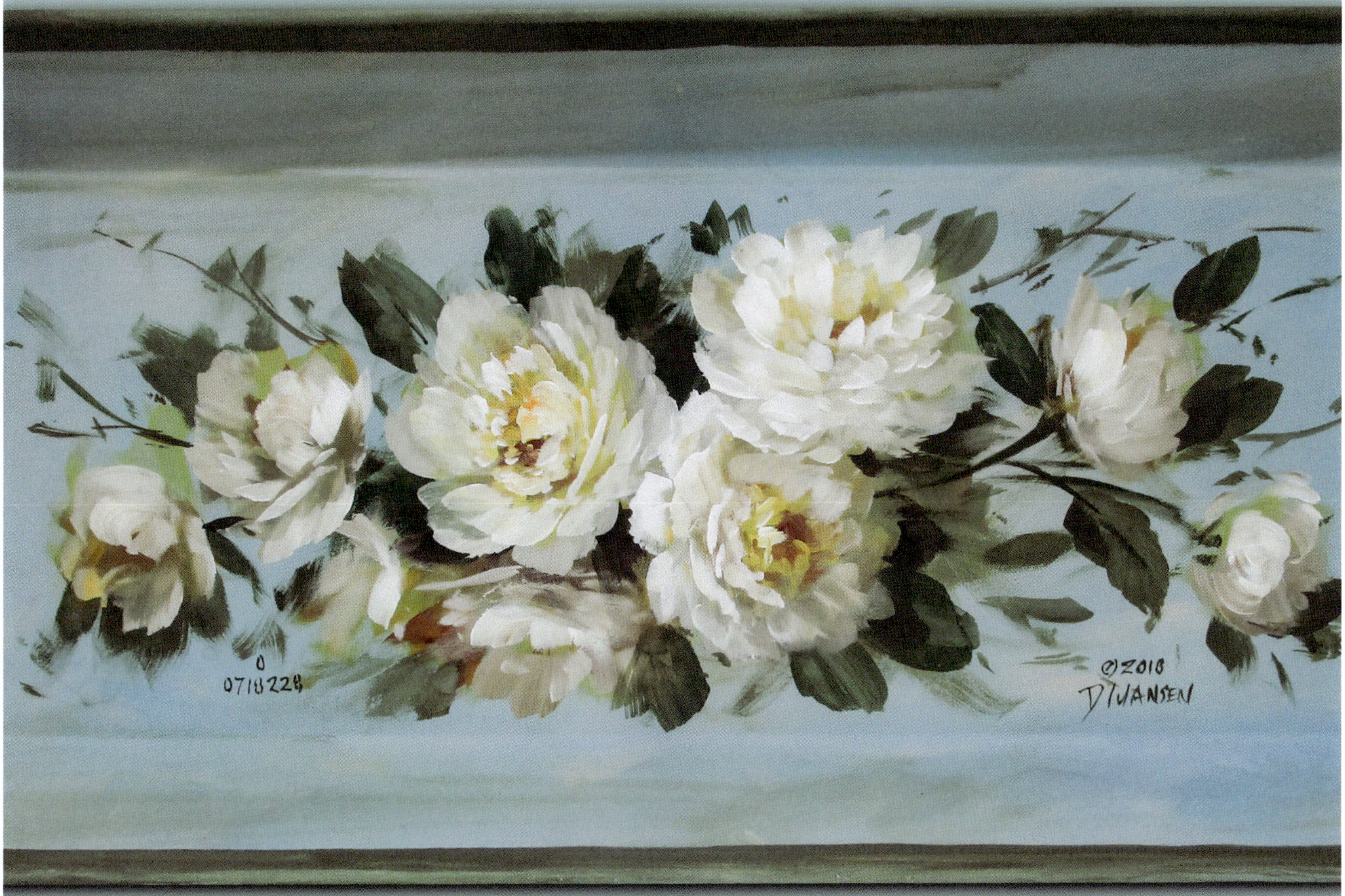

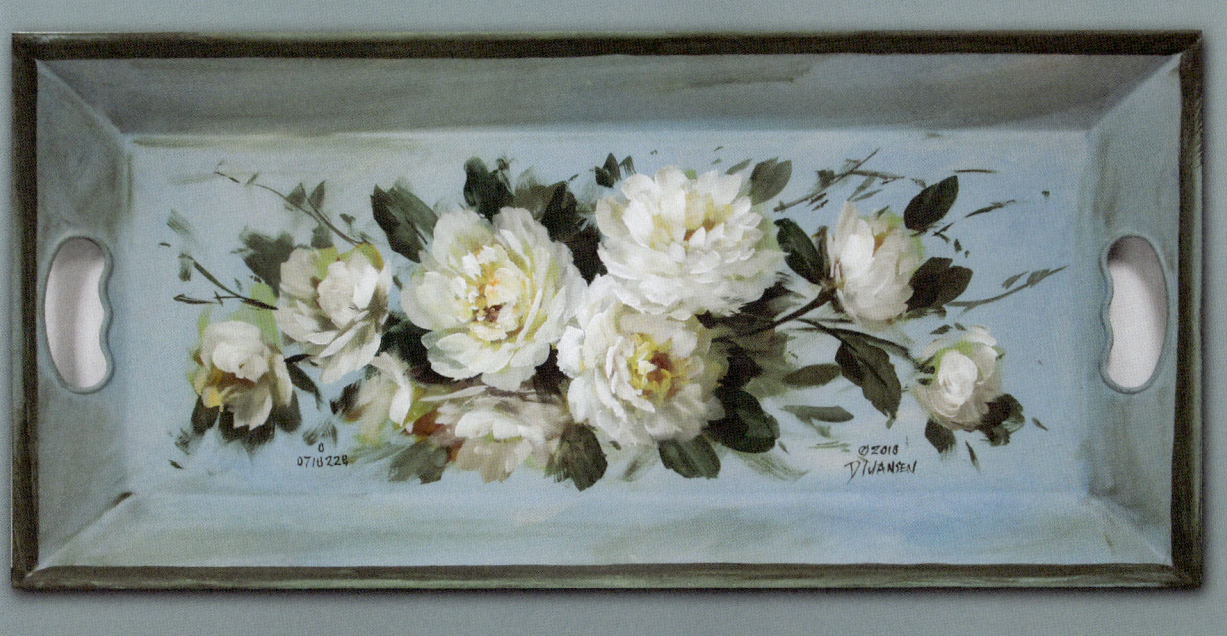

Lesson 2

Rosa Imogen- Lots of petals!

I love these roses. They are almost like mums. To paint them, we need to control our values so we that have many colors to work with to establish petals. We will also use the shadow glazes to create simultaneous contrast. (See photo below)

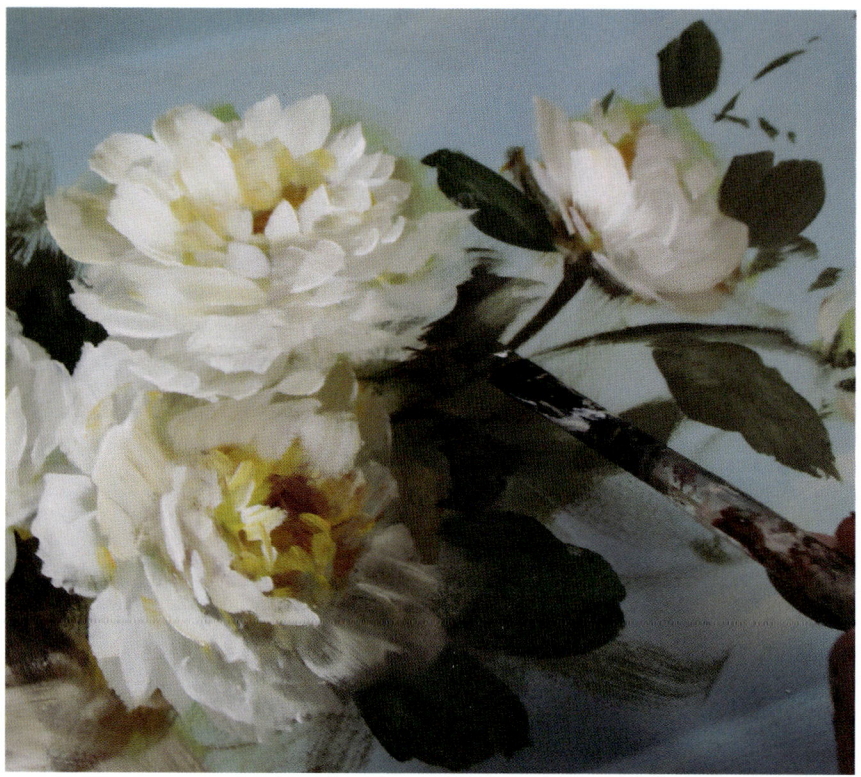

With simultaneous contrast, the darker tones make lighter tones appear lighter. By painting these flowers on a light to medium value background, we visually have more whites to work with. It works!

To paint these successfully we need to be very stingy with our white. Don't apply too much to the petals at a time. Slowly progress through the values as you build the petals.

We will also use a tinting technique to push back some the light petals to give us more room to make value adjustments.

It takes a plan to paint a group of white multi-petaled flowers. You must control the white. Watch the values I use in each photo. Tint where necessary and control your white. It is a great practice piece! Let's give it a try!

Paint It Simply Palette
Base Color- Light Grey

Palette Colors

PAINT IT SIMPLY COLORS
Naphthol Red Light
Red Violet
Titanium White
Carbon Black
Phthalo Blue
Hansa Yellow

OPTIONAL COLORS
Yellow Oxide
Diarylide Yellow
Pine Green
Quinacridone Violet
Burnt Sienna
Phthalo Green Blue

Painting Surface
Large Metal Tray

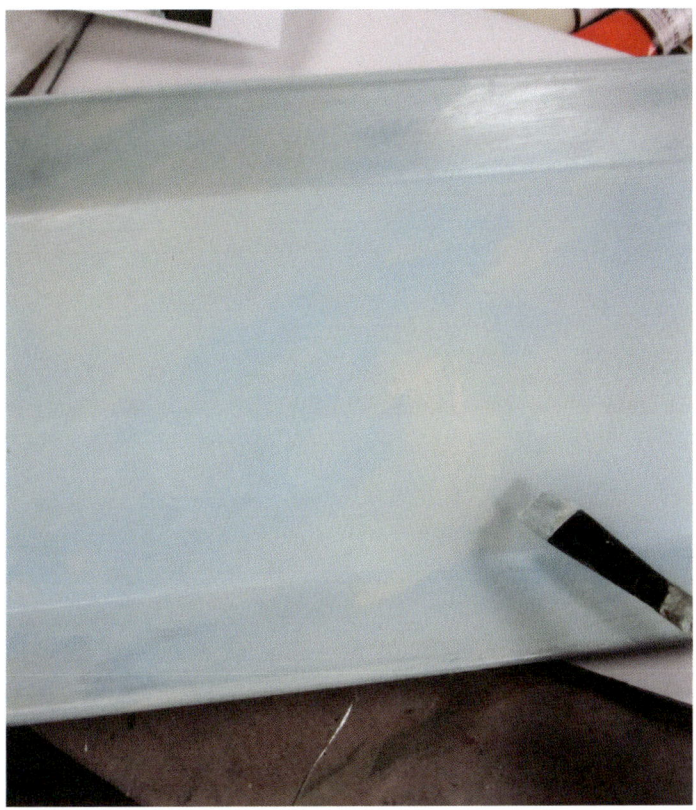

Step 1 I based a rectangle tray with Heritage Light Grey. Mottle a light blue from Phthalo Blue and White. Add to the surface of the tray leaving some of the Light Grey showing.

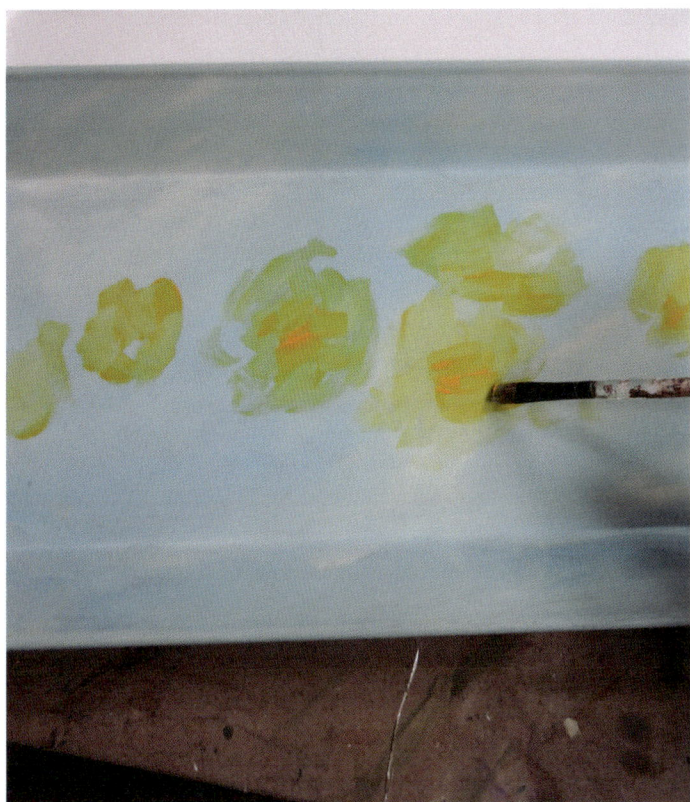

Step 2 Mottle the brush with Diarylide Yellow and make circle shapes to define where the imogen roses will be.

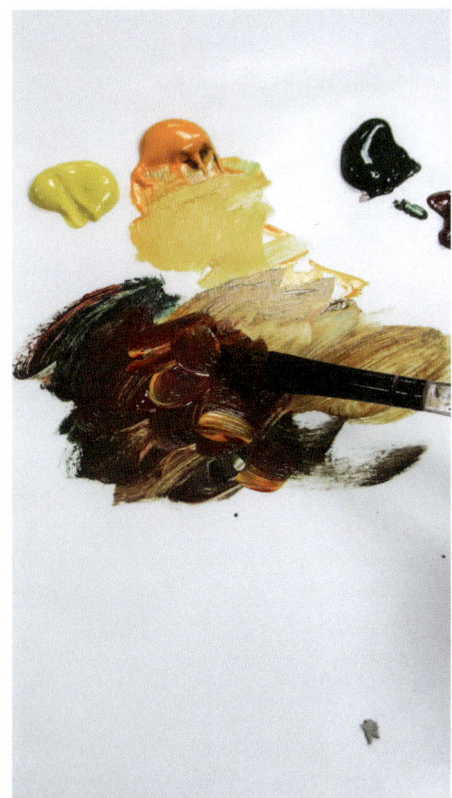

Step 3 Mottle the brush with Burnt Sienna and tone with touch Phthalo Green Blue.

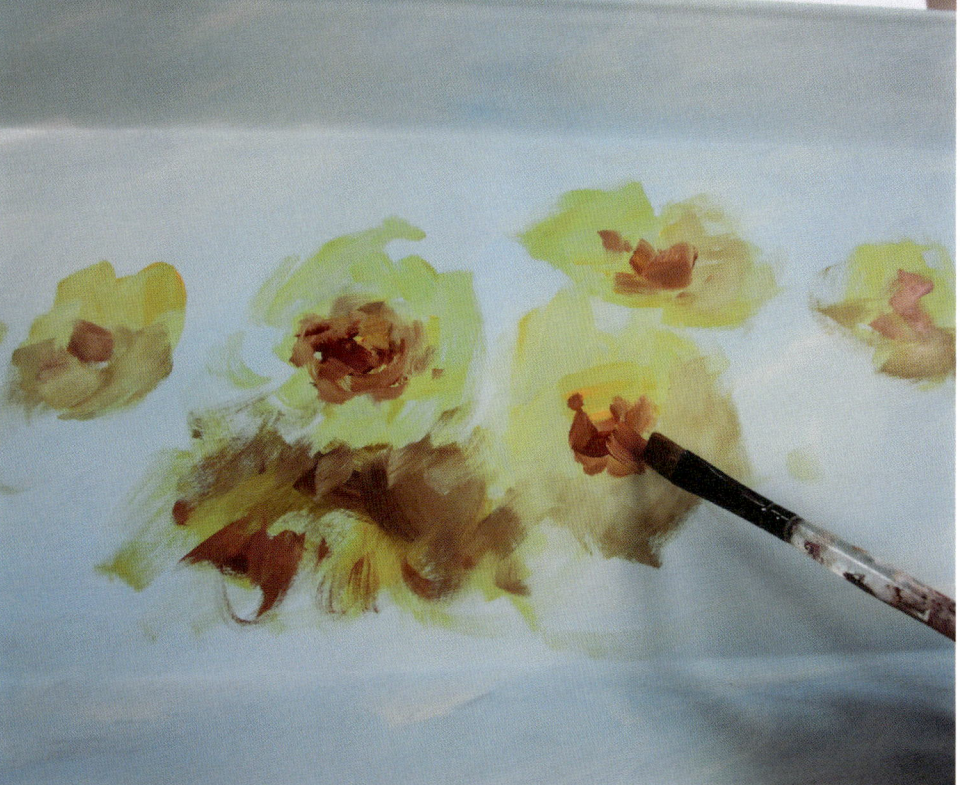

Step 4 Use this dark toned Burnt Sienna to create some contrast in the centers of the imogen roses. I am using a # 8 flat. Mottle the color so you get lots of variation in the color. Darker in the center.

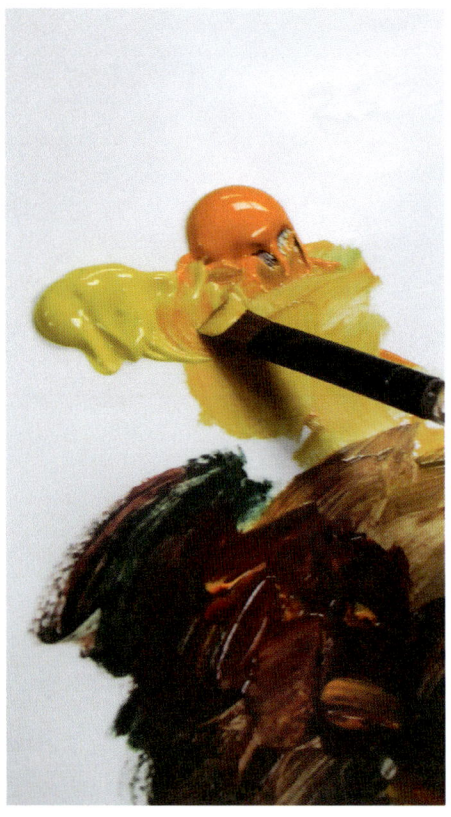

Step 5 Mottle the Diarylide with Hansa Yellow. Do not over mix the colors.

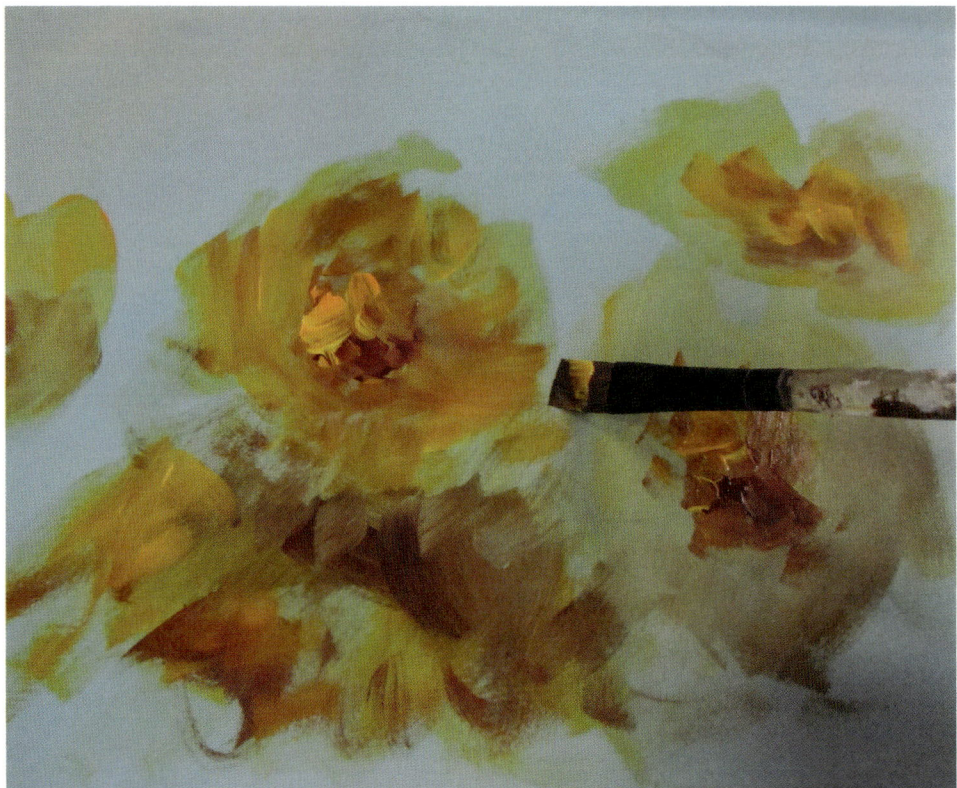

Step 6 Tap the color into the centers of the roses where we just deposited the darks. Since the colors are semi-transparent they will allow the darks to show through a little. Let this happen. It makes very interesting centers.

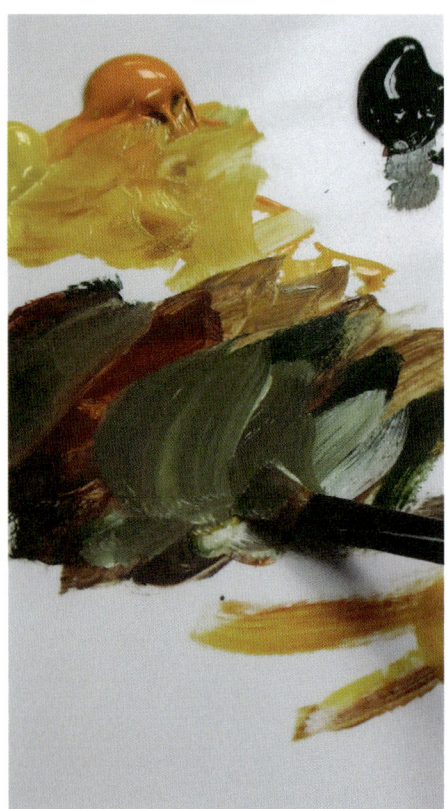

Step 7 Mottle Phthalo Green Blue into the yellows and Burnt Sienna. Lighten with touch white.

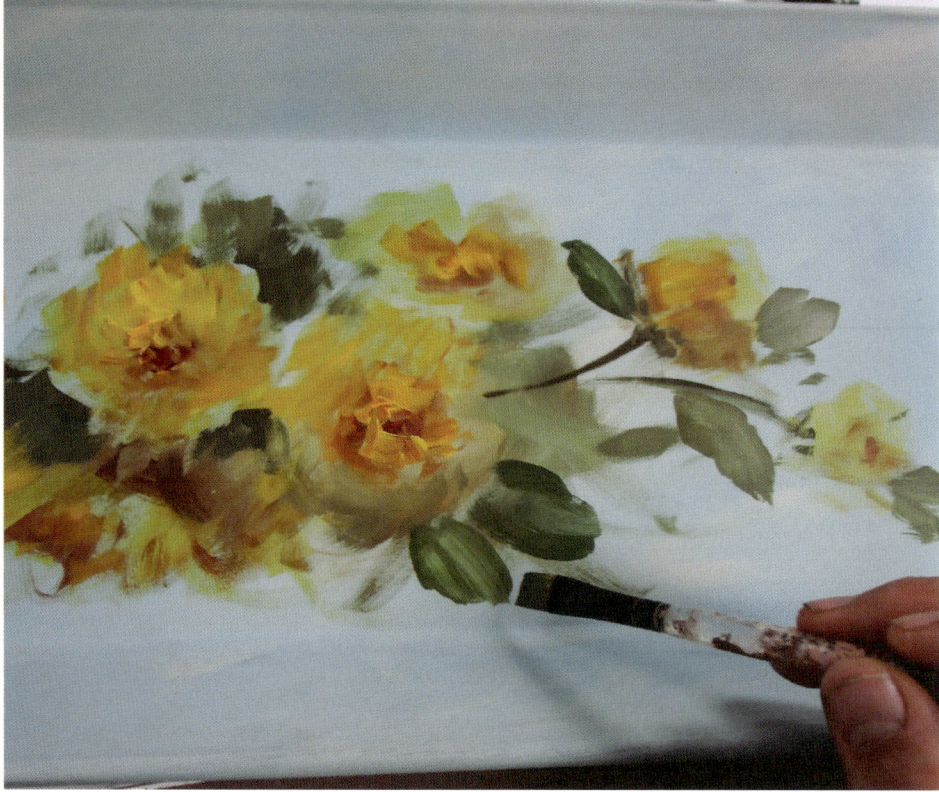

Step 8 Add the shapes of the leaves. I used 2 to 3 strokes to base in the oval shape of the leaves. Allow the streaks to show through. You can soften with your finger as we did with the last lesson. Vary the colors. More grey to the outer edges.

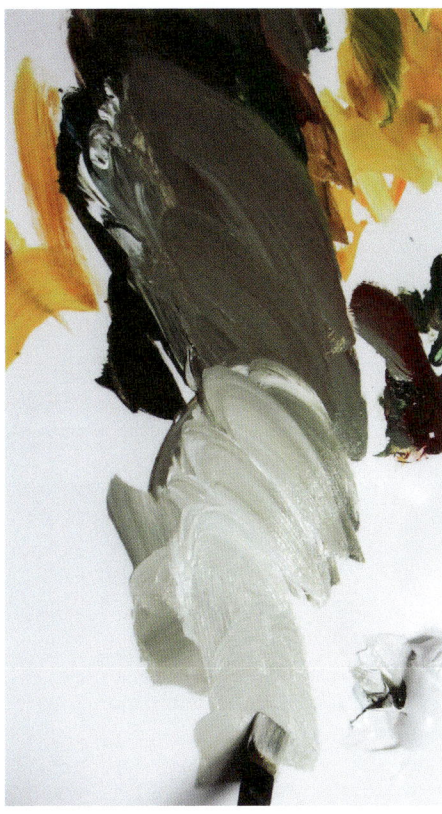
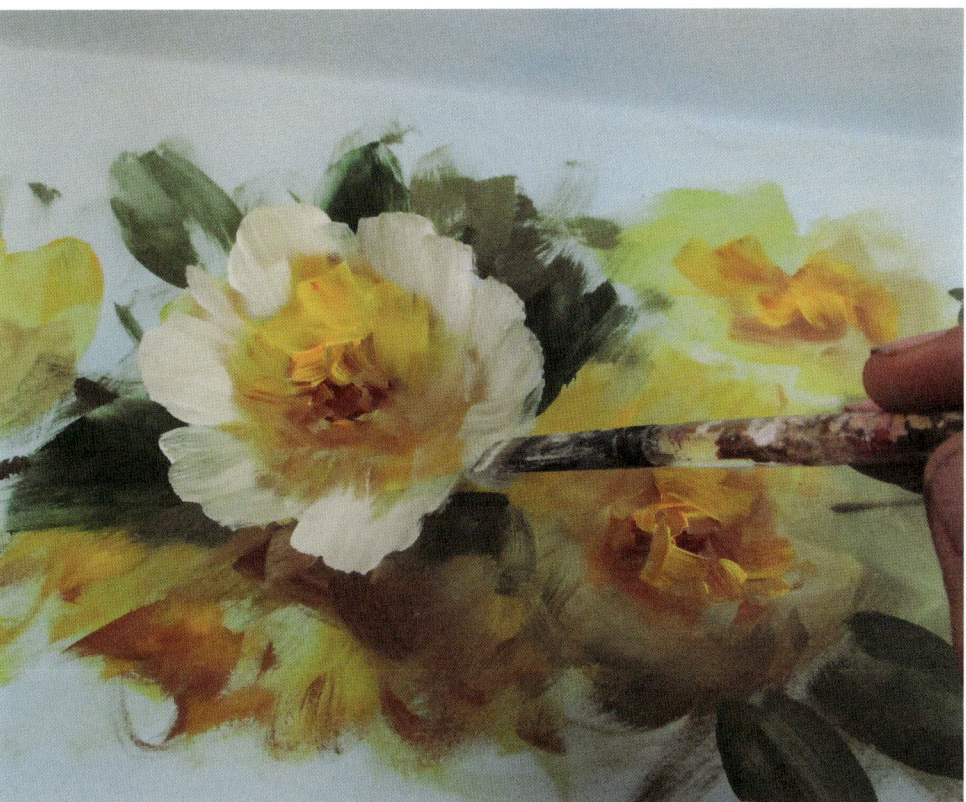

Step 9 Mottle all the colors to make a grey. Burnt Sienna and greens. Lighten with white to value close to background.

Step 10 Begin the outer petals of the roses. Notice how sometimes I will pull in toward the center and sometimes pull out leaving a soft edge. Also notice that the white is very close to the color of the background to keep these outer petals soft looking.

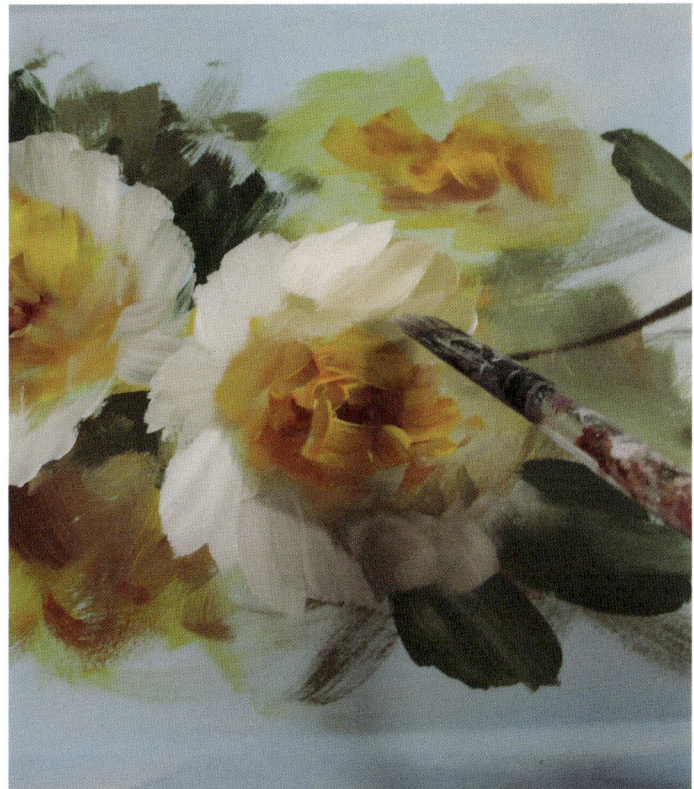
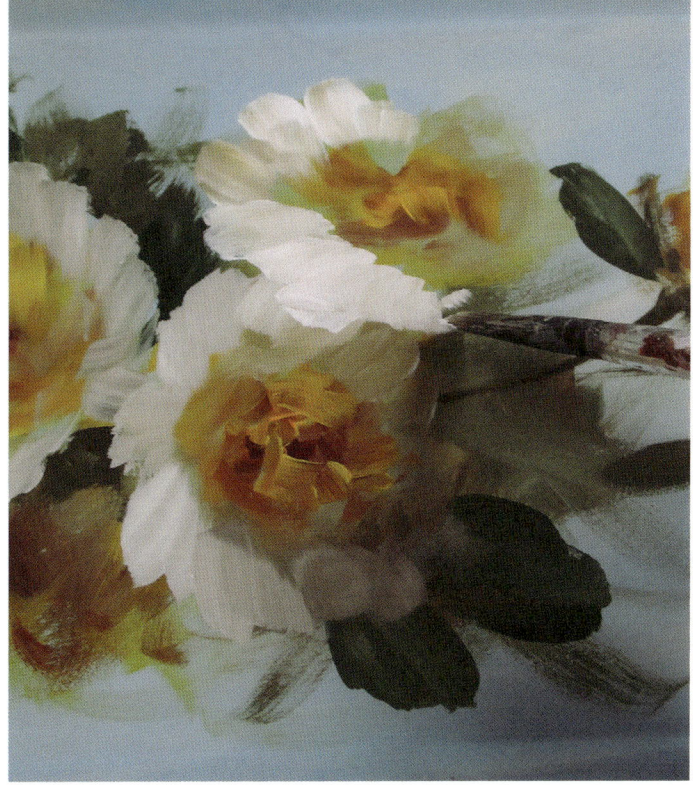

Step 11 Lighten the color with a little more white and add additional thicker color to the side of the roses that face the center. This starts our center of interest.

Step 12 Here you see me starting the outer petals on the next rose. Let the streaks happen in the roses. This adds interest to the petals.

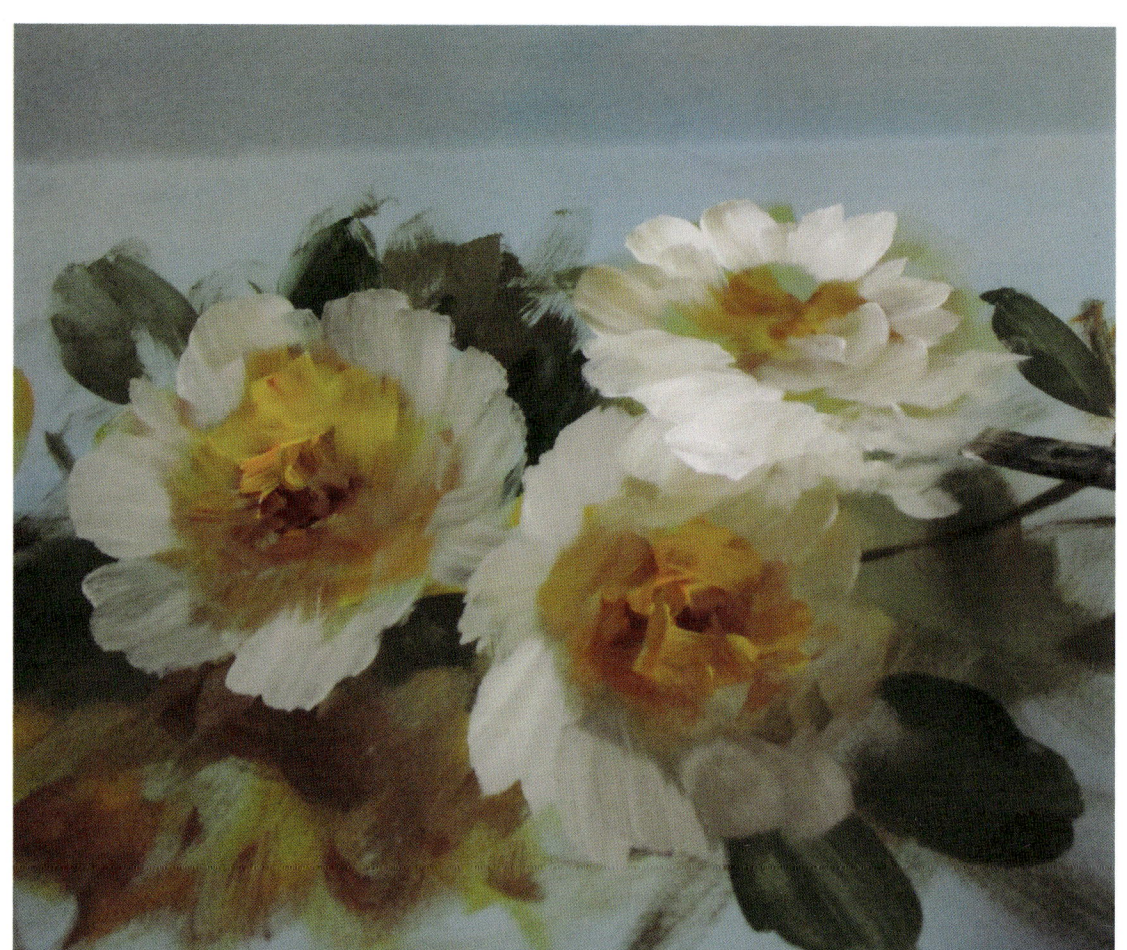

Step 13
Mottle the greys a little darker. Using 2 or 3 strokes per petal, begin to fill in the rose heading toward the center. This can be the most difficult part of these roses. Try to make each petal a little different. Work into the center and cover some of the outer yellow areas. If you get too much, do not worry we will add more yellows with the next step. Vary the sizes and colors.

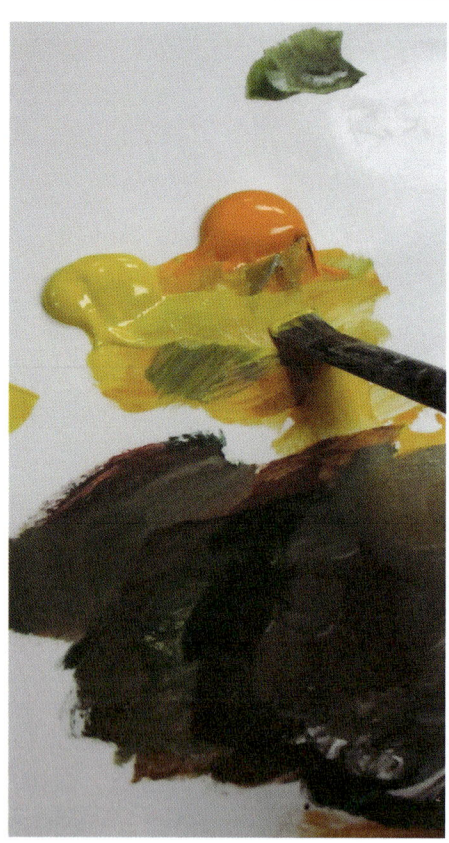

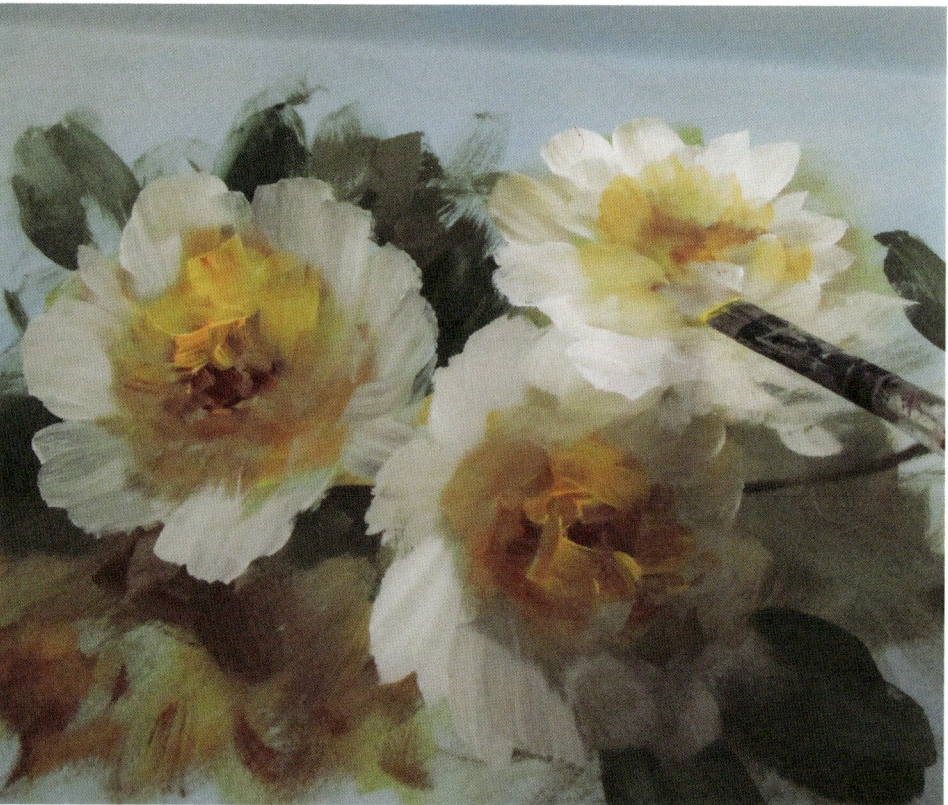

Step 14 Mottle the 2 yellows together again. Do not over mix the colors. I used just a little more Hansa this time.

Step 15 Tap these colors into the center of the rose we just added the petals to. I like to work back and forth between the whites and the yellows to create some depth and interest to the roses. Use just the tip and corner of the brush for the small center petals.

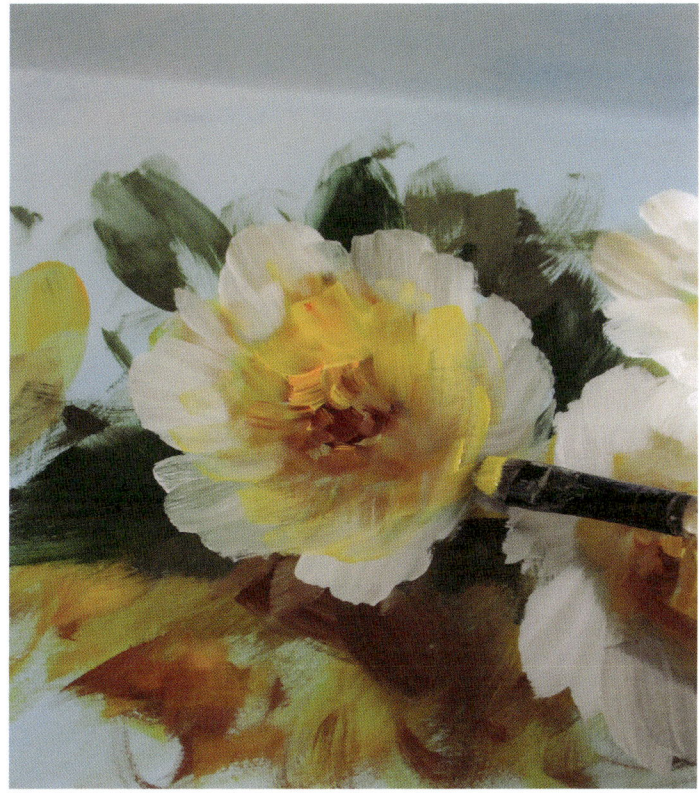

Step 16 Add additional yellows to the center of the next rose. Here I am using the same yellow I just used on the last rose. A little more Hansa in the mix to make a touch different.

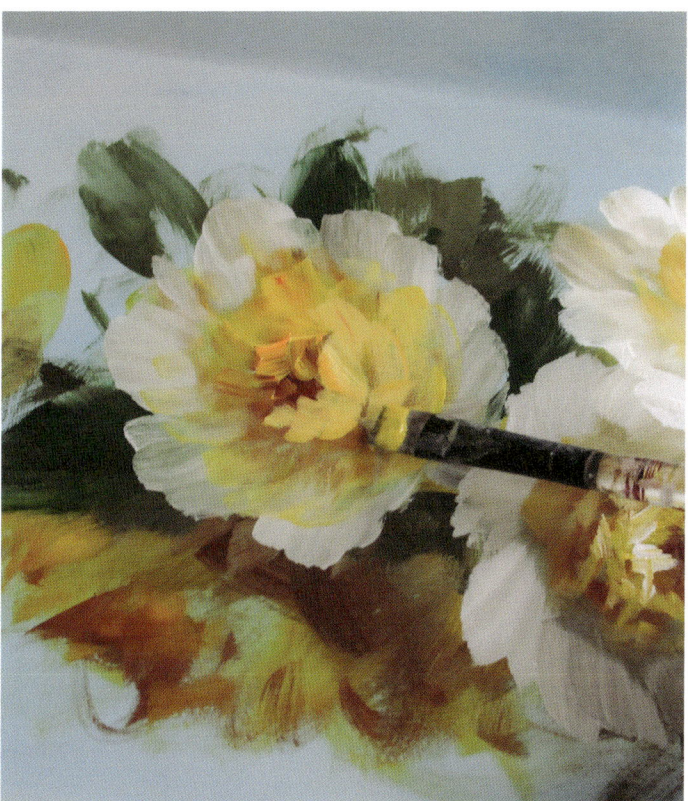

Step 17 Build more Hansa in the center areas to suggest center yellow petals. Short strokes with the tip of the flat brush.

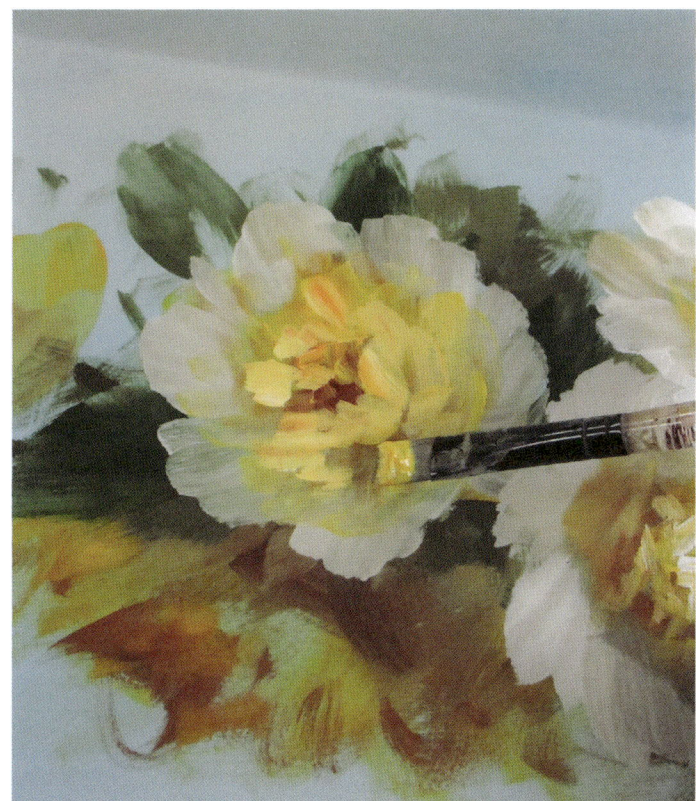

Step 18 Mottle with more white and add more petals slightly lighter that the first ones. Vary the colors. Restate the Burnt Sienna darks if you get too many.

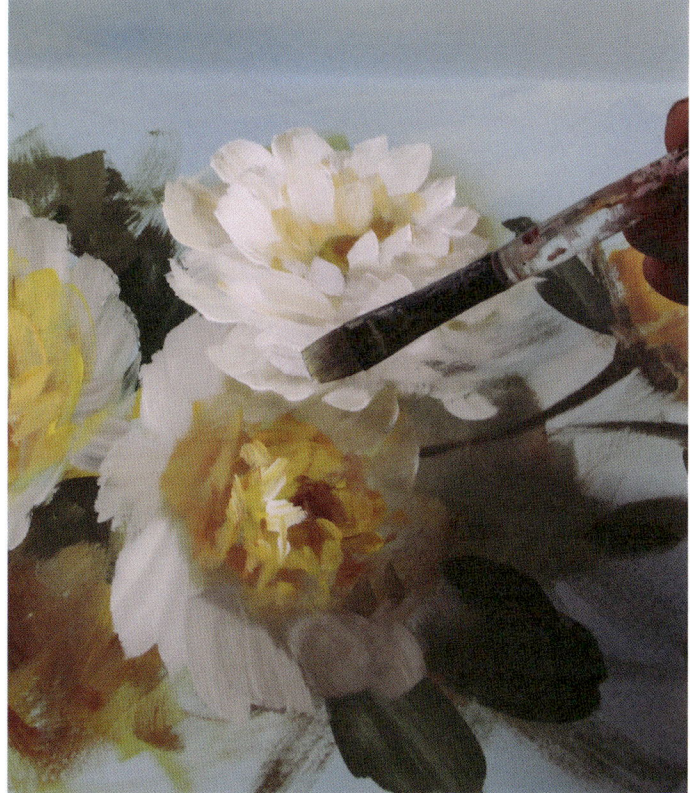

Step 19 Add these yellows to the next rose. Then use the corner of the flat and white to "draw" the edges of the top rose. Use petal edging technique.

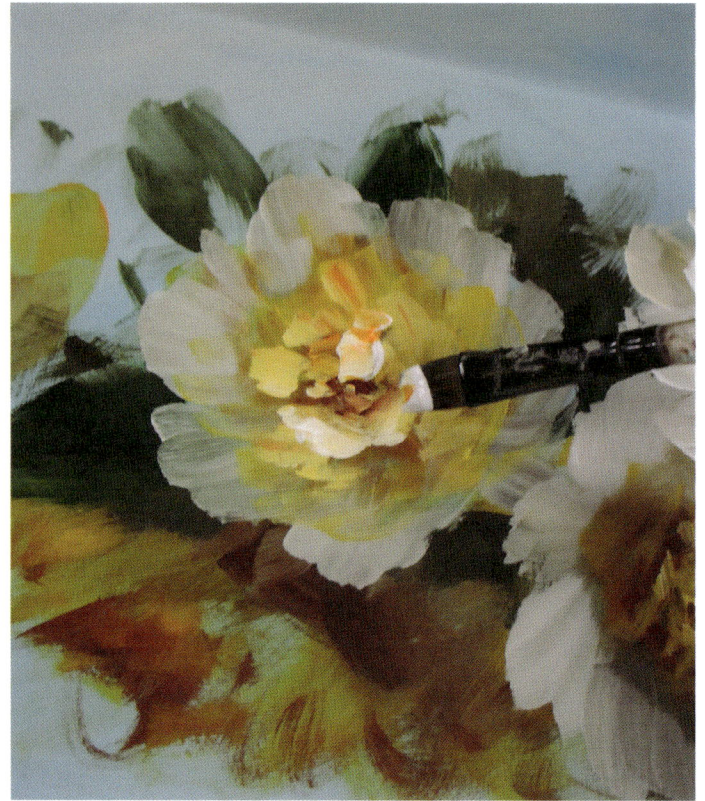

Step 20 Notice the mottled brush with yellows and white. Begin tapping some petals around the center to make smaller lighter petals. Thicker paint now. More opaque petals.

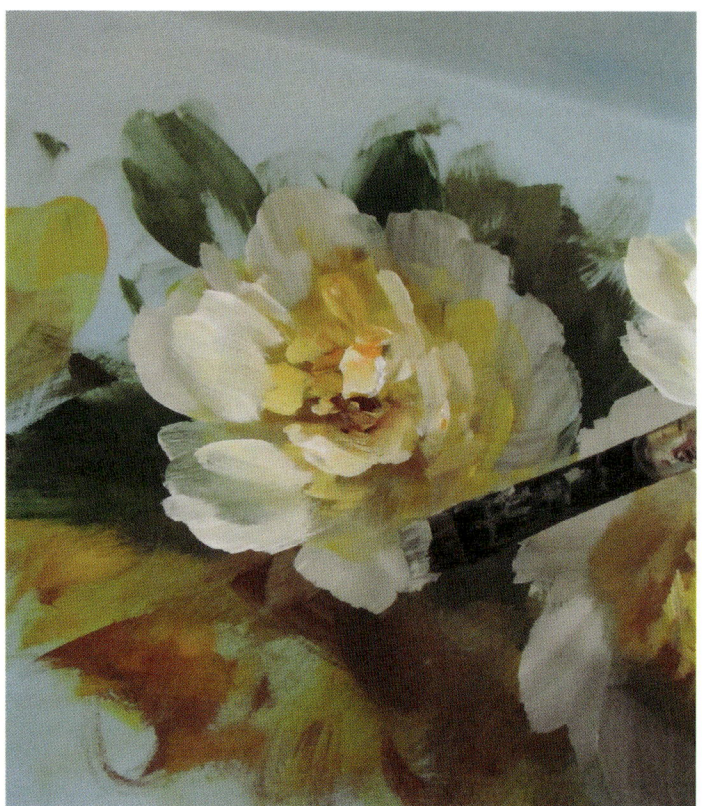

Step 21 Mottle the color more grey and begin the next rows of petals. Vary the sizes and shapes pulling in toward the center.

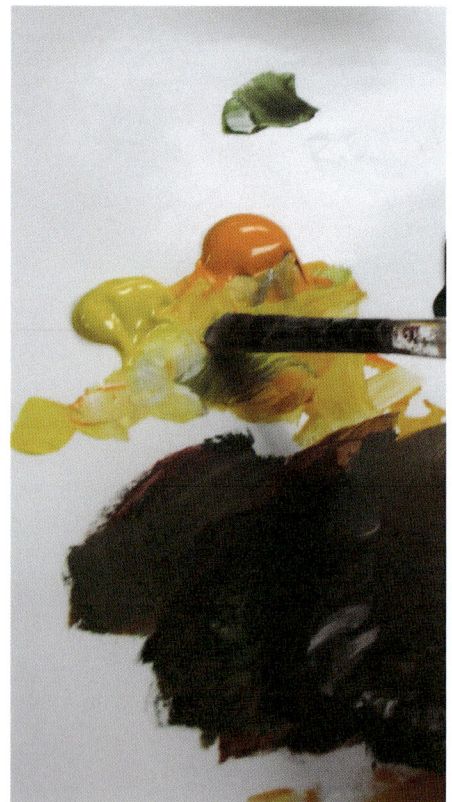

Step 22 Mottle the brush with the yellows again. Always vary the colors slightly.

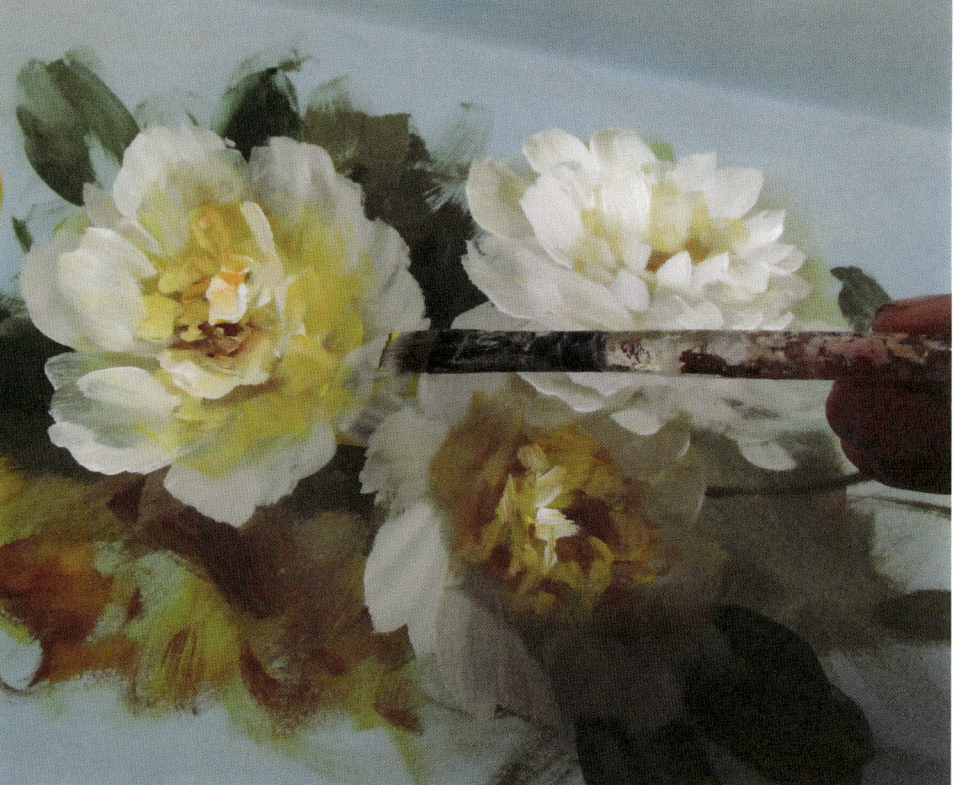

Step 23 Restate the yellows over the center area of the rose. This will add yellows below the upcoming white petals and make the center flower a little more interesting than the first rose that we painted.

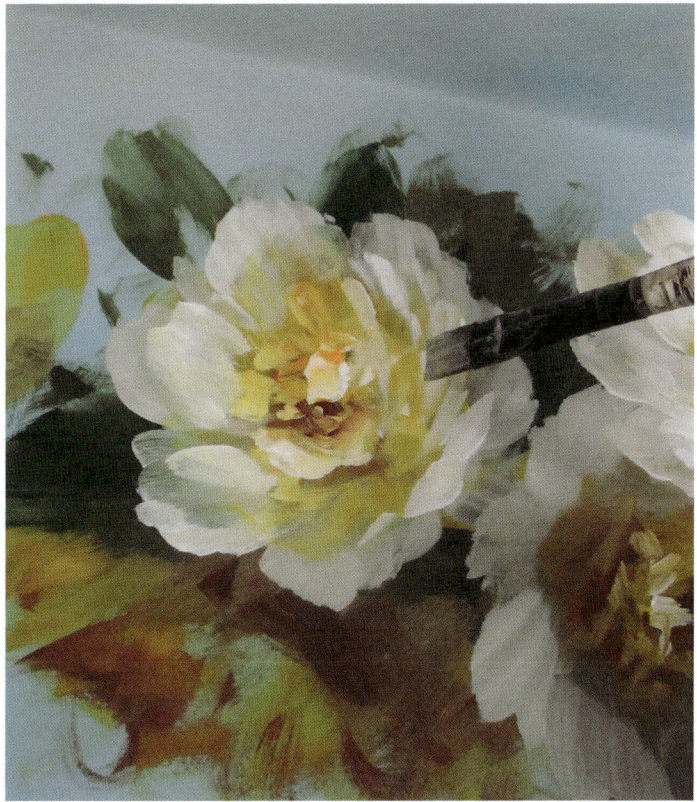

Step 24 Mottle the brush with lighter whites. Not pure white yet. Use the chisel to help turn some of the petals and make the rose look like it is gazing down.

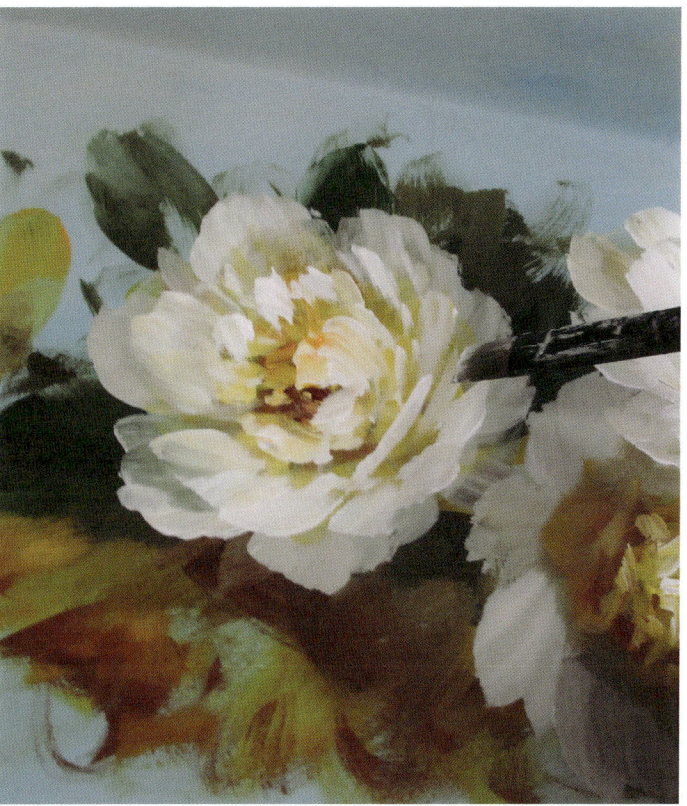

Step 25 Add additional chisel edges to fill in petals between the first outer row and the center. Vary the sizes and placement to make all the roses look different.

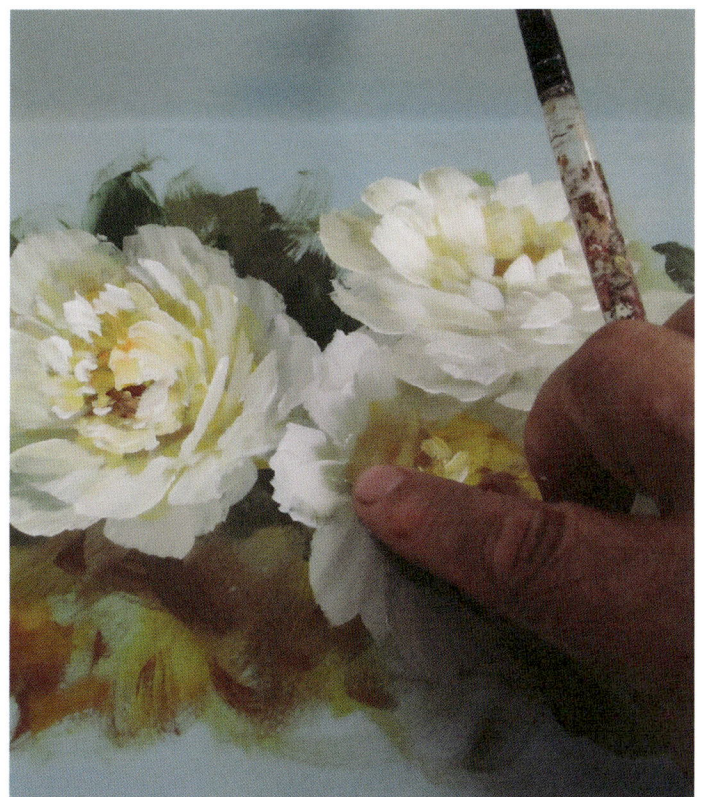

Step 26 Begin the next rose by adding some lighter color. Here I am pushing in and out of the center with the color to establish movement. I like to do this to vary the look.

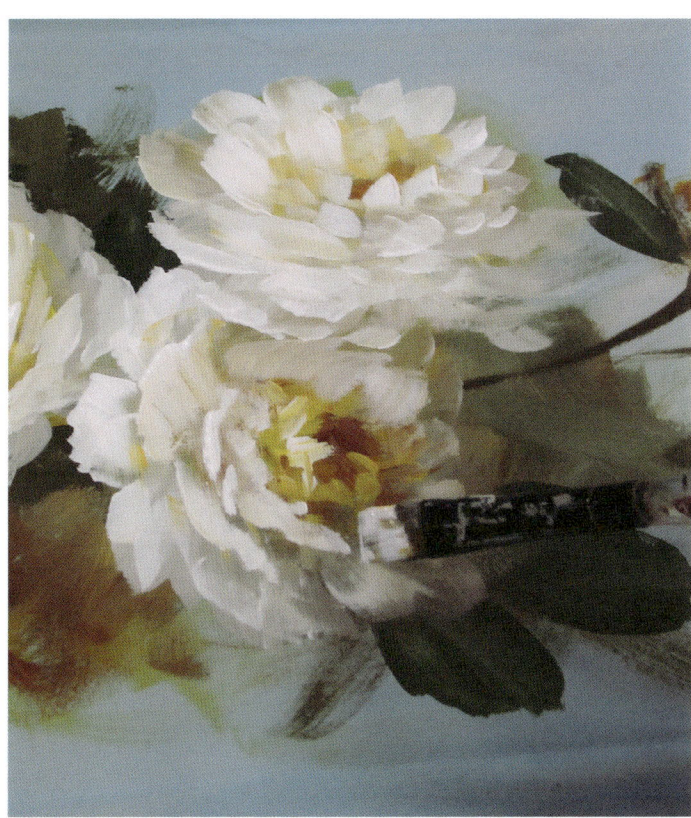

Step 27 Use the tip of the flat to create additional petals. Try to vary them. Make different shapes with the corners and edges of the brush.

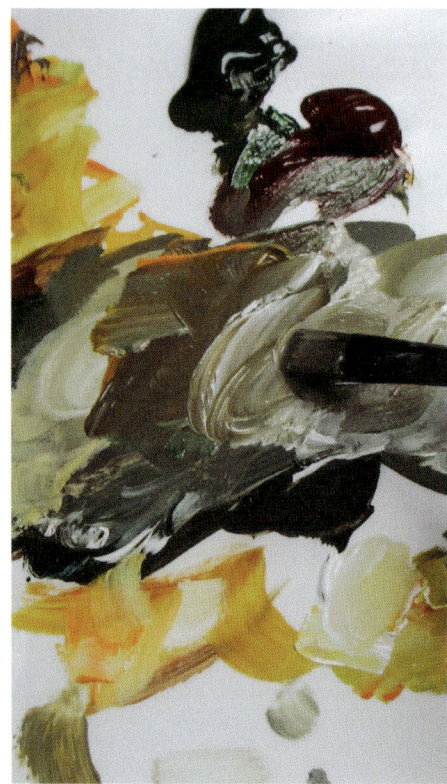 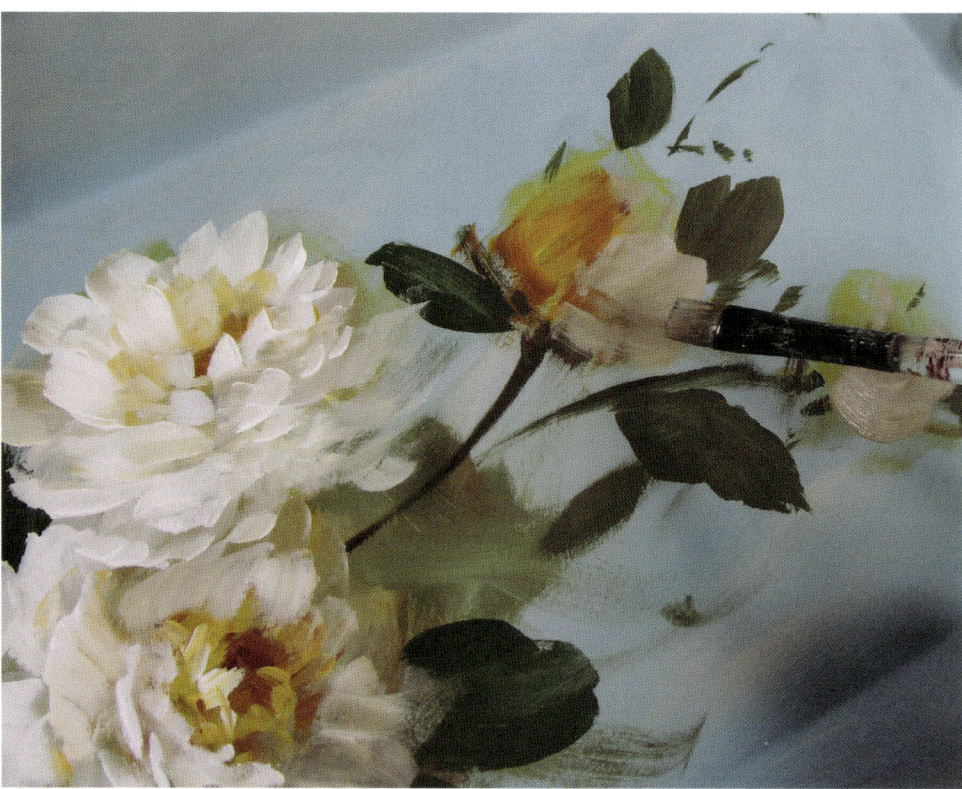

Step 28 Mottle greys with all the colors, a little more greens, then lighten a little with white.

Step 29 Using a color of grey that is no lighter than the background, begin the outer roses and rose buds with large soft strokes. Create less movement and petals on these outer flowers.

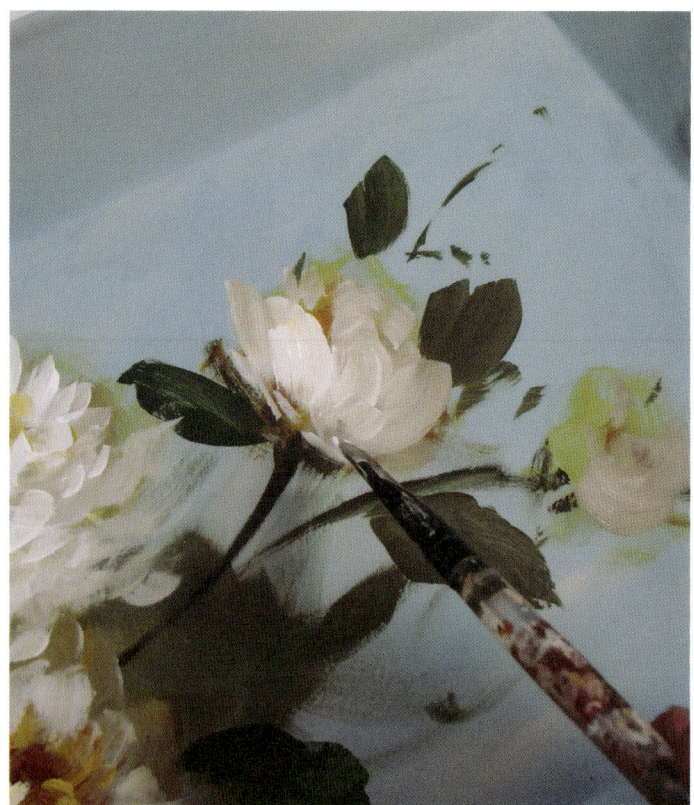 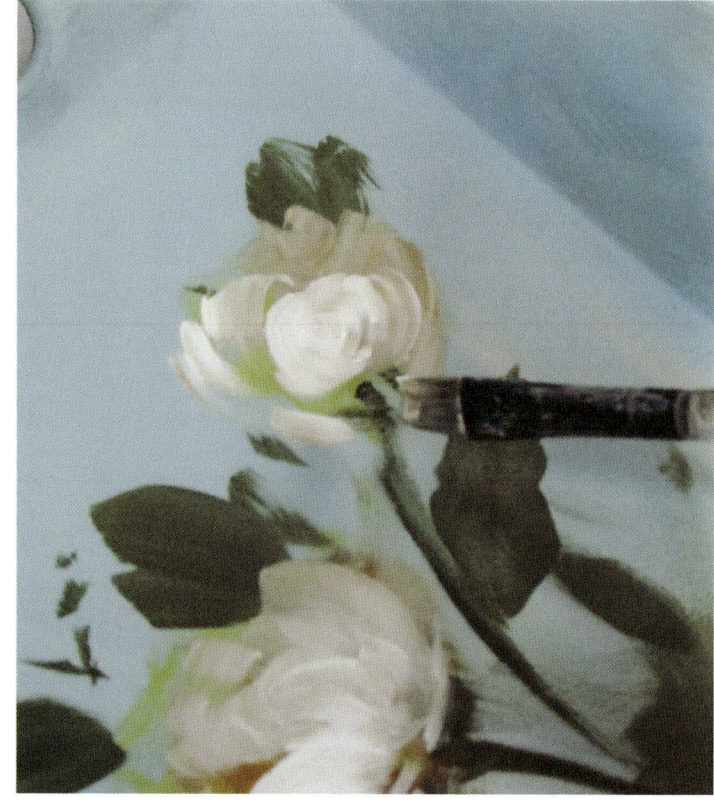

Step 30 Lighten the color and slowly build the petals toward the center of the rose bud. More light in the center petals. Use dark greens for the stems.

Step 31 Vary each rose bud. Here I make almost a round petal in the front center of the rose. Not as much color or interest on these outside buds.

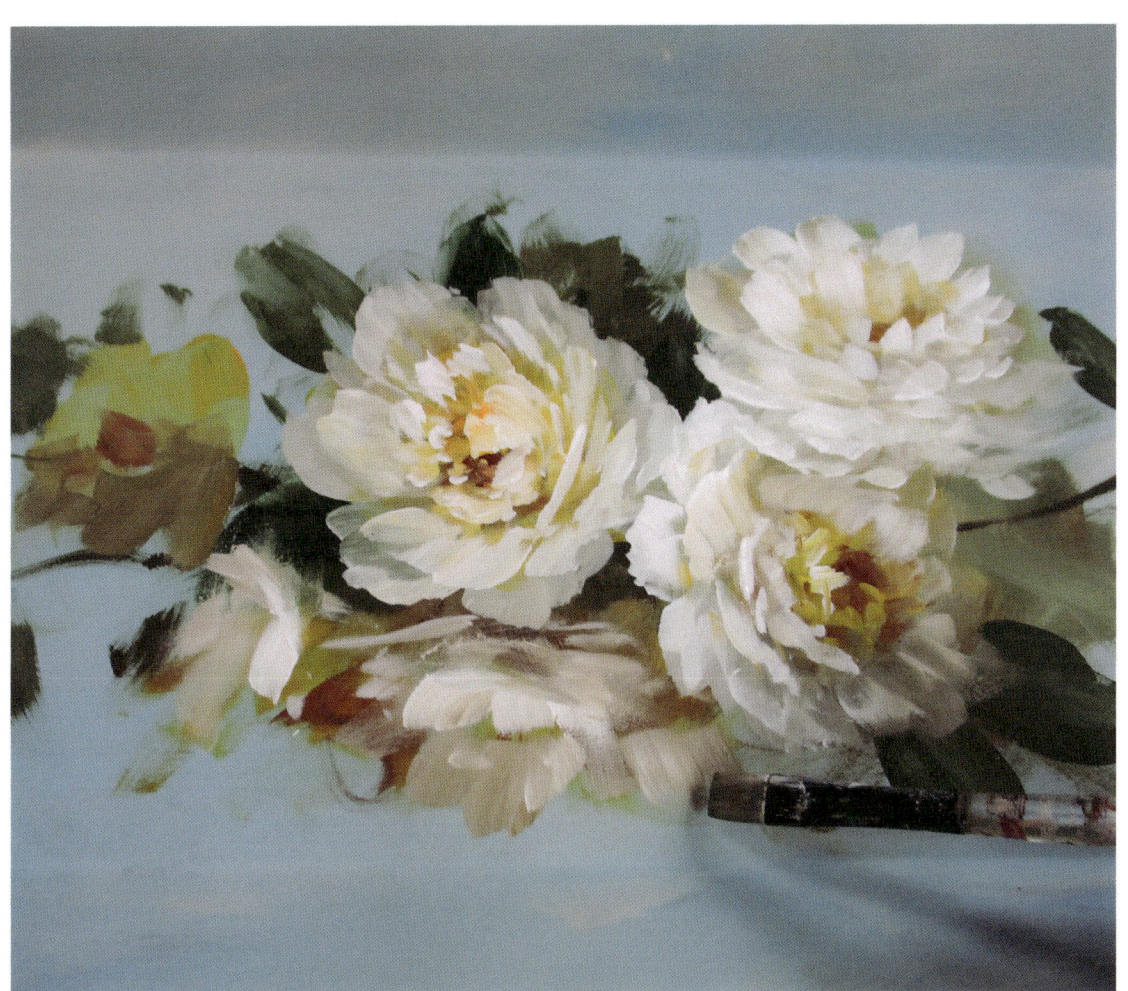

Step 32 Here is an open imogen rose. Just paint for movement. Try not to add too many details. Just paint movement to some petals. We already have beautiful center of interest roses and these will suggest the shapes of the other roses to the viewer. All you have to do is to make movement that will suggest a flower. Do not paint much detail so the lower flower stays soft.

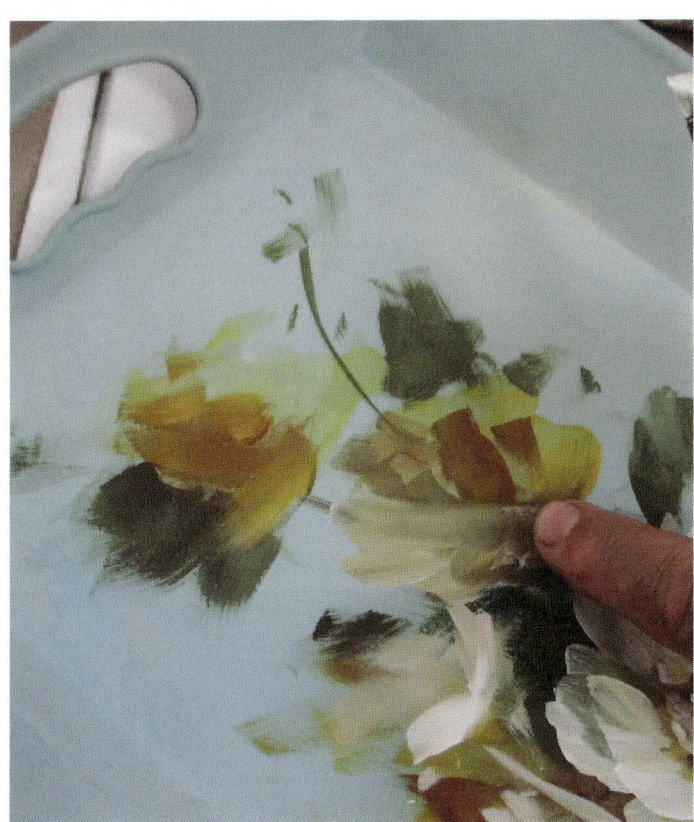

Step 33 To paint the outside buds, I mottle the yellows and the Burnt Sienna. I push the colors around to start the interest. Then begin to add the lighter colors and push them around.

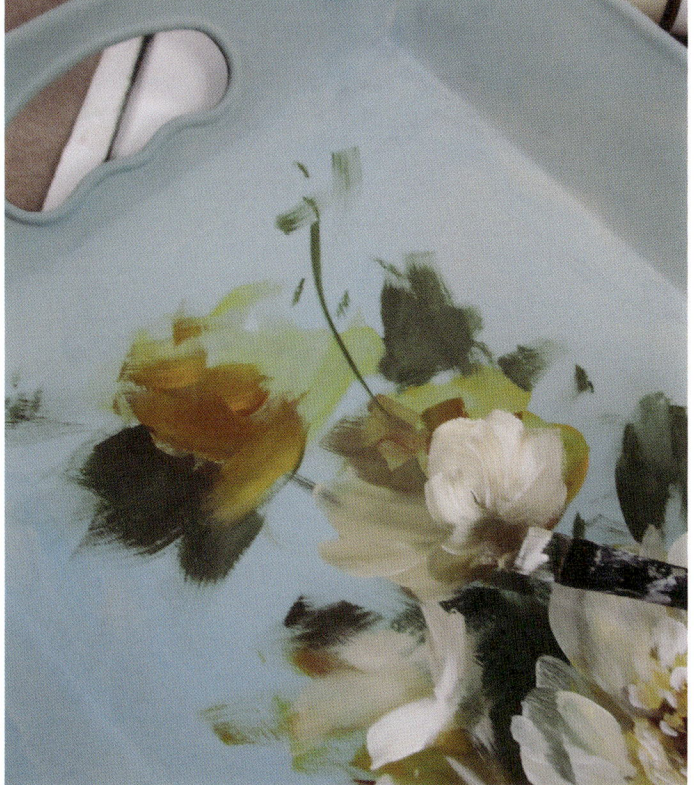

Step 34 Mottle the brush with more color and begin some forward petals. No lighter than the outer petals on the main roses. We must keep these softer and less detailed.

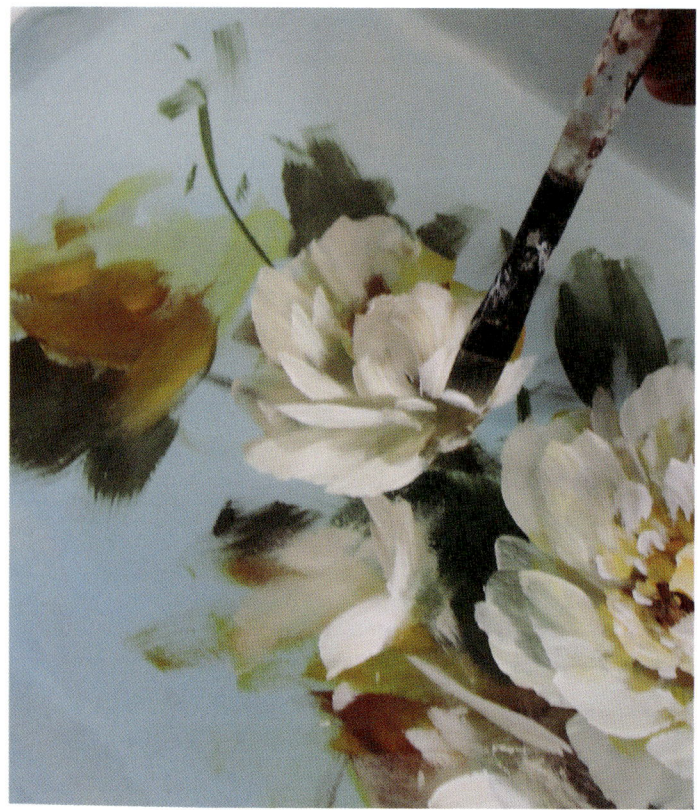

Step 35 Use the chisel of the brush to add additional petals to the bud. Make chisel petals between the reaching and the center petals.

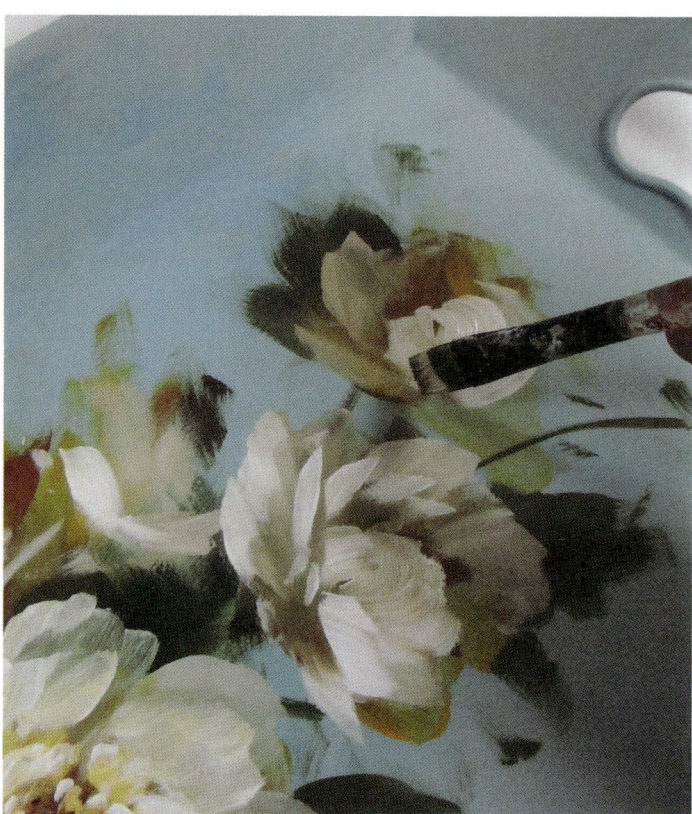

Step 36 Mottle some darker yellow greys and add petals to the next rose bud. Keep them soft. We are moving out in the composition.

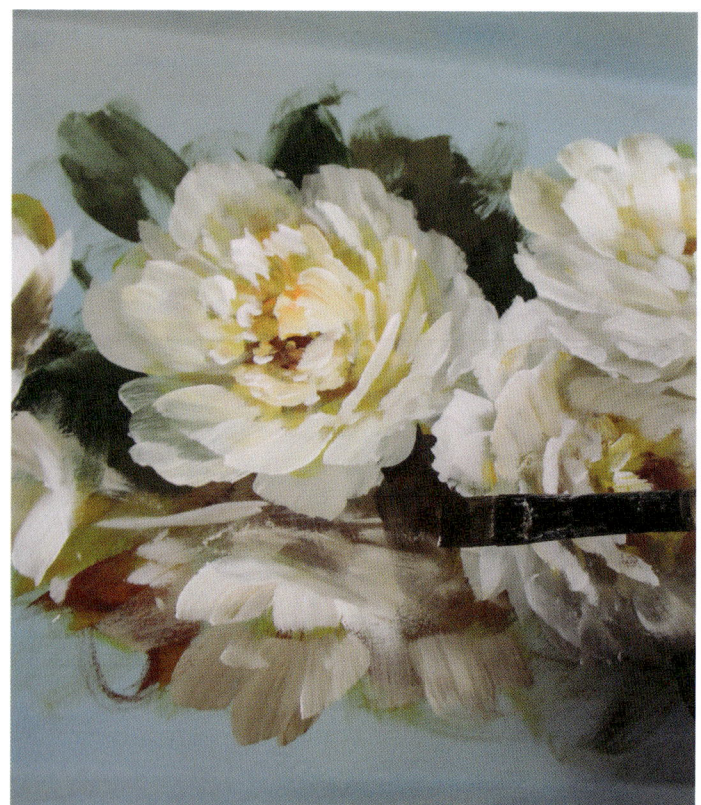

Step 37 Here I use the negative painting technique and dark colors to creat contrast in the flowers. This dark color will also make the whites appear lighter.

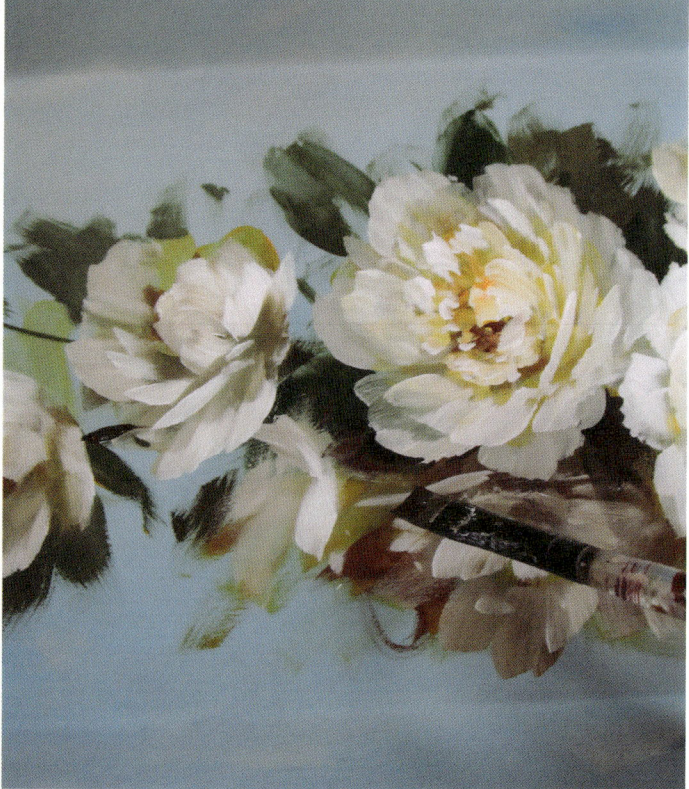

Step 38 Use Phthalo Green Blue, Burnt Sienna and then cool with Red Violet to make the dark cool colors in the center. Vary that amounts to vary the color.

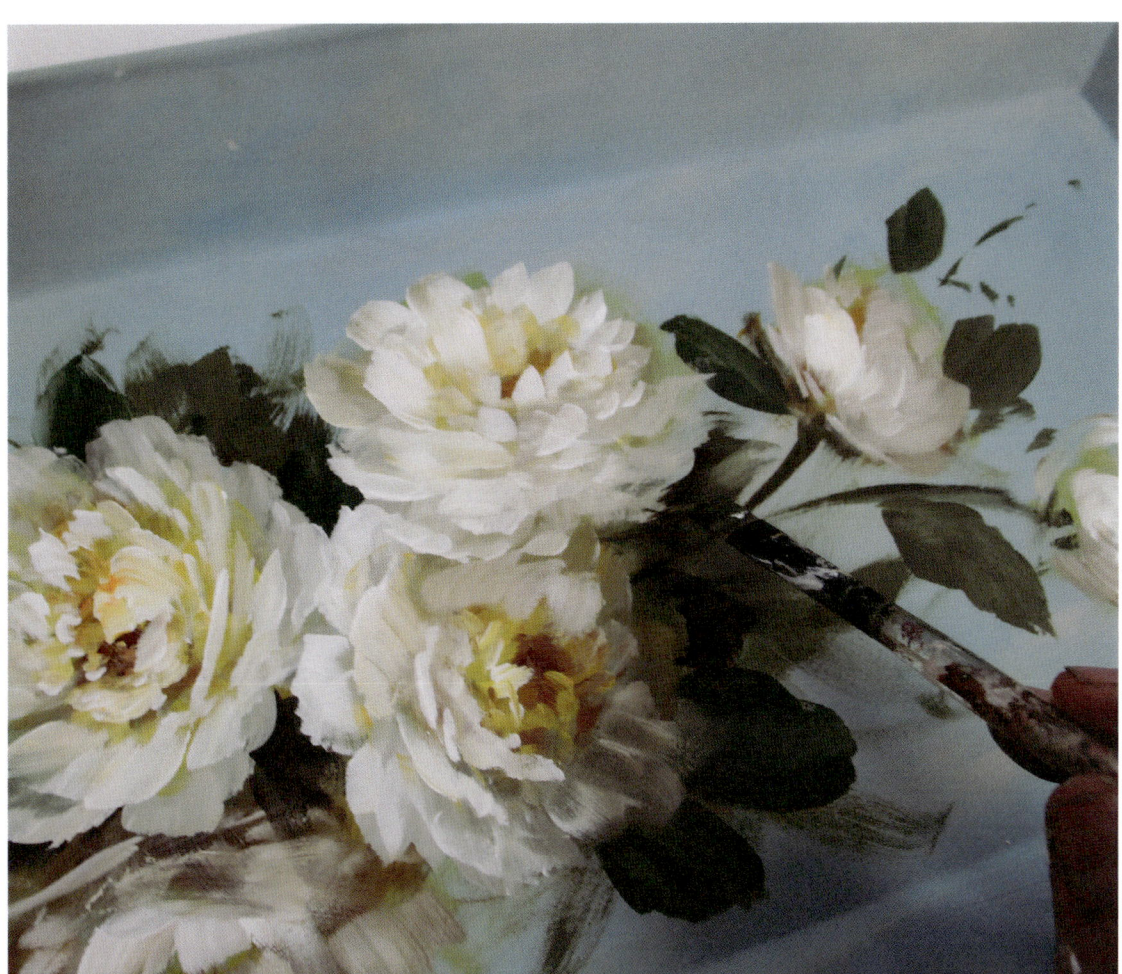

Step 39
Here I use the color a little transparently and wash over the shadow side of the roses. Then I make the color a little more opaque and move into the rose to shadow and shape those petals. This transparent wash of color will set a shadow on this side of the composition and create more interest.

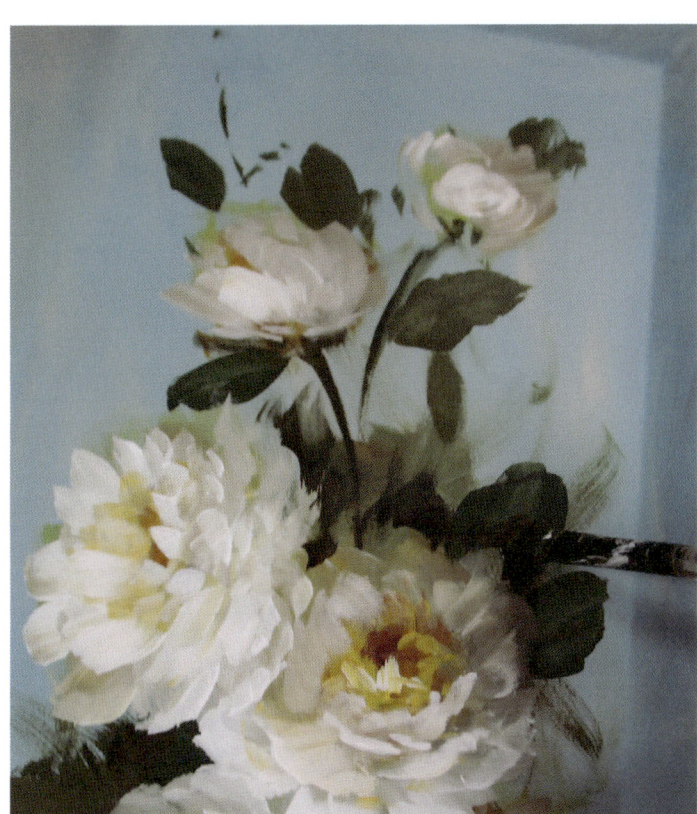

Step 40 Darken the color and use a little more opaque as you add shadows to the leaves and shape the bottom petals.

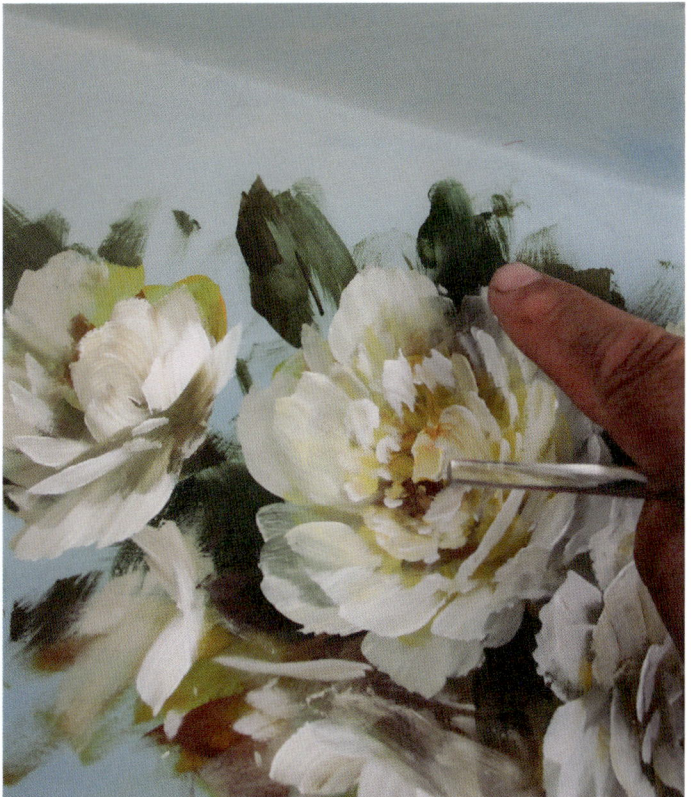

Step 41 After I add darks to the roses, I like to revisit the center of interest with more color and more white to make additional contrast.

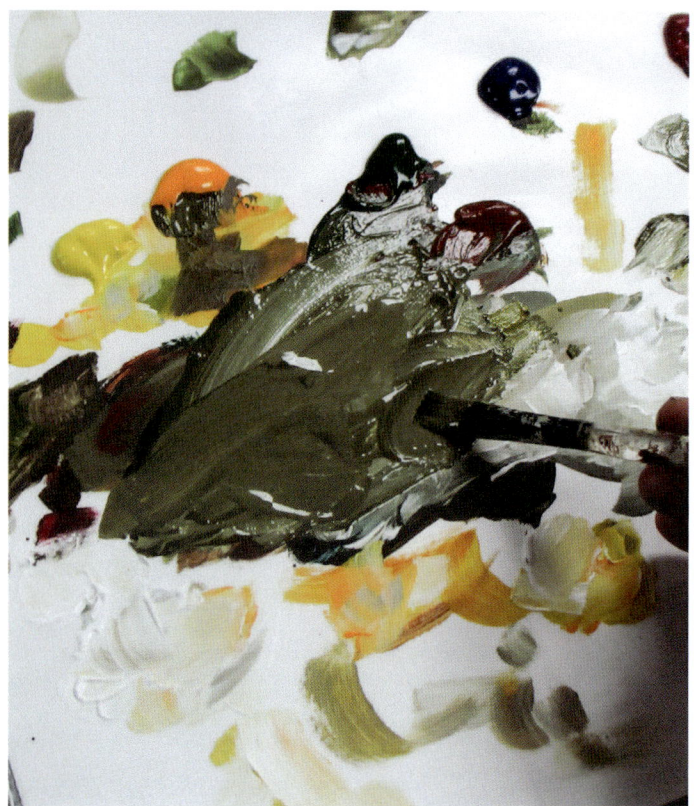

Step 42 Mottle a greyed green with all the palette colors. Lean more toward green with Hansa Yellow and touch Phthalo Green Blue. Tone with the reds and Burnt Sienna.

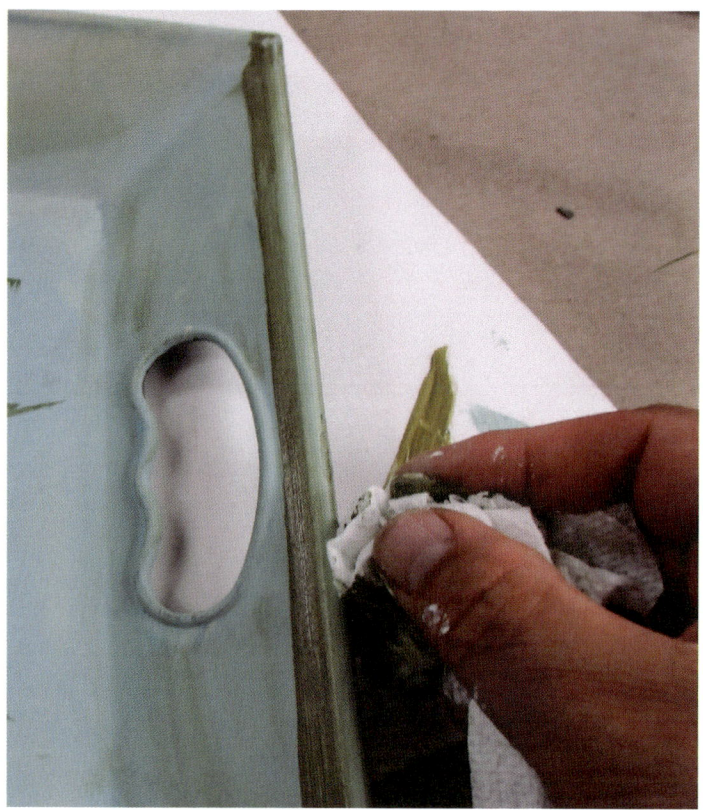

Step 43 I added this as a trim color to the outside edge of the tray. I then wiped down with a paper towel to create a little transparency, movement and interest.

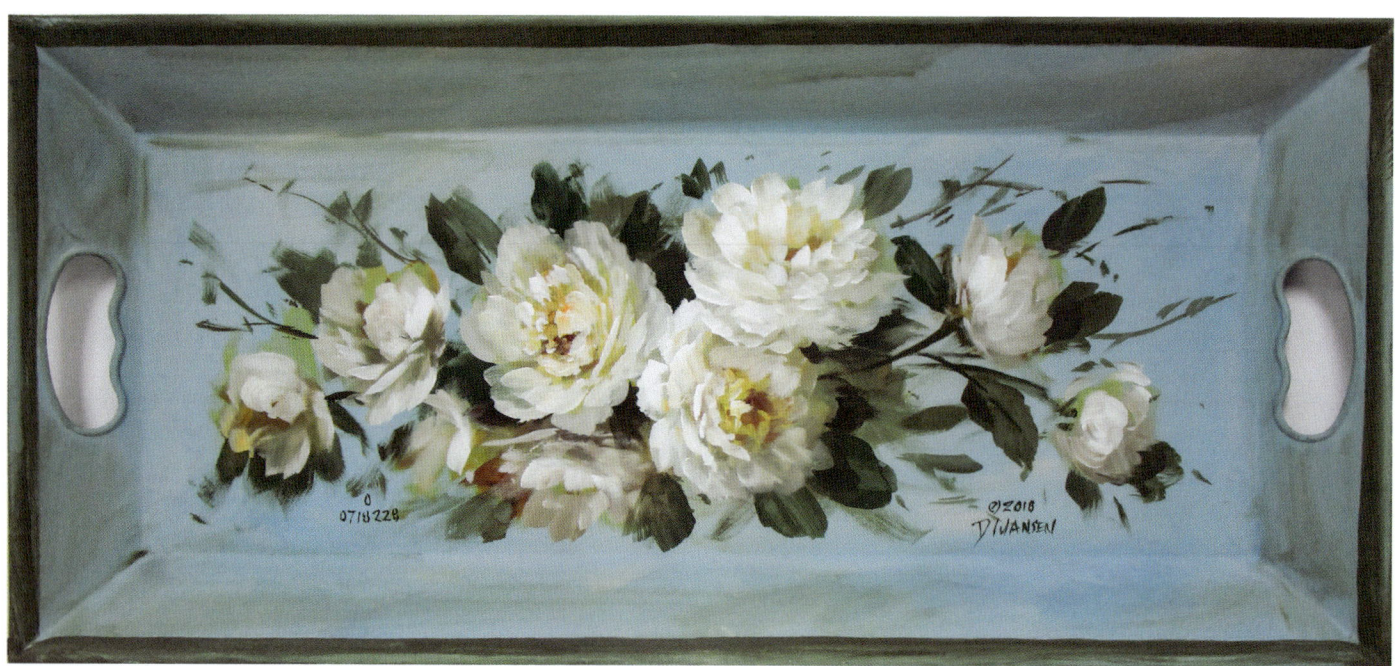

Step 44 Here you can see the completed tray. I brushed a little of the outside trim color transparently around the outside sides of the tray. This carried some of the greens and added movement which I liked. You could also do a soft solid color if desired. Enjoy!

Lesson 2
Pattern

Copyright © 2018 David Jansen

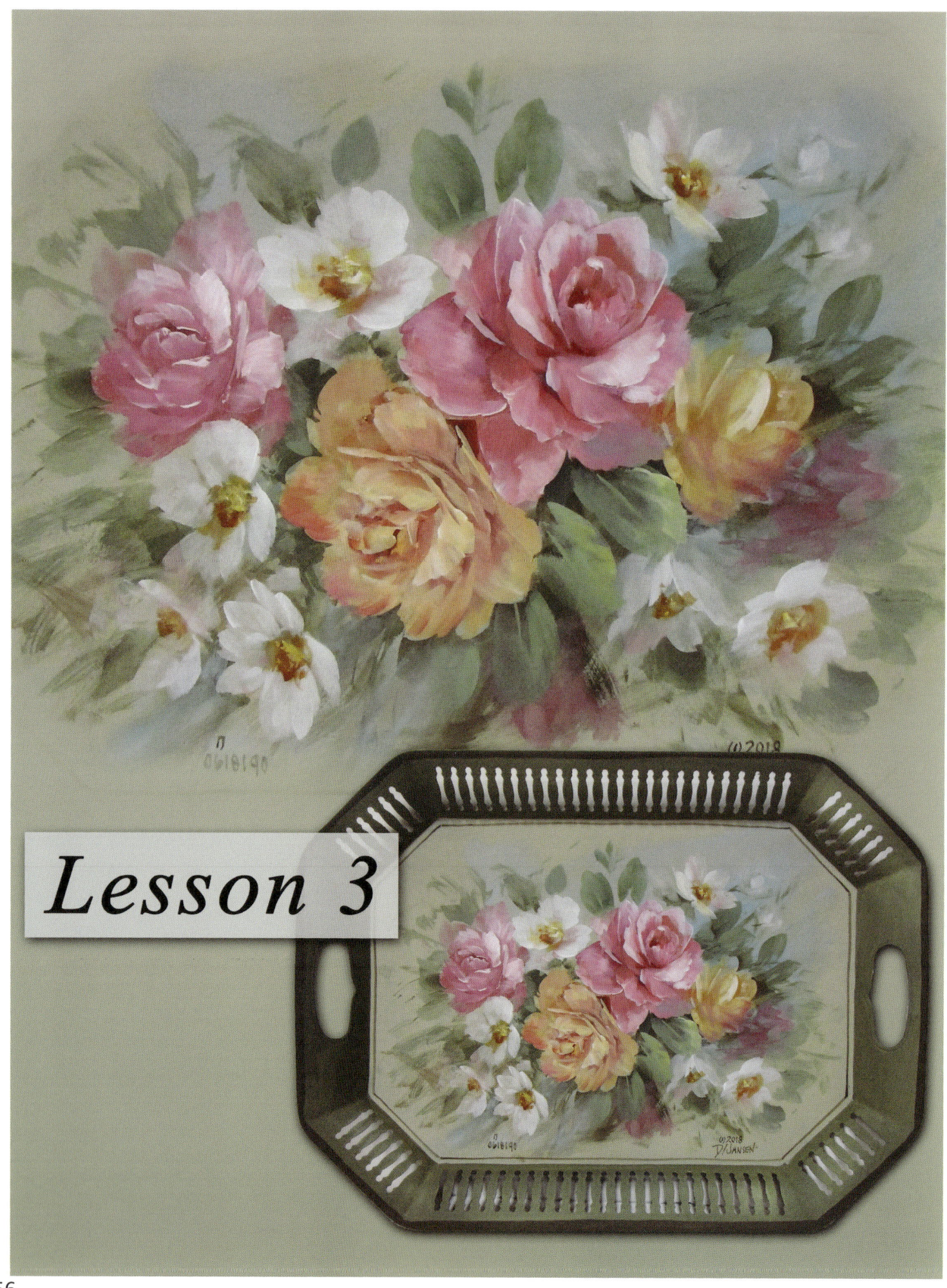

Negative Painting

This is an amazing technique that I use on almost everything I paint.
You have two ways to refine the edges of a petal. One way is to make positive shapes with techniques such as "petal edging." Drawing petals with clean lines increases the contrast.

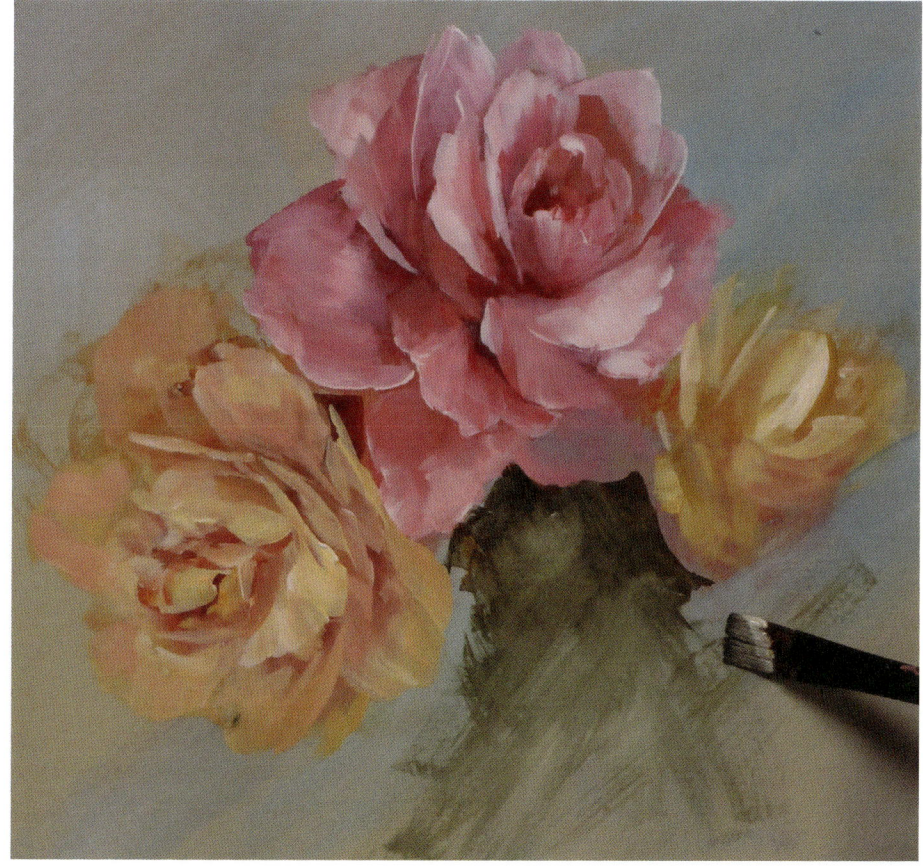

The other way is to negative paint with the background color. This method allows the artist to work different tones into the petals and then clean up the edges with the background color creating a sharper edge for more contrast.

I started doing this with the Heritage porcelain technique a few years ago. It is a technique that porcelain artists use to create beautiful light colored roses. Since they do not have white paint on their palette, they negative paint with darker values to create sharp edges. The dark contrast makes the flower appear lighter in value. A great technique! Let's give it a try!

Paint It Simply Palette
Base Color- Light Green Grey
White + Touch Hansa Yellow and Black

Palette Colors

PAINT IT SIMPLY COLORS	OPTIONAL COLORS
Naphthol Red Light	Yellow Oxide
Red Violet	Diarylide Yellow
Titanium White	Pine Green
Carbon Black	Quinacridone Violet
Phthalo Blue	Burnt Sienna
Hansa Yellow	Phthalo Green Blue

Painting Surface
Large Metal Tray

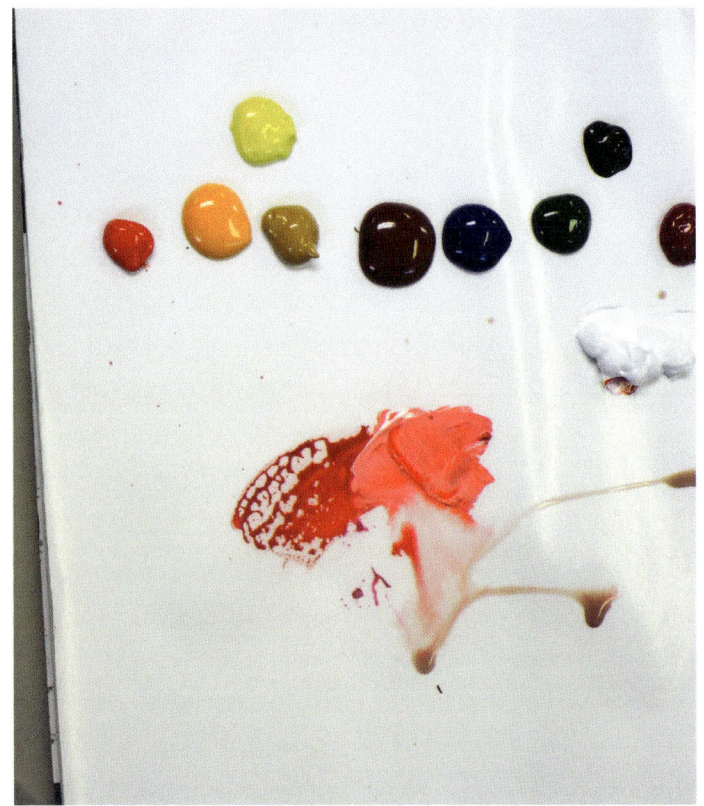

Step 1 Mottle a light red with Naphthol Red Light and touch white. Vary with touch Quinacridone Violet. Add some water to thin the color and allow for some transparency.

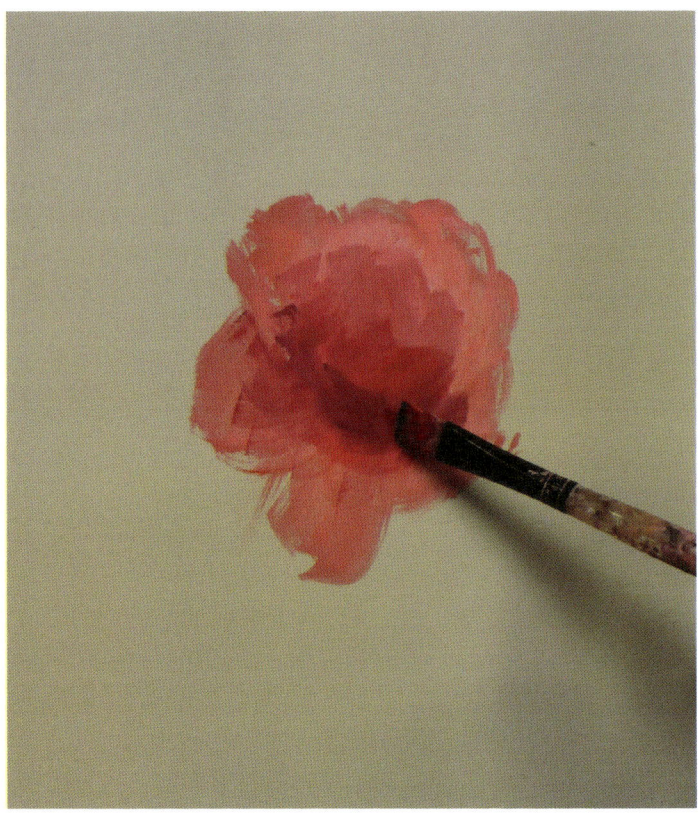

Step 2 Begin the shape of the red rose. Mottle the color with additional Quinacridone Violet and touch Red Violet. Add the darker center to the rose.

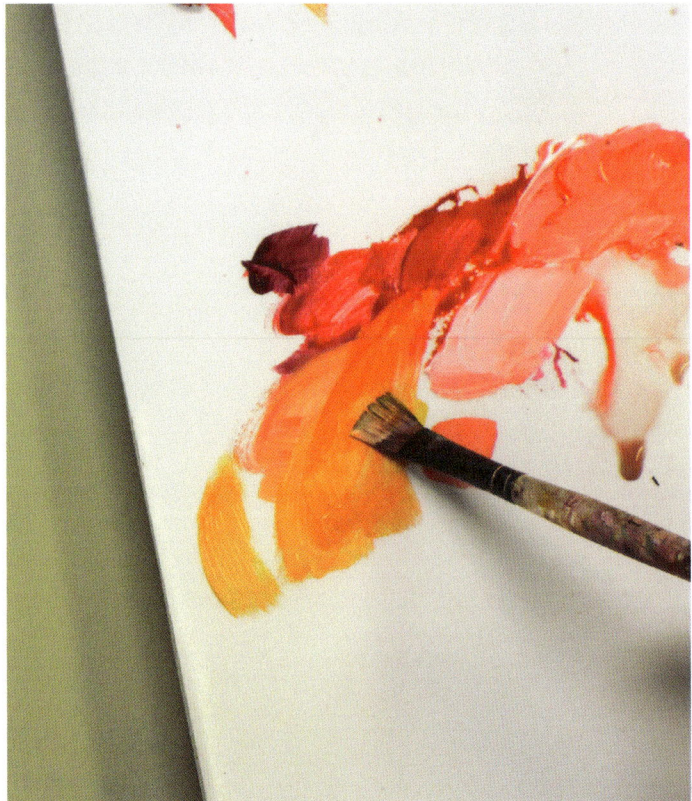

Step 3 Mottle the reds with a touch of Diarylide Yellow. Do not over mix the colors.

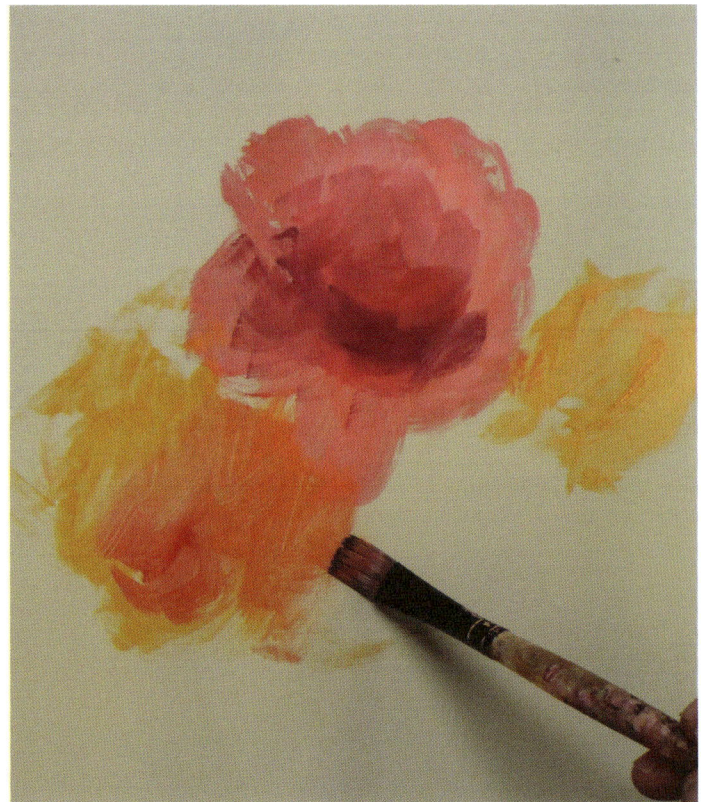

Step 4 Brush these colors into the shapes of the roses. Let streaks happen for movement.

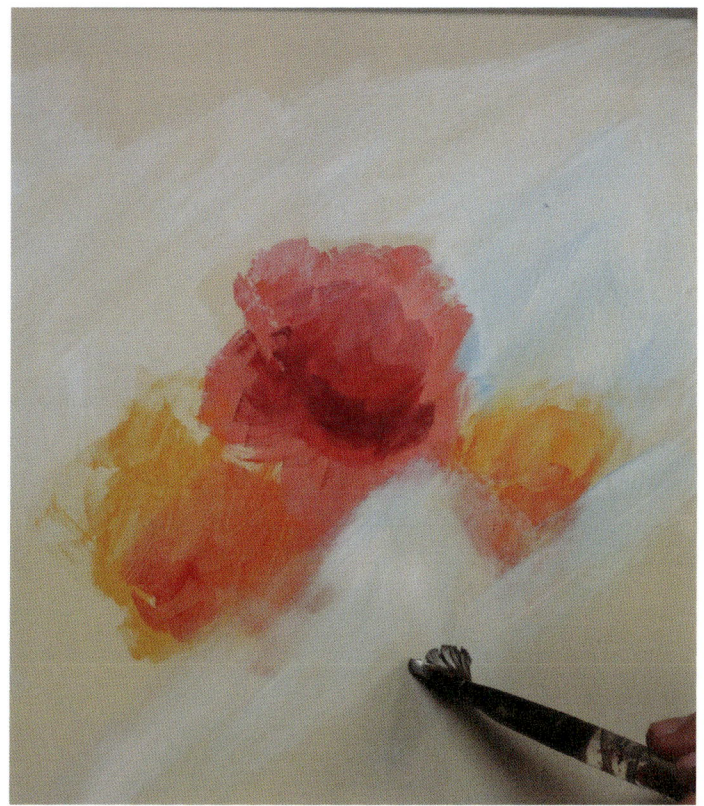

Step 5 Lighten Phthalo Blue with touch white and using the 3/4 inch brush, go over the areas around the flowers. This is a soft negative painting which helps establish soft rose edges.

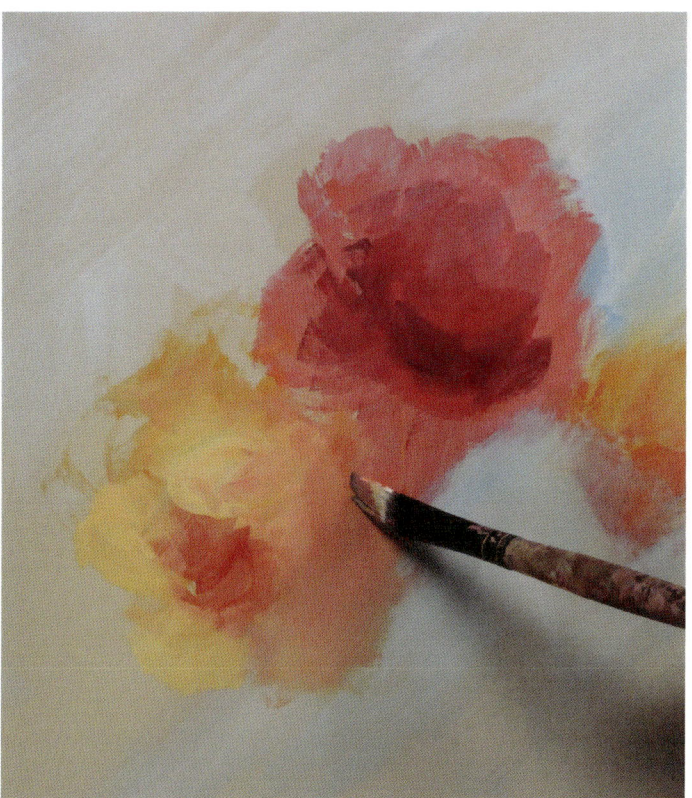

Step 6 Mottle the yellows a little lighter and begin to build the front of the yellow rose. Not too light. We have a long way to go.

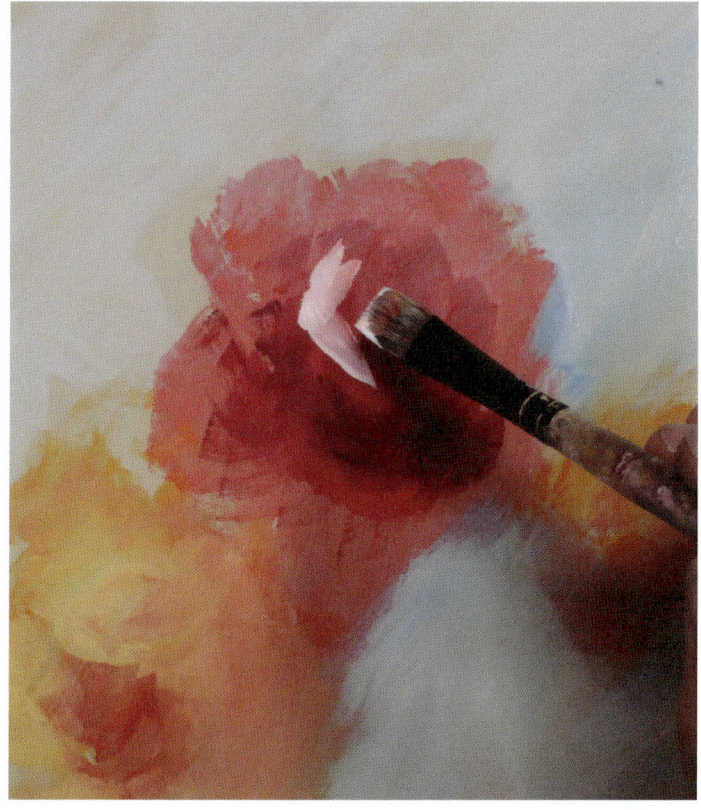

Step 7 Mottle the brush with the reds and then lighten one corner with a little white. Strike across the front of the red rose to set the color contrast for the rose.

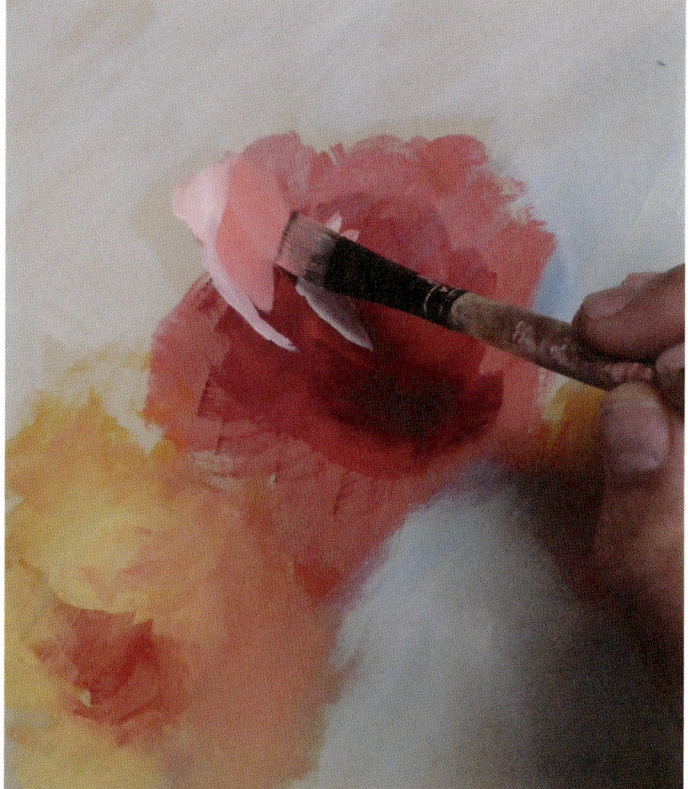

Step 8 Make the color a little darker than the first strike with more mottled reds and begin the outside to inside reaching petals.

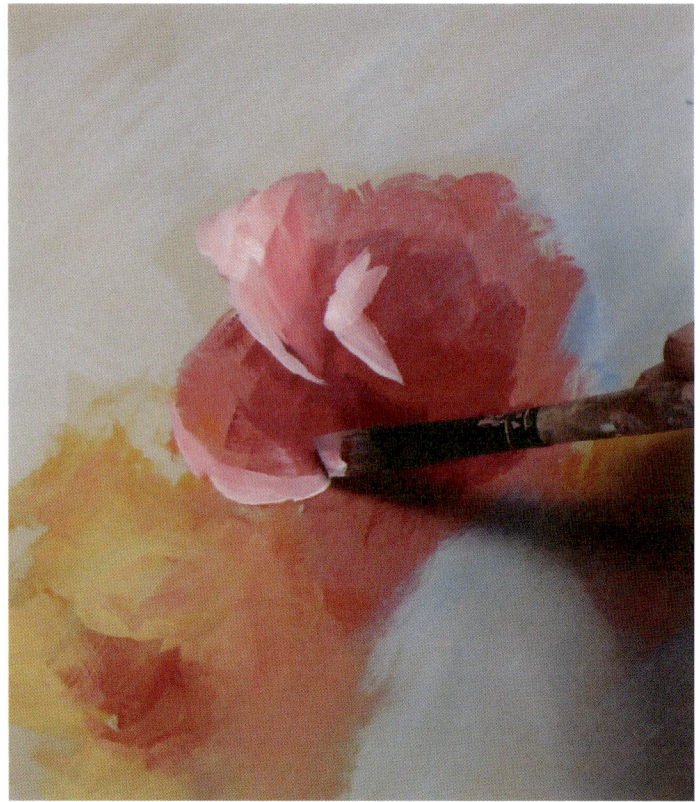

Step 9 I use the light corner of the brush to "draw" the shapes of the petals. Stroke through the rose petal to give movement and interest.

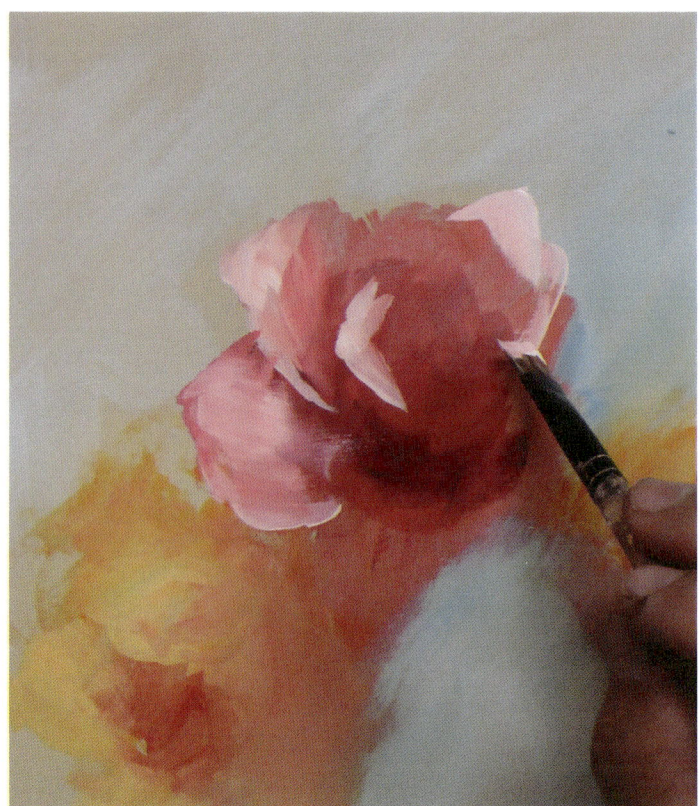

Step 10 Lighten the color across the brush and add back petals. Soften the color with darker values and apply along the light to soften.

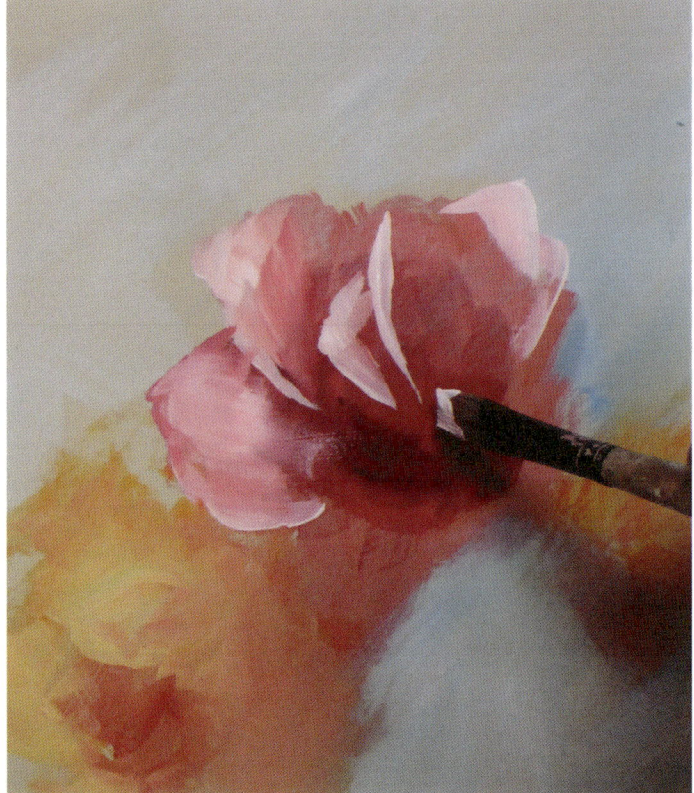

Step 11 Mottle the color lighter and then using the chisel of the brush, add the center petals to the rose. The light makes the edge of the petal.

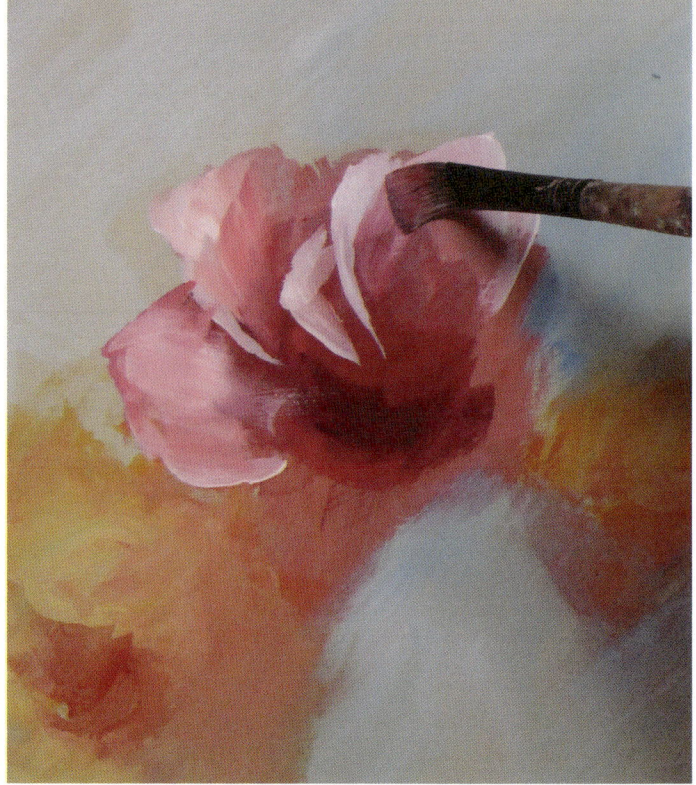

Step 12 Mottle the brush a little darker with reds. Brush along the light color to soften the light petals and shadow the inside of the bowl.

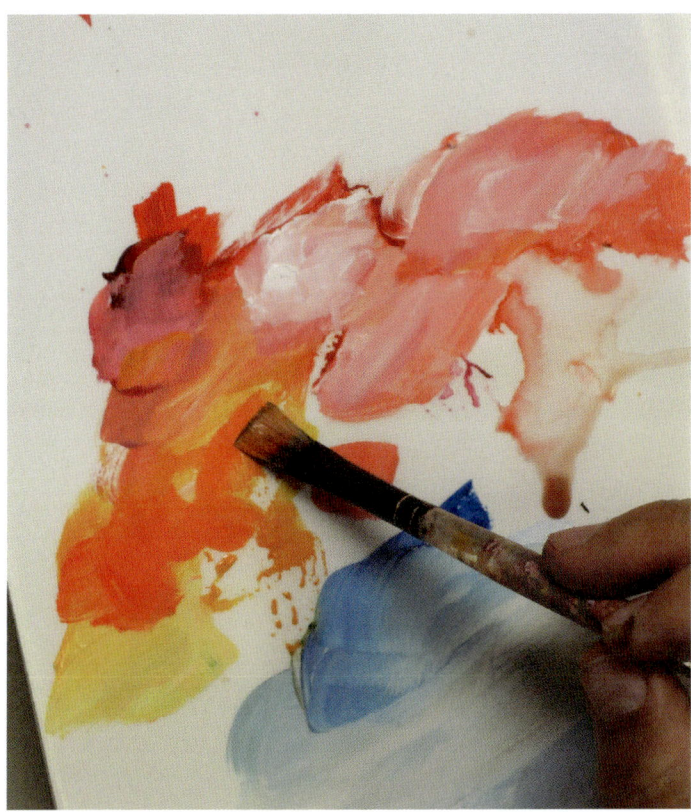

Step 13 Mottle the reds with warmer yellows to make a light warm pink color. Warming the color on the highlight side is a wonderful way to add more color interest to your roses.

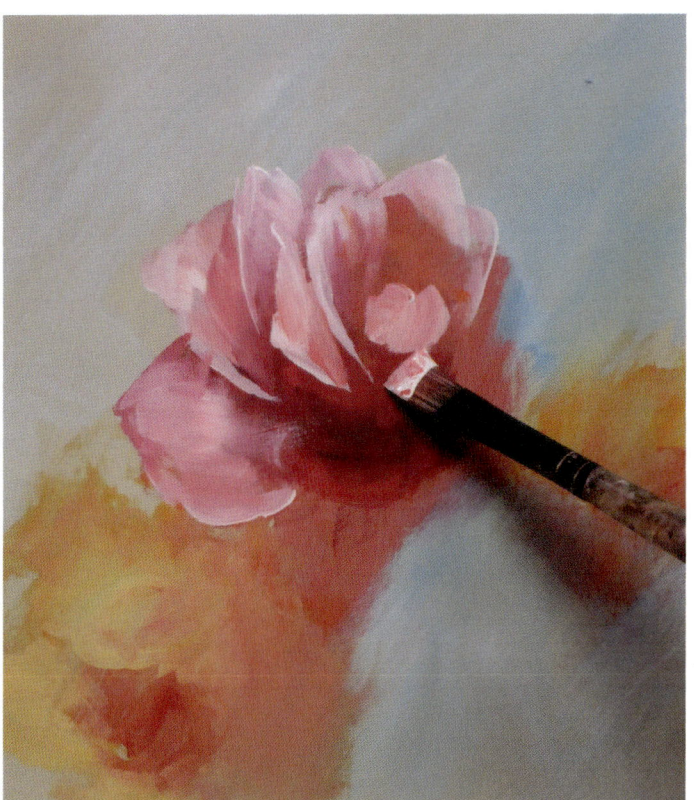

Step 14 Mottle the warmer light reds on the brush and then add the center petals to the rose.

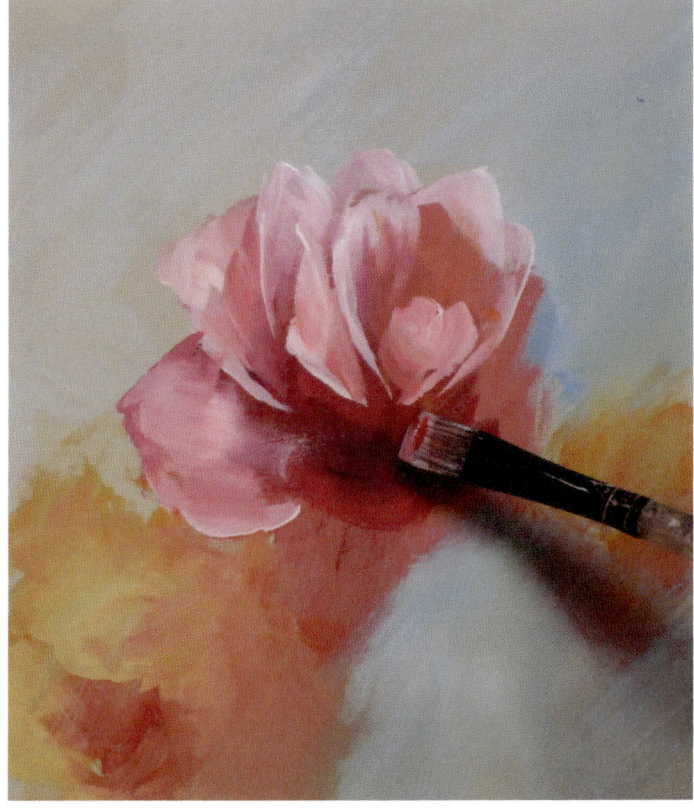

Step 15 Mottle the brush with cooler Red Violet and Quinacridone violet. Add shadows to the bottom of the rose to keep the roundness to the bowl.

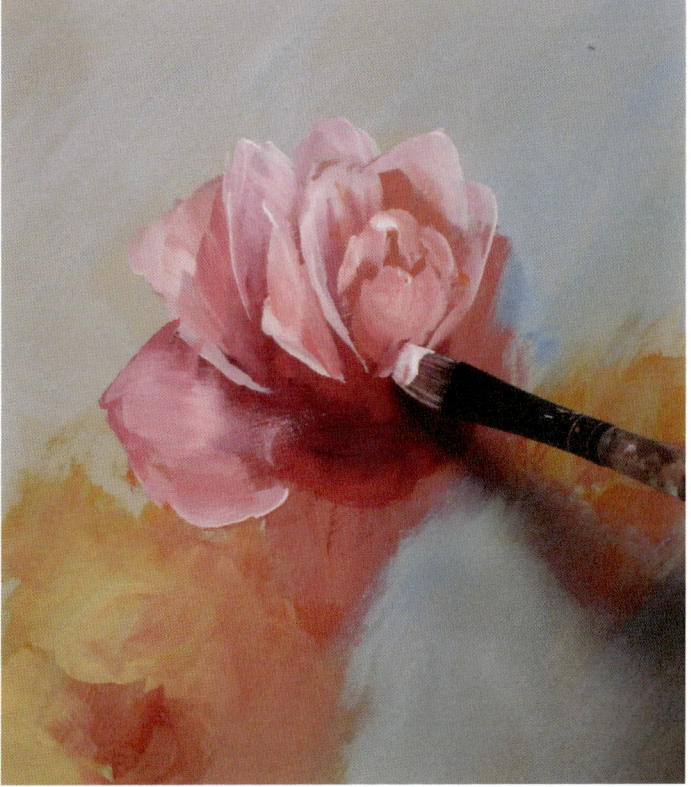

Step 16 Work back and forth with the reds to soften the color exchange between the light petals and the shadow of the bowl.

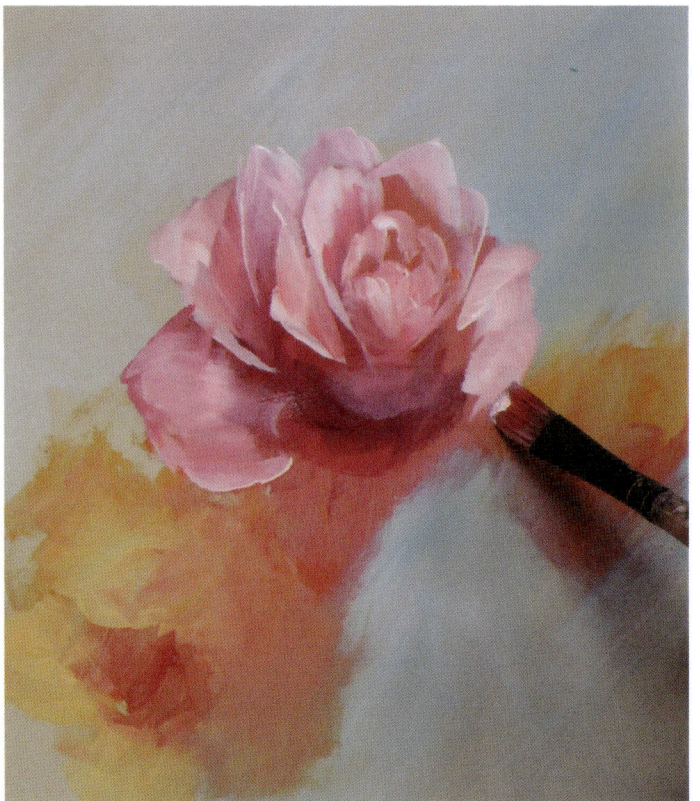

Step 17 Mottle the color lighter with touch more white on the warm side and begin reaching petals.

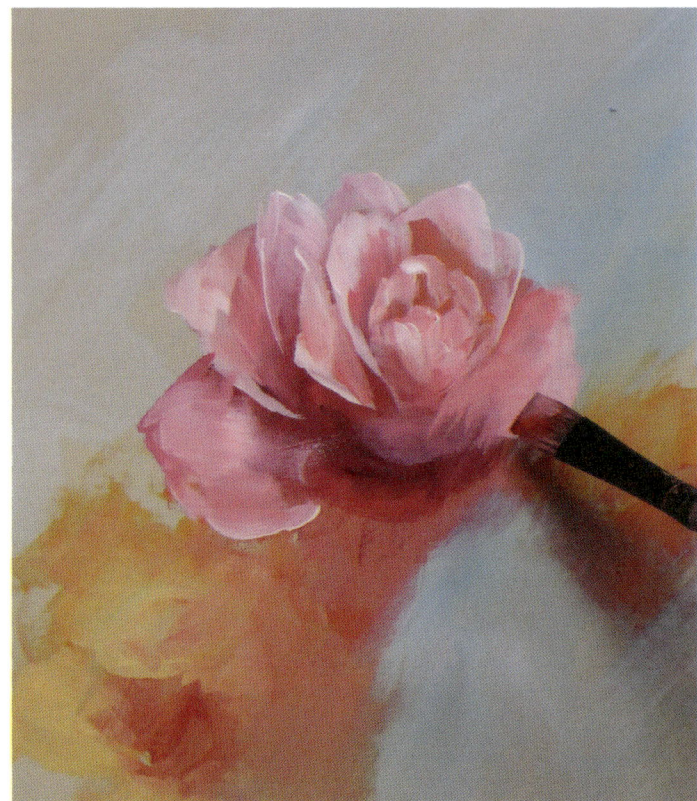

Step 18 Mottle with softer shadow and incorporate the shadows into the warm highlights. I don't blend them, I leave a lot of streaks for interest and movement.

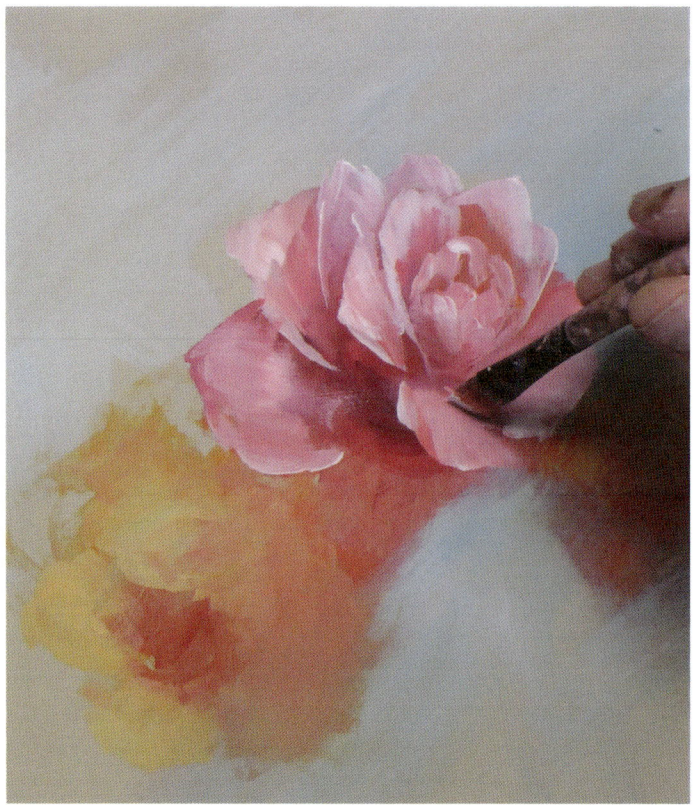

Step 19 Use the chisel of the brush and the light warm color to make additional petal edges. Then begin to build the front petals coming out from the bowl shadow.

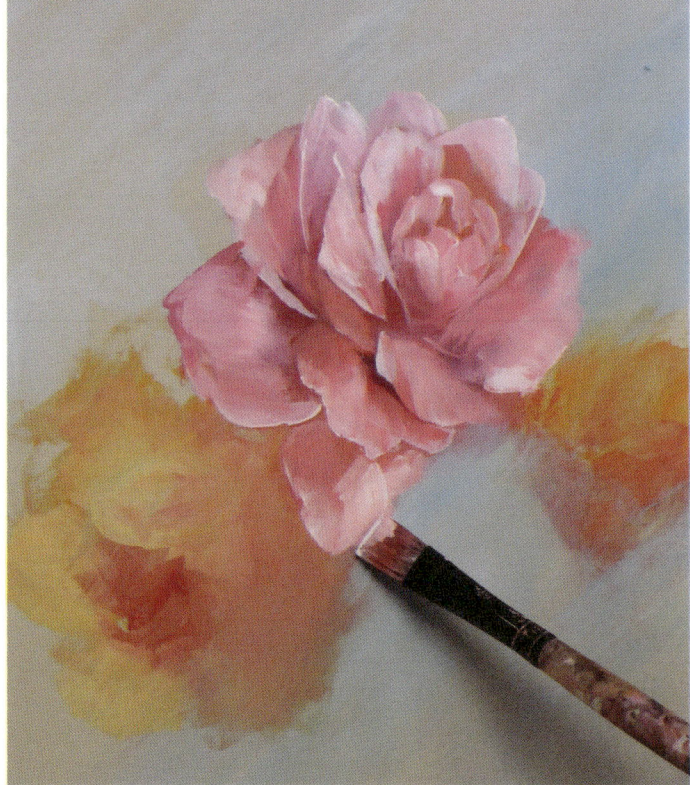

Step 20 Add the warmer (orange side) petals to the front of the rose pulling the color in and out of the bowl shadows. Lighten the tips of the petals with more white.

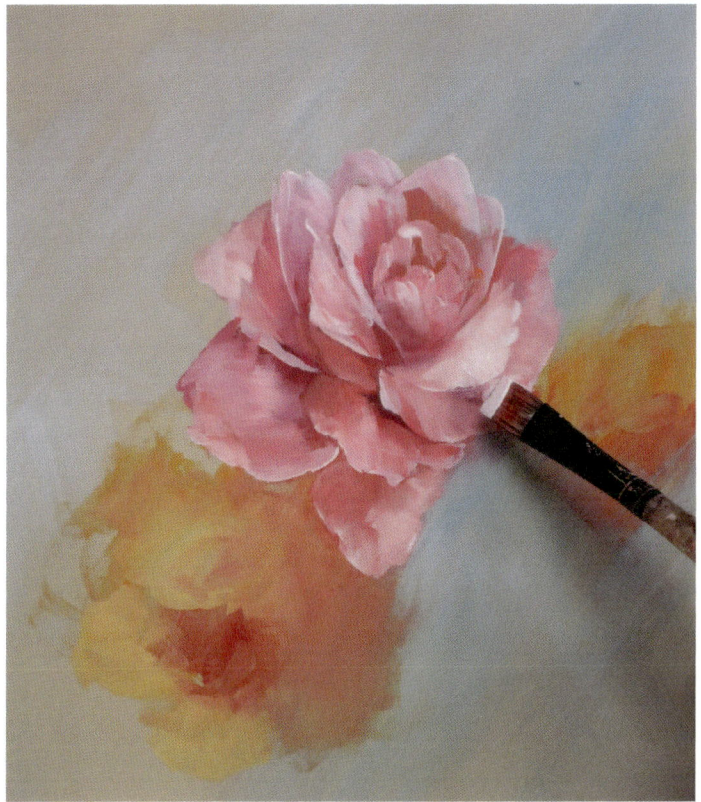

Step 21 Mottle the color lighter with more white and begin the light front petals. Here I am pulling out to keep the outside edges soft.

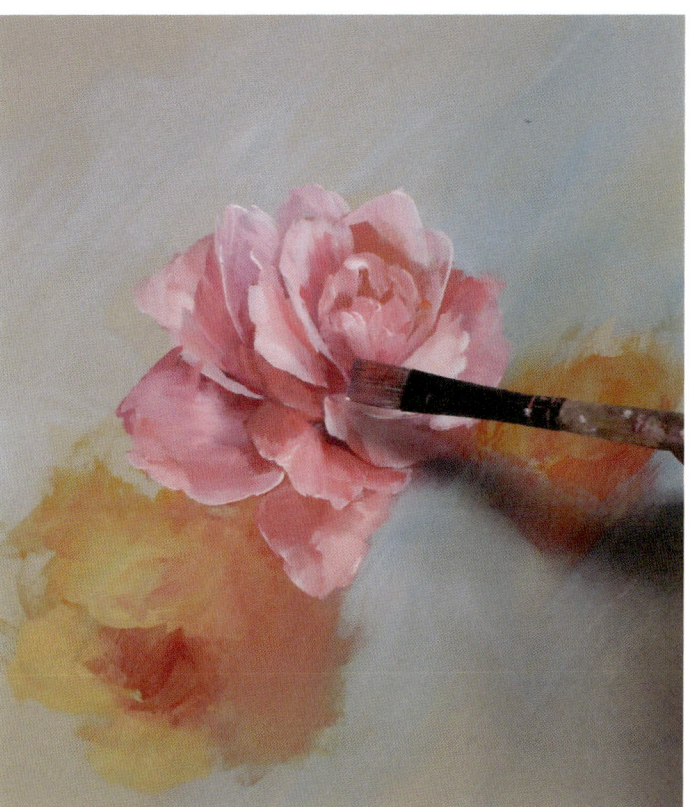

Step 22 Restate the bowl shadows with the violets. Soften into the light petals with medium tones.

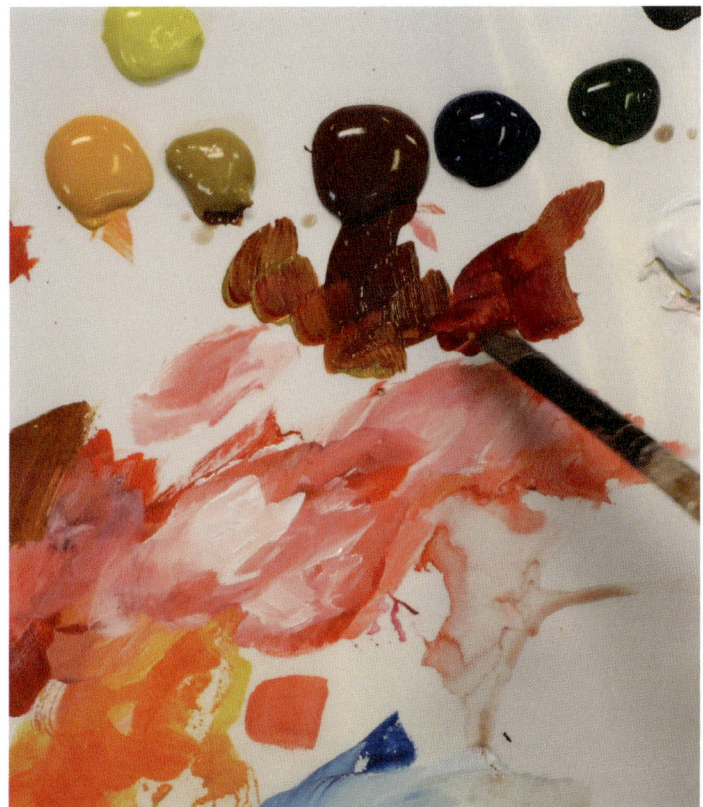

Step 23 Mottle Burnt Sienna with the violets to cool the color so we can use it in the shadow areas.

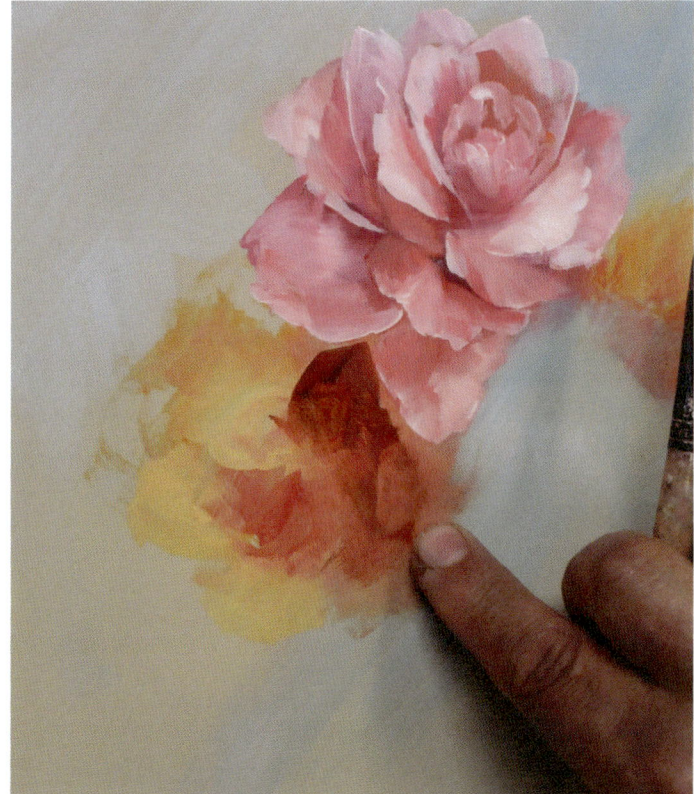

Step 24 Add to the bowl shadow next to the pink rose and soften the color into the background with your finger. Shear technique.

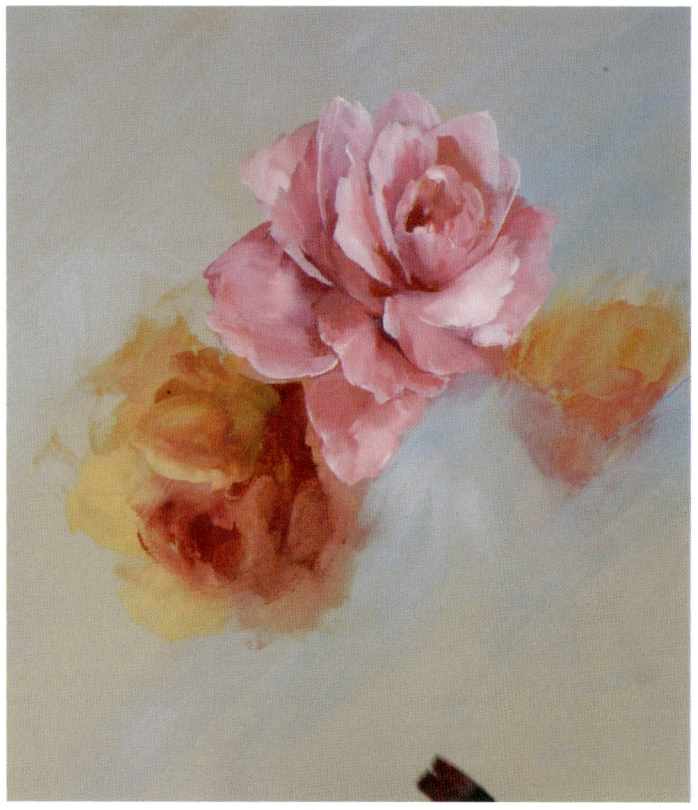

Step 25 Add additional shadows to the center of the rose. Here you can see the cool contrast on the yellow rose.

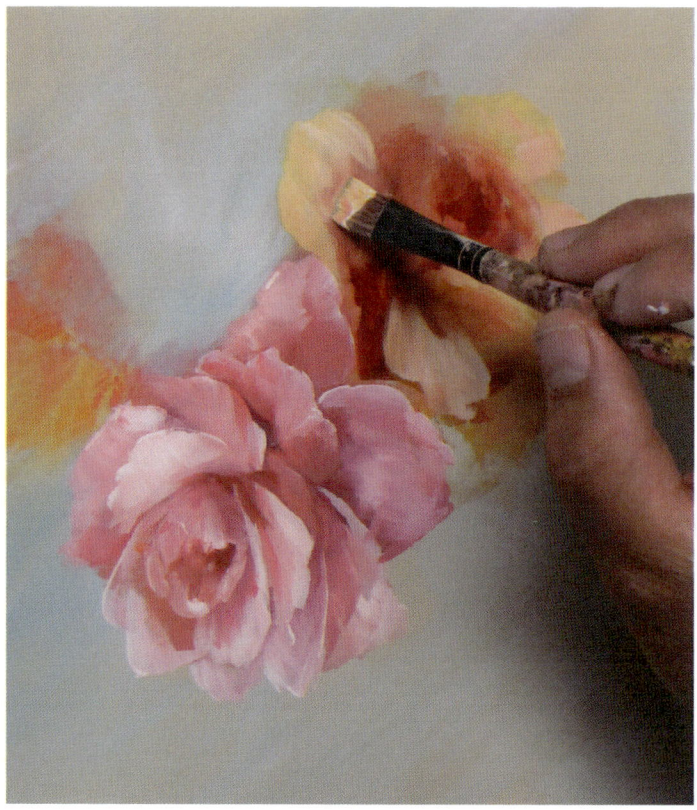

Step 26 Mottle the yellows, oranges and lighten with touch white. Begin shaping the petals on the yellow rose. Pull in towards the bowl shadow we just applied.

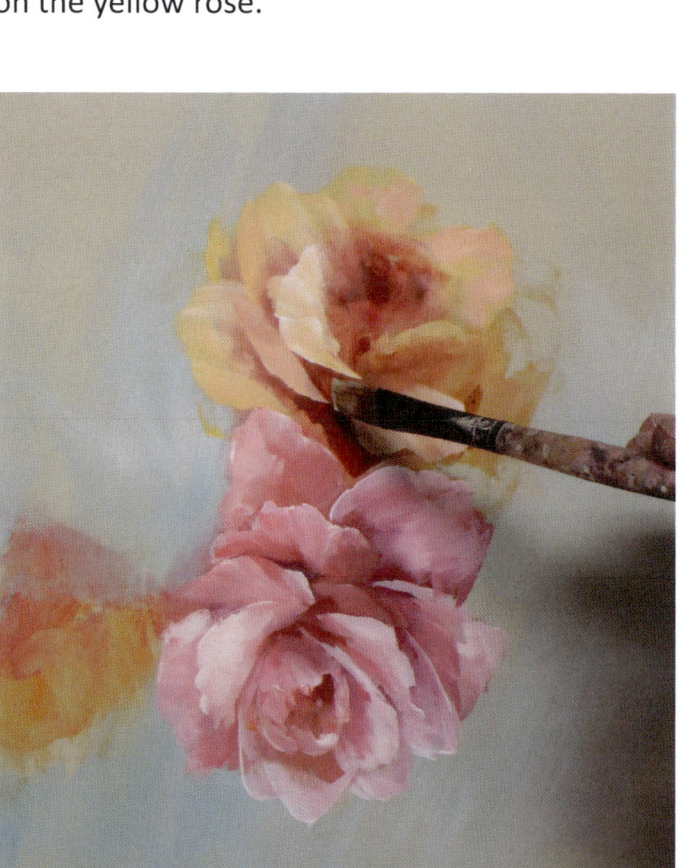

Step 27 Lighten the color with more white and add the next row of petals pulling in. Vary the shape of the petals by using the flat and chisel of the brush.

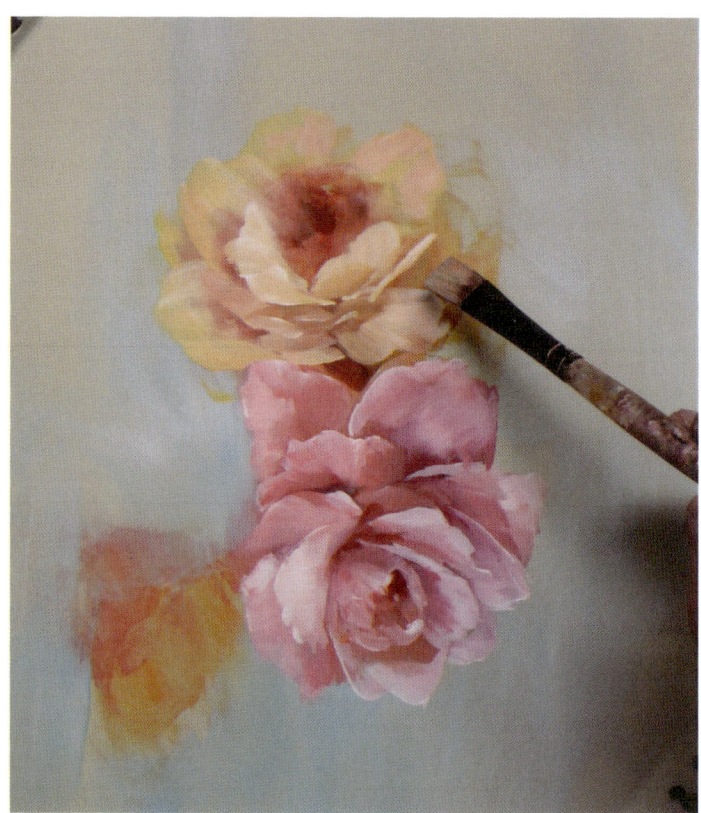

Step 28 Lighten the color further with more white. Vary with yellows. Using the chisel add the tips of the petals to the front of the rose.

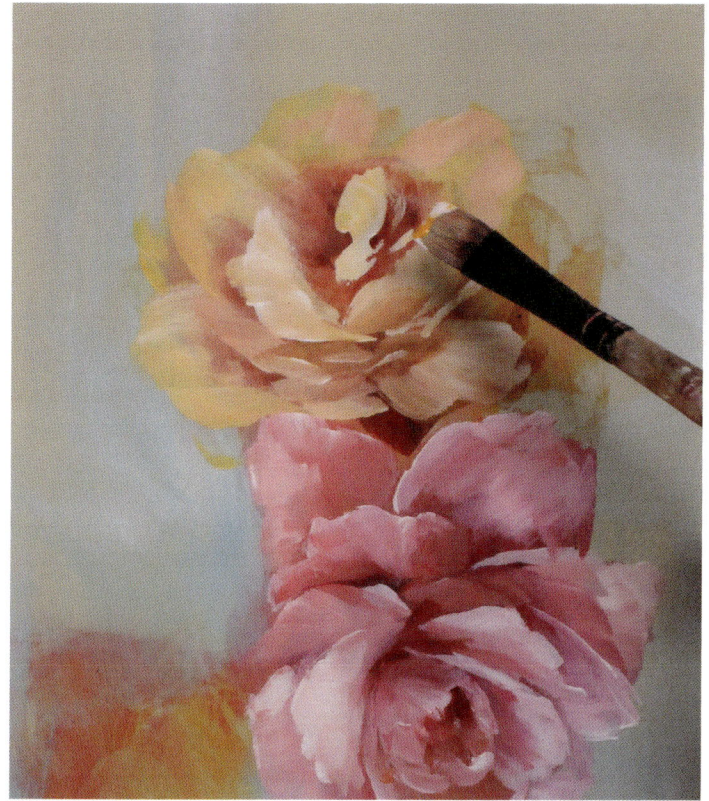

Step 29 Add light colors to the corners of the flat and then use the corner to "draw" the smaller petals in the center of the rose.

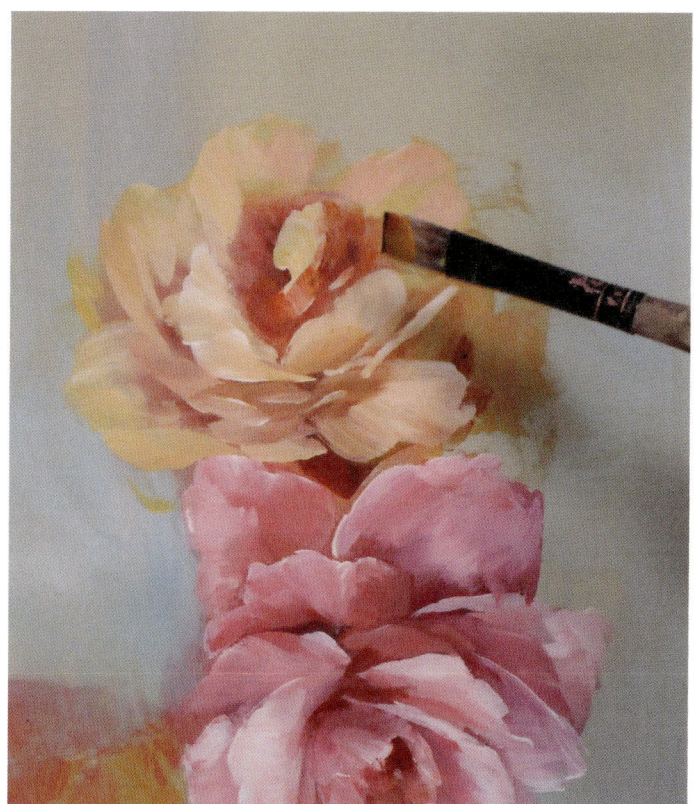

Step 30 Mottle the brush with shadow violets and incorporate the light petals into the shadows. Leave some violets showing in the center for the cool shadow contrast.

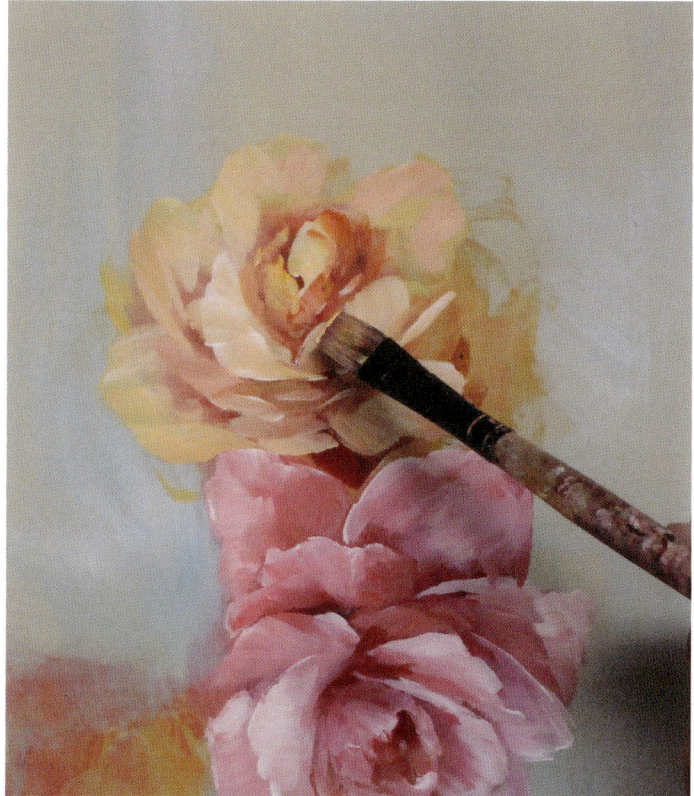

Step 31 Mottle the brush with additional yellows and add to the center of the rose for more interest. Varying the colors in the key interest.

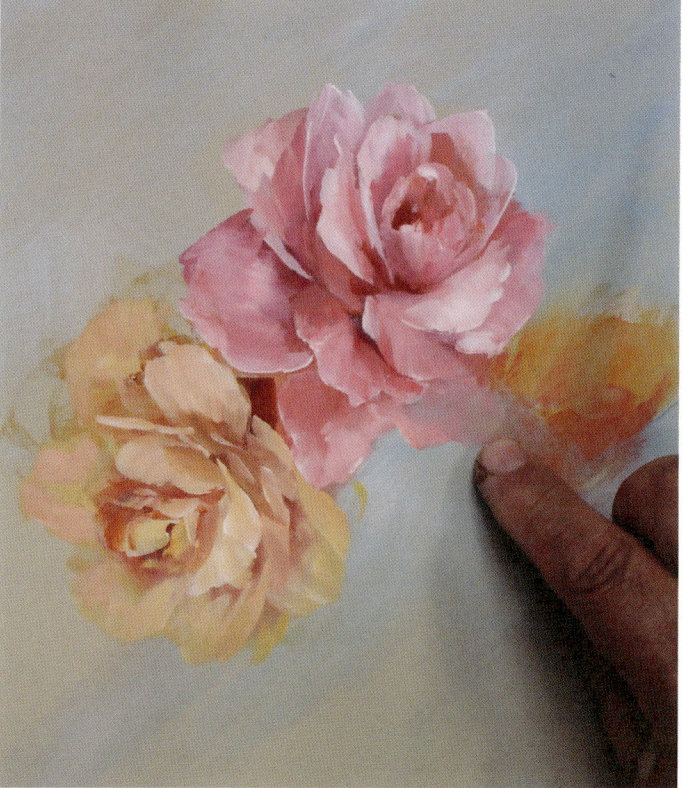

Step 32 Mottle the brush with light blues from the background and add to the edges of the roses. Use your finger to incorporate the colors together and create soft petal edges.

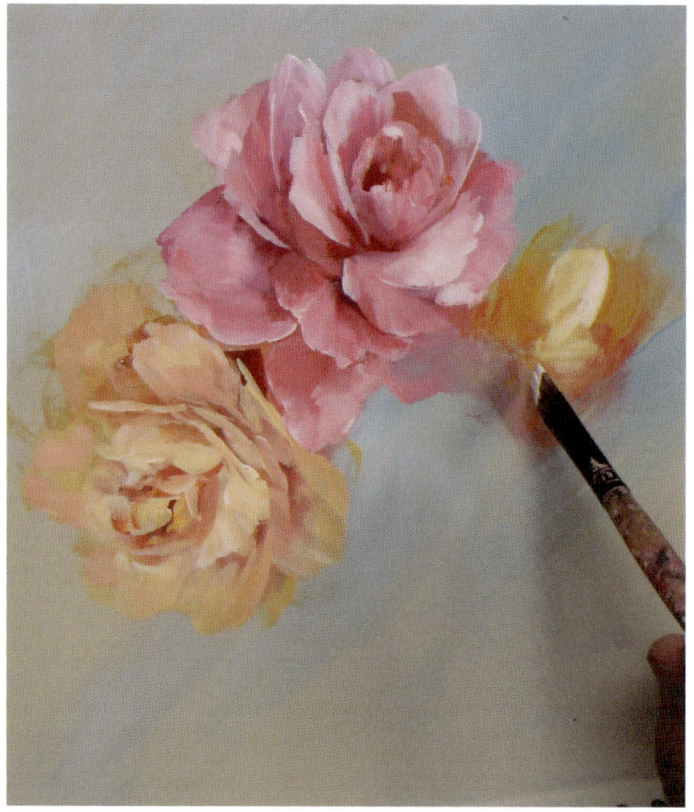

Step 33 Lighten the yellows with more white and add the front petals of the smaller rose bud.

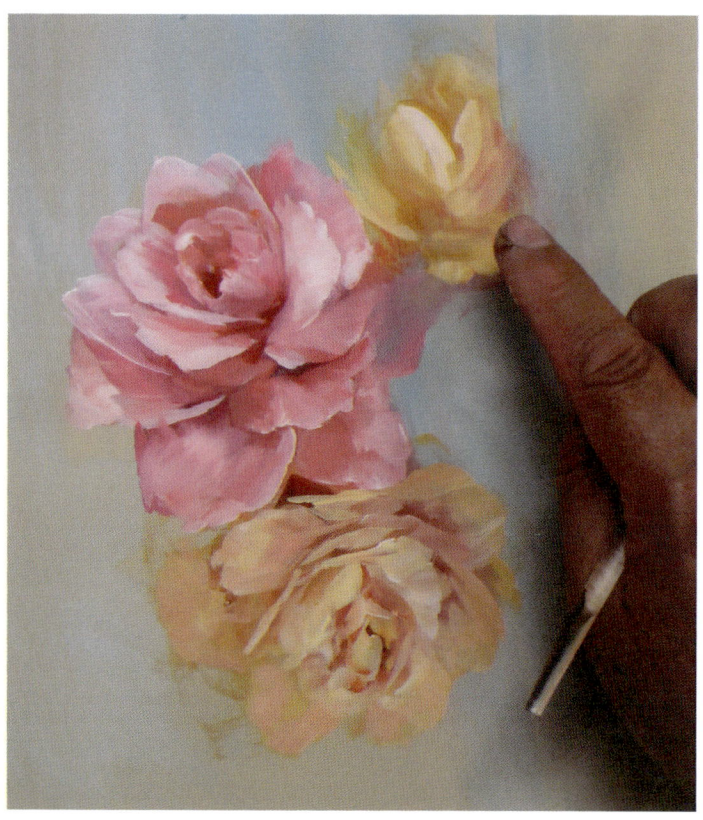

Step 34 Soften the outside edges with your finger into the background.

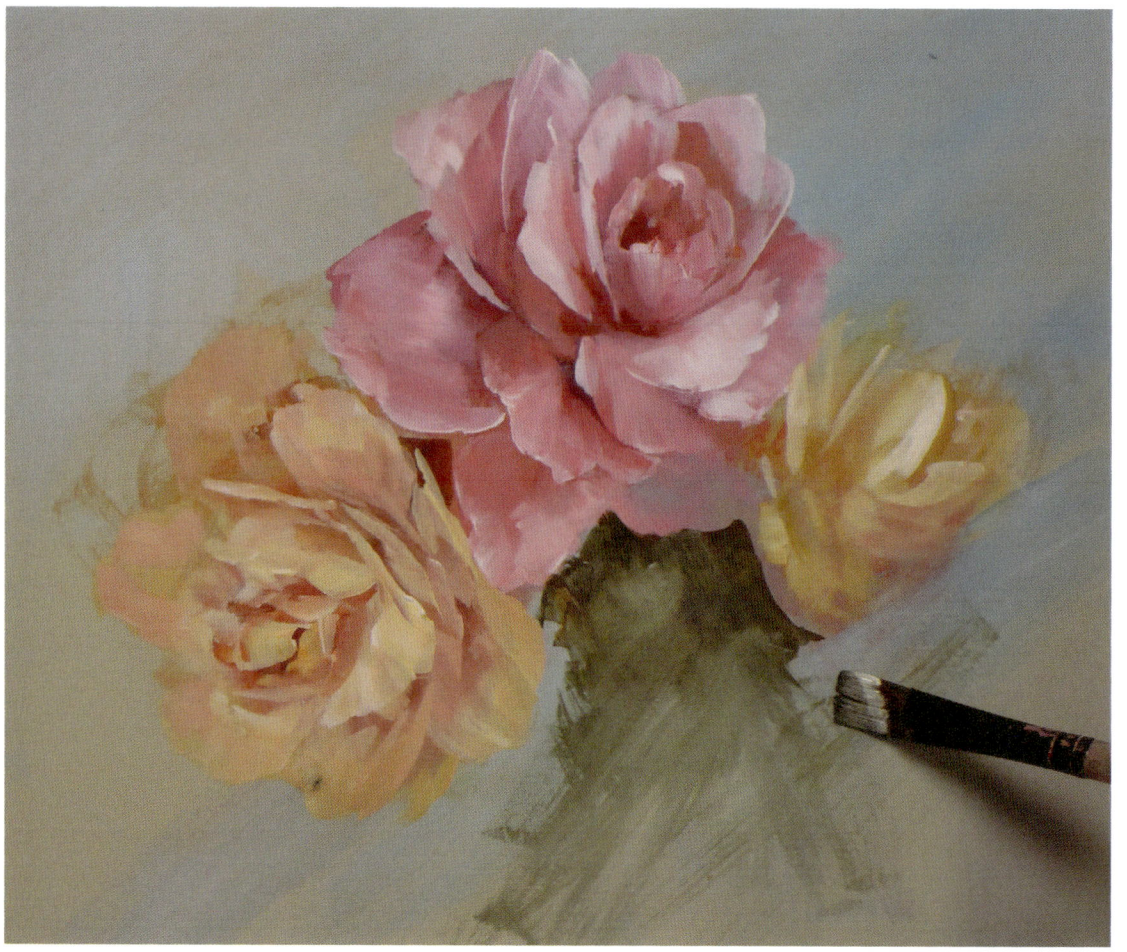

Step 35 Mottle various greens that we can use to do the negative painting around the roses for details. I mottle Pine Green with touch Burnt Sienna and then cool the color with a touch of violet. You can use either violet. Here you have a choice: lighten the color slightly with white or use it transparently, as I did, to begin the shadows. Negative paint around the roses for contrast.

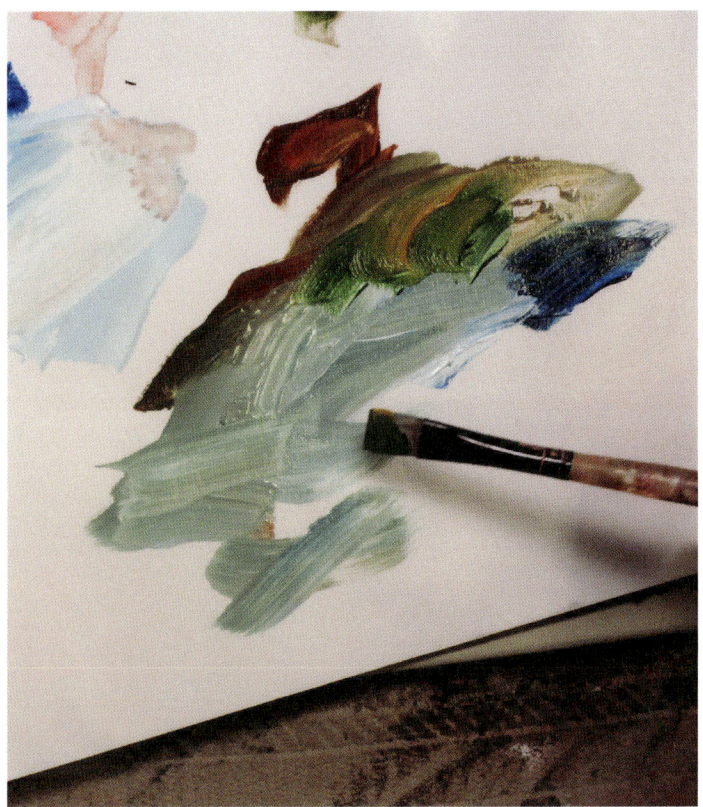

Step 36 Mottle the light blue from the background with greens, yellows and Burnt Sienna on the palette.

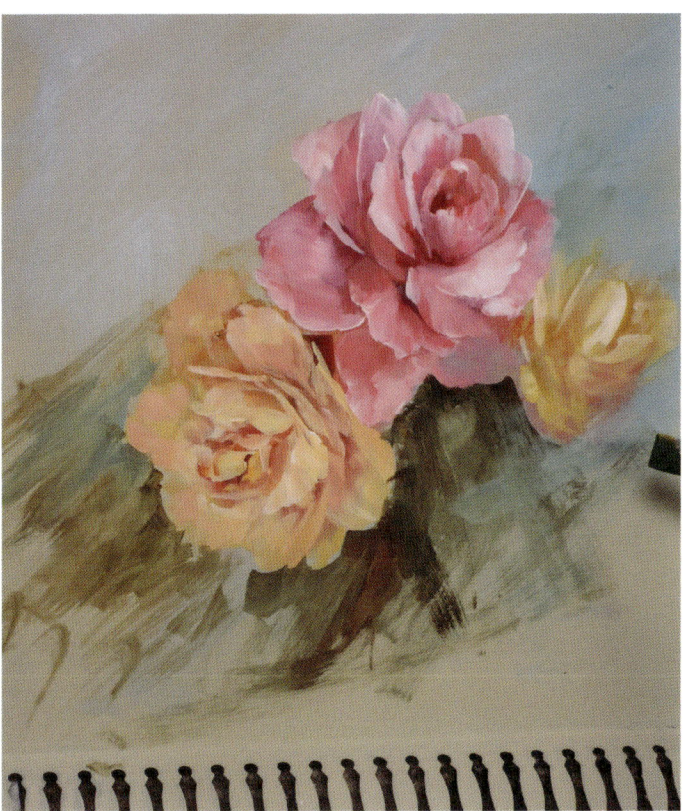

Step 37 Use this color to soften the edges of the cool greens with just applied. This helps reduce the contrast as the viewers eye leaves the roses.

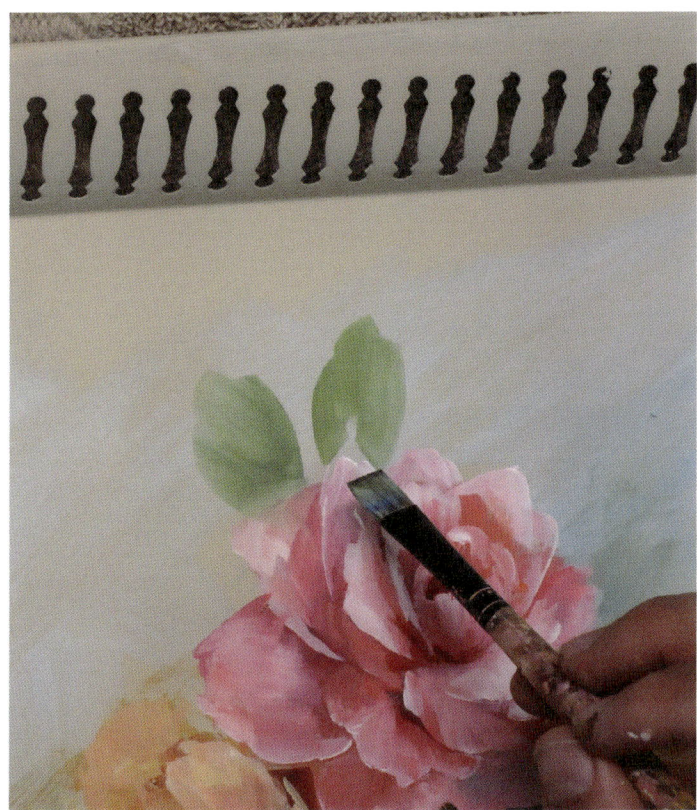

Step 38 Mottle a soft green and begin the oval shapes of the leaves. I use 2 or 3 strokes pulling to the rose. I sometimes soften one side with my finger before it dries.

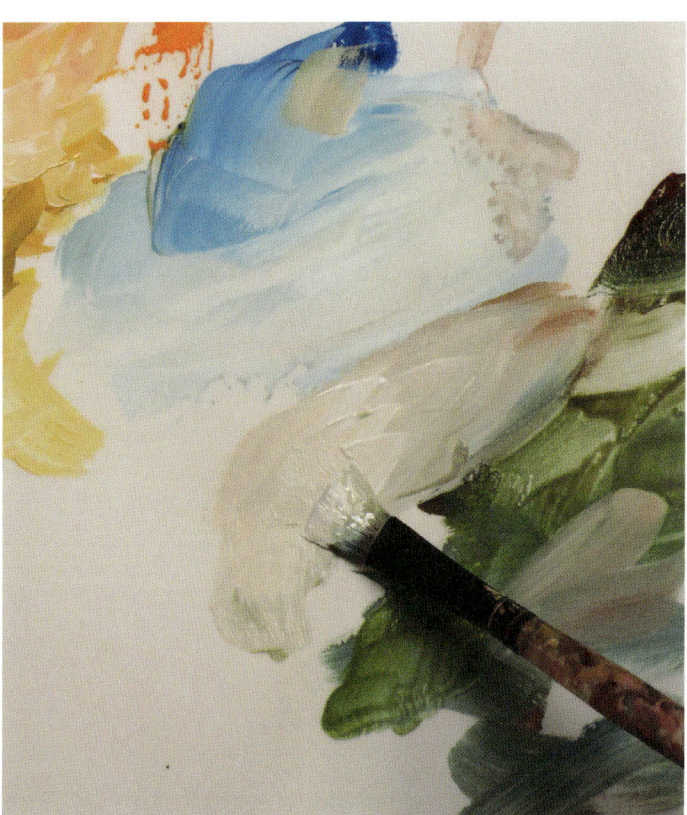

Step 39 Mottle a soft grey with the greens, blues and touch Burnt Sienna. Lighten with white to about the value of the background.

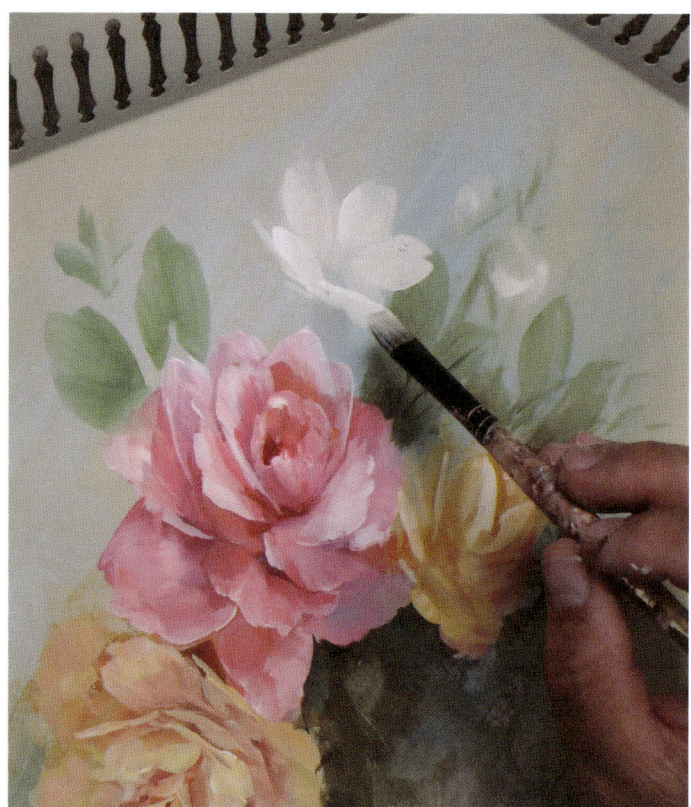

Step 40 Start the smaller white blossoms. Vary the petals using the float to the chisel of the brush.

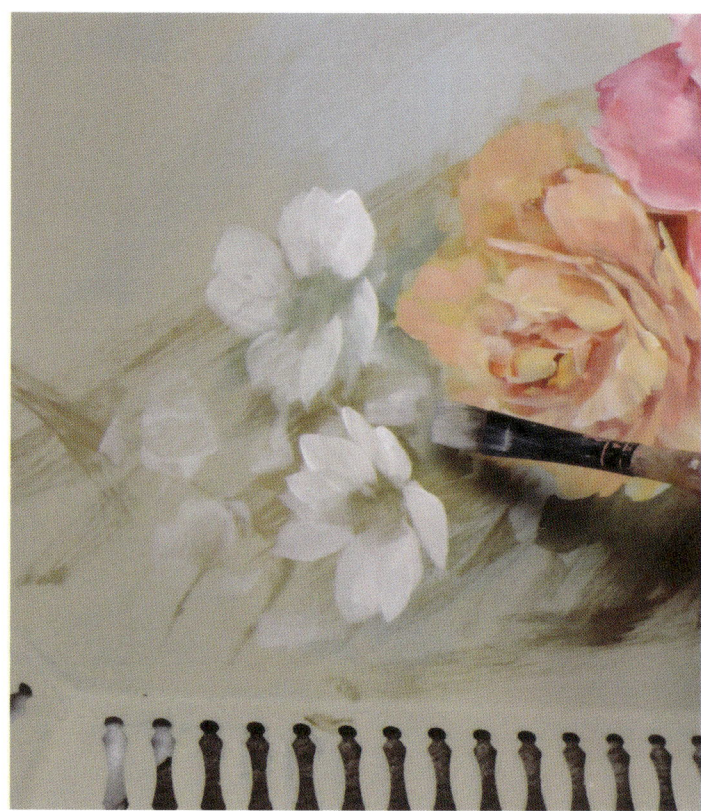

Step 41 Mottle the color a little lighter with more white and add the front light petals to the blossoms. Tap the brush around to create more movement and suggest back blossoms.

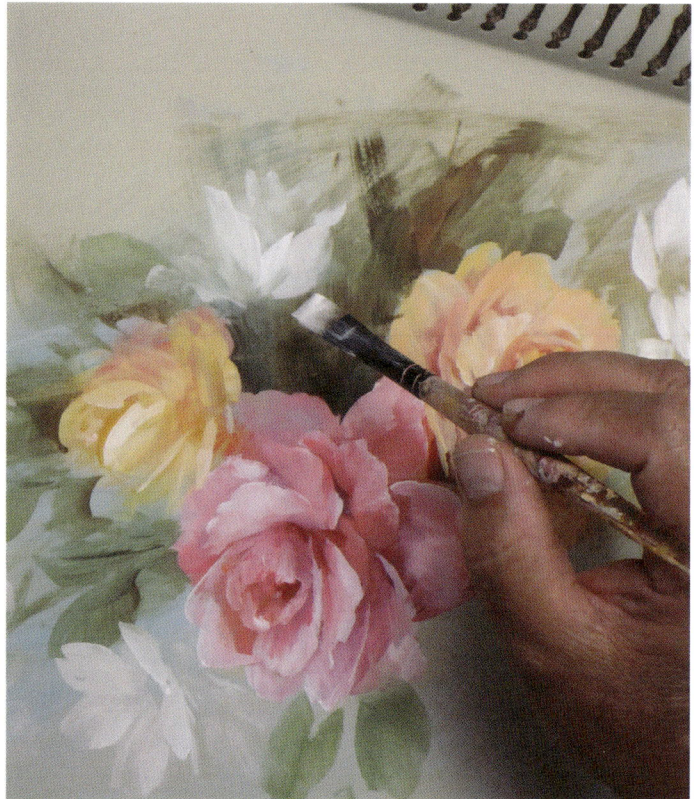

Step 42 Add strokes of the light to the bottom of the composition to suggest more flowers. Always use different parts of the flat to create more interest.

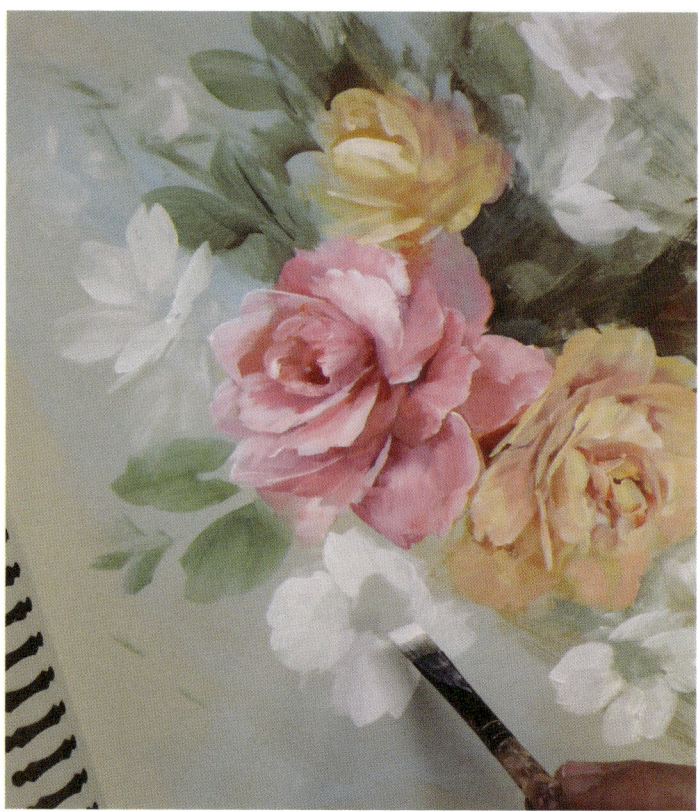

Step 43 To keep some blossoms soft, use the flat of the brush and a soft white. Having soft blossoms helps with the interest in the composition.

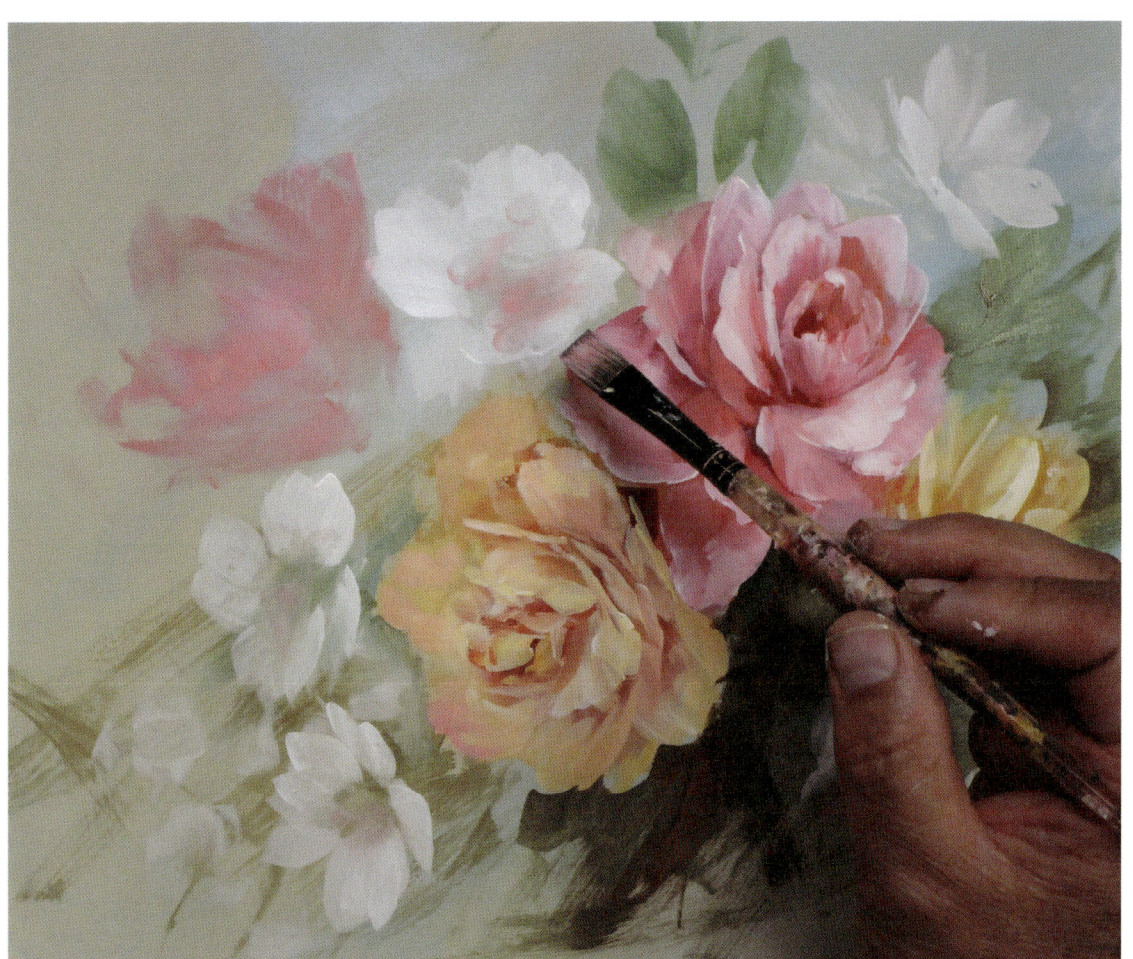

Step 44
Here I decided to add another rose to the composition. I felt that the one pink rose looked a little lonely in the bouquet. Mottle a light cool pink and push the color into the shape of the rose. Notice all the streaks.
To incorporate the pinks into the composition and move it further through the flowers, I decided to add pinks to the centers of the white blossoms.

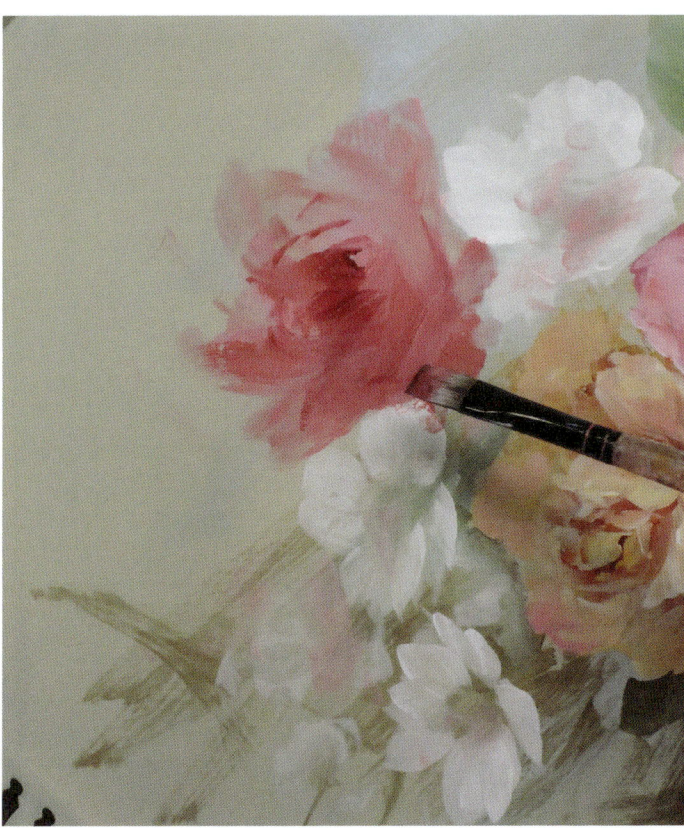

Step 45 Mottle the brush with more violets to cool and darken and add the center and bowl shadow to the rose.

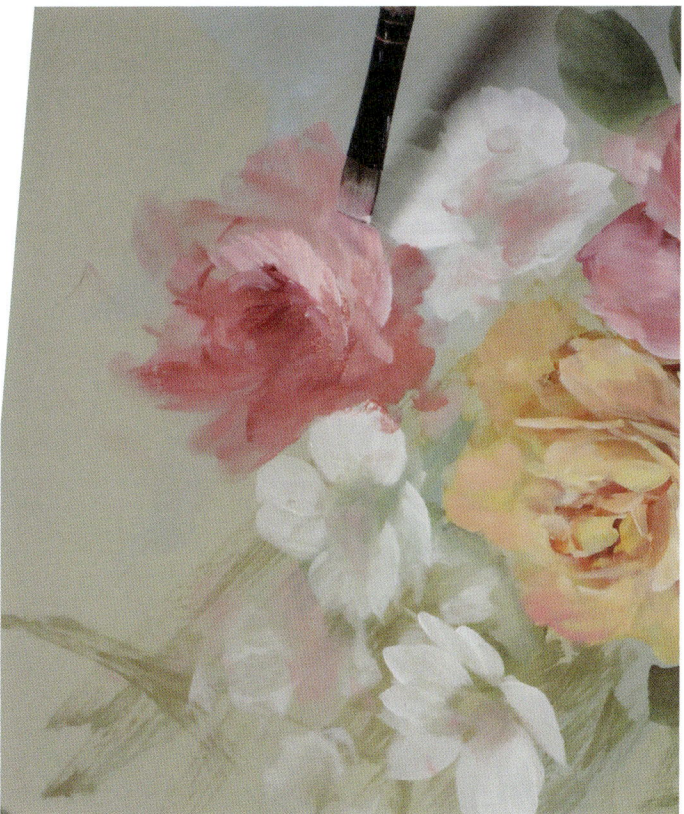

Step 46 Mottle the color lighter with white and touch yellows to warm and begin to build the front of the rose.

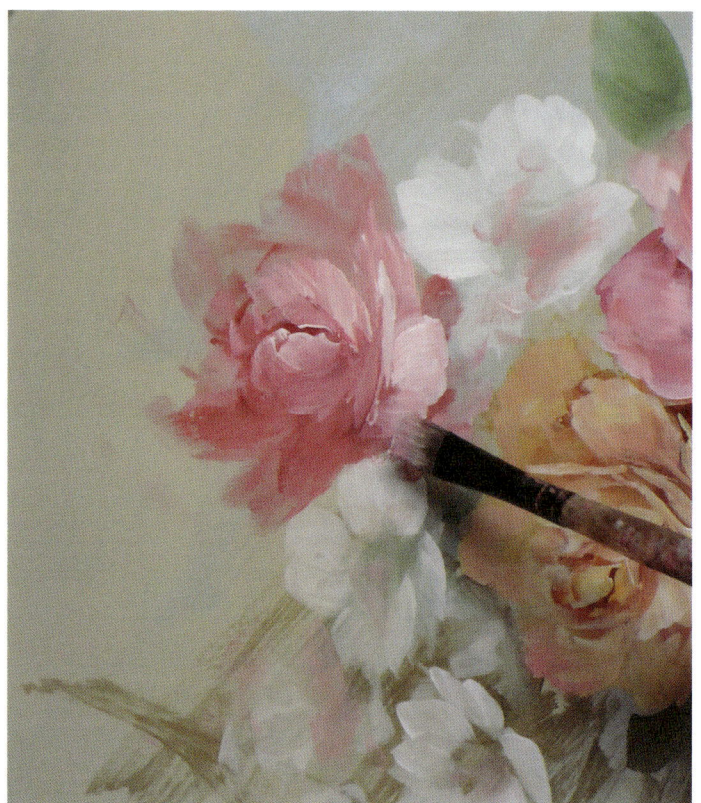

Step 47 Mottle the color lighter and add the front reaching petals to the rose.

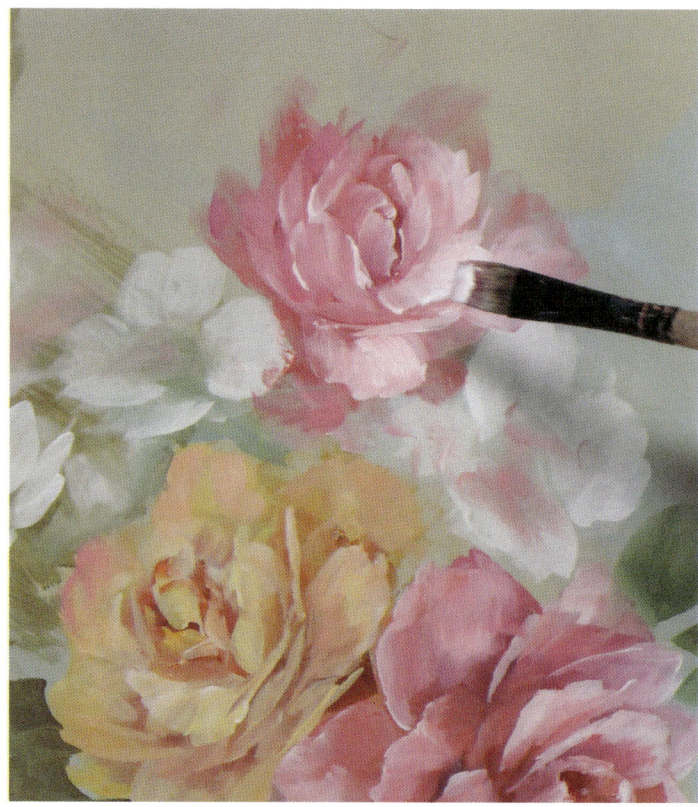

Step 48 Mottle the color lighter. Remember you can also increase the warmth with a touch of yellow. Add lighter petals.

Step 49 H
Here are the flowers at this point. I added more yellows to the centers of the blossoms. Also, I stated some reds on the lower part of the composition to move the pinks down the design. The petals on the pinks have a lot of contrast but I kept the shadows on the center pink rose darker. This give it just a little more contrast than the other one. Darks contrast against light backgrounds.

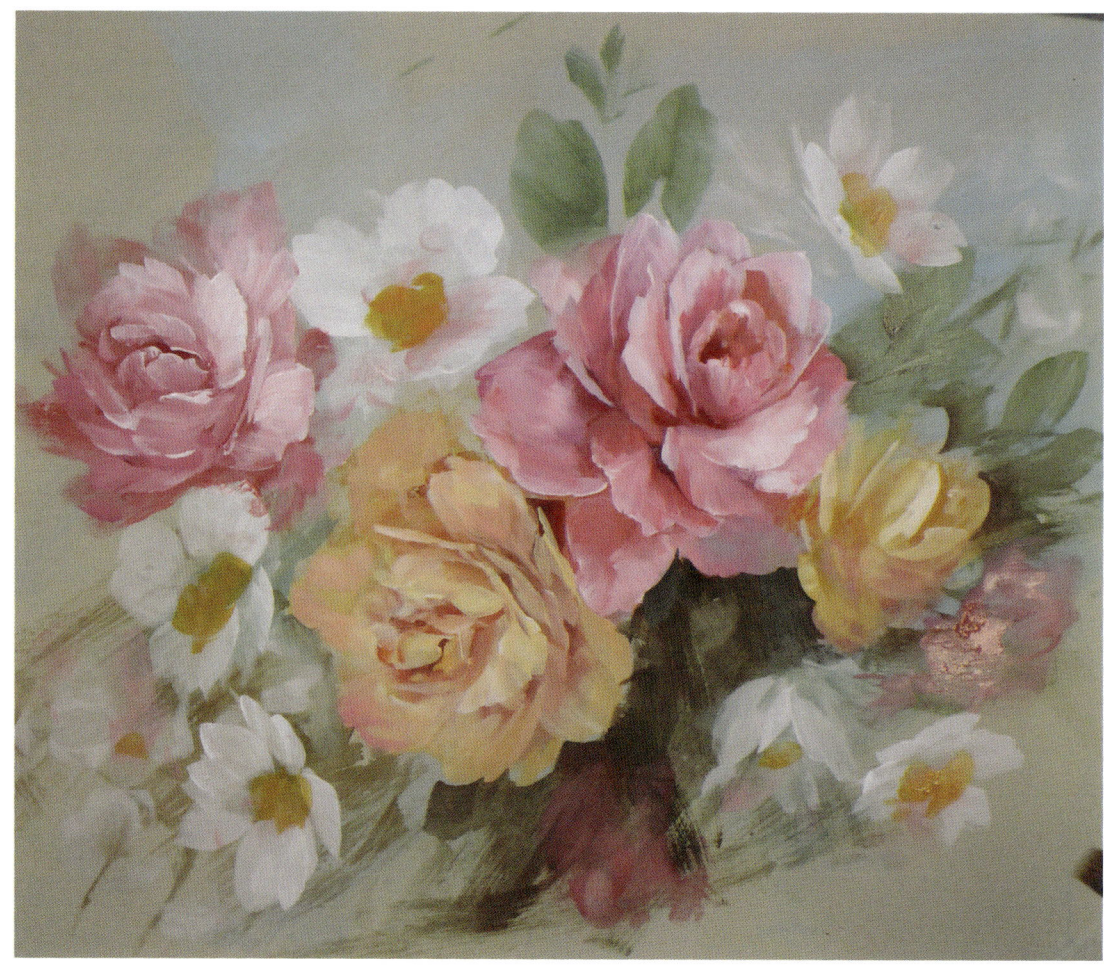

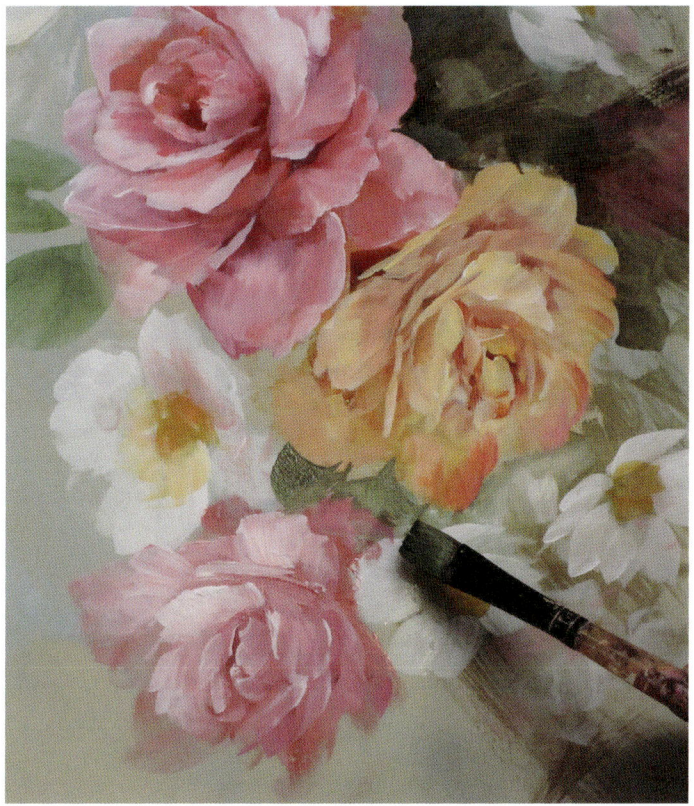

Step 50 Add washes of softer greens to negative paint around the roses. To the outside. Keep the darks in the center for contrast.

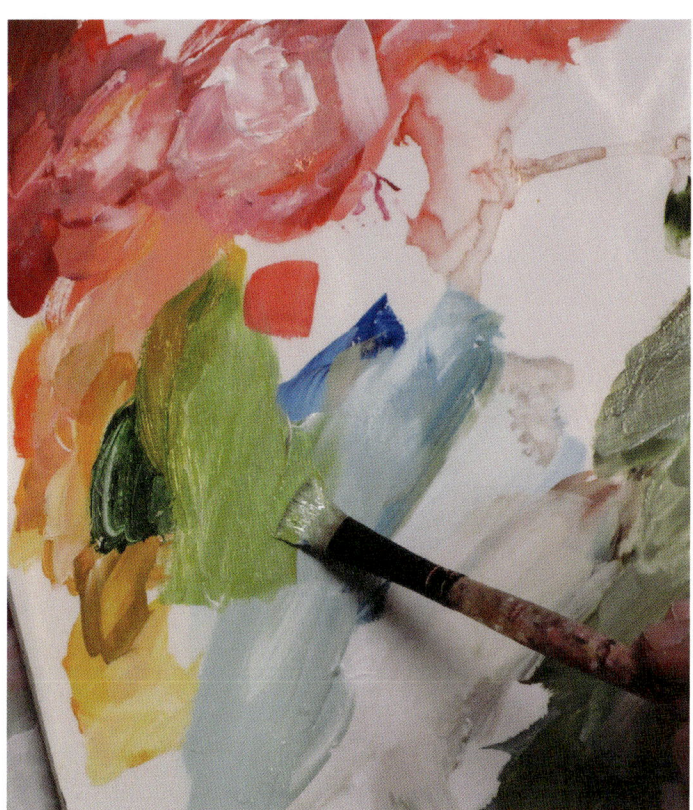

Step 51 Mottle a lighter green with the yellows and touch Pine Green and white.

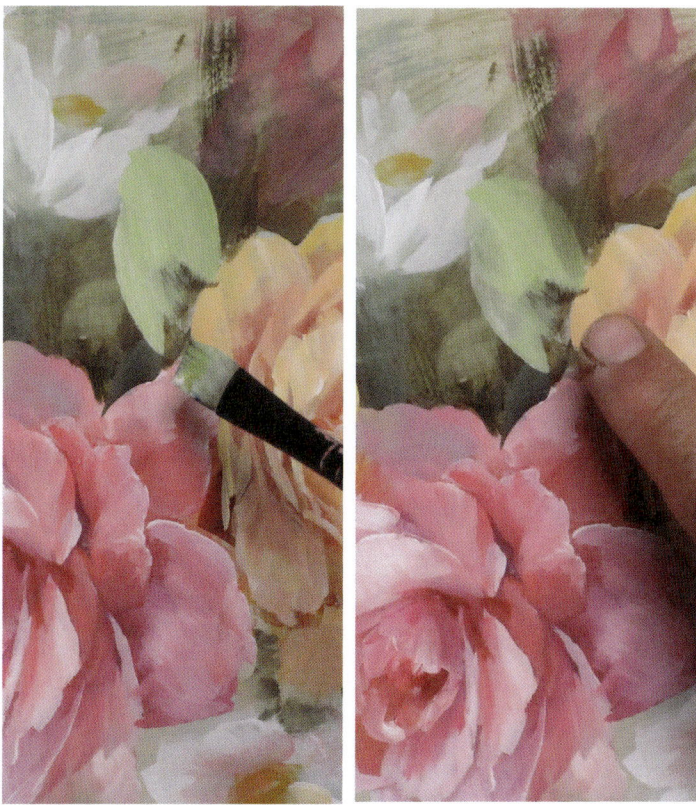

Step 52 Use this to add additional light colors to the leaves and then soften the movement in and out with your finger. Allow some areas of highlight to become transparent.

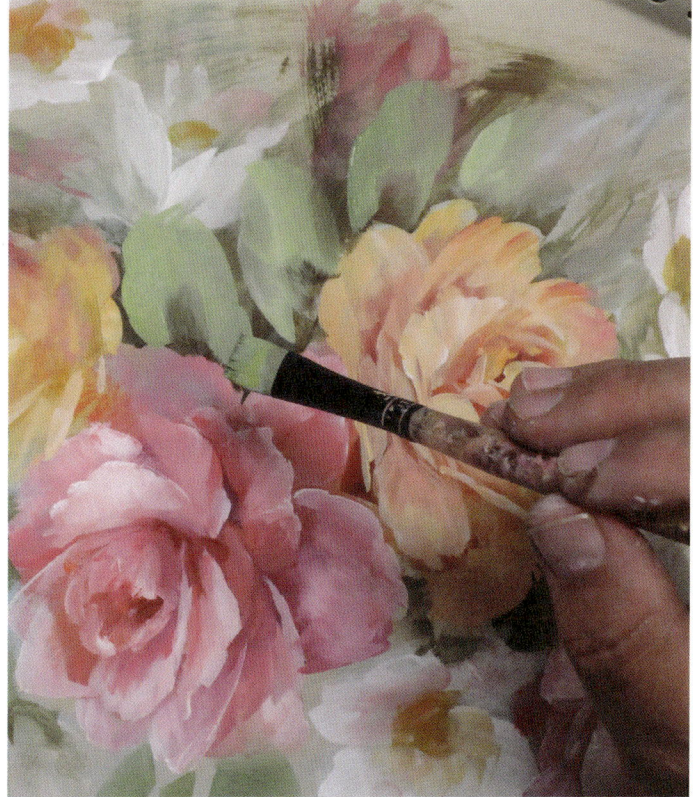

Step 53 Work the greens around the leaves in the center of interest. This will give them more contrast with the darks. Soften with your finger like we did in the last step.

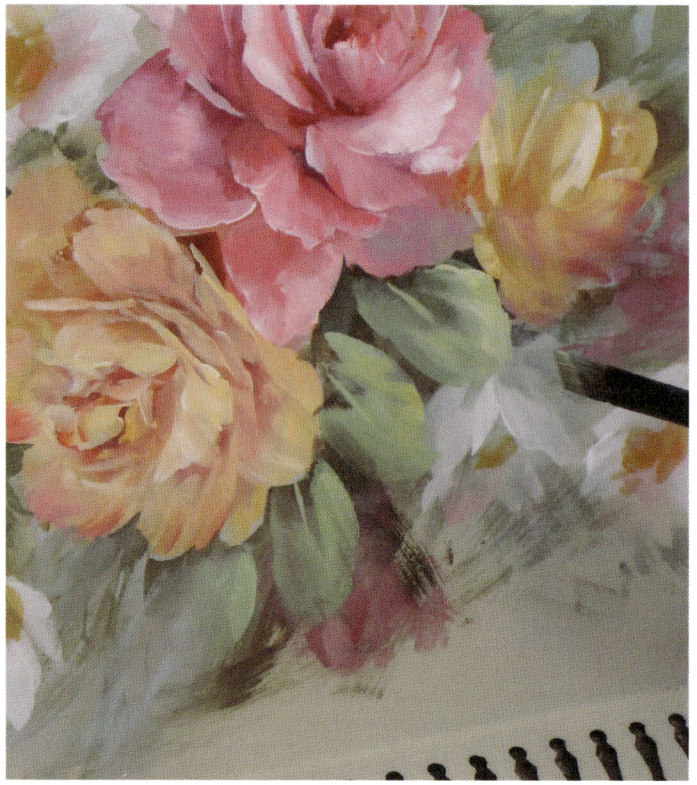

Step 54   Add soft whites and pinks to the bottom flowers to carry the tones down there. Keep soft and "blur" the edges with your finger.

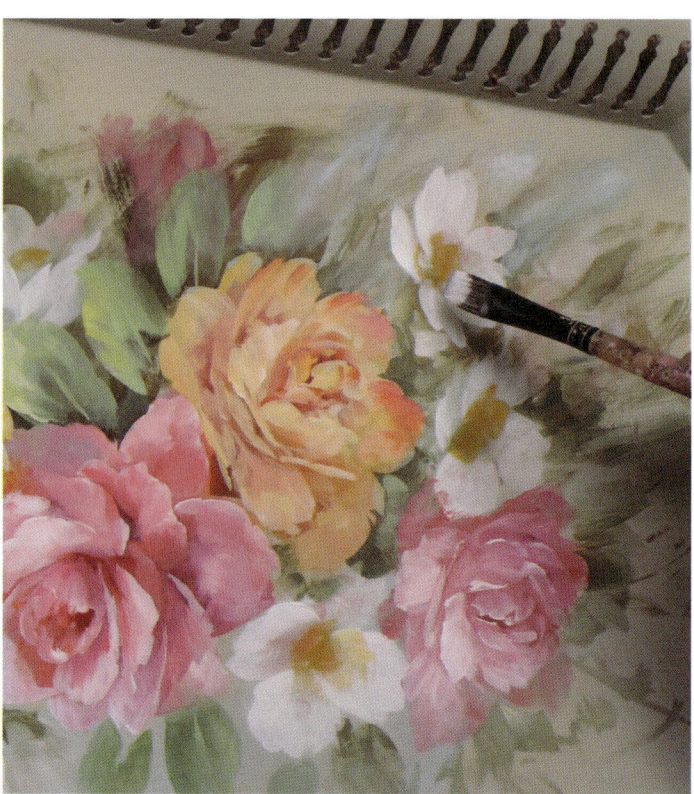

Step 55   Add final light highlights to the white blossoms giving a nice shapr edge on the petals that are pointing to the center of interest. Keep the outside petals soft.

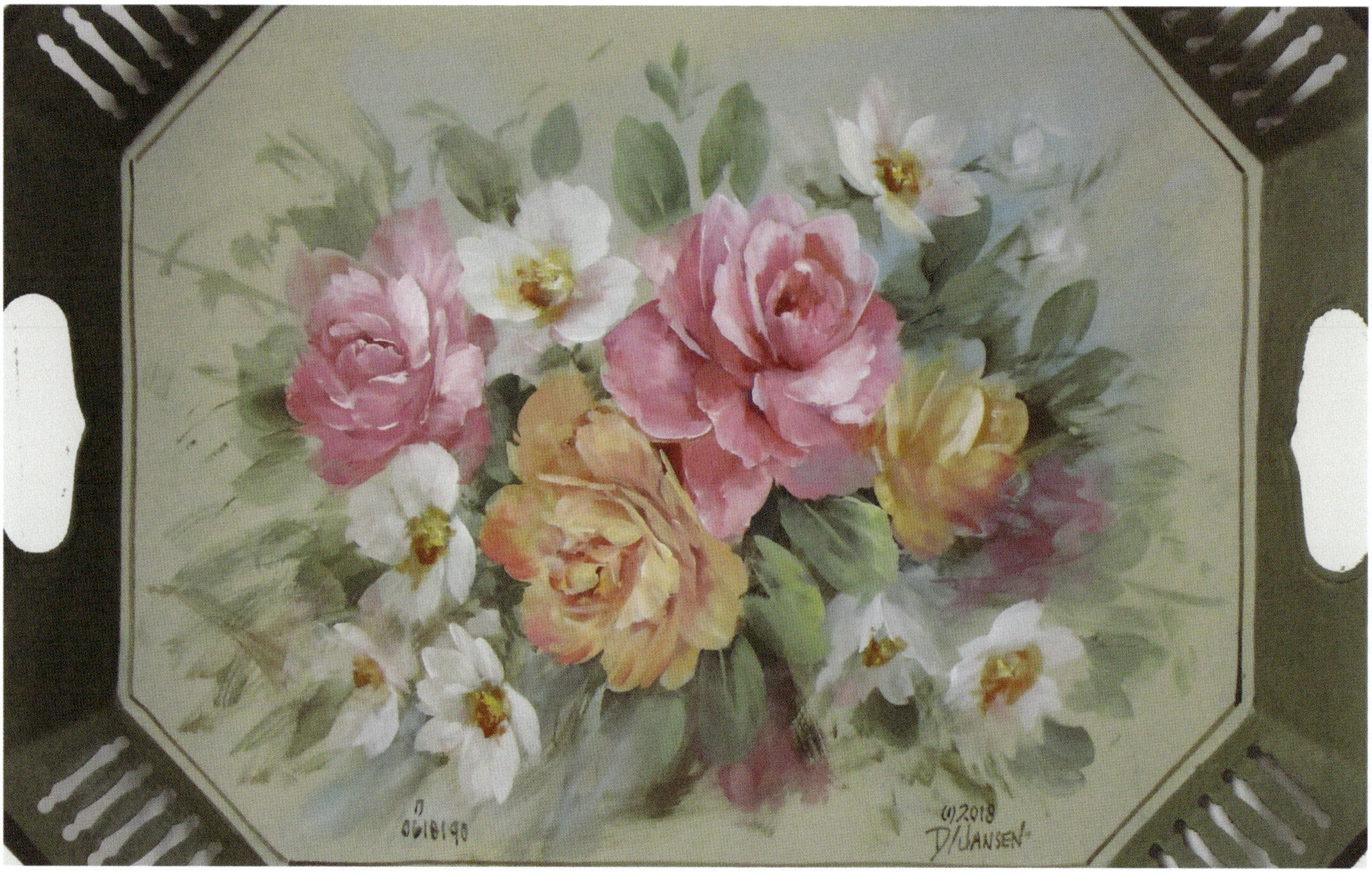

Step 56   I tapped in Hansa + White into the centers of the blossoms. I also added a touch of Burnt Sienna and Violet to the shadow side. Finish the edges as desired. I use toned green. Enjoy!

Lesson 3
Pattern

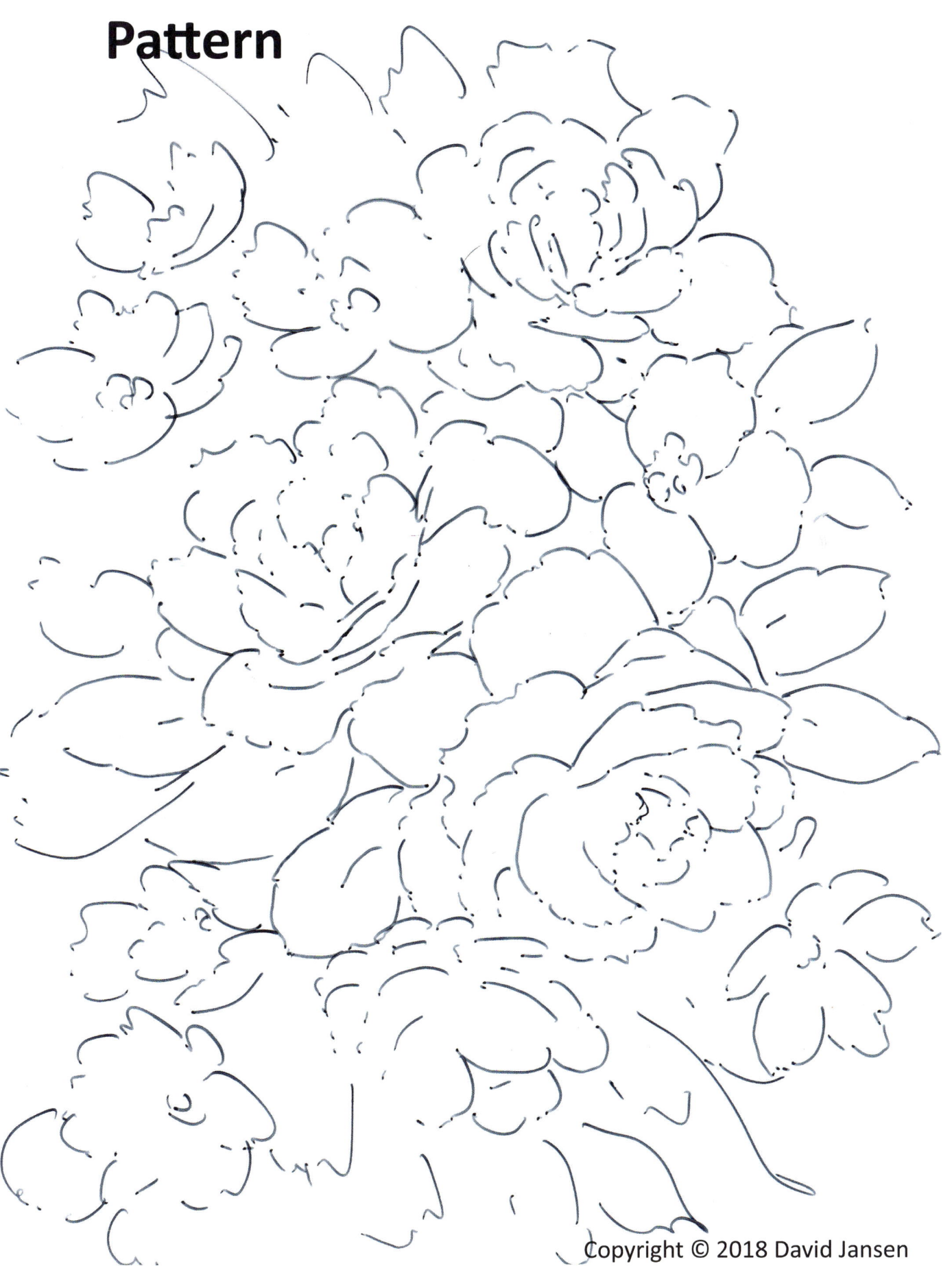

Copyright © 2018 David Jansen

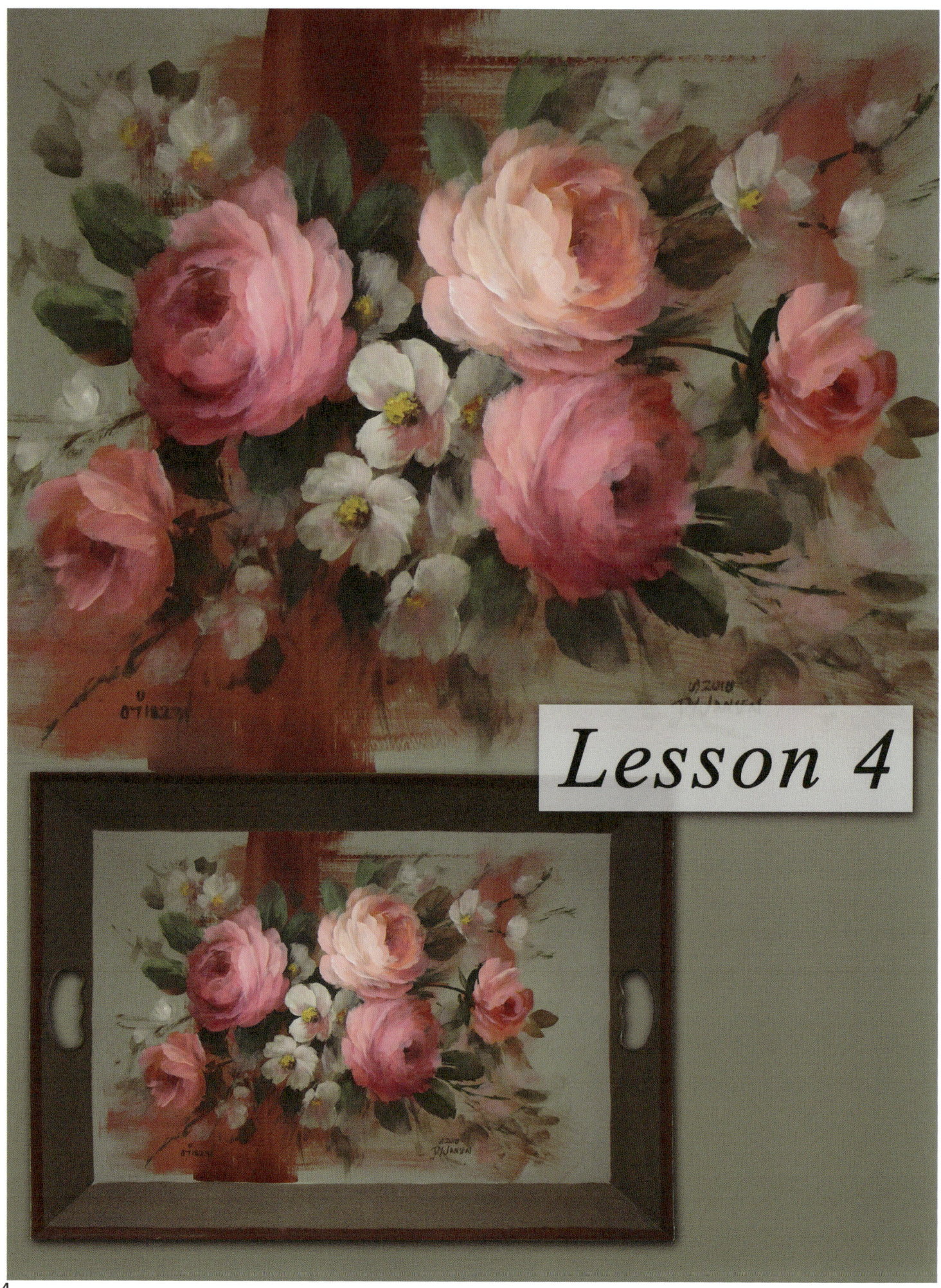

Lesson 4

Step Shear Technique

In the beginning of the book, I explained the shear technique. I began using this method a few years ago, however, we designed Heritage Acrylics specifically for this type of painting.

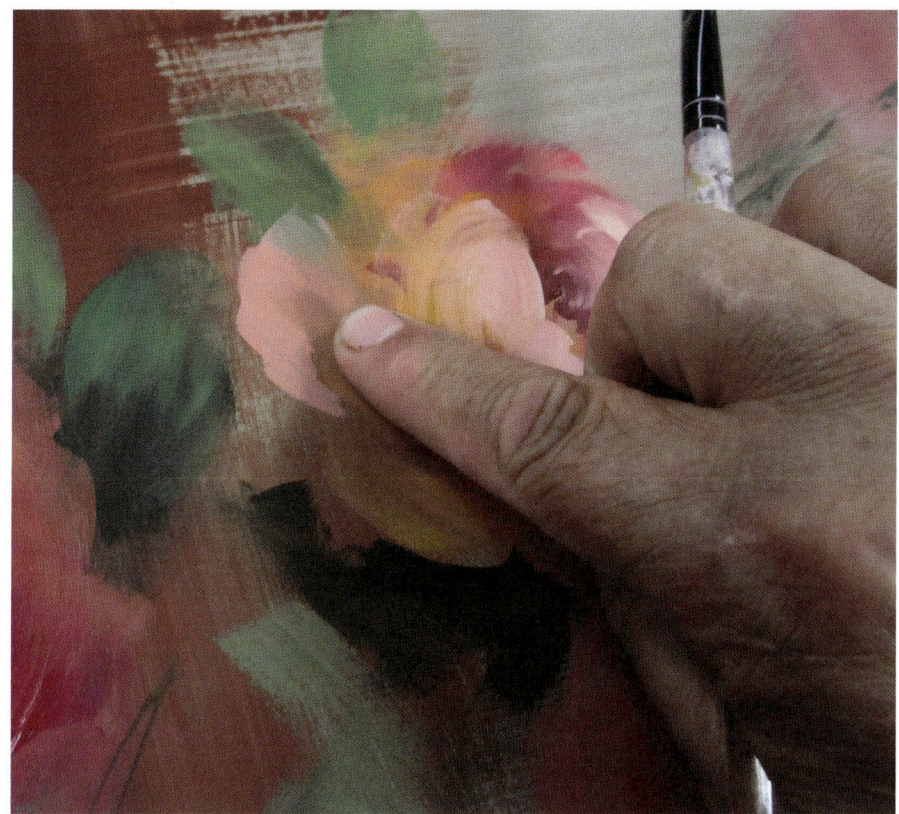

For these roses we use the shear technique to add movement and soften the receding edge of the petals. A receding edge is the edge of the petal that is heading away from the viewer, such as into the background or into the bowl shadow. (See left photo).

This lesson will add one more element. It is the "step". This is where you slowly lighten or darken the petals in successive steps while using the shear technique.

As you can see in the final photo, this can give roses the look of blended oils. However, with this technique, you can paint exciting compositions much faster with acrylics than oils. However, it takes practice. The key is no more than 2 values lighter between petals. Slowly lighten and the petals will shear and give you the blended look! Let's give it a try!

Paint It Simply Palette
Base Color- Light Green Grey
White + Touch Hansa Yellow and Black

Palette Colors

PAINT IT SIMPLY COLORS	OPTIONAL COLORS
Naphthol Red Light	Yellow Oxide
Red Violet	Diarylide Yellow
Titanium White	Pine Green
Carbon Black	Quinacridone Violet
Phthalo Blue	Burnt Sienna
Hansa Yellow	Phthalo Green Blue

Painting Surface
Large Metal Tray

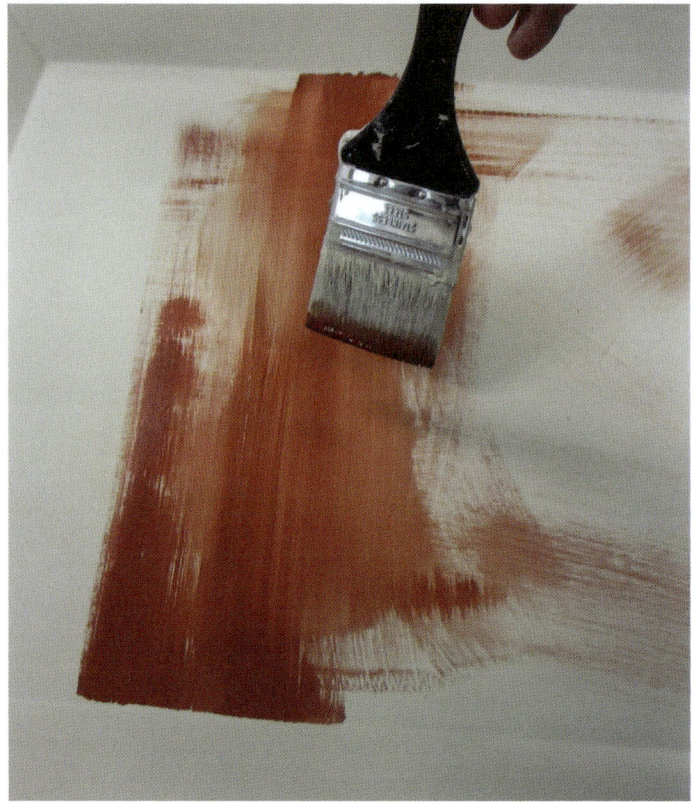

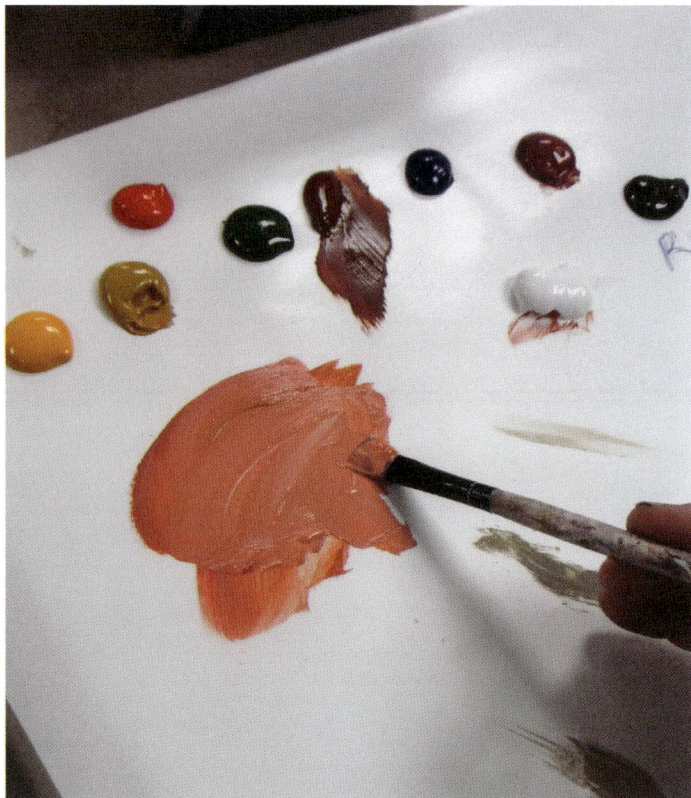

Step 1 After you have base coated the tray with a light grey green, use a large brush with Burnt Sienna to create the movement in the background. Leave it very streaky!

Step 2 Mottle Burnt Sienna with reds and a touch violet. Lighten with a touch of white. You want the color just a little darker than your grey green background.

Step 3
Use an 8 or 10 fusion flat begin to shape the roses with the reds. I also added a few touches of Hansa Yellow to vary the colors. Let the edges of the roses blur off into the background.

I also like to push the colors around with my finger to create movement. Leave some spaces between the flowers to make the design more "airy". We call this informal design.

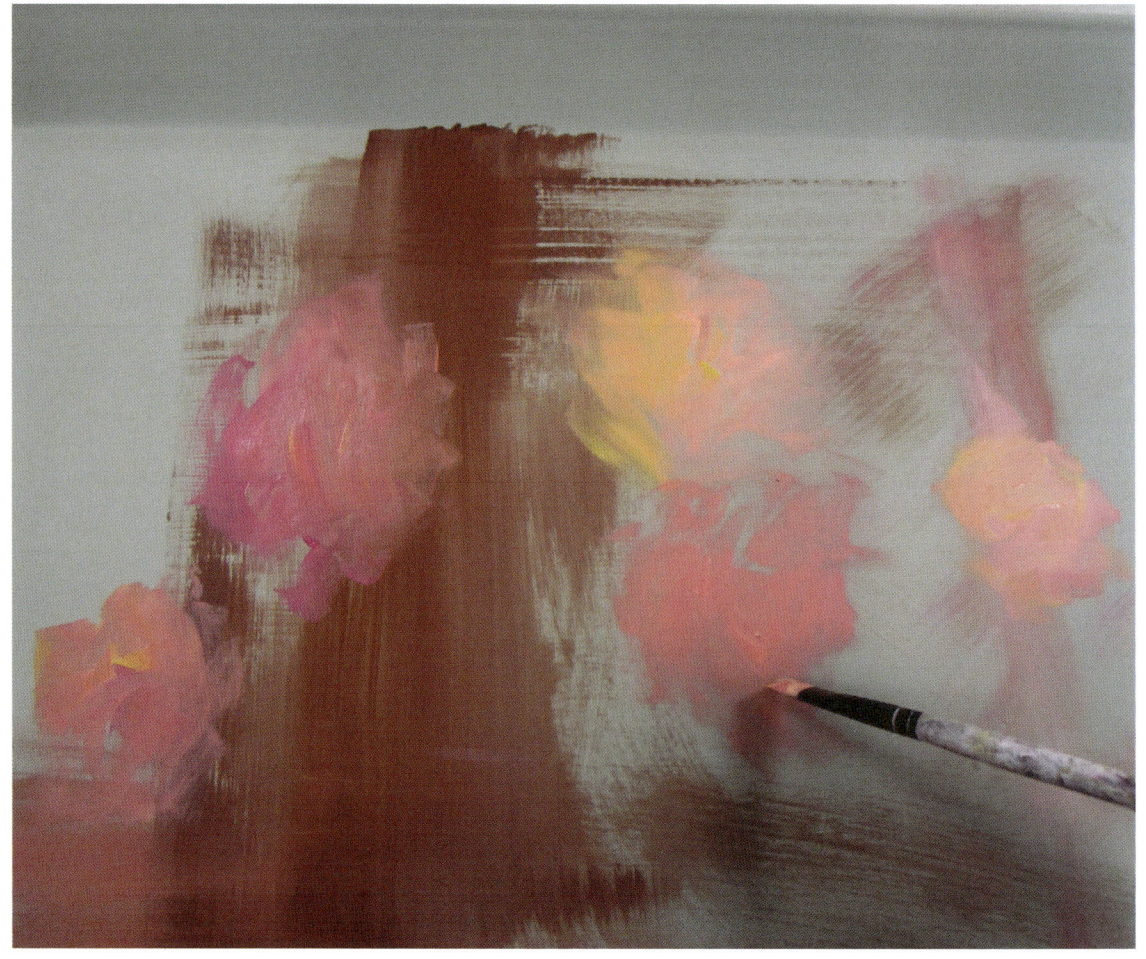

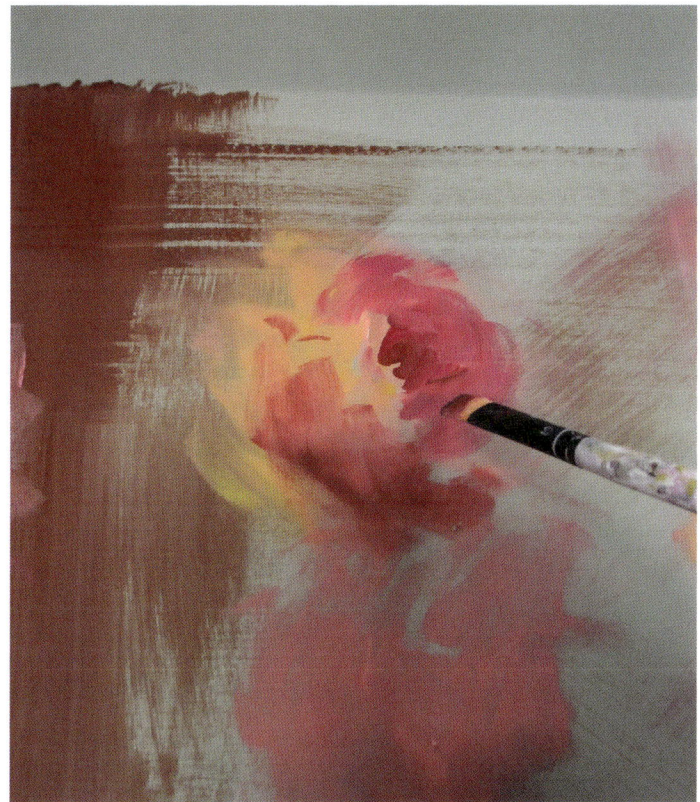

Step 4 Mottle the brush with the violets to cool and darken. Add the center shadows and then the bottom bowl shadow for the rose. Notice how the bowl shadow is not as bright.

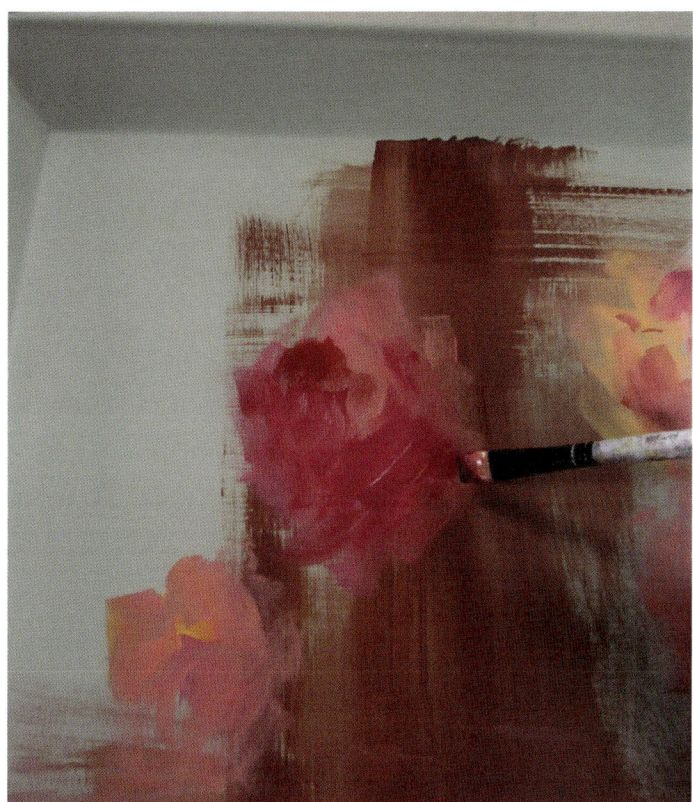

Step 5 For this rose I went extremely casual on the shadows. I let the bowl and the center shadow combine which will give a different look to this rose.

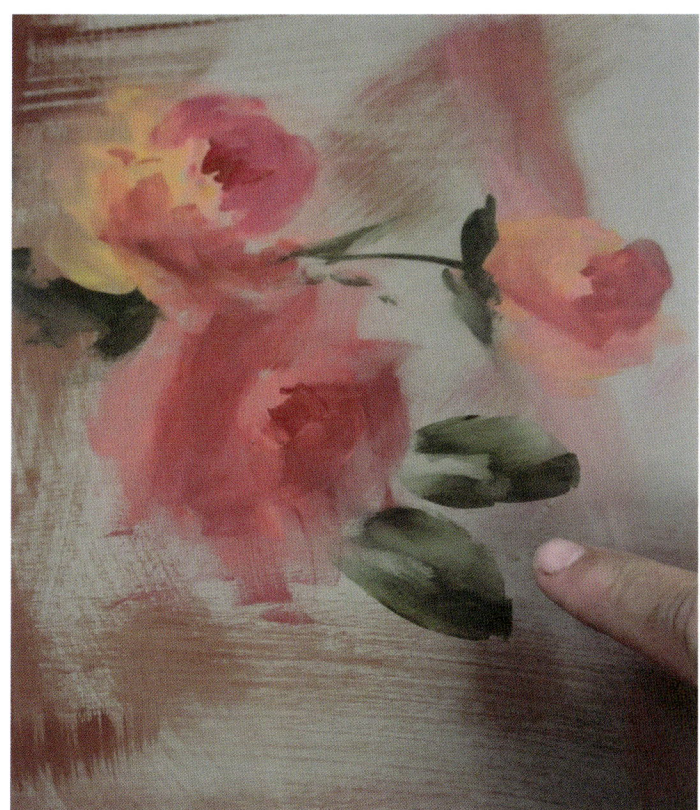

Step 6 Mottle Pine Green with touch Phthalo Green Blue. Use 2 or 3 strokes to form the leaves like the last lessons. Use your finger to push the color and add transparency.

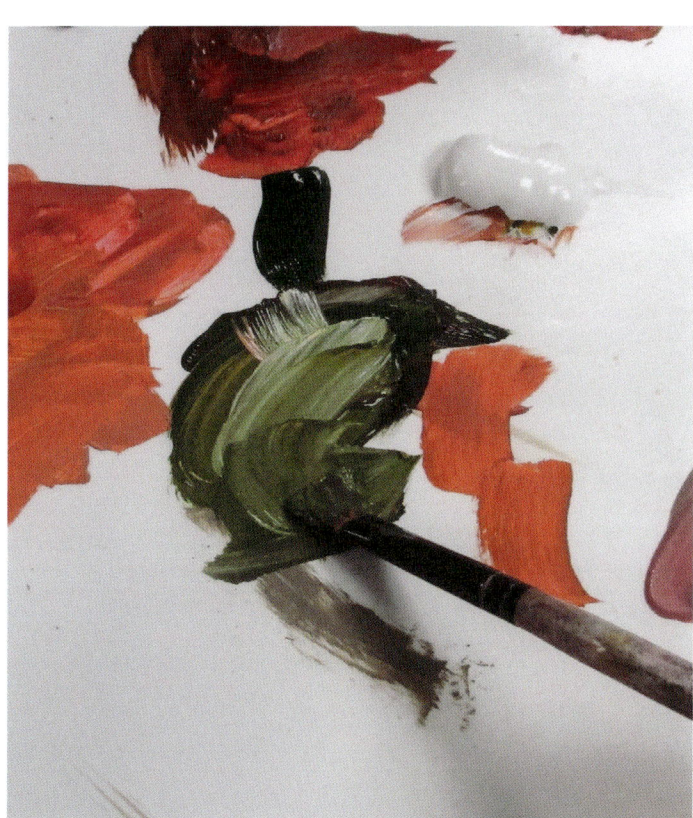

Step 7 Mottle the greens. Change the color with small additions of yellows and white.

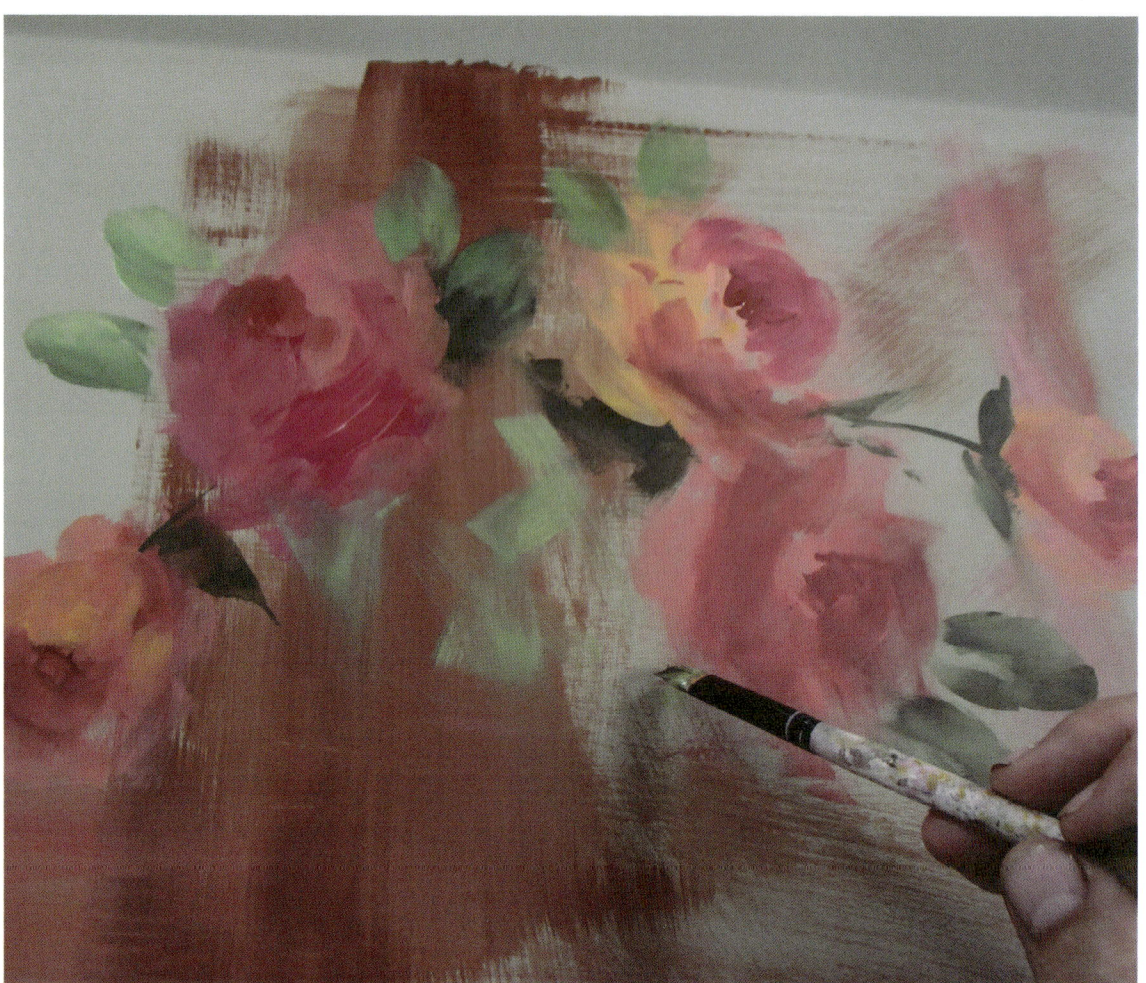

Step 8
Add lighter leaves mixed in with the darker leaves. I do this for interest in the composition. I also strike some light greens through the center of the composition. At this time I am not too sure what the center leaves will finally look like. I add some color which I can change later as needed.
Use the chisel to add stems and smaller leaves.

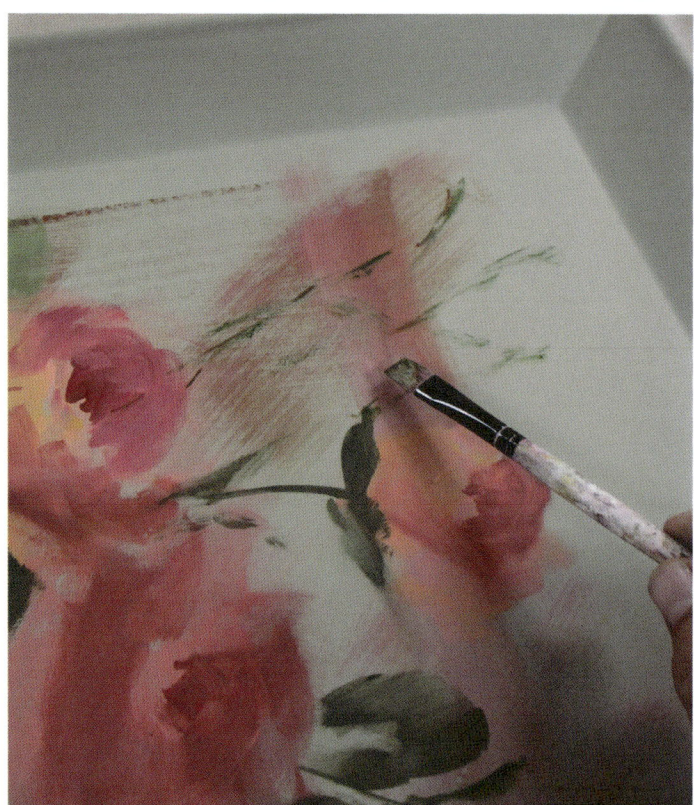

Step 9 Here I use the brush mottled with greens to add some casual touches of green into the background for additional movement of color.

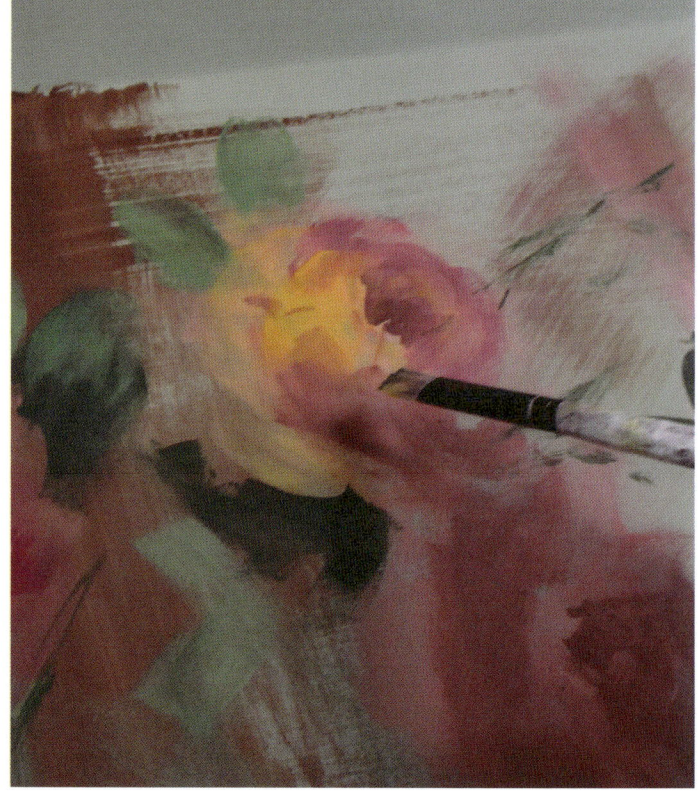

Step 10 Mottle the brush with Diarylide Yellow and wash over the yellow rose. Notice how this beautiful pigment doesn't opaque out all the shadows. Excellent color for doing this.

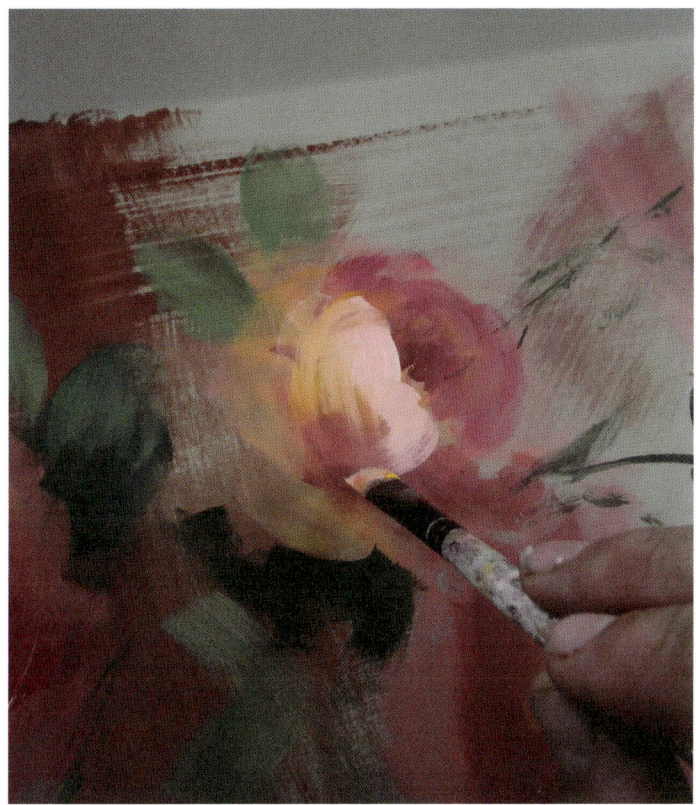

Step 11 Lighten the color with white and begin the front petals on the rose. I use my finger to shear the bottom of the petal where it starts into the shadow.

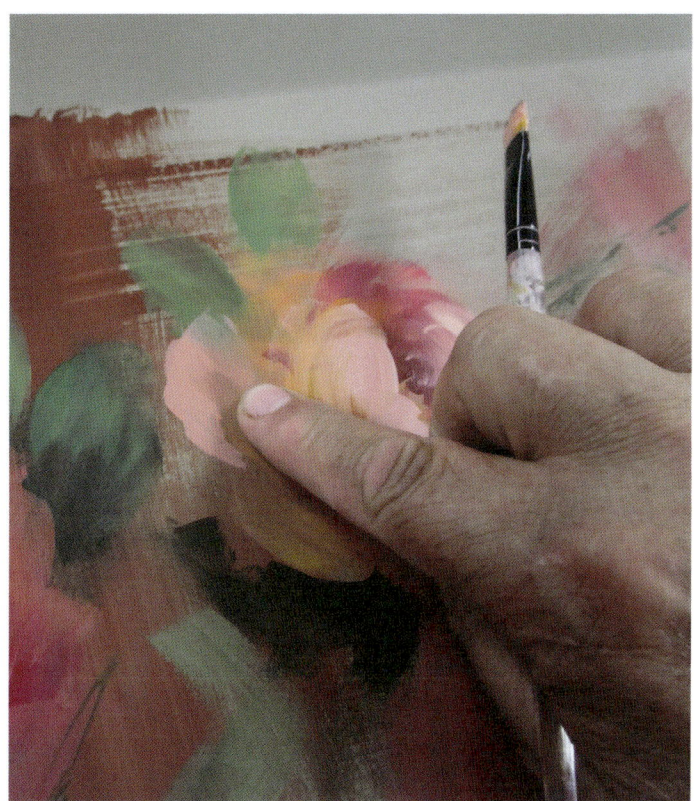

Step 12 Add the first reaching petals by stroking in towards the bowl. Use your finger to shear the color as it goes to the shadow and also push in and out to add movement.

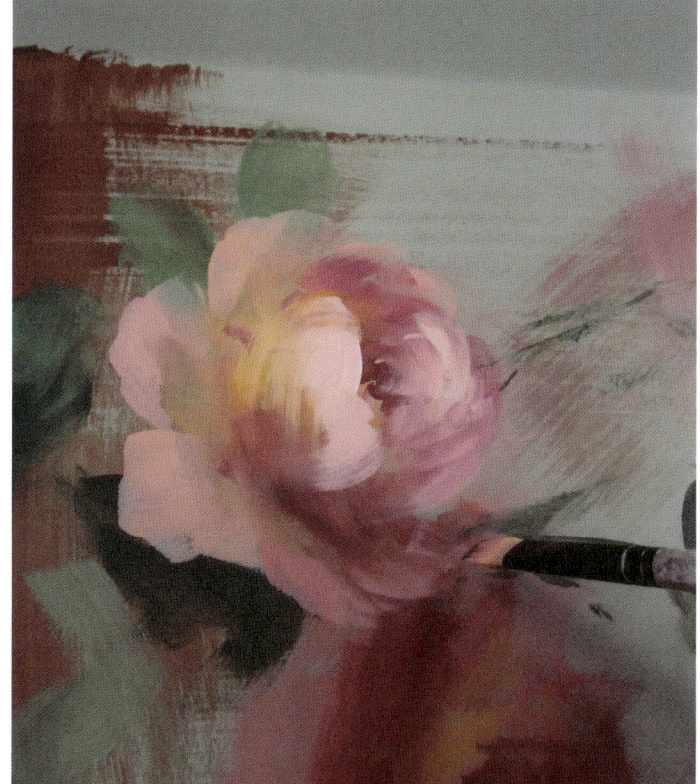

Step 13 Mottle the color a little darker and cooler as you go around to the shadow side of the rose. I also pull out on the petals to make softer edges.

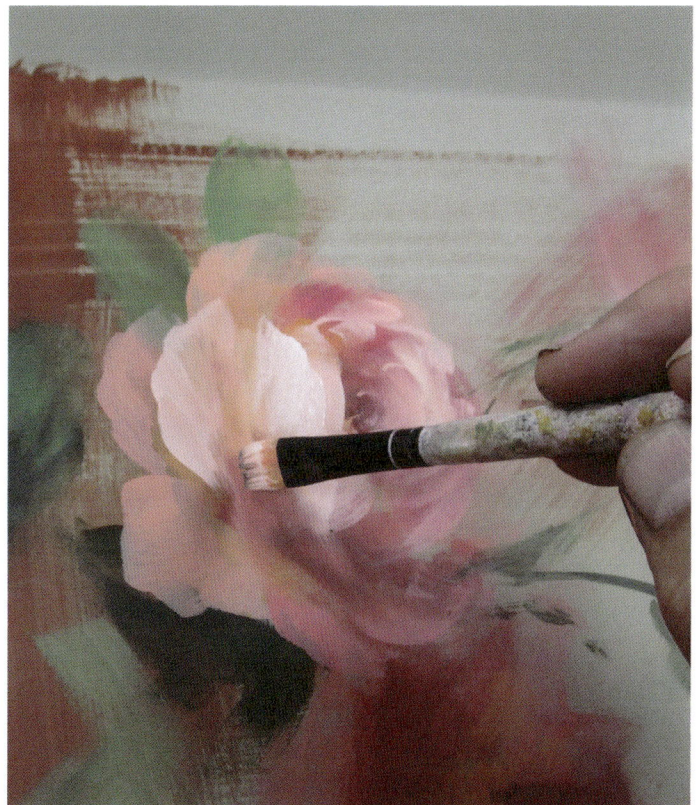

Step 14 Lighten the color with a little more white and warm with touch yellow. Begin next layer of petals pulling towards bowl. Shear the edges.

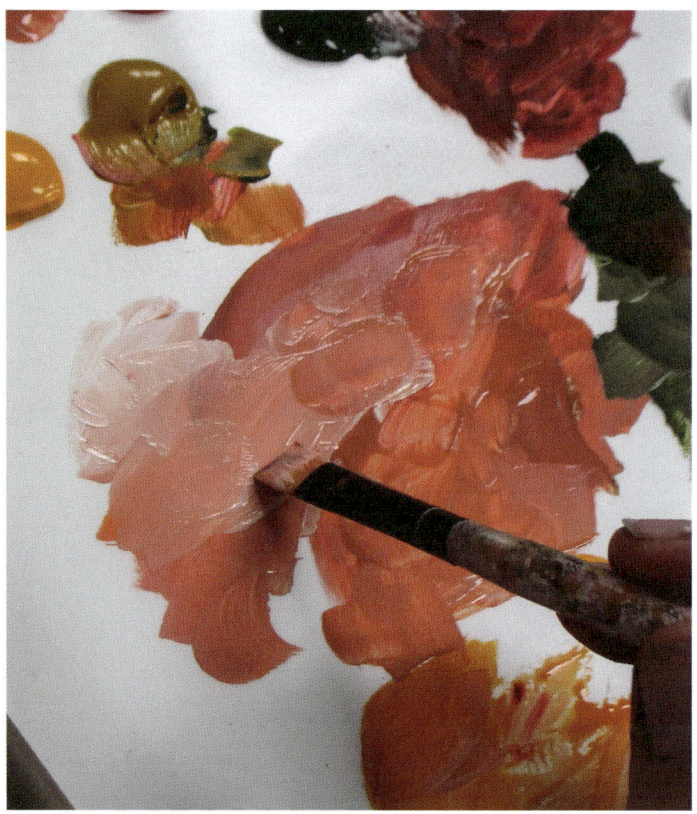

Step 15 Here you can see how I like to use my palette. As I make colors lighter I step off to one side so I can see the value change. Lighten color with more white.

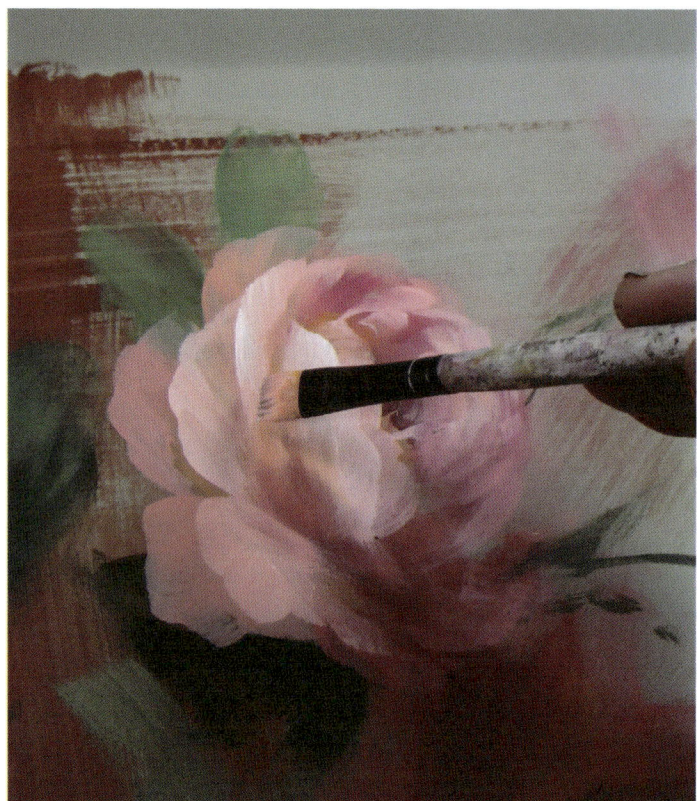

Step 16 Begin the next row of petals using the chisel as you go around to the front of the flower.

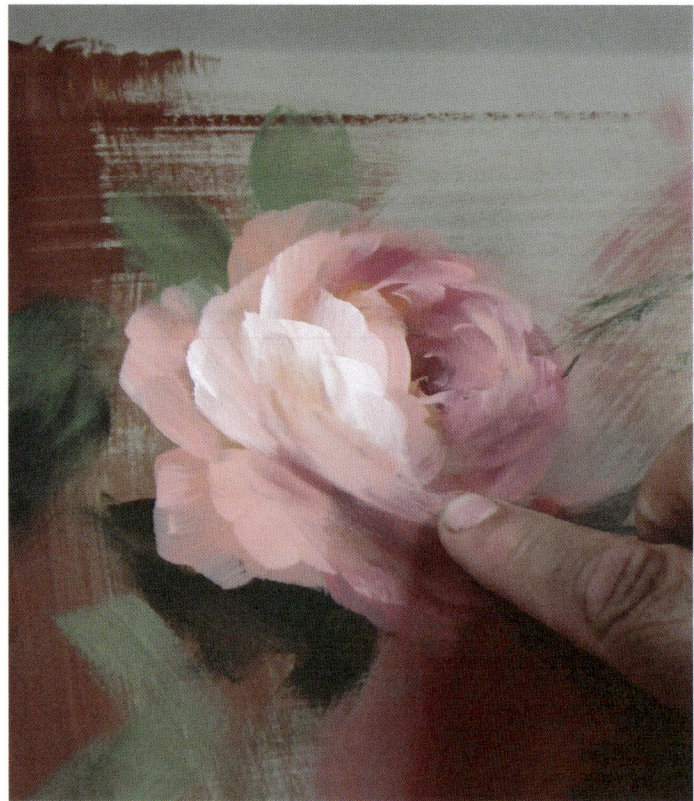

Step 17 Use your finger to push the round shape on the bottom of the bowl. Restate shadows if you need to.

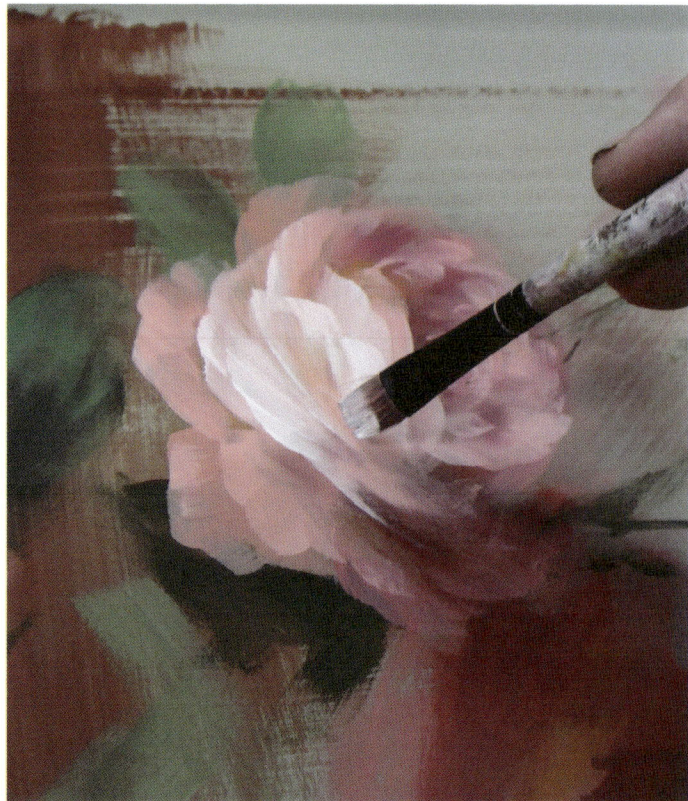

Step 18 Lighten the color with more white and add some chisel petals in the front to suggest the front petals.

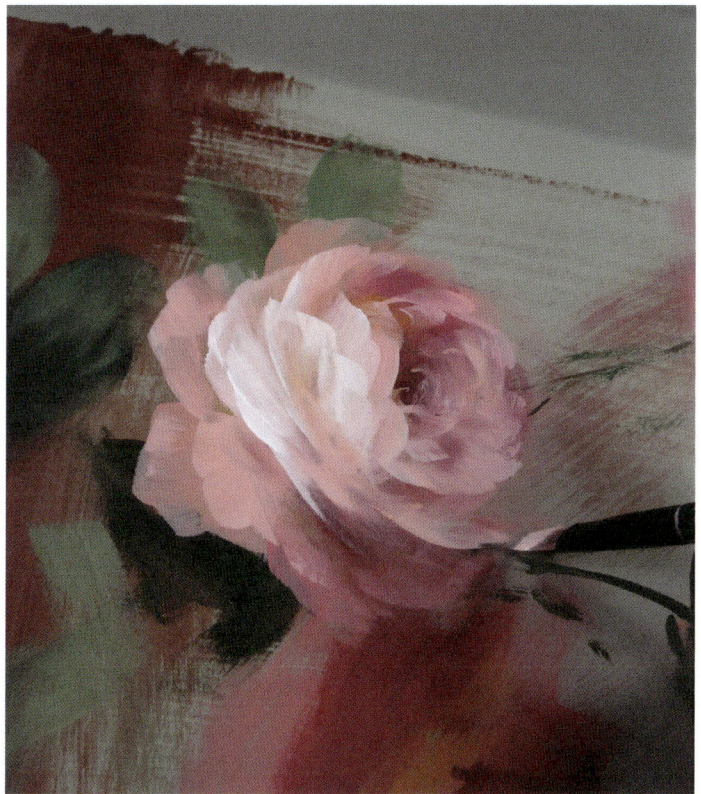

Step 19 Darken the color slightly with violets to cool. Pull out on the shadow side leaving the edge soft and undefined.

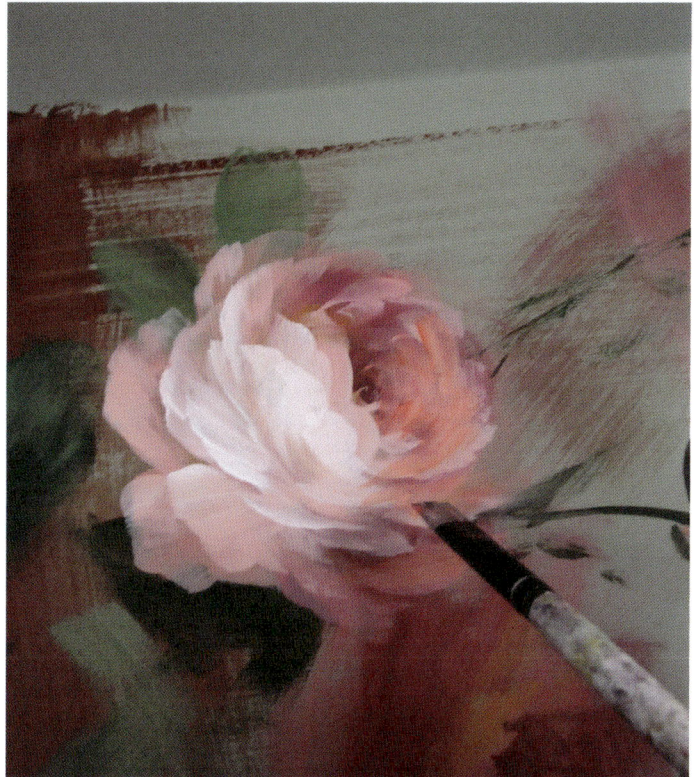

Step 20 Here I add a little warmer Diarylide Yellow and reds (orange) to warm some of the rose. Use the chisel of the brush to work between petals.

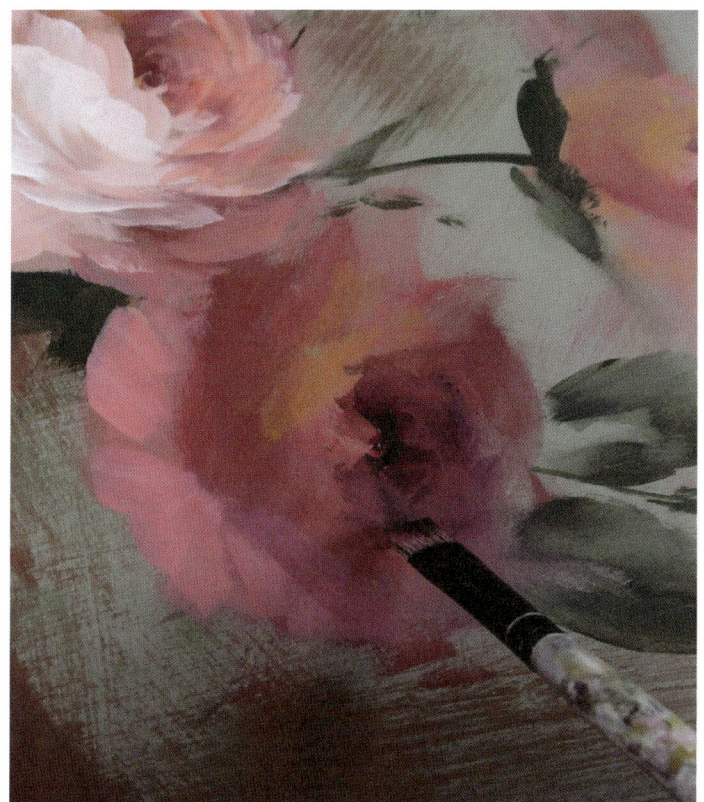

Step 21 Time to start the next rose. Mottle the brush with Red Violet to make darker and cooler. Add to the center of the bowl. Add a little to the bowl shadow.

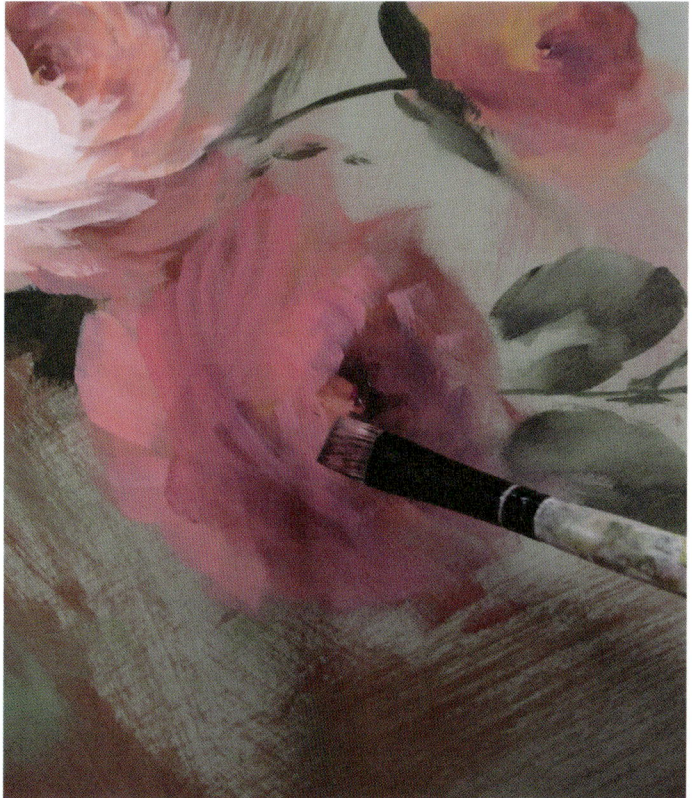

Step 22 Mottle a lighter red with violets, red and white. Make color a little different than last rose. More violets. Lighten the front of the rose.

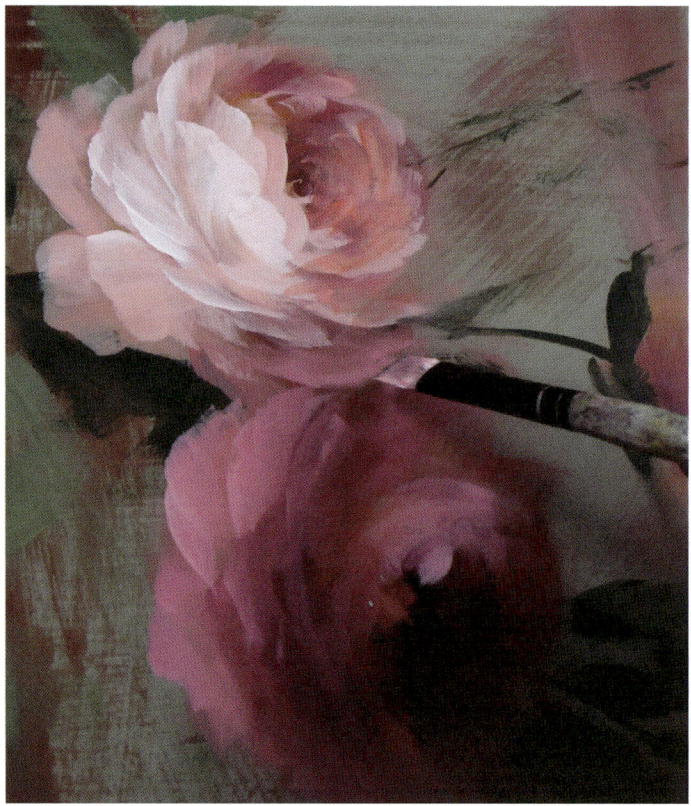

Step 23 Add a few reaching petals on the bottom rose. Then stroke a few lighter petals on the top rose that hang over the bottom rose to set the depth.

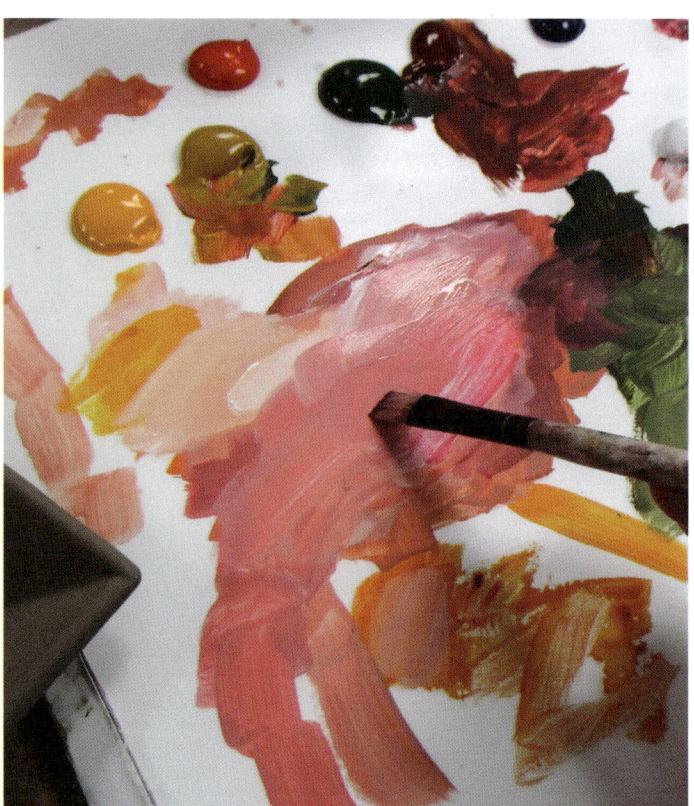

Step 24 Here I am cooling down the color I used before so they will look different on the nest rose. Cool with more Quin or Red Violet.

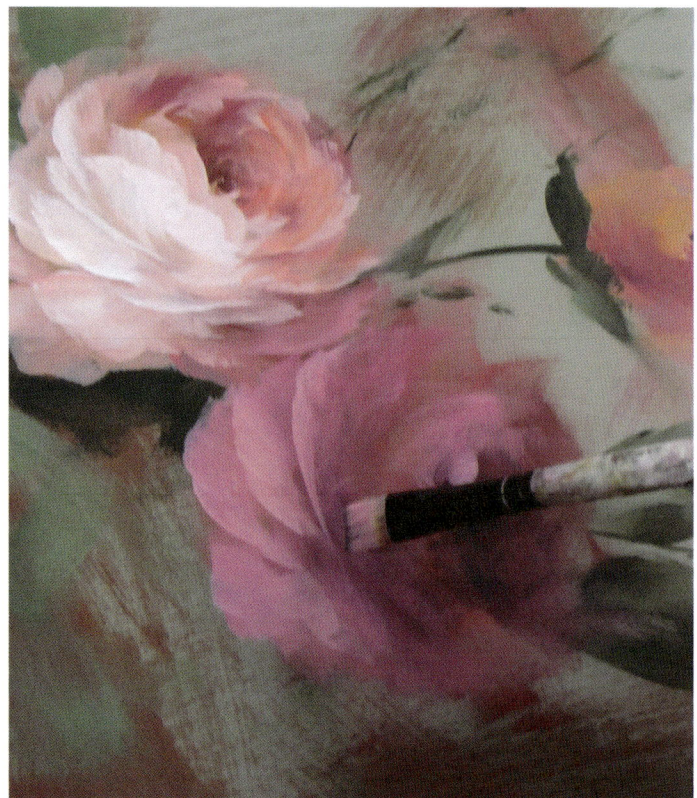

Step 25 Build the petals like we did on the first rose just with slightly cooler and darker colors. Try not to use the same petals shapes.

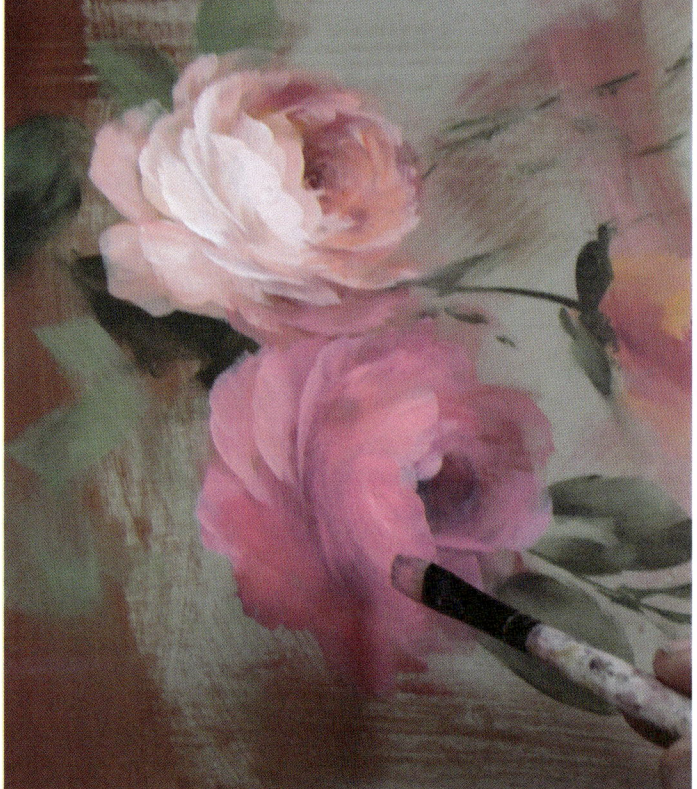

Step 26 Tint some cool Quin. Violet over the bottom reaching petals to preserve the shadows.

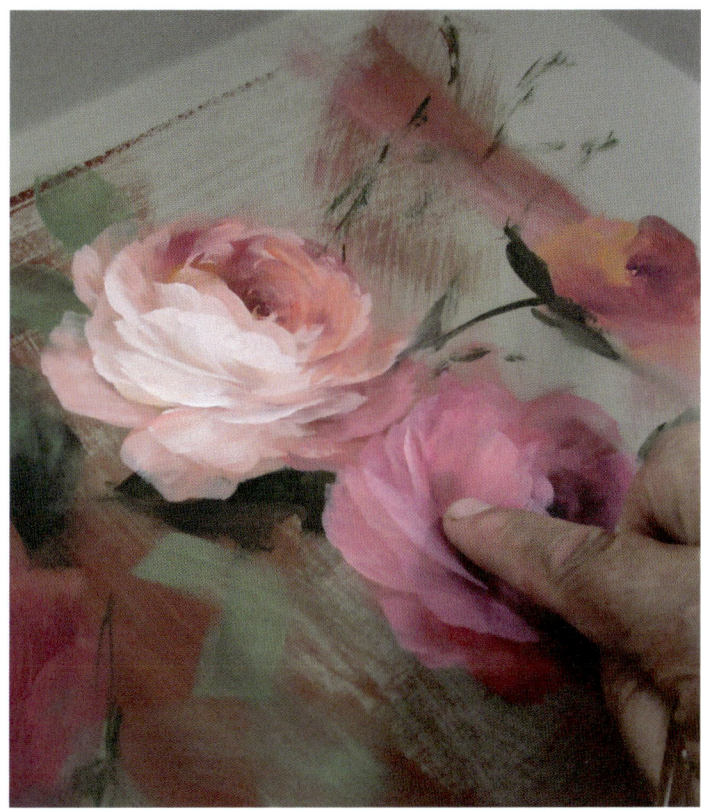

Step 27 Add the next layer of light petals and then use your finger to incorporate the petals into the round bottom of the bowl.

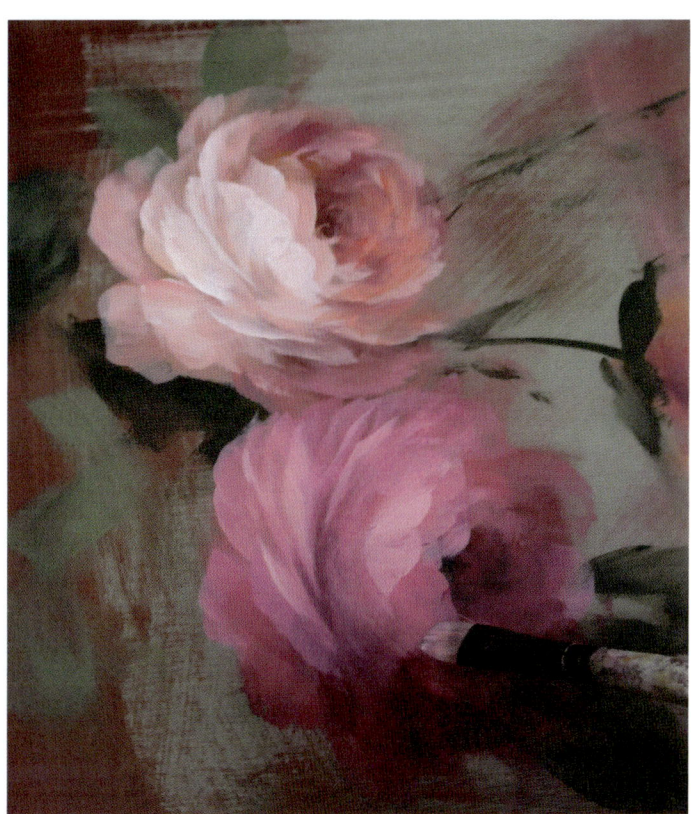

Step 28 Slowly lighten the front of the rose, but do not make it as light as the one on top. Make smaller lighter petals. Also keep them cooler.

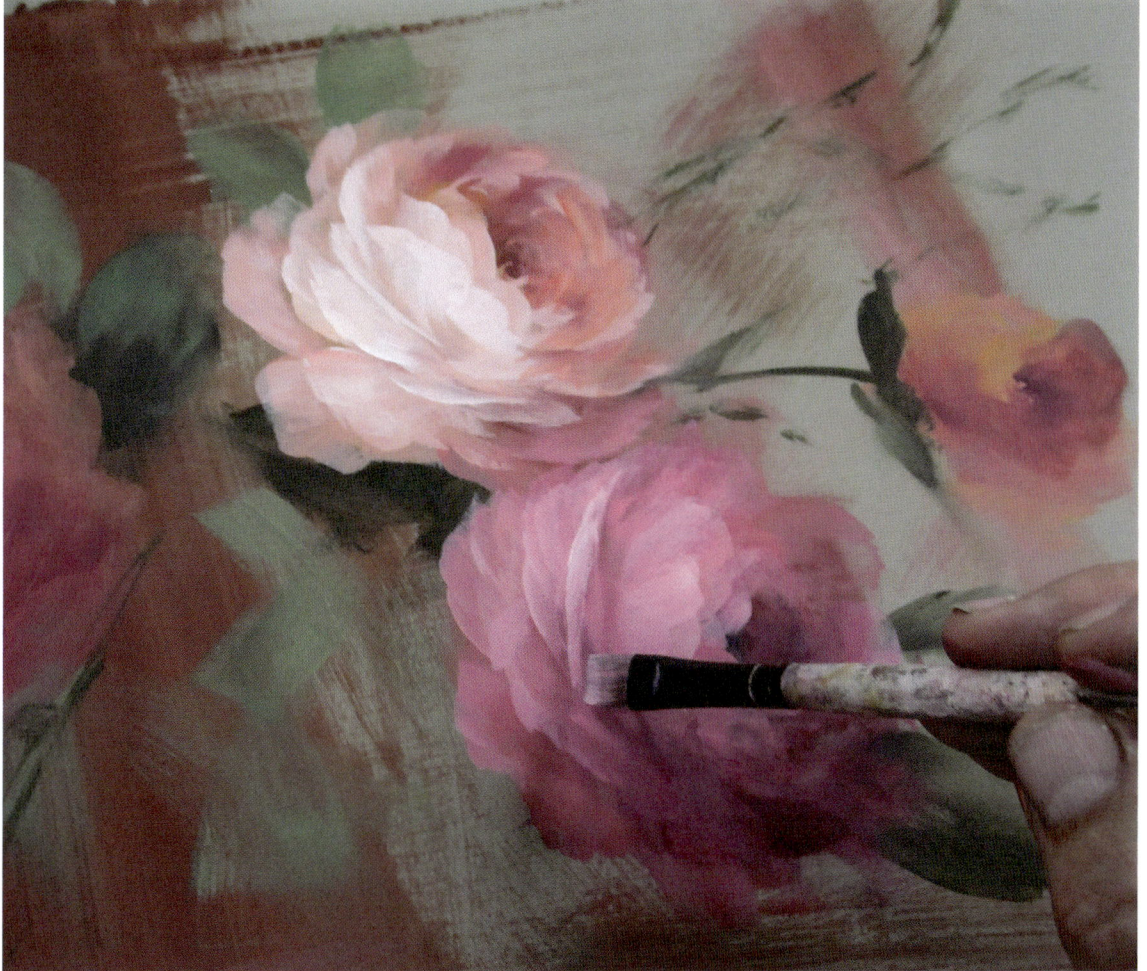

Step 29
Use the chisel of the brush to make the petals in the front. I think of this as weaving the petals. In Rosemaling we do what we call "weaving scrolls". This is where the scrolls cross over each other and come together to form the flow. I think of this concept as I paint the crossing and weaving petals in the front using the chisel of the brush. Weave them together.

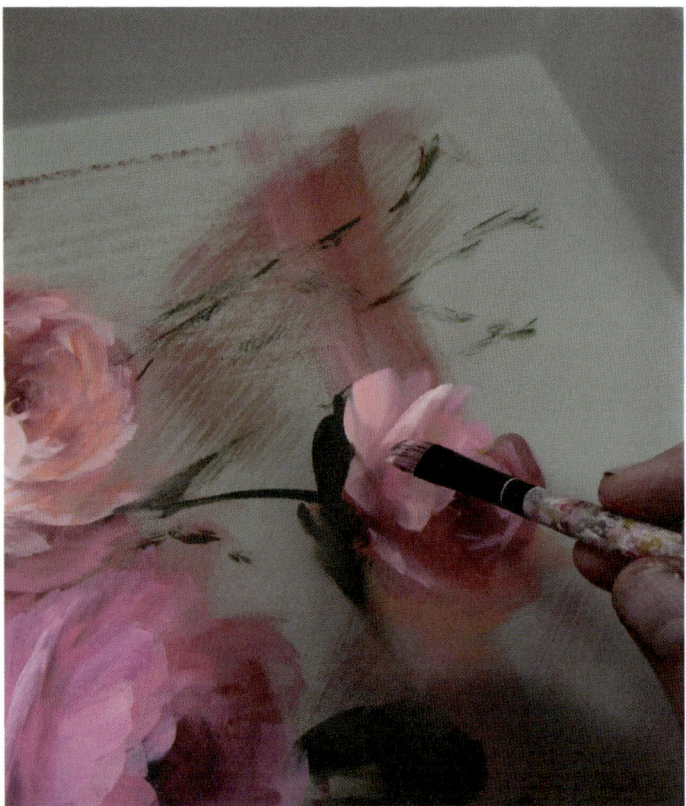

Step 30 Bring the next rose to the outside using the same techniques. Vary the color a little. Here I made it warm and cool. Lighten the top side to show the light source.

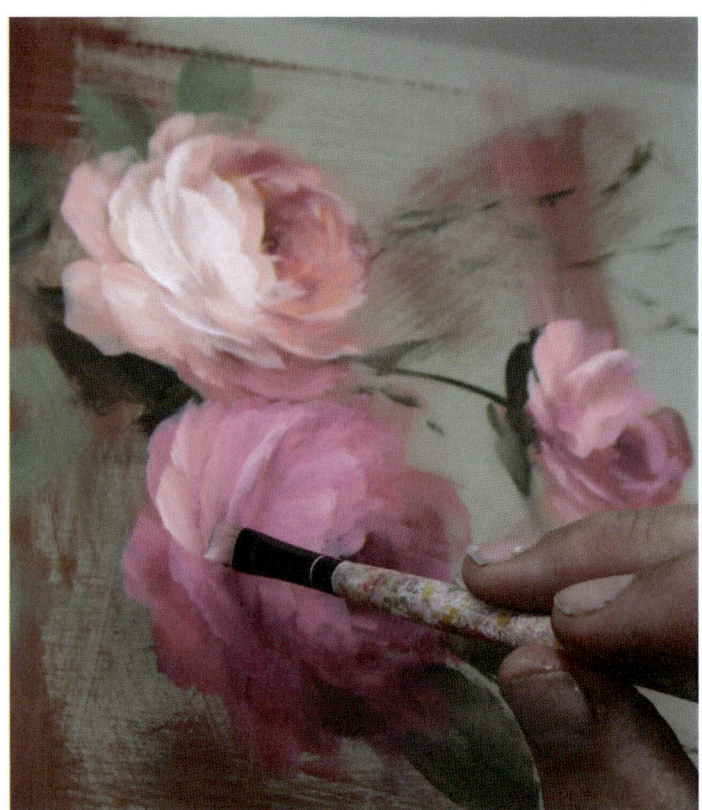

Step 31 Use a little of the light color from the smaller outside rose bud on the front of the bottom cool rose. This help harmonize the roses together with common tones.

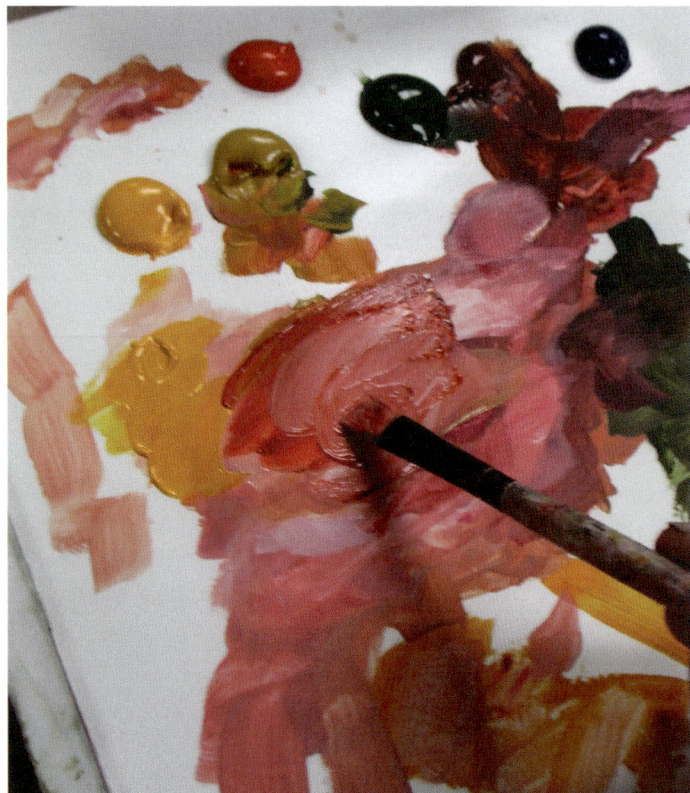

Step 32 Time for the next rose. Mottle the colors a little differently. This time I use a little more red and touch Diarylide Yellow. Lighten with white.

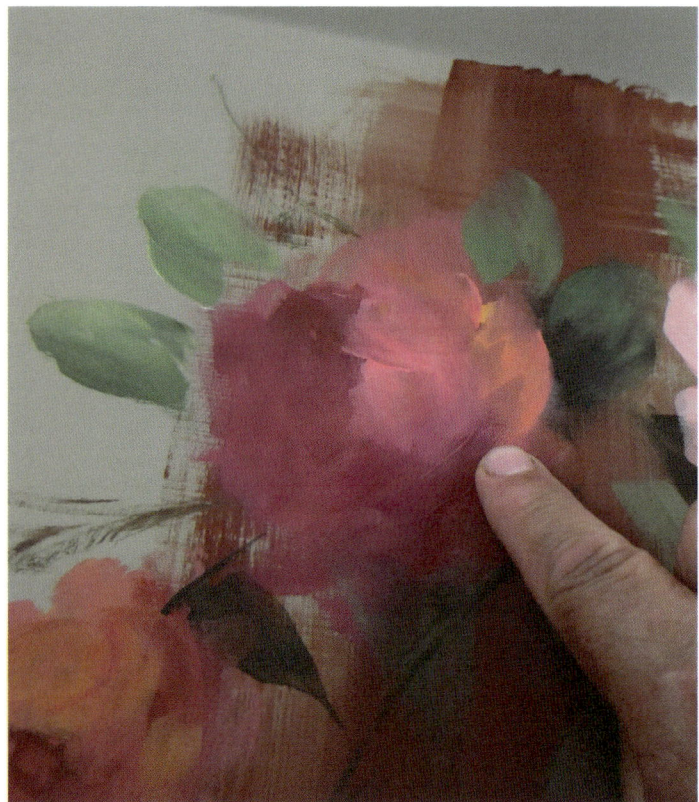

Step 33 Begin to build the front of the rose on the top side. This is the light source side. Use your finger to incorporate the colros and push for roundness.

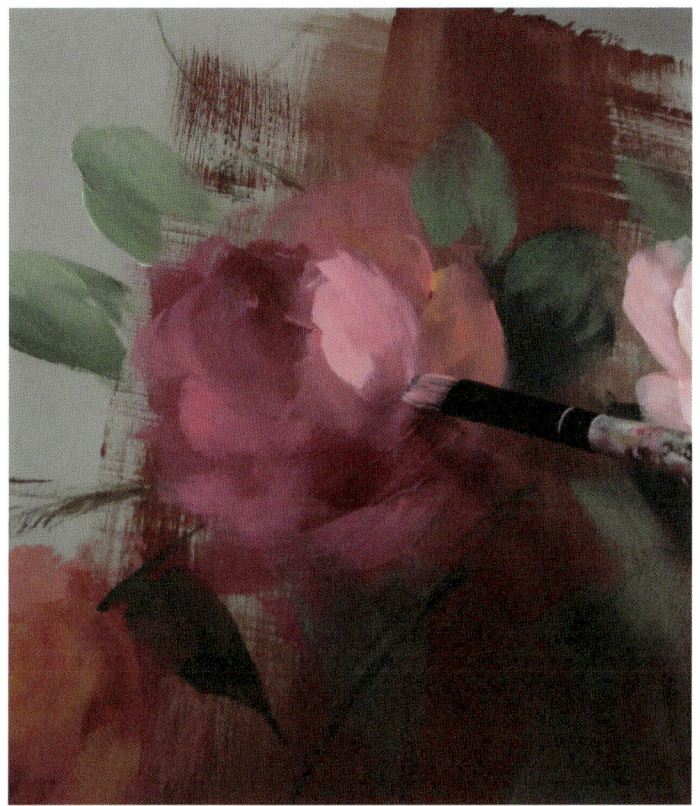

Step 34 Lighten the color with more white and begin the top petals. Shear the bottom of the petals where they go into the bowl shadow.

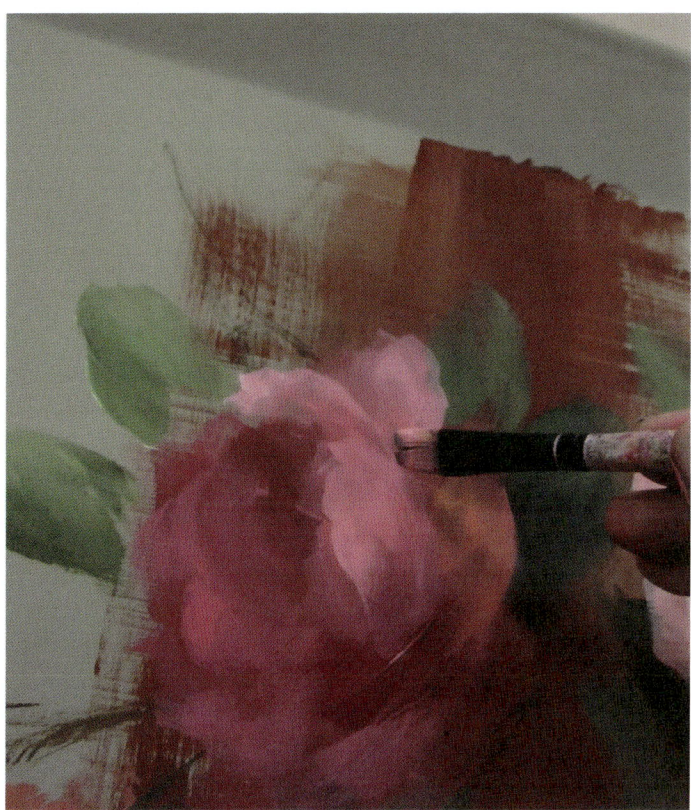

Step 35 Lighten the color further. Add petals to the light side like with did with the other roses. Vary the petals so it looks different.

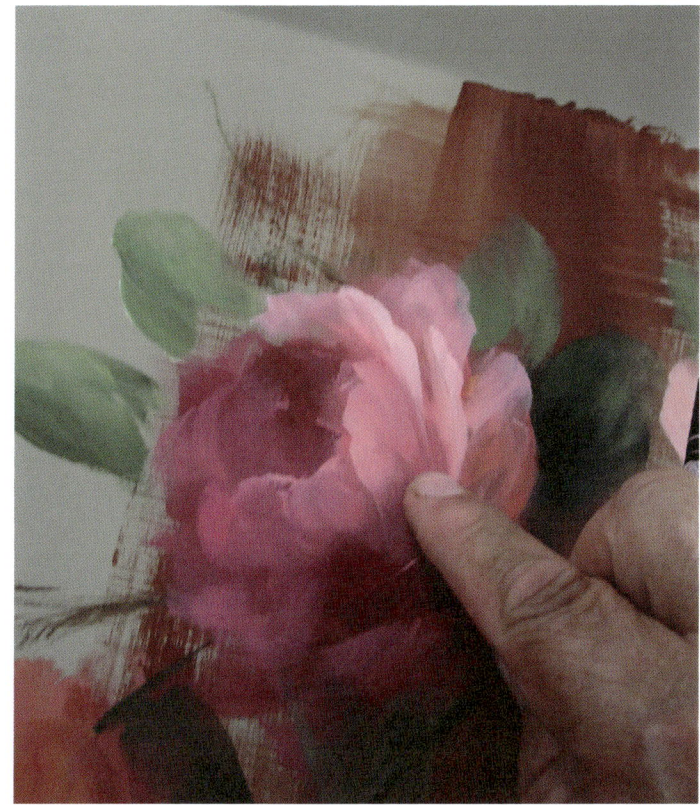

Step 36 Push the petals with your finger into the shape of the bowl of the rose. I use a rounding shape on the sides and bottom.

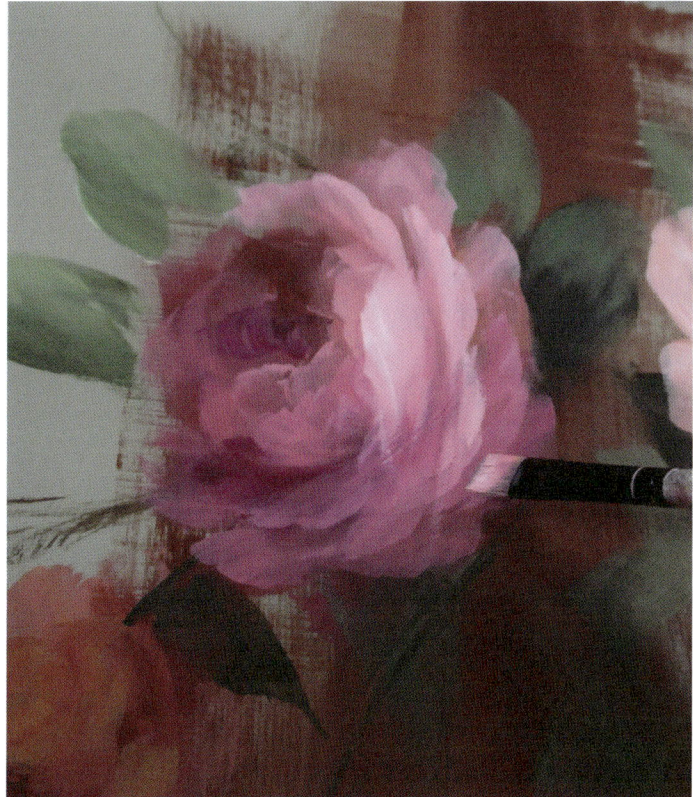

Step 37 Use the chisel of the brush in the front of the rose to make the forward front reaching petals.

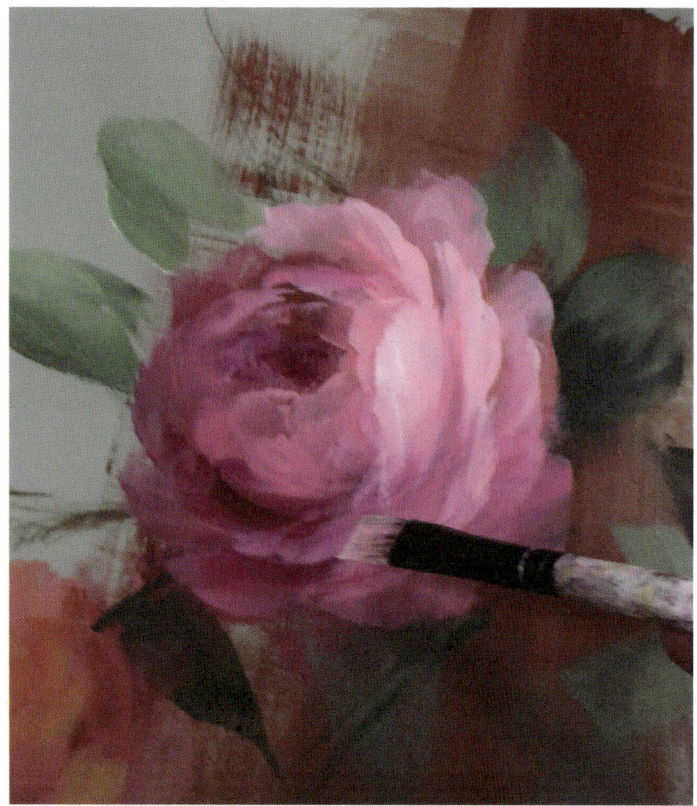

Step 38 Cool the color on the shadow side with violets and darken as well. Add a few reaching petals but keep them soft by pulling out.

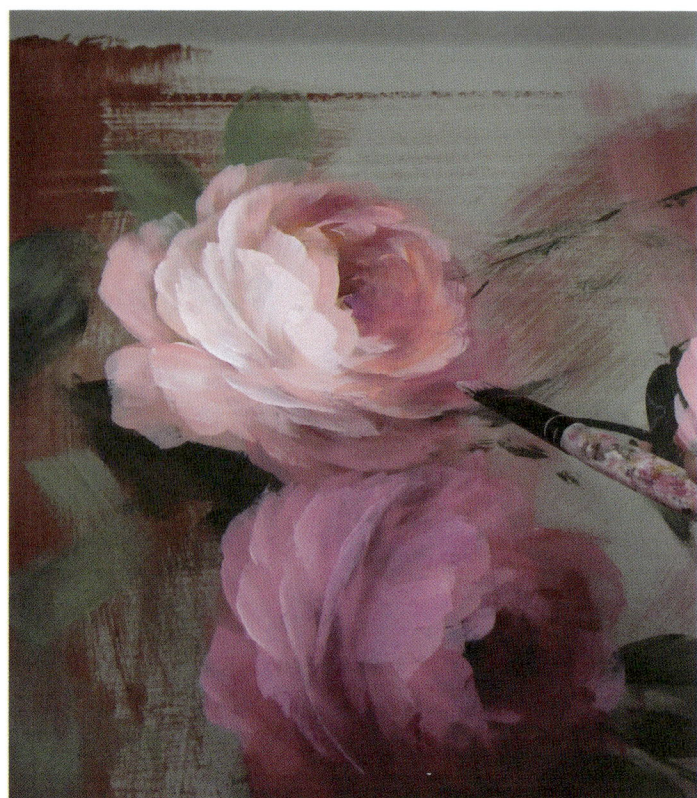

Step 39 Here I use a little of the cooler tones from the last rose on the back of the main top rose. Again, this harmonizes the roses by carrying some common tones.

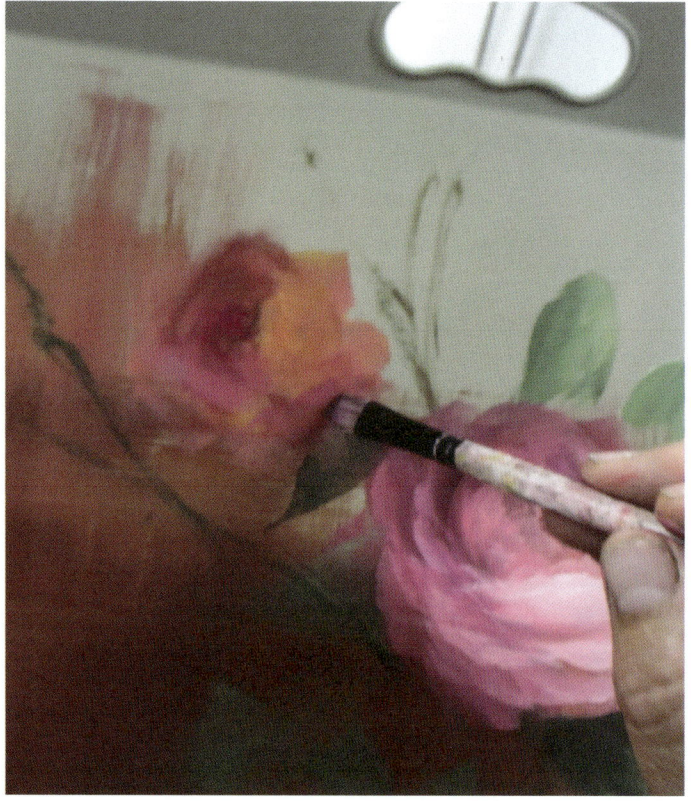

Step 40 Begin the next outside rose bud. Vary the colors and keep it simple. Violet shadows on the bottom to show the light source.

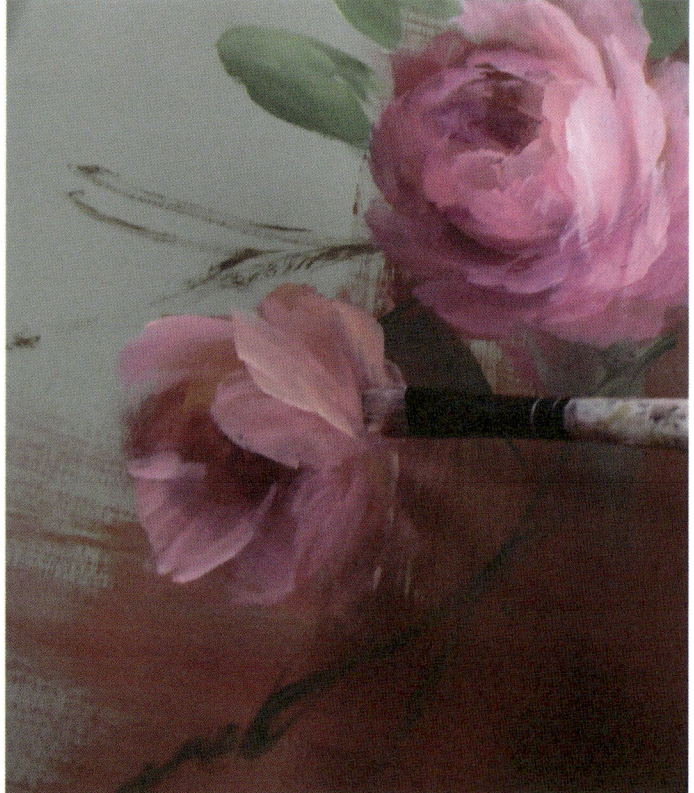

Step 41 Petal the rose with simple and limited petals since this is a rose that is just opening. Keep the bottom petals cooler with more violets.

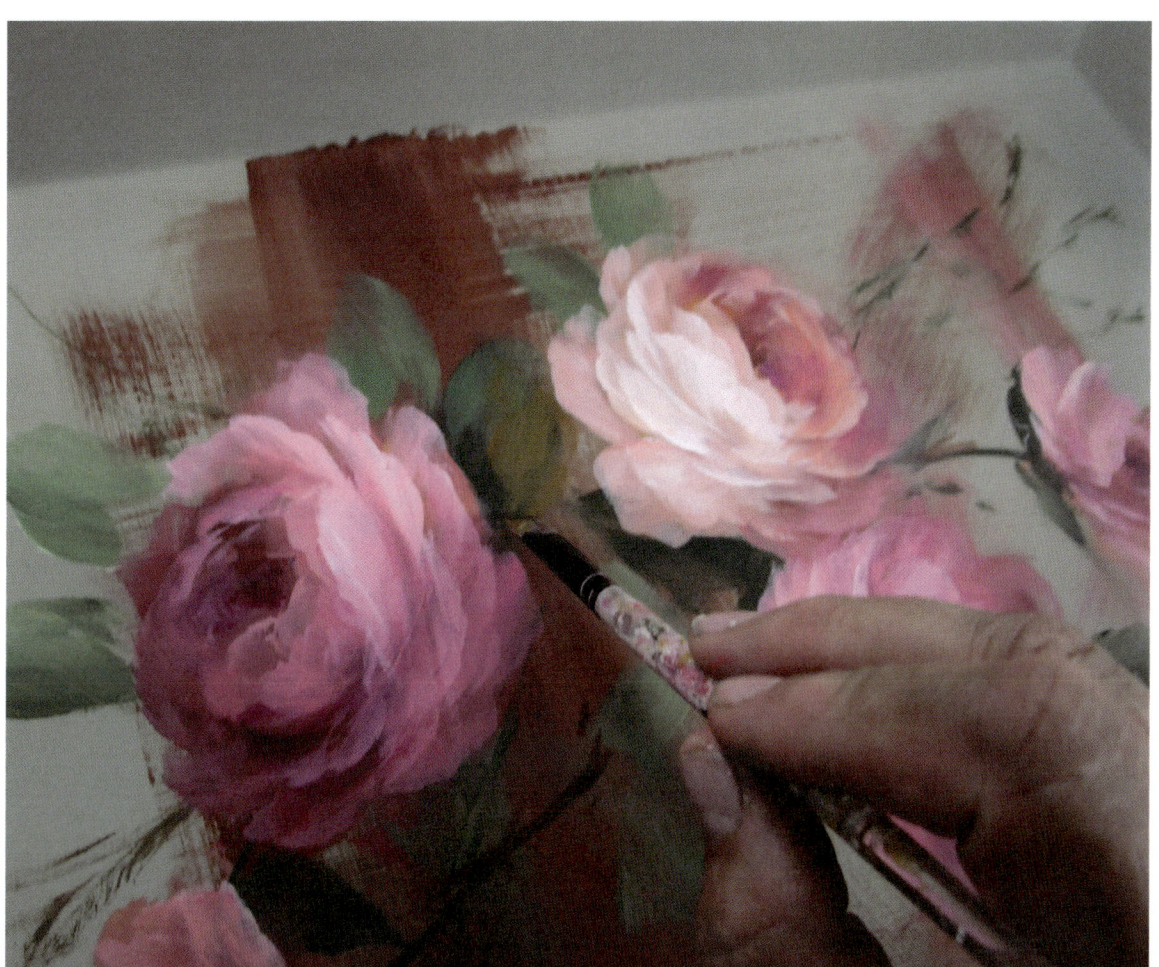

Step 42
Mottle greens and yellows and add these tones to the leaves. This will add more interest in the center of our painting. Vary the colors. I like to add Burnt Sienna to the greens to give a Fall look to the colors. This is also very warm. Cool and darken any colors with the violets. Best floral paintings vary the leaves. Just mix a little at a time and your colors will vary!

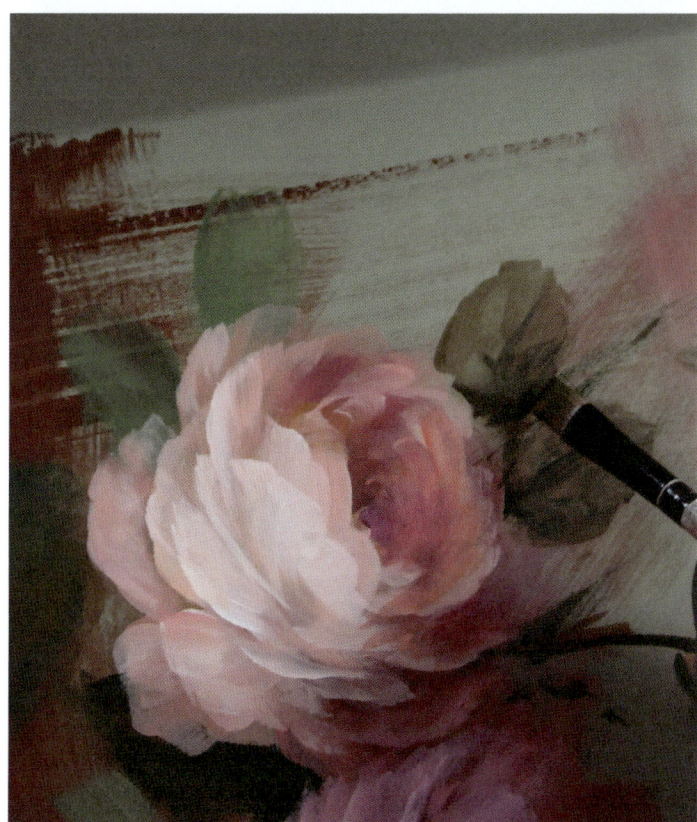

Step 43 Add a few Diarylide Yellow tones to the green and add to a few leaves. This yellow makes some beautiful leaves because it leans slightly yellow orange. Different colors!

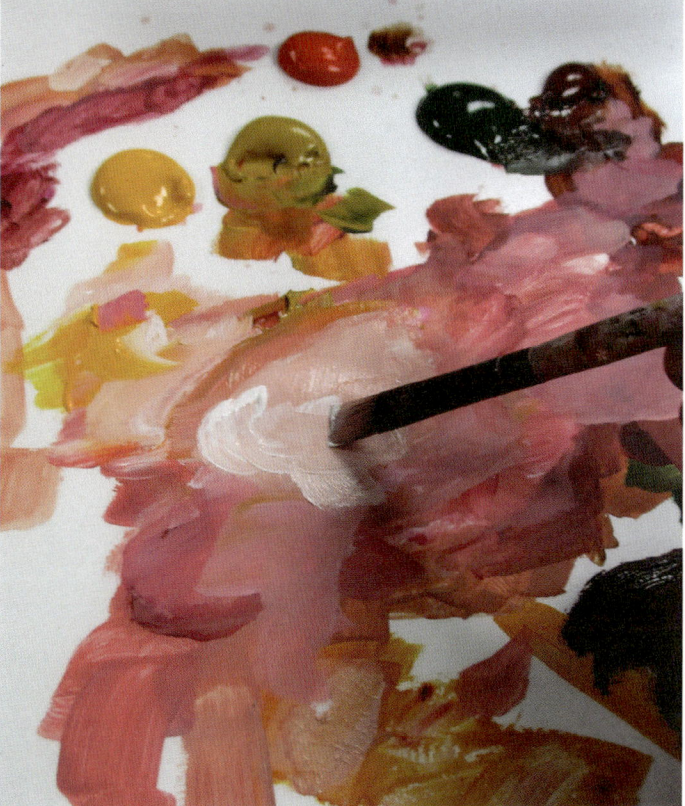

Step 44 Mottle the reds on your palette with touch of yellow and then lighten with white.

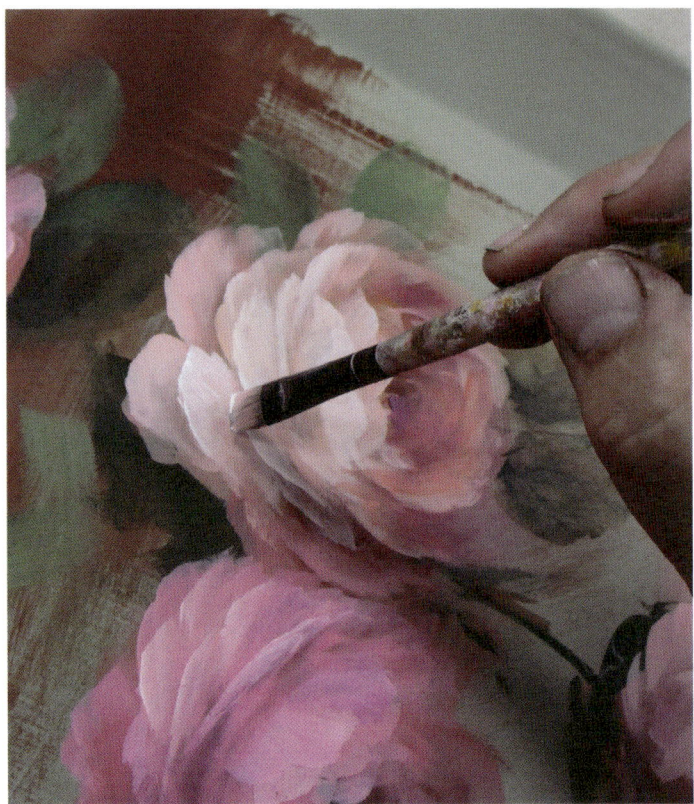

Step 45 Add additional highlights to the front of the main front roses. Pull in leaving the tips of the petals lighter and shear off the petal as it approaches the shadow.

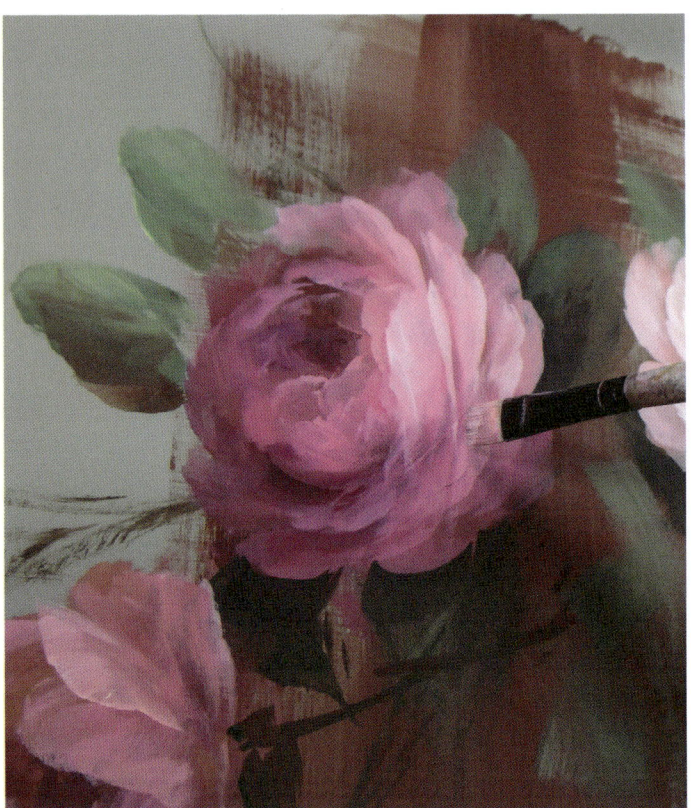

Step 46 Use the chisel on the petal in the front. I am working all the petals in the roses (front) lightening them and giving more contrast to the composition.

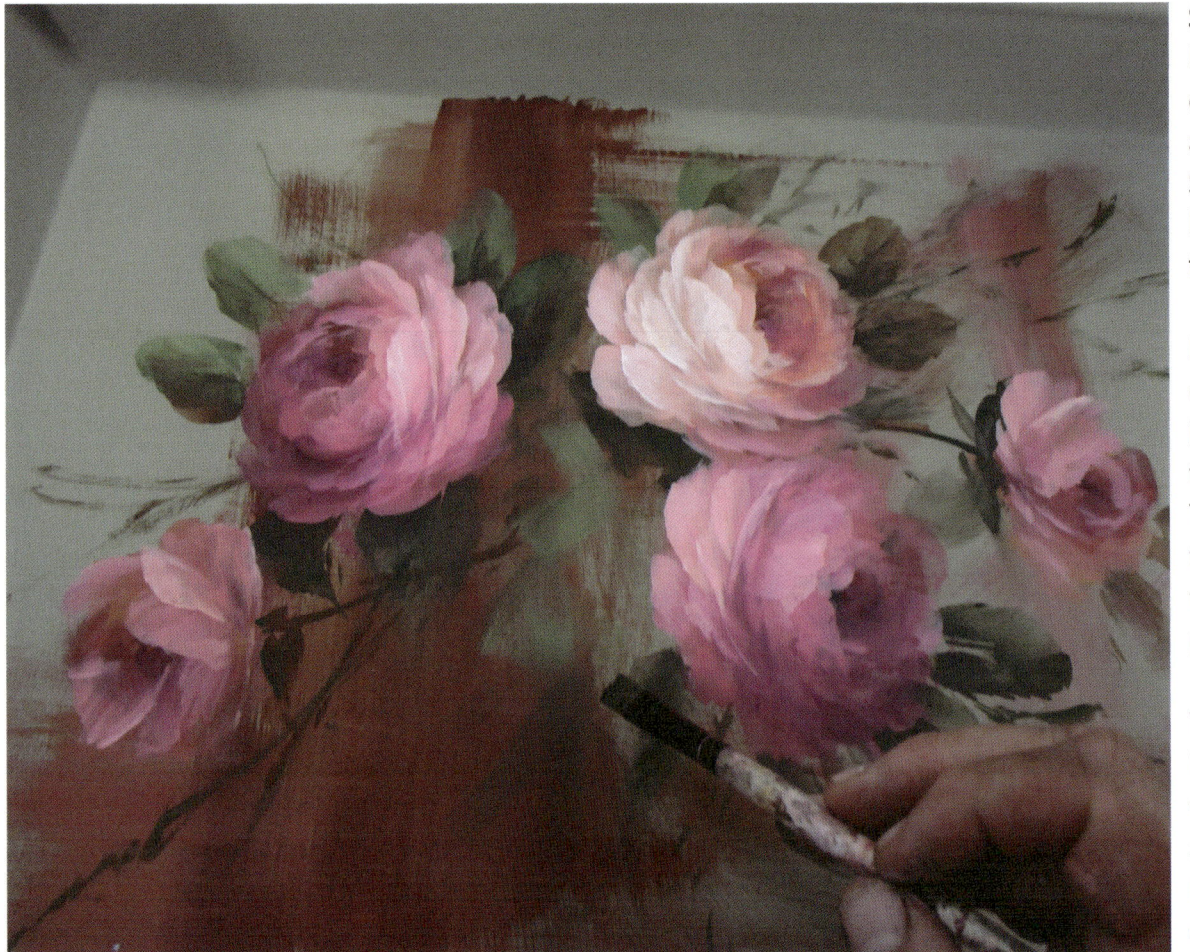

Step 47 Use the chisel of the brush to add more stems. Slowly add more leaves to the center of the painting.

In this picture you can see the building the lights on the top 2 roses. This is presenting the light source in the middle of the painting.

The top right rose is the queen. It will be the lightest and control all the highlights on the other roses.

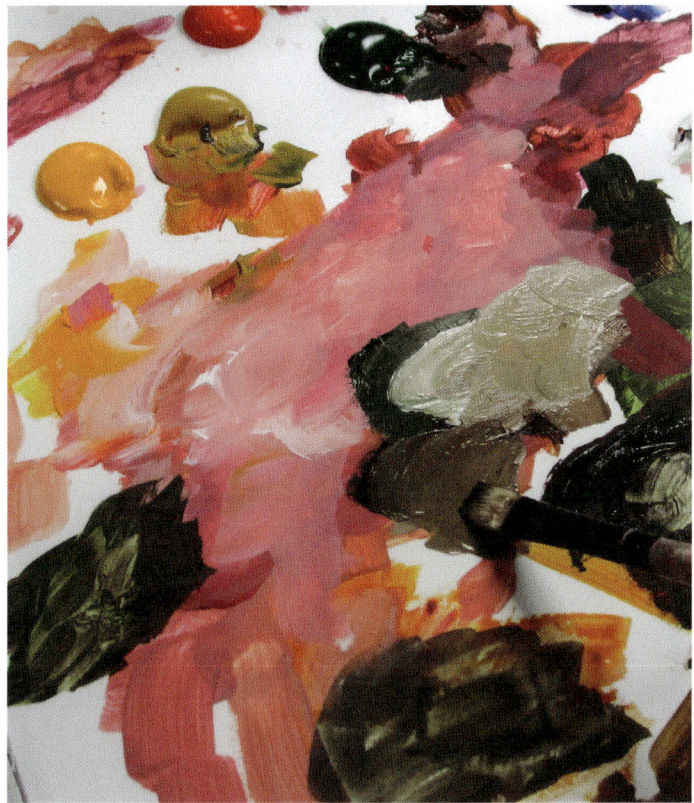

Step 48 Mottle a dirty white with the greens and reds. Lighten with a touch of white. Not too light. This is the base and not the light value.

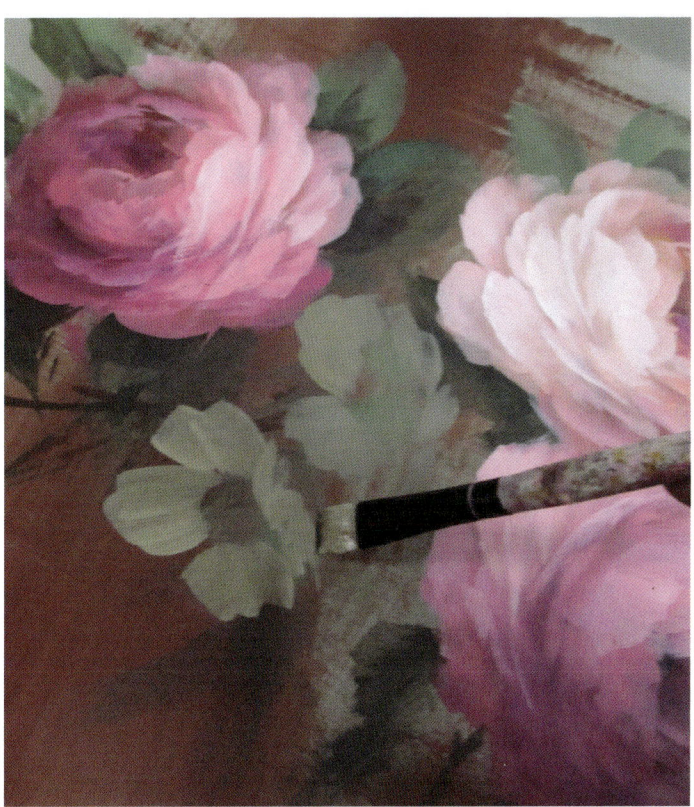

Step 49 Shape the blossoms with strokes pulling in the out of the center as we have done in the other lessons.

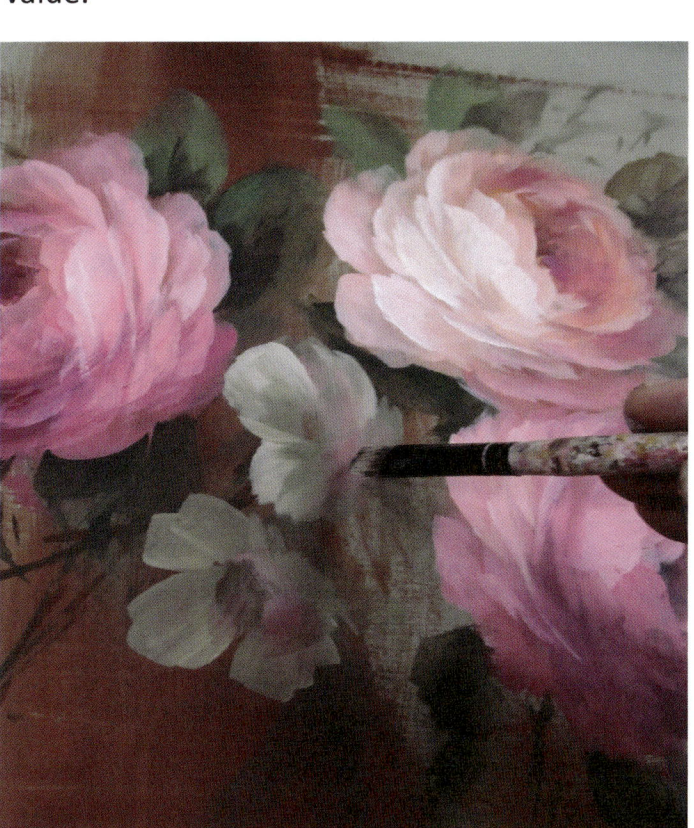

Step 50 Mottle the brush with some pinks and tint into the blossoms to carry the rose colors. Lighten the color with touch more white and begin the highlights on the blossoms.

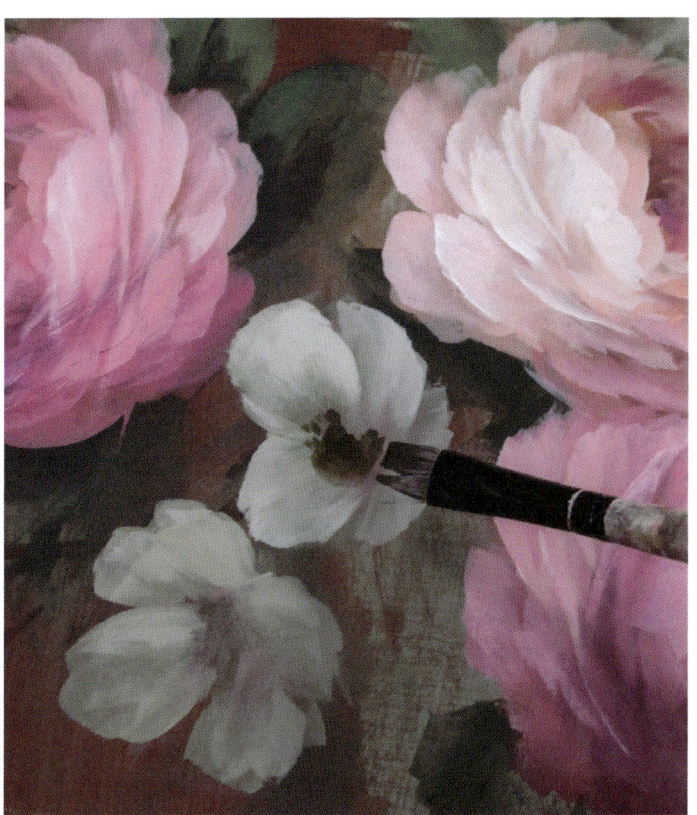

Step 51 Mottle the brush with greens and Red Violet to make a dark cool green. Add to the center of the blossoms, pushing with your finger to shear off the edges.

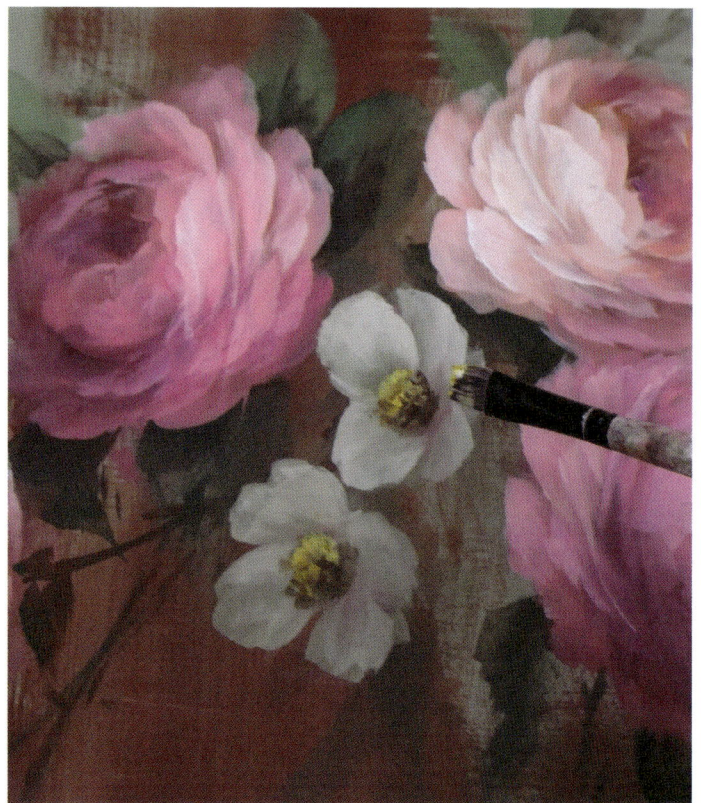

Step 52 Mottle the brush with the yellows. Tap the corner of the brush in more Hansa Yellow. Use this to slowly tap around the center of the blossom.

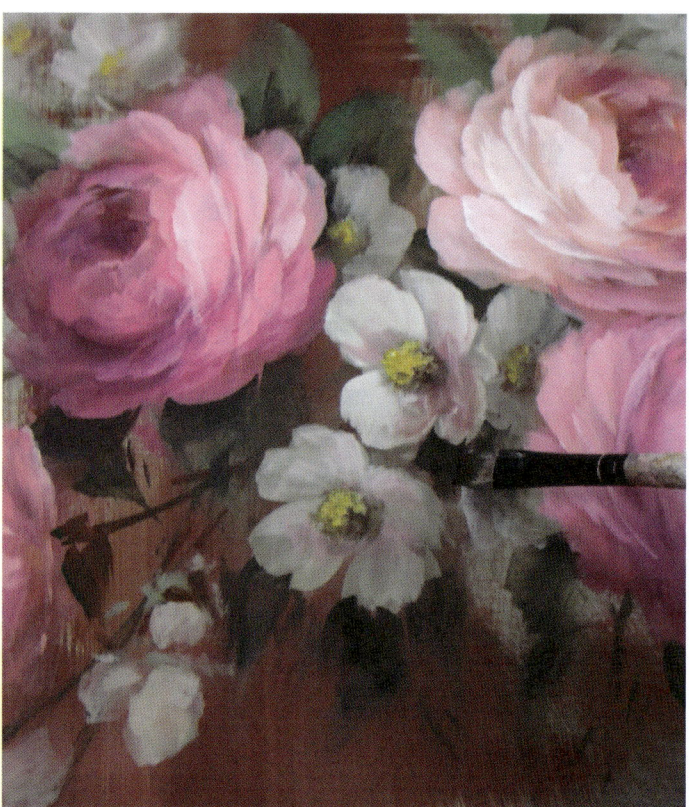

Step 53 Make the centers lighter on the top with Hansa + Touch white. Use greens cooled with Red Violet to negative paint around the blossoms to increase contrast and shape them.

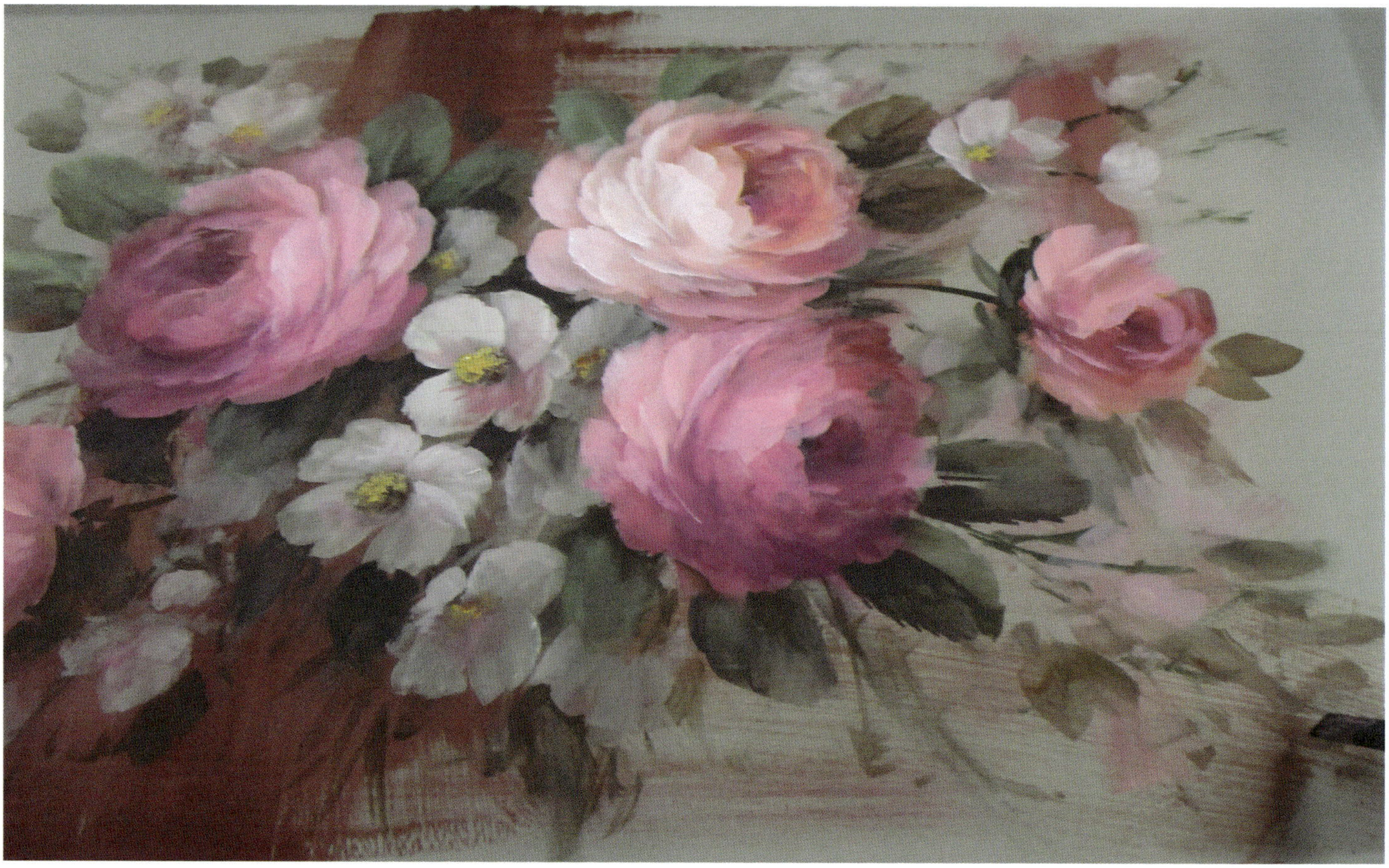

Step 54 Finally, using the brush mottled with different palette colors, streak and softly blur the outside of the composition. Just add movement to increase interest. Enjoy!

Lesson 4
Pattern

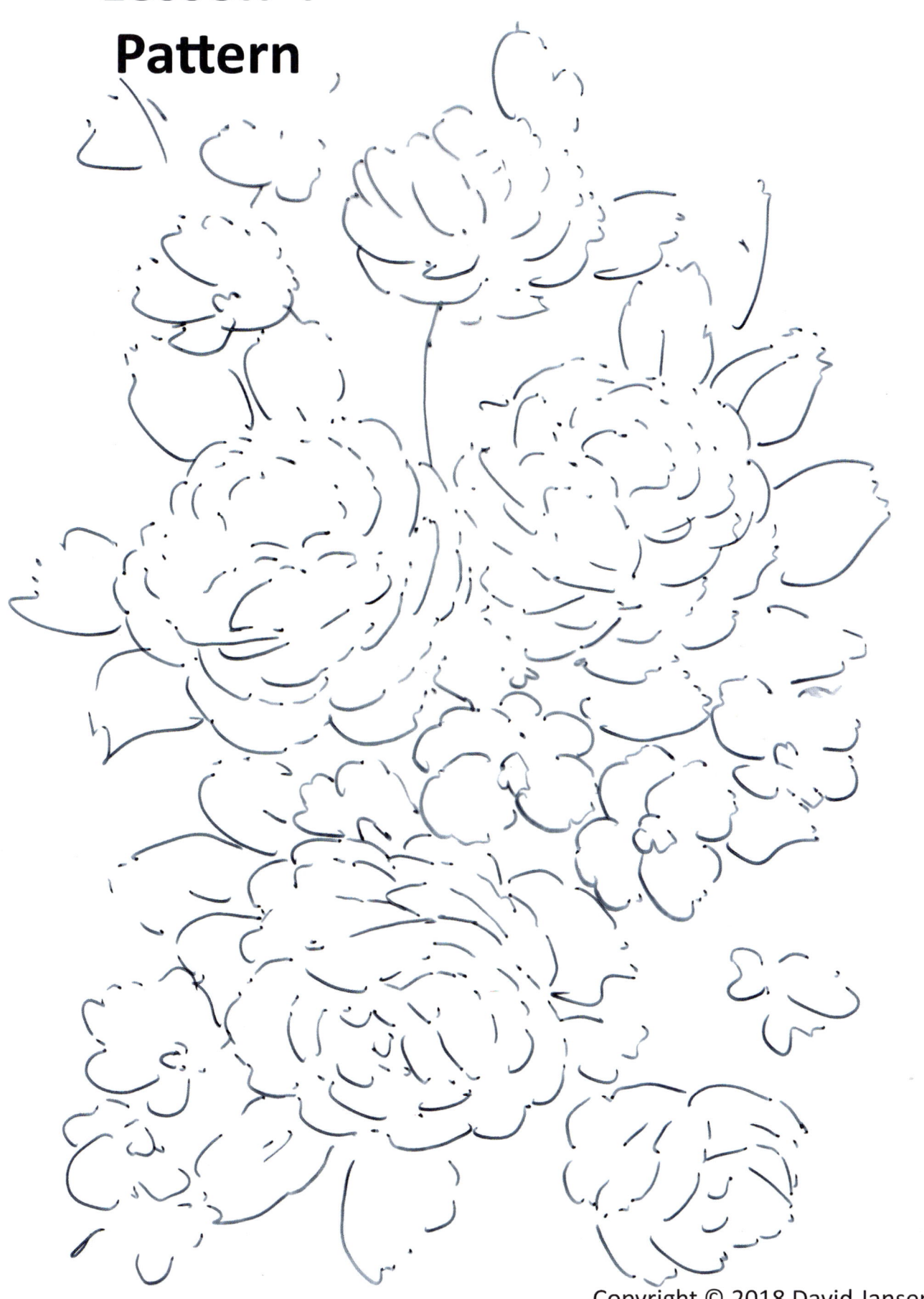

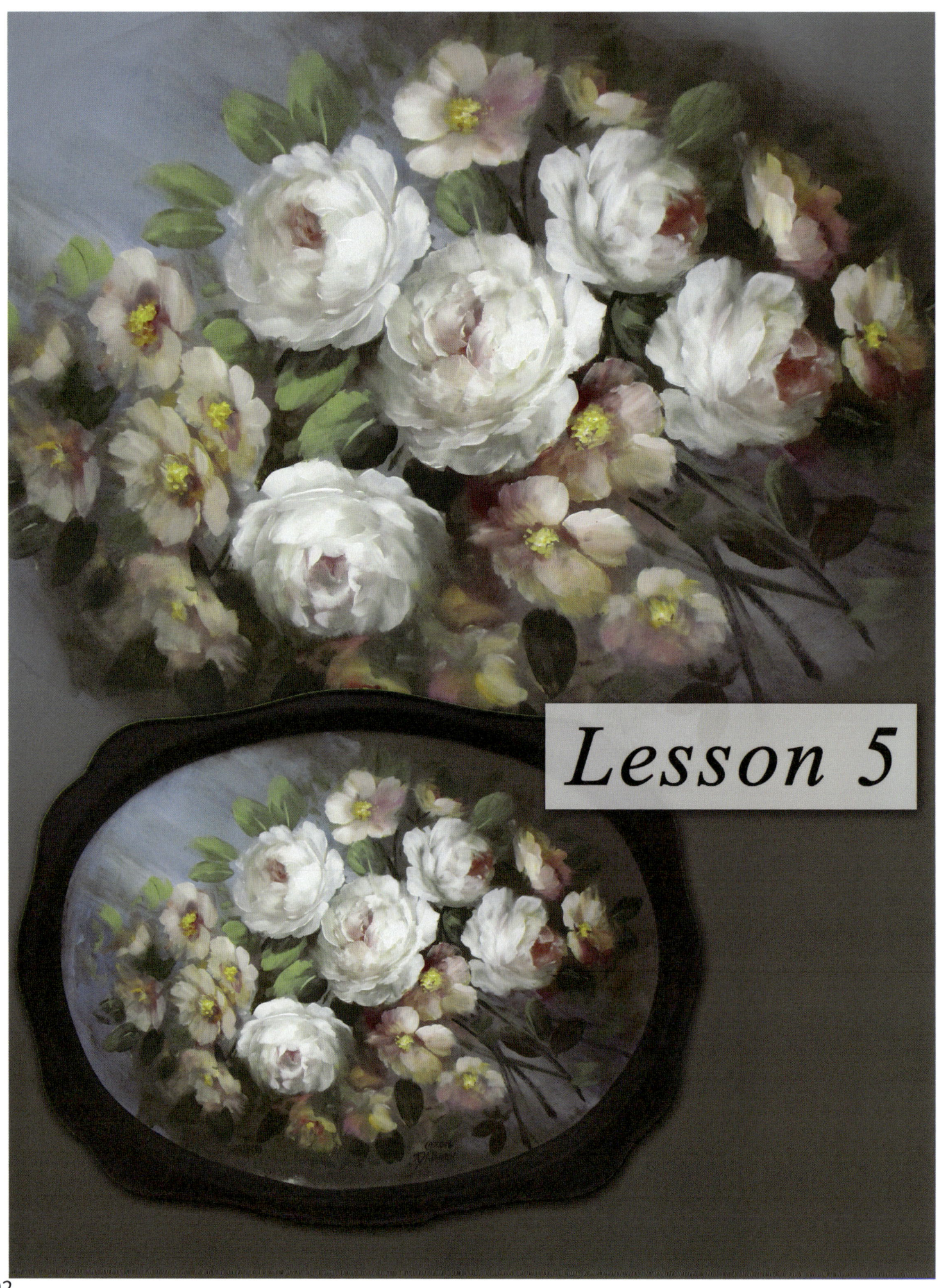

Lesson 5

Reaching Bouquet - Movement

In the last couple years, I have added more movement to my paintings. For many years I used plain basecoated backgrounds. Now, I love the movement in a composition. You have to build more contrast in your flowers with larger value differences and bigger shifts between warm and cool colors.

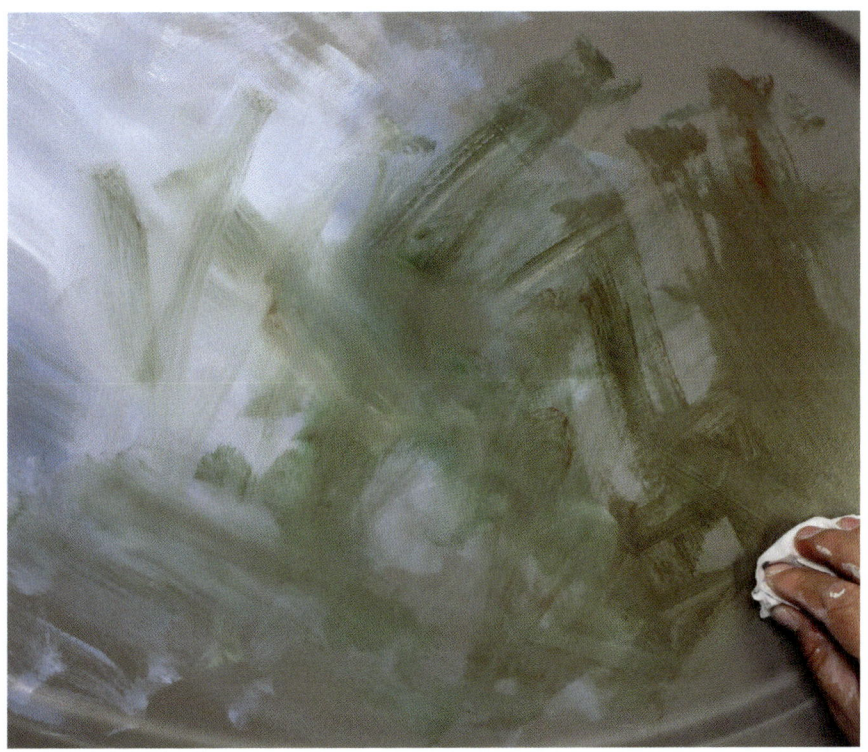

This large tray would be boring with just a plain background. By adding movement to the background colors from the start, we establish more interest and a balanced light source.

When I start a painting like this, I use large, broad strokes to establish some of the movement. I then use smaller strokes to support the movement in other directions.

The bouquet is reaching towards the light in the upper left hand corner. To support the reaching bouquet, you want a powerful movement to the upper left in the background. However, you also want to let eye travel to other flowers in the design.

Learning various ways to add background movement unifies your composition to the background. It also increases the beauty and grace of the composition. Let's give it a try!

Paint It Simply Palette
Base Color- Light Green Grey
White + Touch Hansa Yellow and Black

Palette Colors

PAINT IT SIMPLY COLORS	OPTIONAL COLORS
Naphthol Red Light	Yellow Oxide
Red Violet	Diarylide Yellow
Titanium White	Pine Green
Carbon Black	Quinacridone Violet
Phthalo Blue	Burnt Sienna
Hansa Yellow	Phthalo Green Blue

Painting Surface
Large Metal Tray

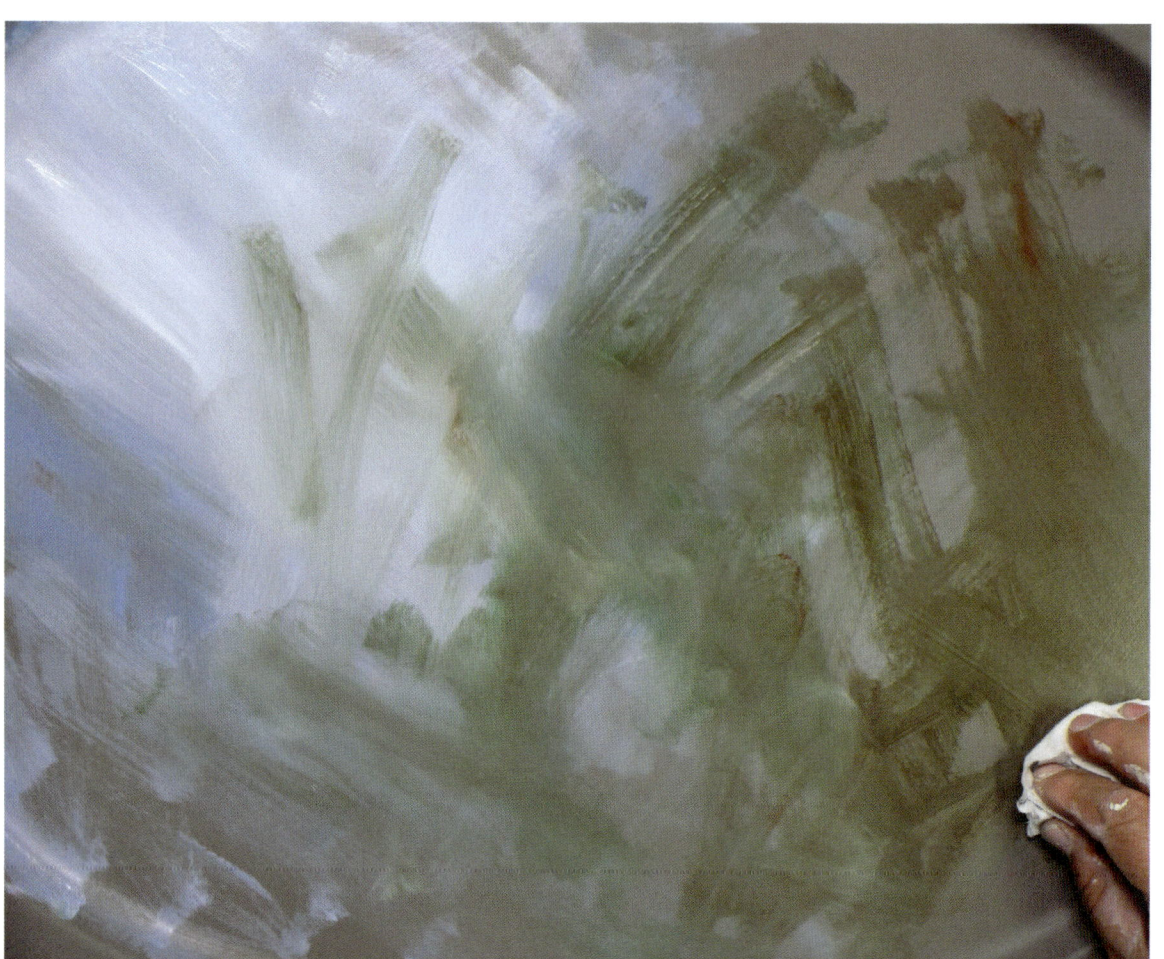

Step 1
Time to create that movement. I based the tray with a green grey. Then I mottled Phthalo Blue and white in the top left corner. Pretty thick paint. You can add extender medium if you are concerned. I used water.
Mottle Pine Green and Burnt Sienna in bottom right corner. I then softened through the colors with a paper towel. Leave streaks.

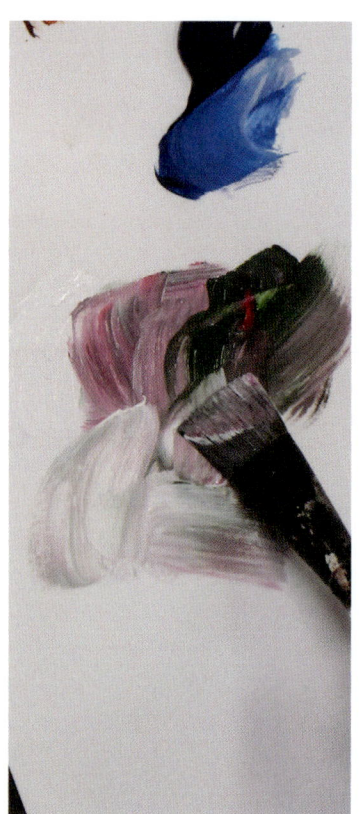

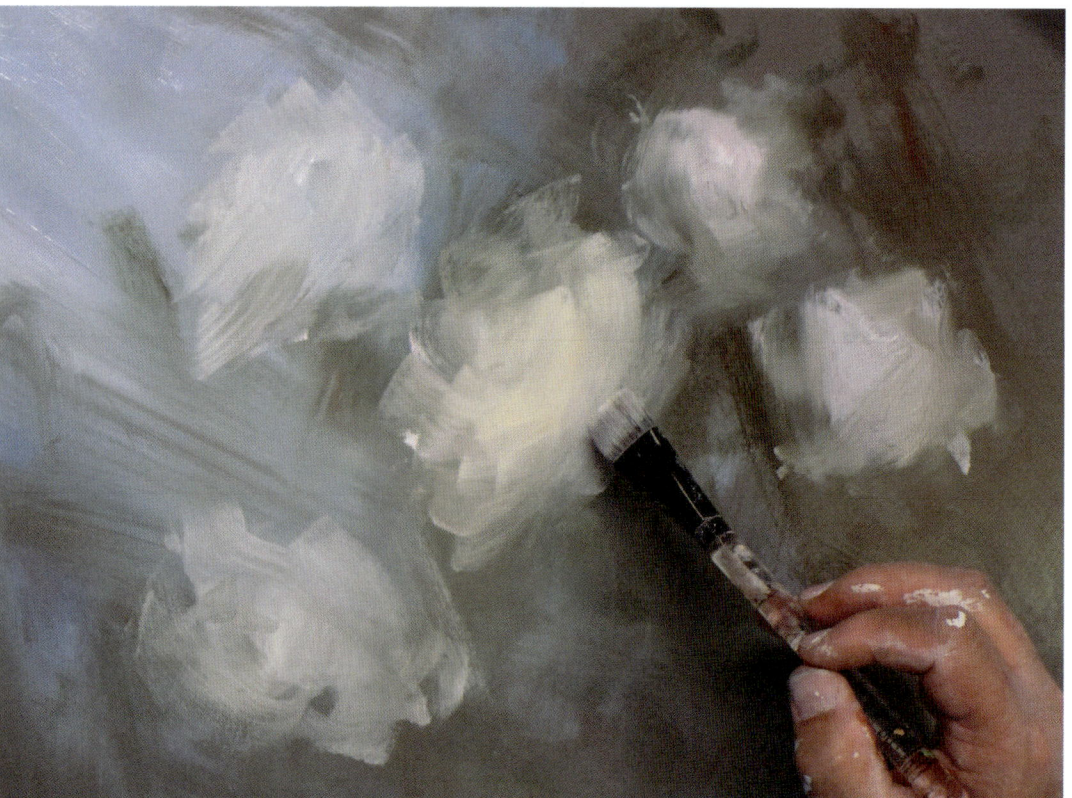

Step 2 Mottle greens and red violets to make grey. Lighten with white.

Step 3 Use the large 3/4 inch brush base the areas for the roses. I build a little more color in the center fronts of the roses where I want them to come forward. Shear off the back and outside edges of the rose to keep them soft against the background.

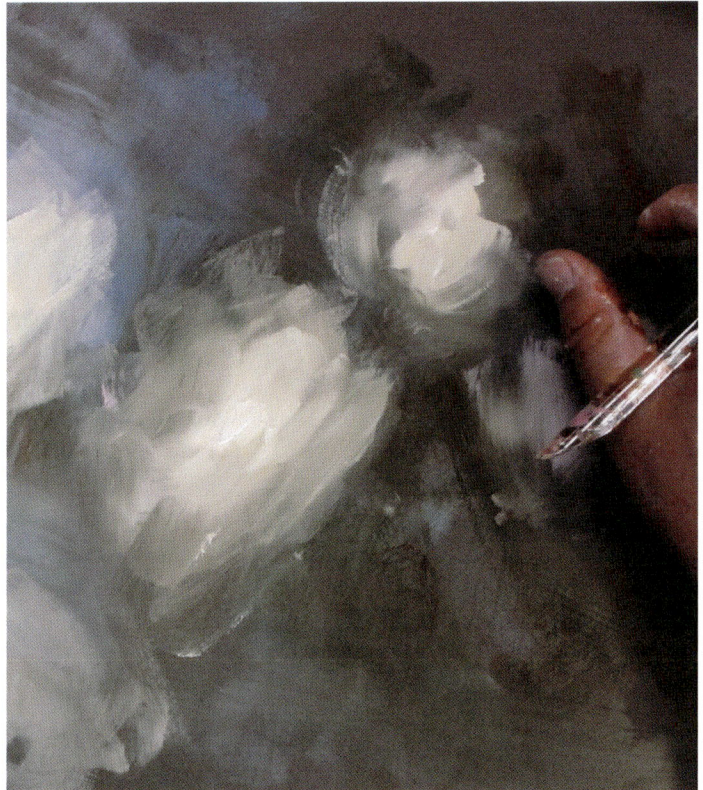

Step 4 Build more white in the center areas. This causes the rose fronts to advance. We will tint these down. Shear the edges with your fingers.

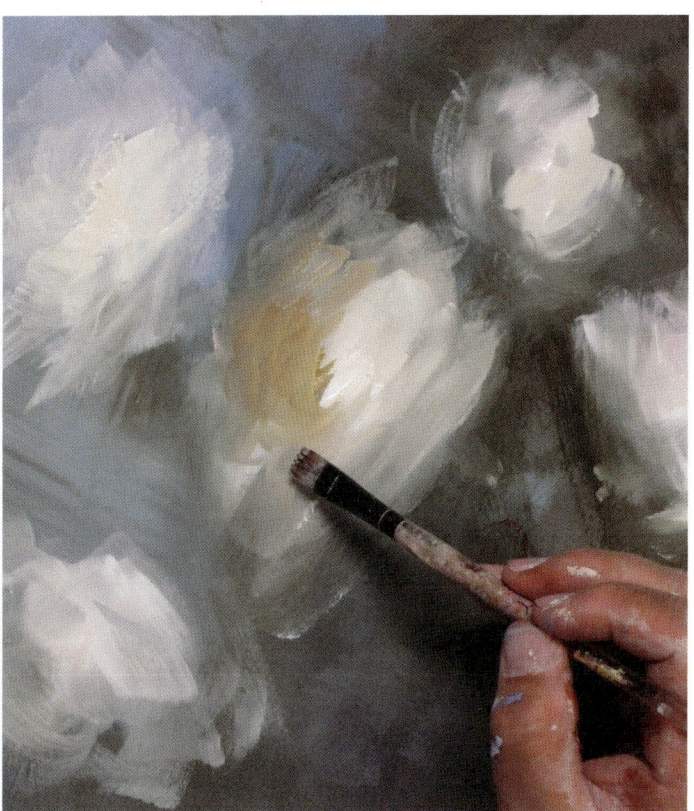

Step 5 Mottle yellows with a little Burnt Sienna to one. Then add a touch of extender to the color make transparent. Wash over the backs of the flowers to recede.

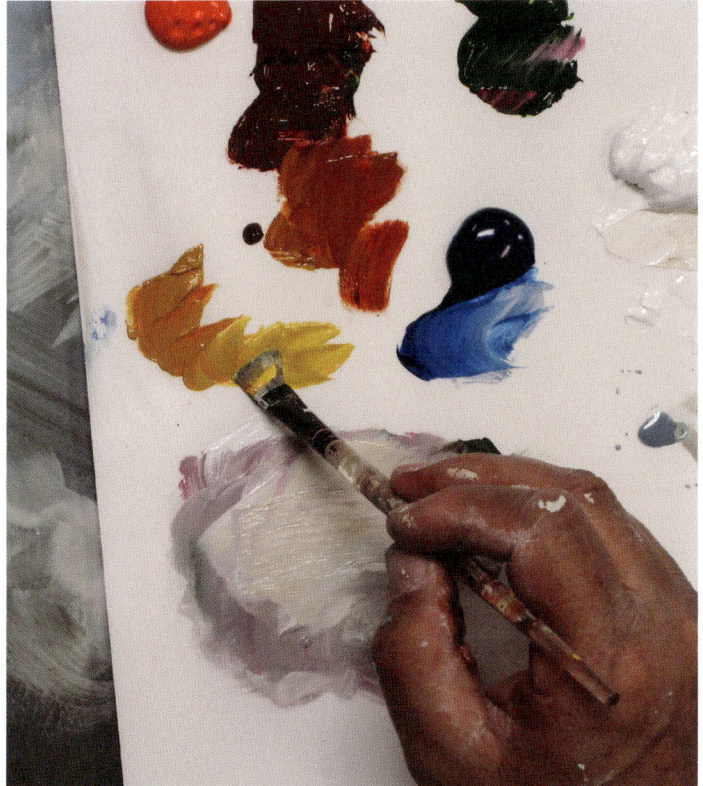

Step 6 Mottle the Yellow Oxide with touch Hansa to brighten and add touch extender.

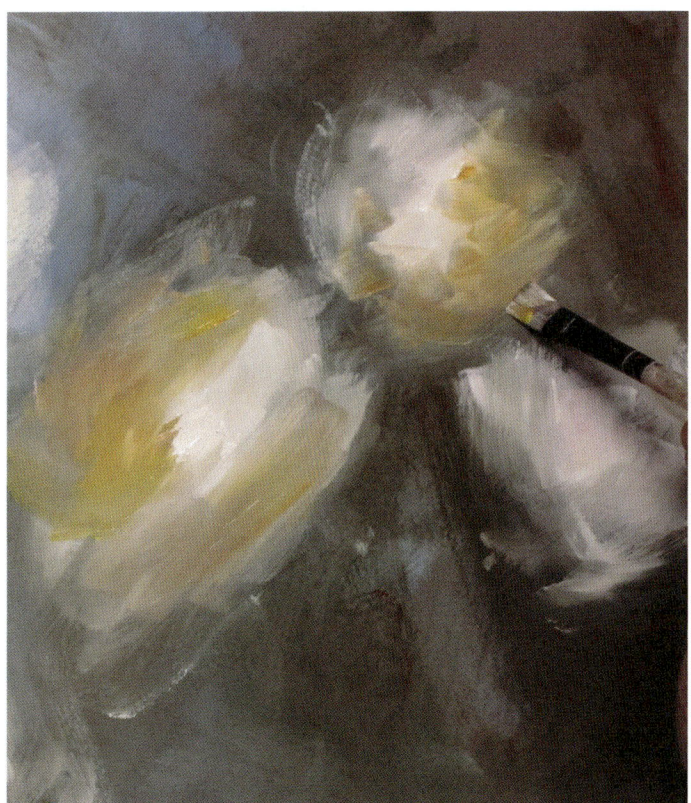

Step 7 Wash over a few of the other flowers to vary the colors. Let the color go into the background a little do soften and recede those areas.

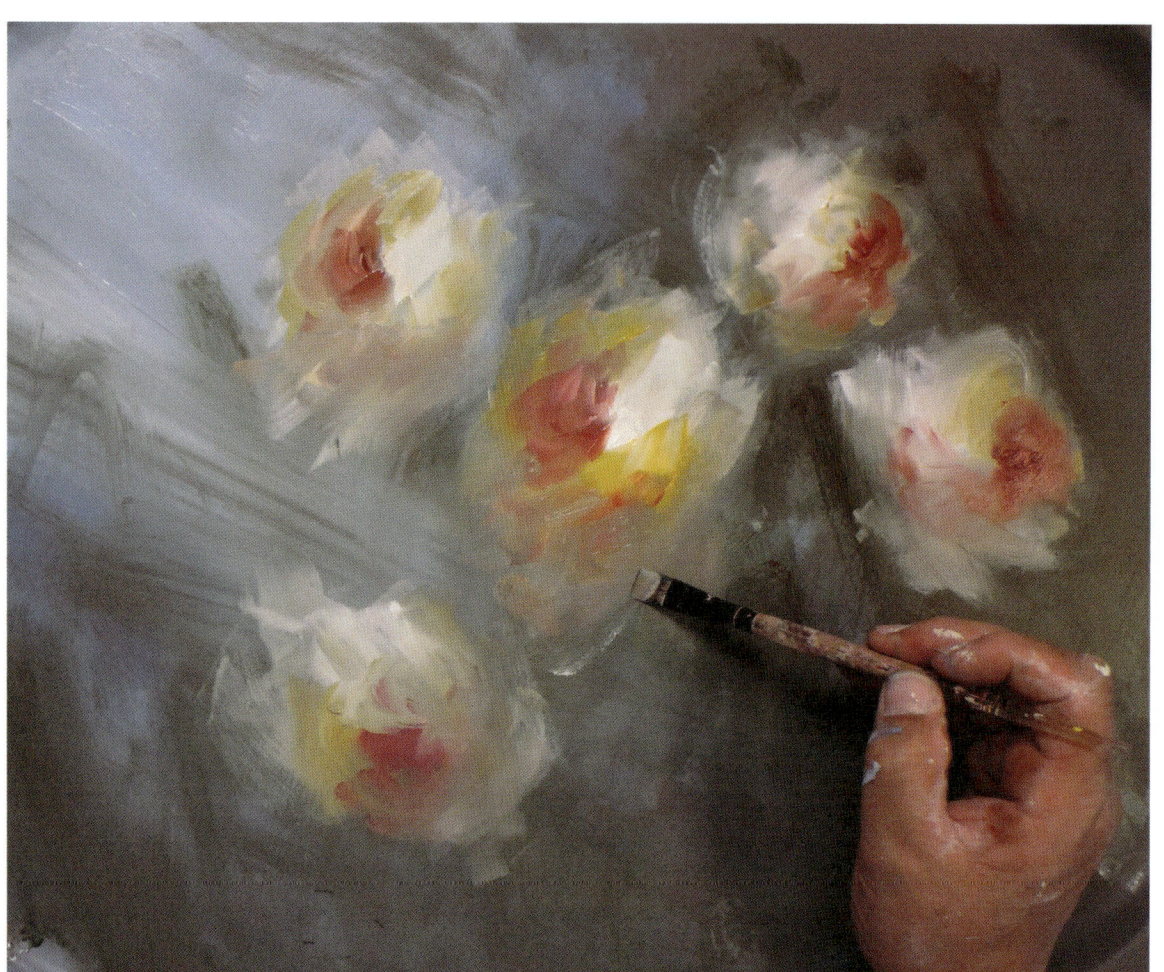

Step 8
Mottle the brush with Reds and Red Violet to darken slightly and cool. Use in the centers of the roses like we have done in previous lessons. Add transparently to the bottom of the bowl for roundness.

Notice how I gaze the roses in different directions and use different amounts of paint to create different looks and opacities.

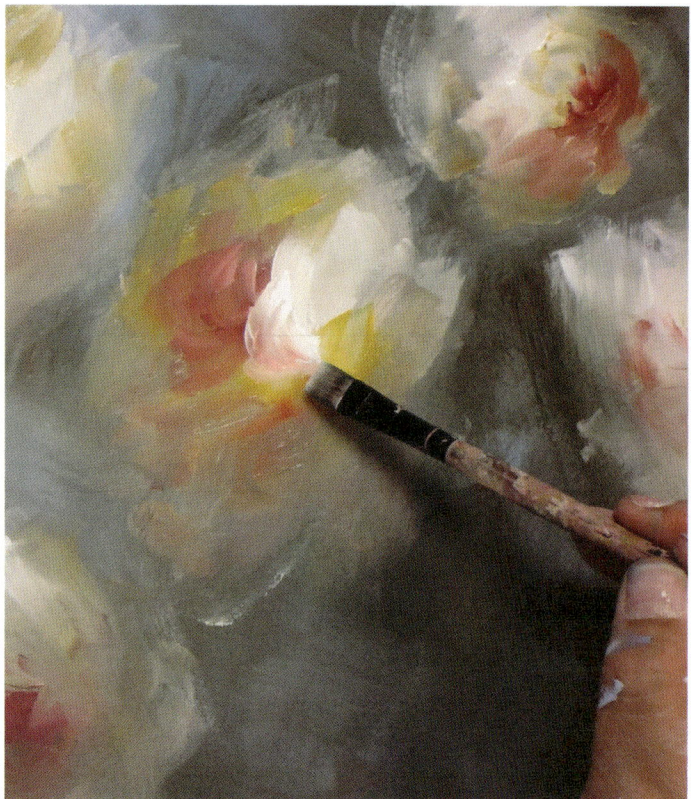

Step 9 Mottle the # 10 fusion flat with more white and begin to build the front of the main rose. Pull the color down and shear off the bottom with your finger.

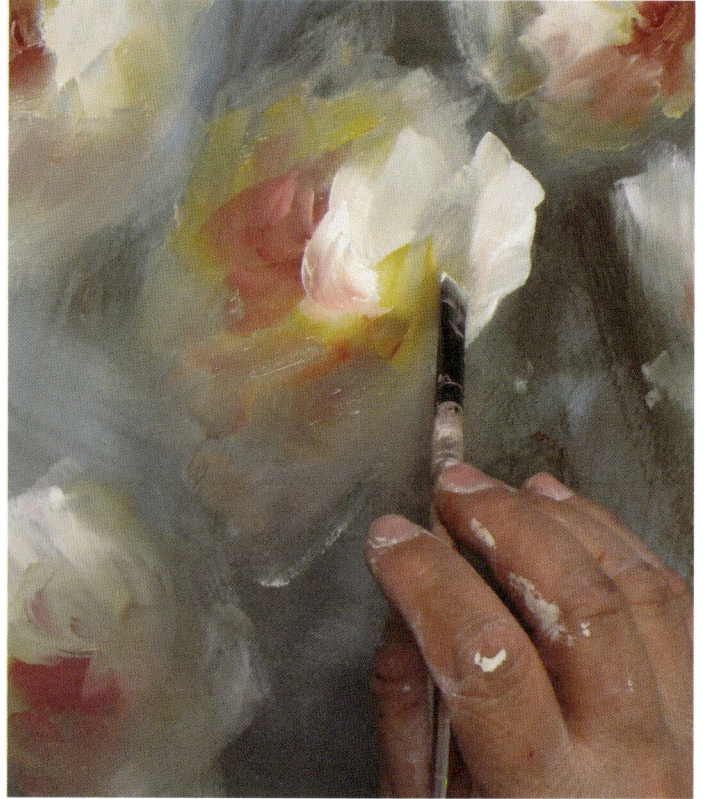

Step 10 Begin the front reaching petals and again, shear off the petal as it approaches the bowl shadow. Keep the more opaque color by the outside tip of the petal.

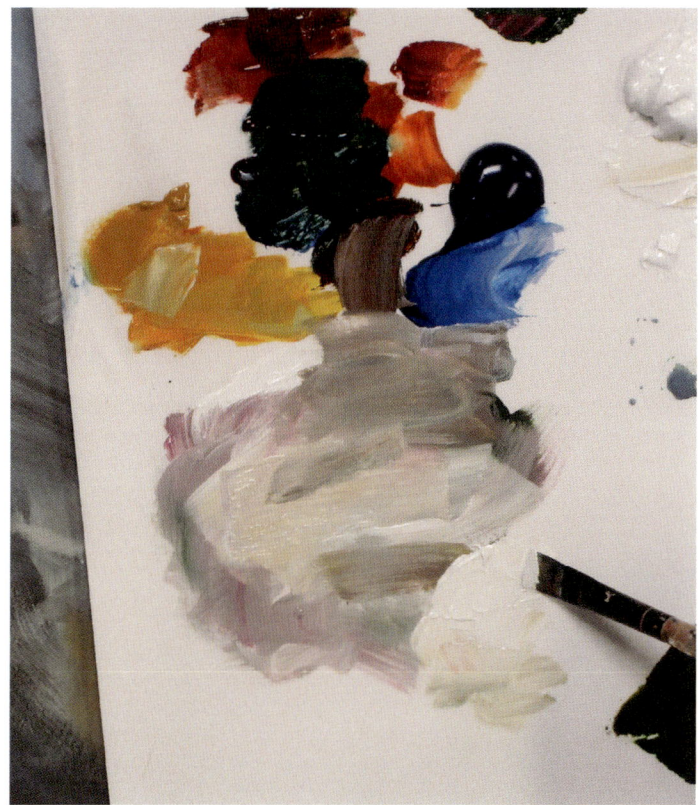

Step 11 Mottle the color with greys we used earlier to tone it down and darken the value.

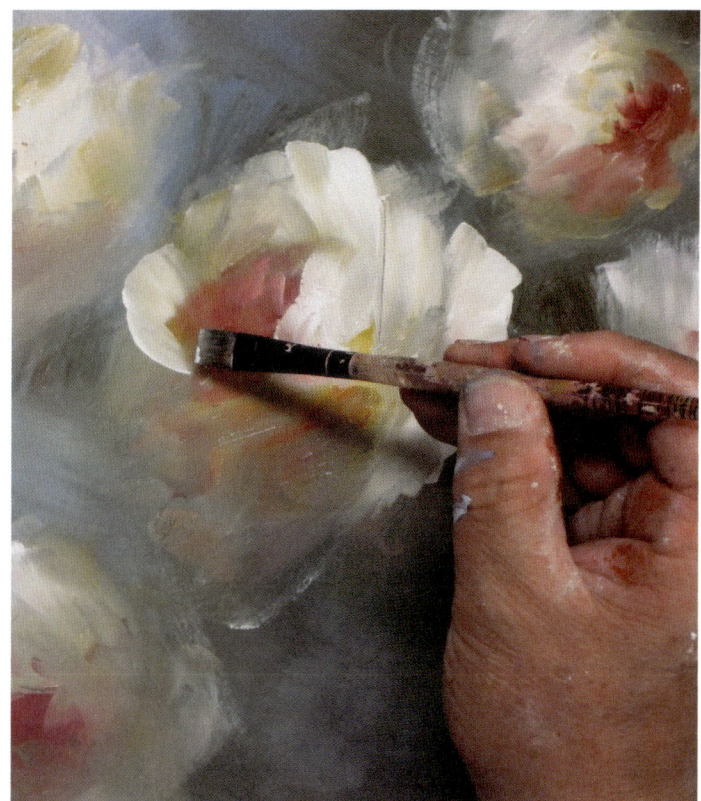

Step 12 Use this darker more toned color to paint the backs of the roses. Vary the looks of the petals. Keep some forward edges while the back should be soft. Shear if needed.

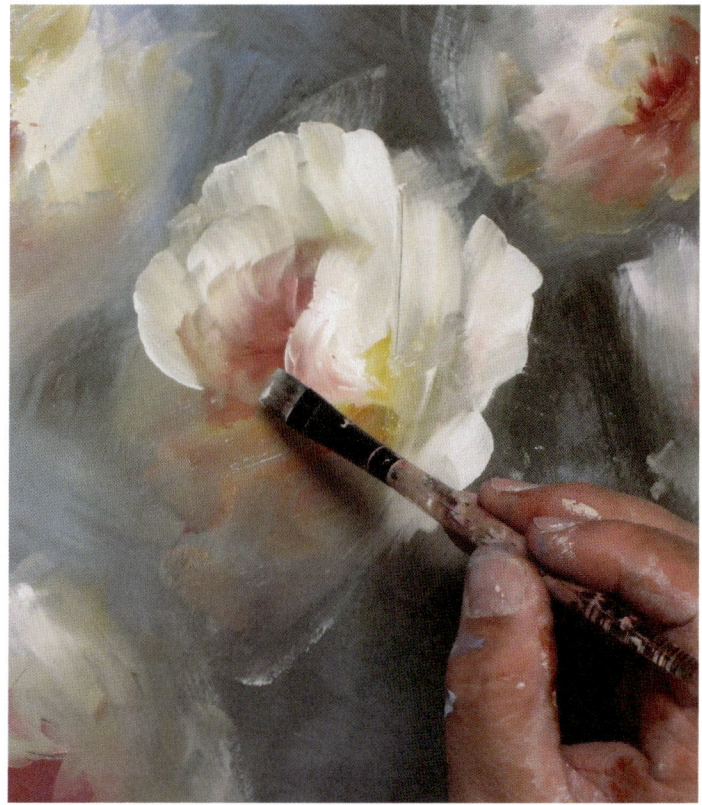

Step 13 Lightly stroke the color into the center of the rose lifting off so you do not cover all the reds. Restate reds if needed. Use just a little paint so the color stays transparent.

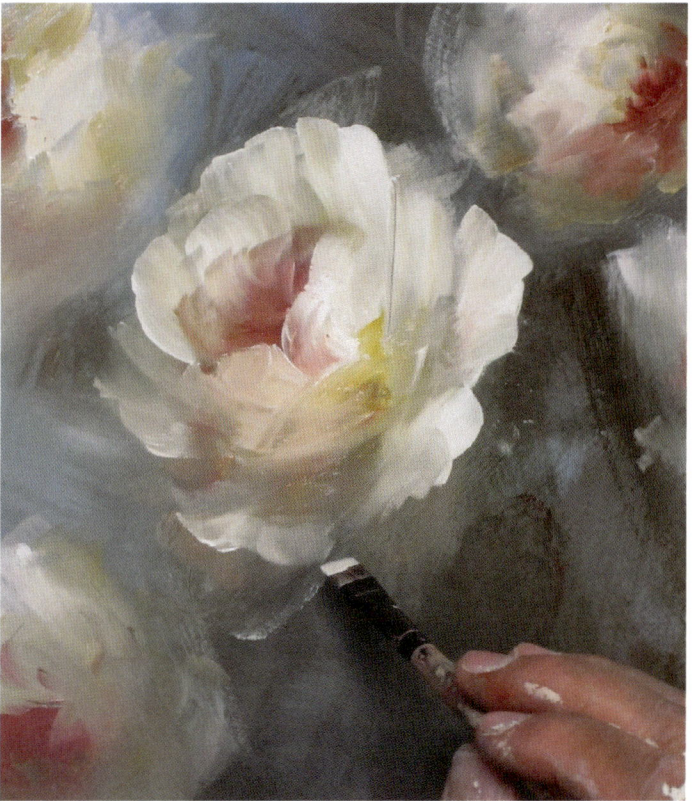

Step 14 Using a little paint and extender for transparency, shape the outside bottom reaching petals. Lift off as you approach the bowl shadow.

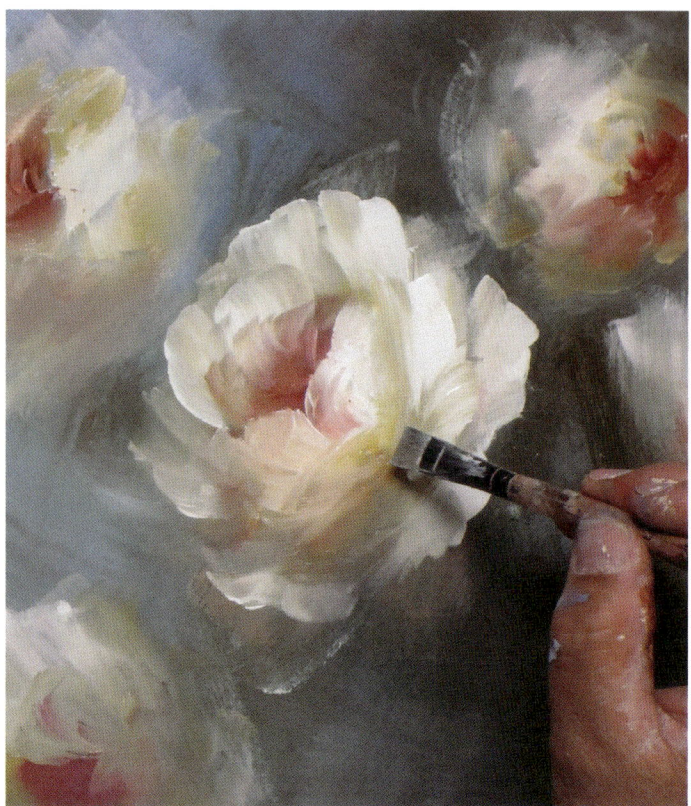

Step 15 Thin Yellow Oxide and Hansa Yellow with a little extender and wash over the bottom bowl to tint.

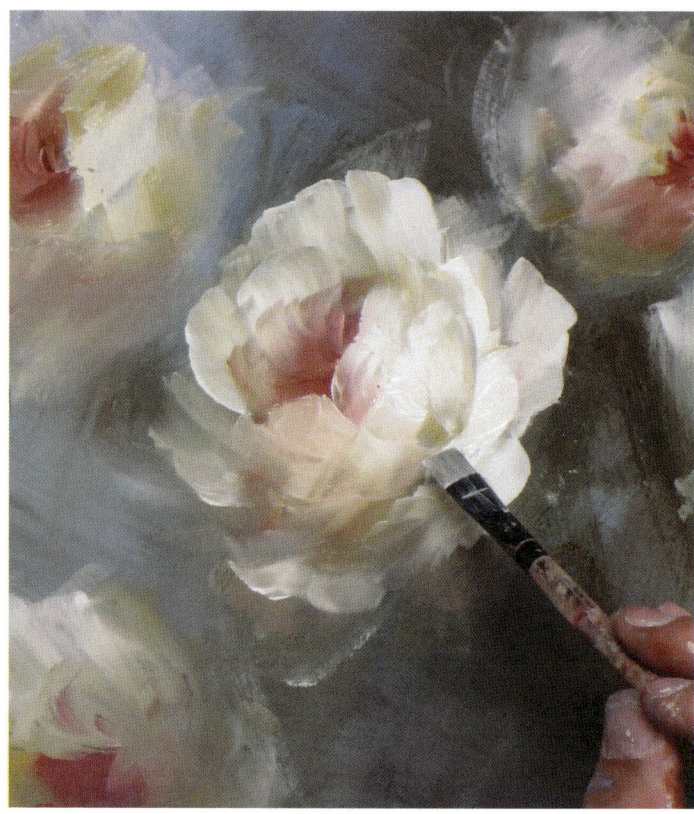

Step 16 While the tint is wet, I mottle the brush lighter with more white and begin to build the front of the rose lifting off at the bottom. Leave some of the yellow color showing.

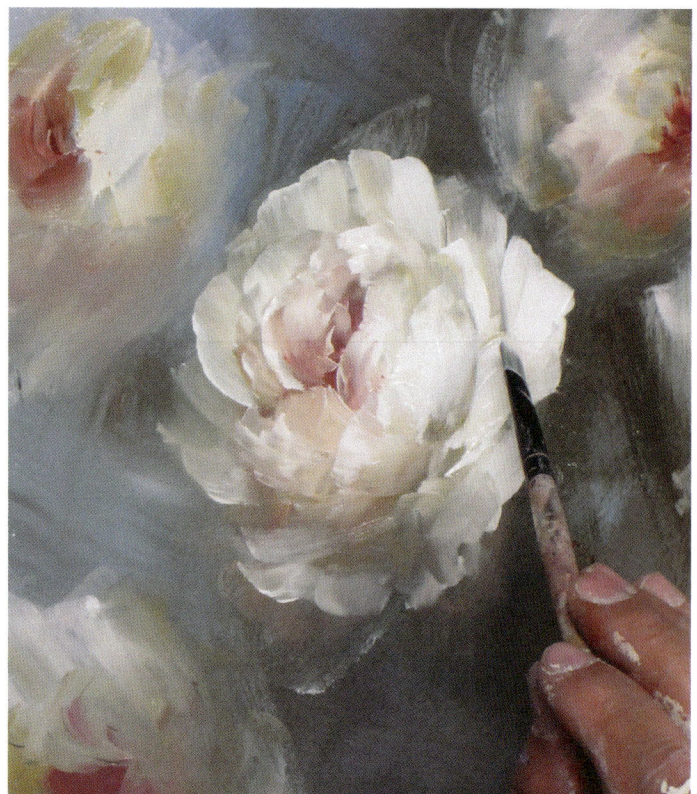

Step 17 Use thicker white on the tips of the reaching petals to give them more contrast and pull them forward. Allow some texture to happen.

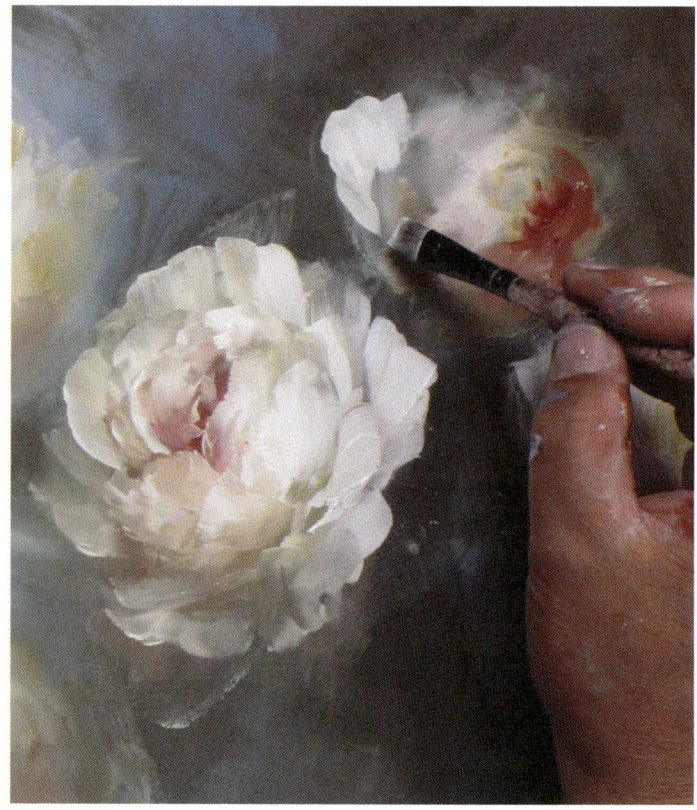

Step 18 Use this thicker white on the top reaching petals of the next rose. Lift off as you get to the bowl shadow to preserve it. Shear the bottom of the petal into the bowl.

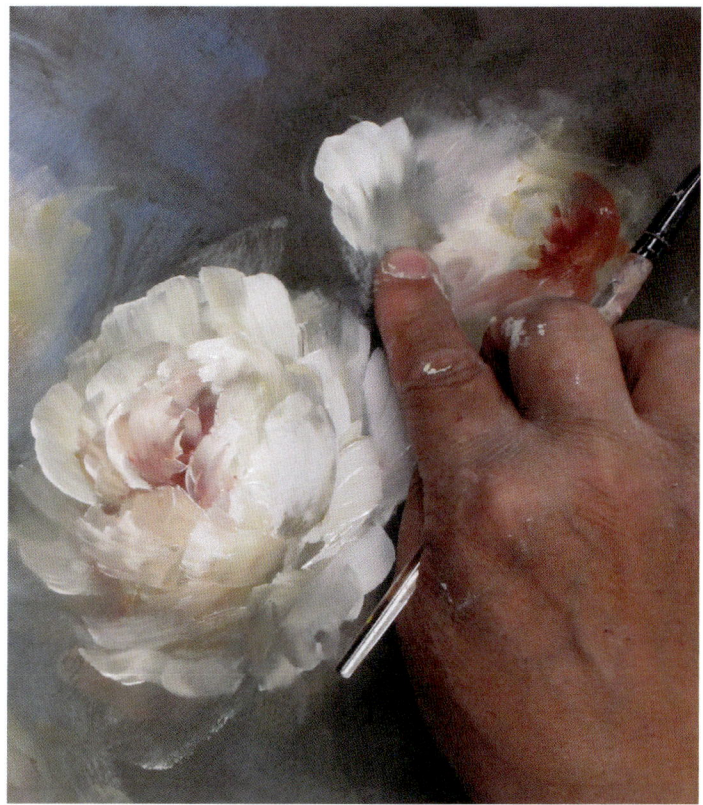

Step 19 Here you see me shearing the petals. Push in and out to create the movement to the petal. Allow the color to be more transparent at the bowl.

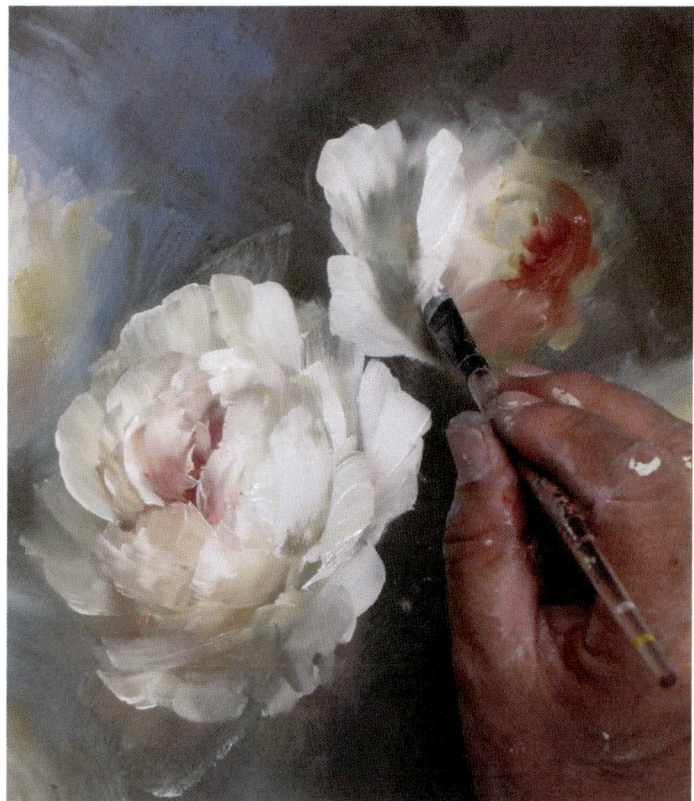

Step 20 Begin building the top bowl petals with more opaque white. Shear off the bottom of the petals as they get to the bowl shadow.

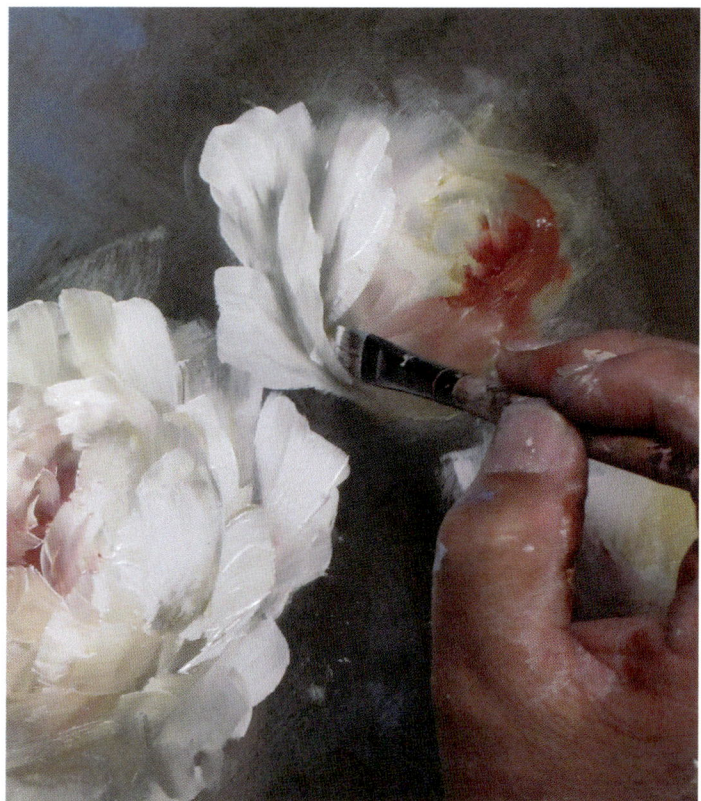

Step 21 Use the chisel of the brush to add the angled petals between the bowl and the reaching petals. Use a little more white on the tips to make them opaque.

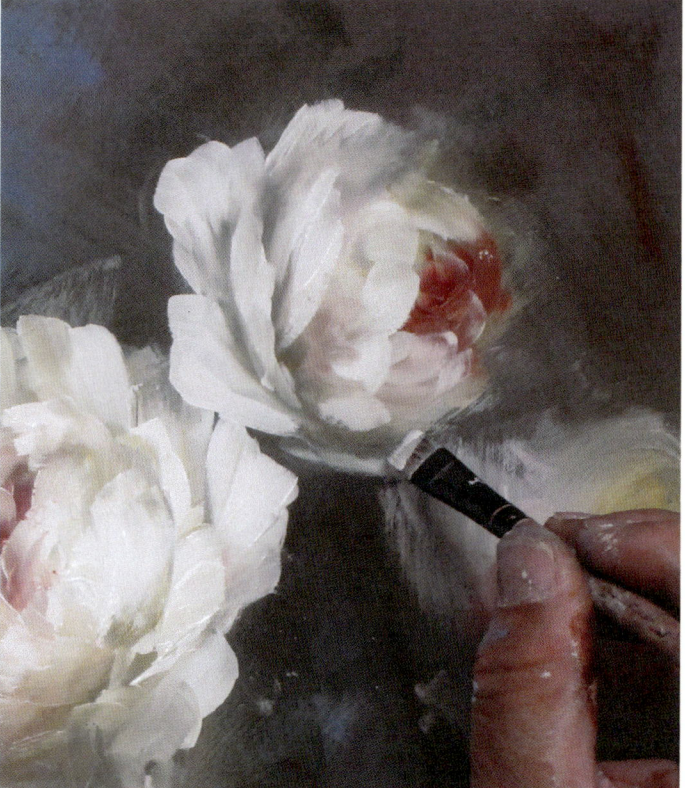

Step 22 Using more transparent color, drag around to the shadow side to just give the impressions of movement. Use just the tip of the brush.

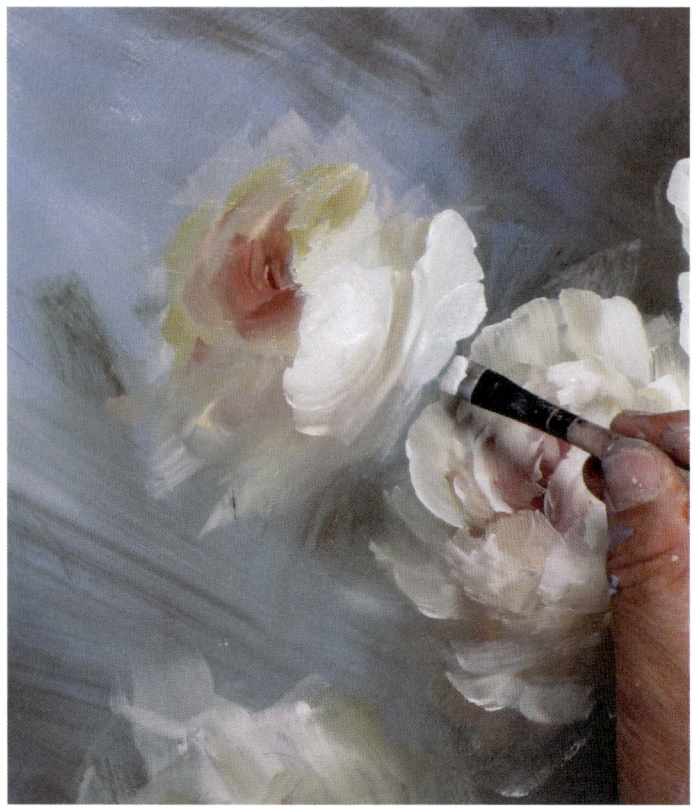

Step 23 Move to the next rose. Add more white out on the tips as it approaches the main "queen" rose. I am pulling out on the petals to give a different look.

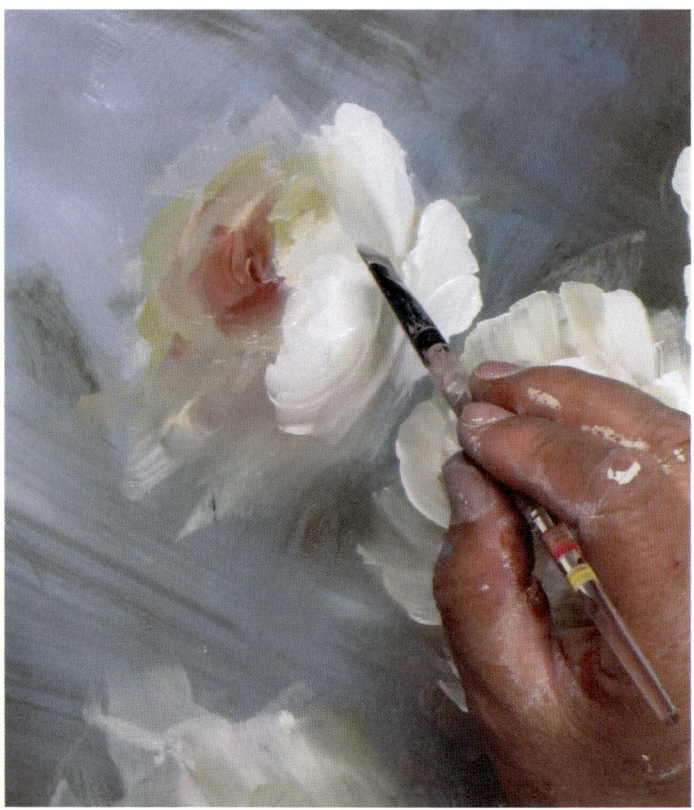

Step 24 Add the reaching side petals. Here I wipe the brush and remove the excess paint from the petal revealing the bowl shadow. Try to always preserve the bowl. It is key!

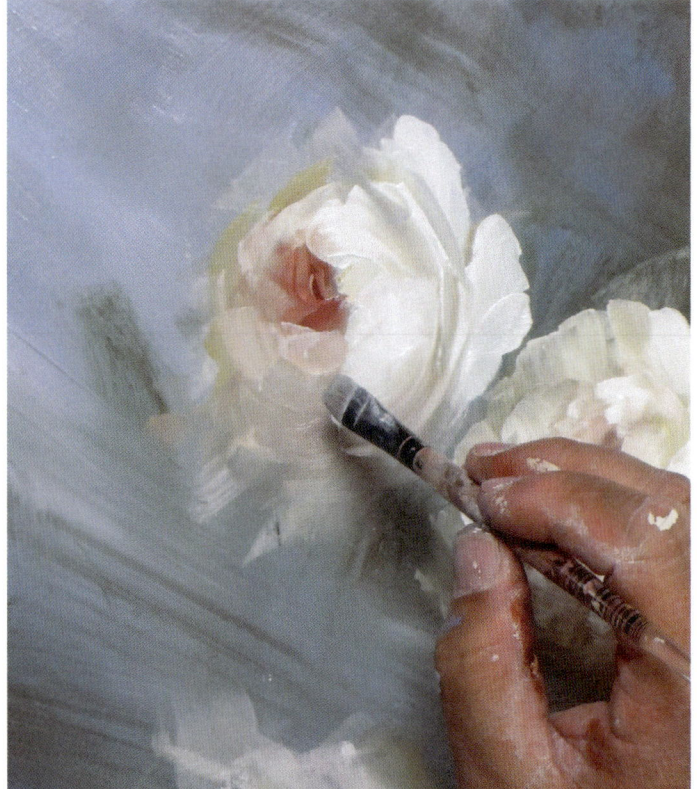

Step 25 Build the front of the rose with more white. I wipe the brush and lift off the paint as it goes around the shadow side. Sometimes I use shear and sometimes lift off.

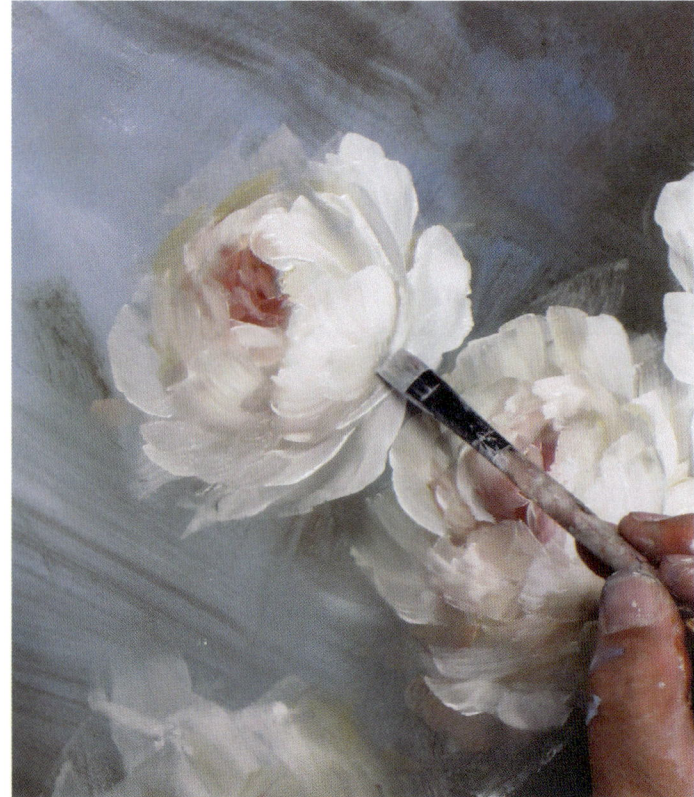

Step 26 Use the chisel of the brush to add the smaller petal tips near the center of the forward reaching petals.

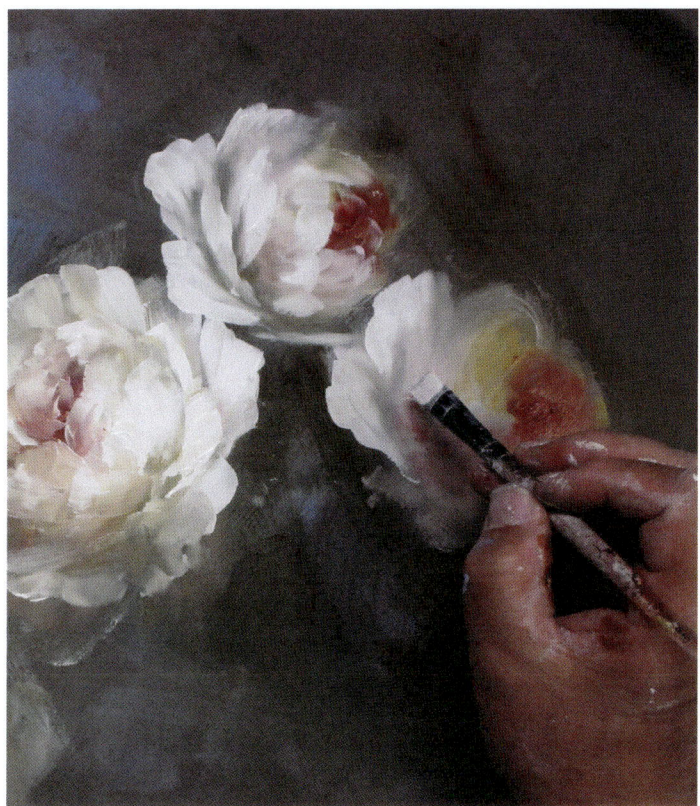

Step 27 Move on the the next rose and begin the same building process. Add the reaching petals and soften the movement with shear using your finger to add movement.

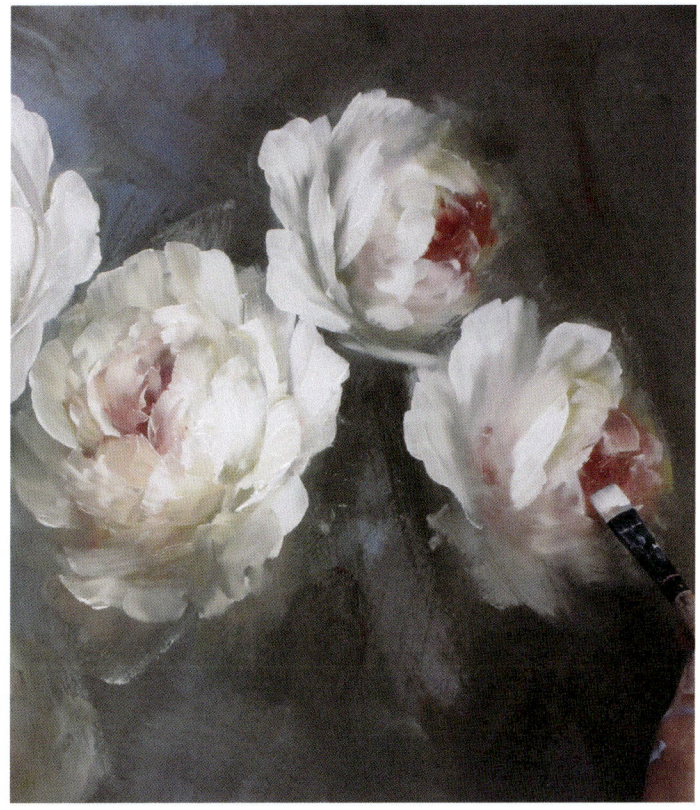

Step 28 Continue to build the rose working around the bowl. Lift off as you reach the bowl shadow.

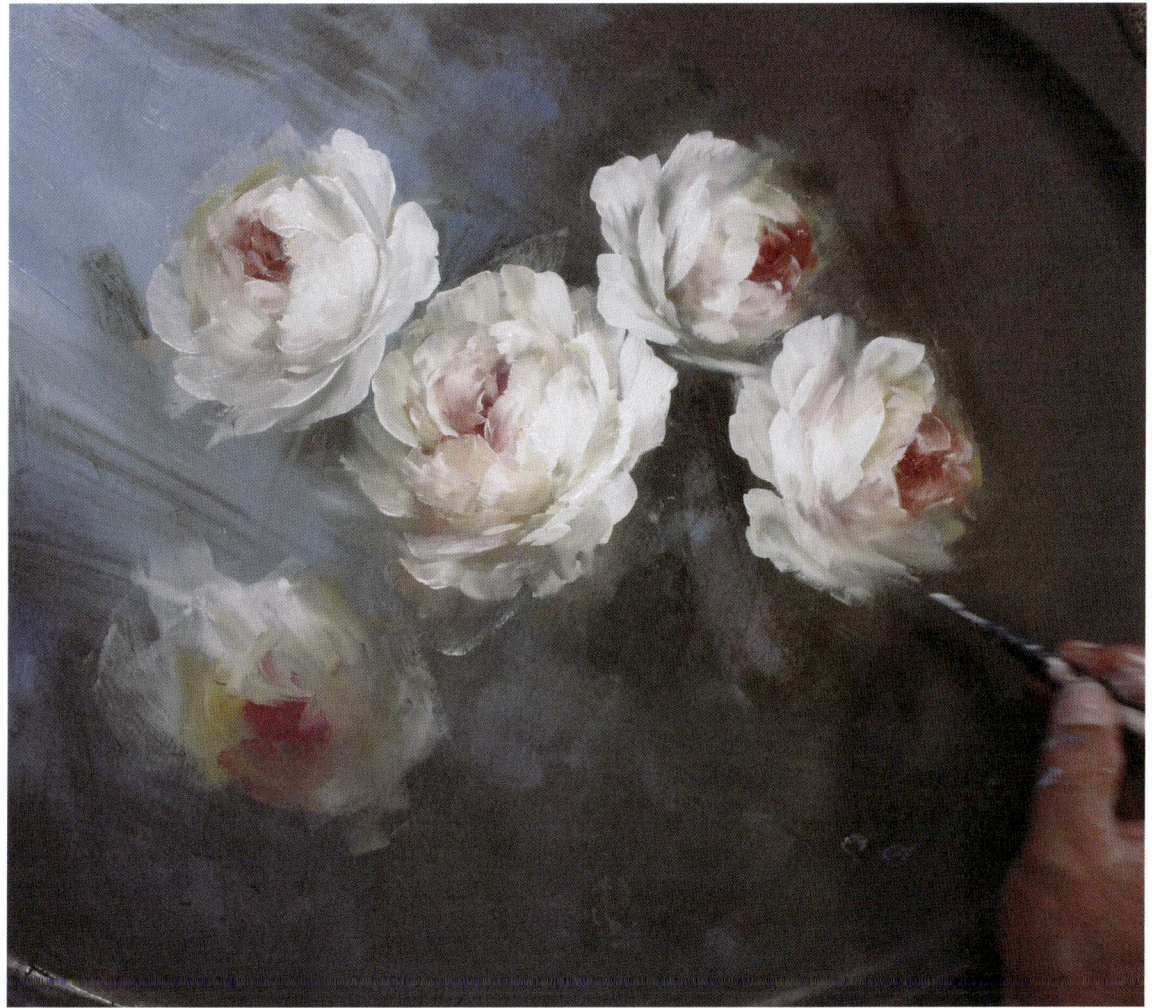

Step 29 Make the color a little transparent with extender medium. Add strokes of the soft grey white to the shadow side of the bowl. This will make transparent reaching petals. I pull out to keep the petals a little softer. You can use your finger to shear off the petals as they reach the background to make them softer and disappear into the composition.

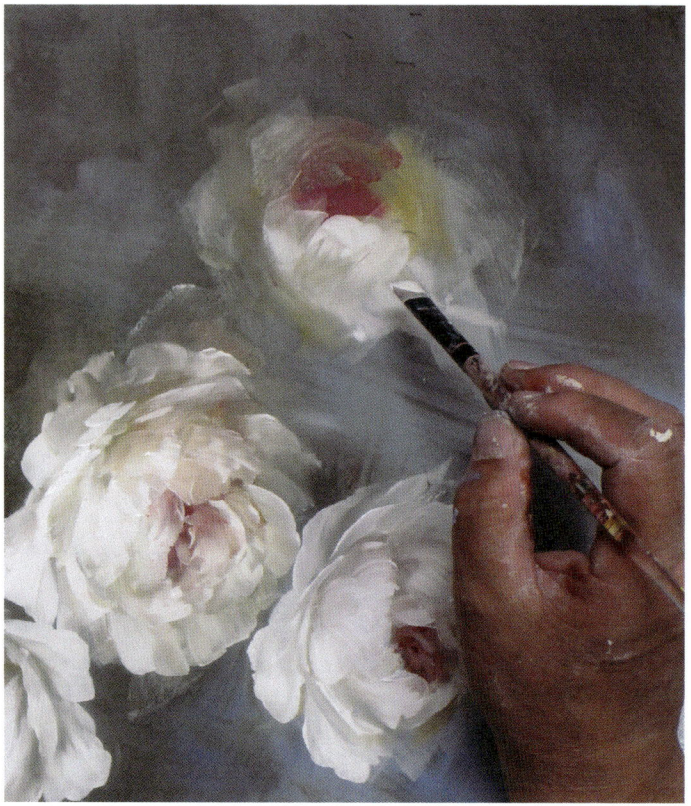

Step 30 Make the the grey white a little transparent with extender and begin the outside roses.

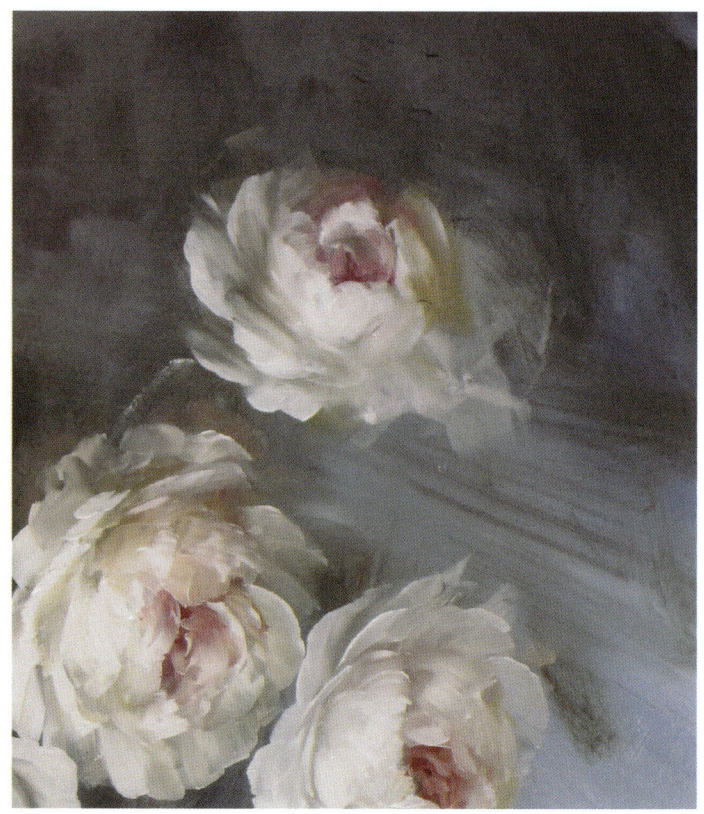

Step 31 Build the rose with the same techniques we did on the other roses. Do not use as much opaque white so the rose stays soft.

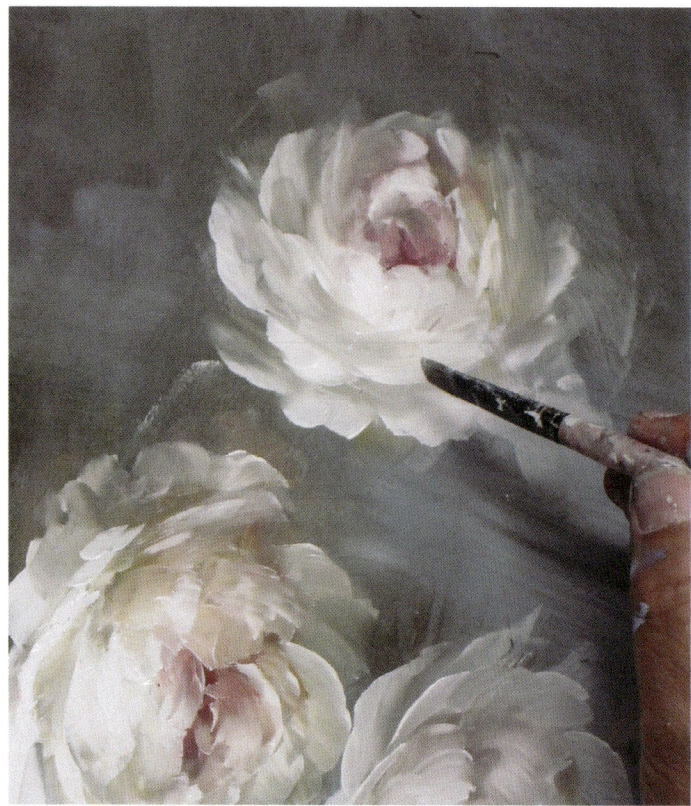

Step 32 Add the final front petals with slightly more opaque white. Use the chisel for the smaller petals in the front of the bowl.

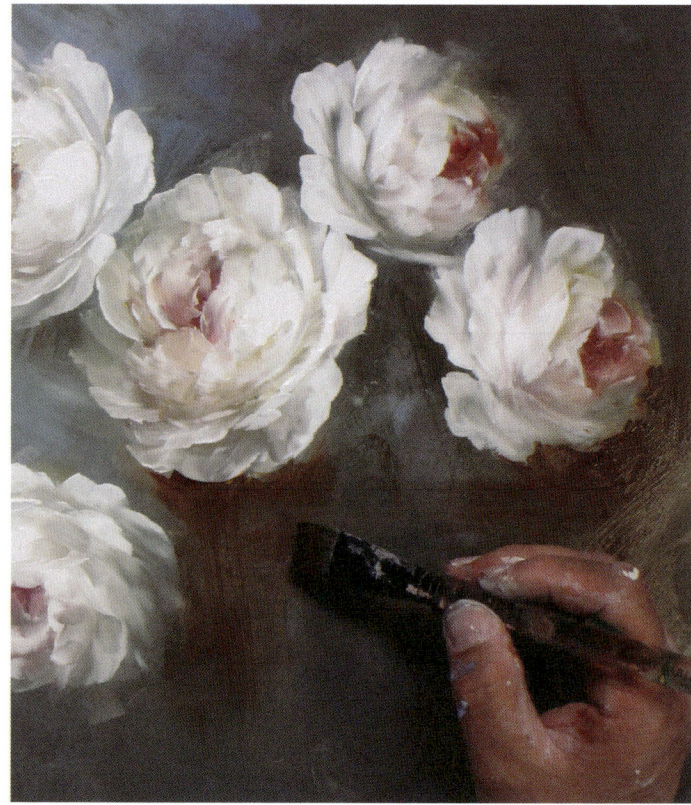

Step 33 Mottle the 3/4 inch brush with Burnt Sienna. Use the negative painting technique to shadow below the roses and shape the front petals.

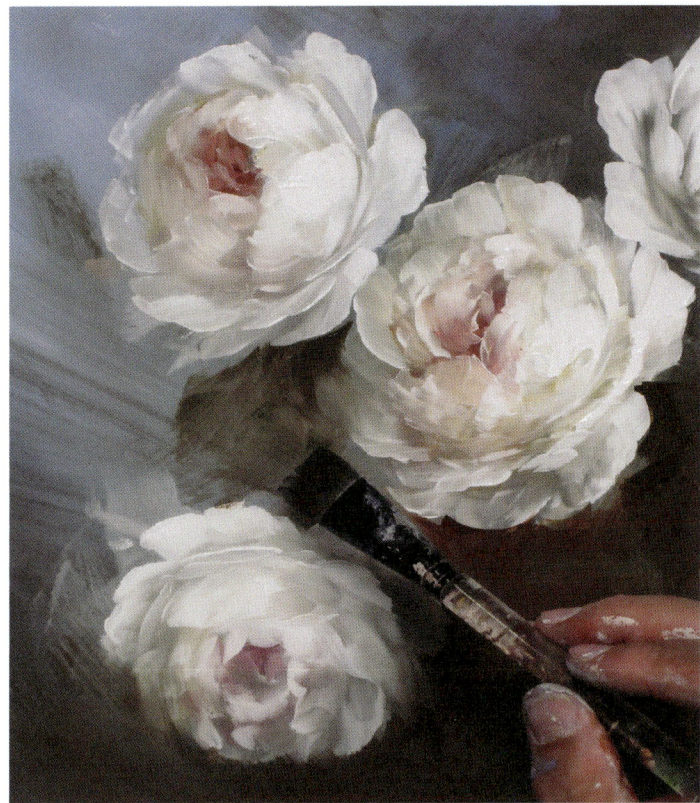

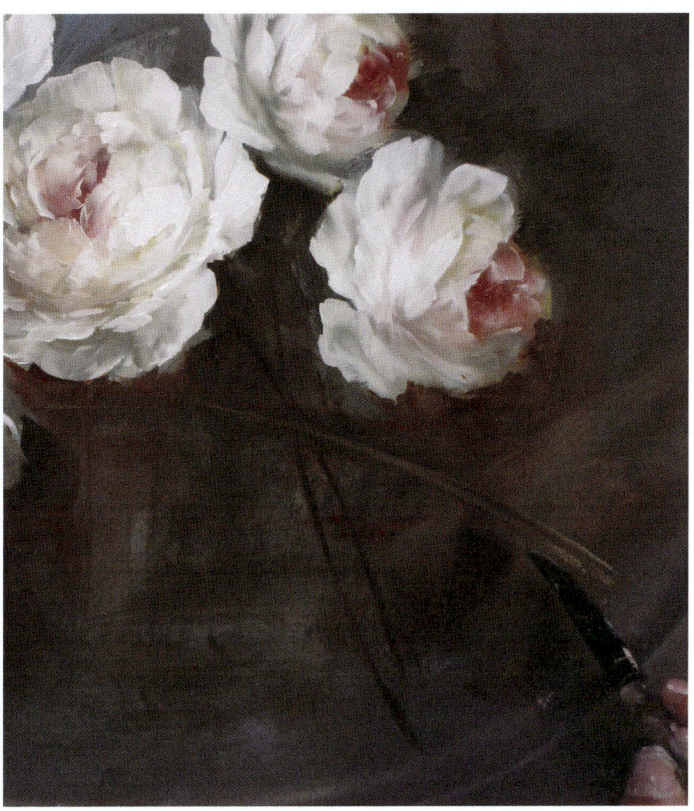

Step 34 Darken and cool the Burnt Sienna with a touch of Pine Green and Red Violet. Use this to add more shadow contrast.

Step 35 Using the chisel of the brush draw some stem movement to the outside edges of the tray. This reinforces the movement we established in the beginning.

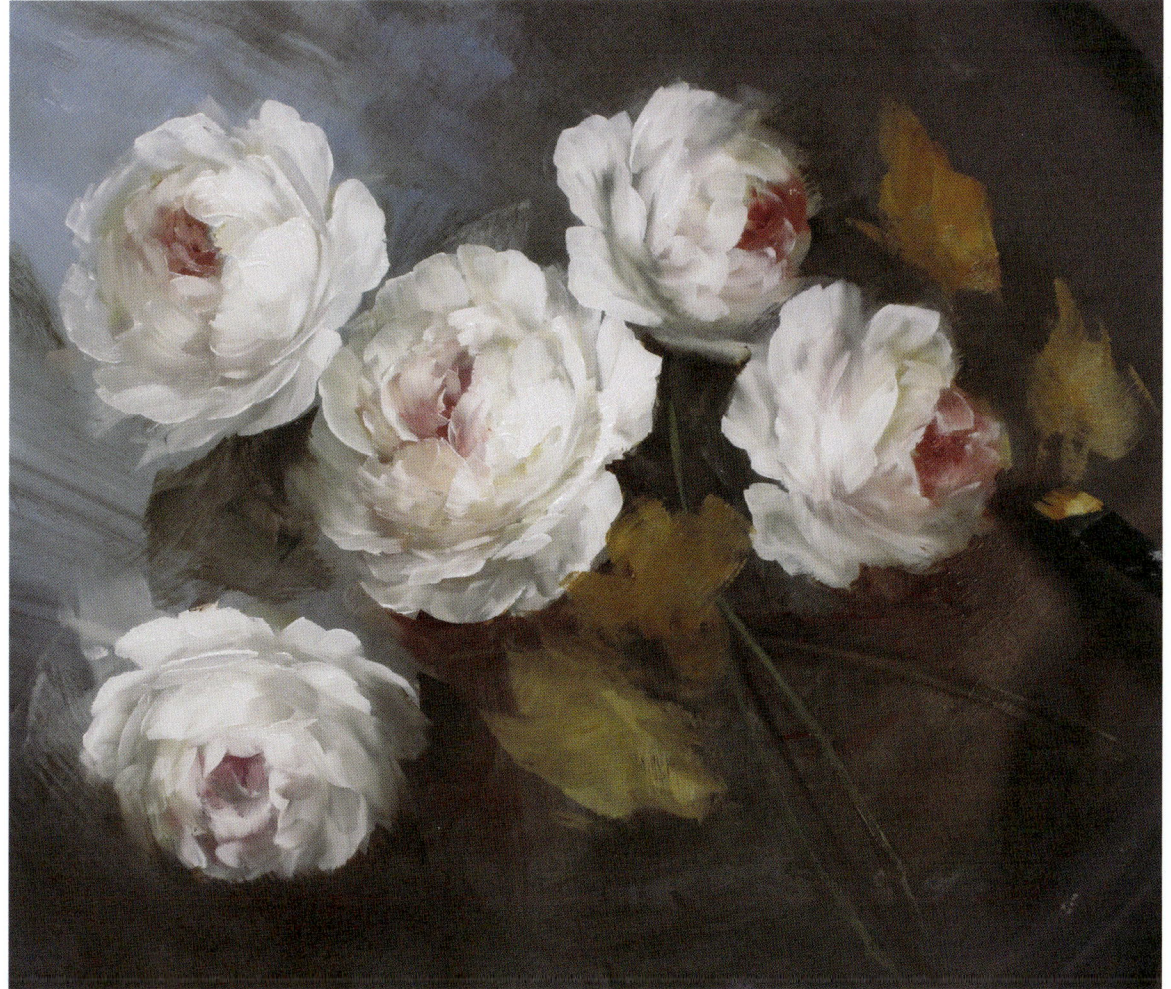

Step 36 Mottle the brush with Yellow Oxide that is toned with Burnt Sienna and cool Red Violet. Mottle in the areas for the yellow flowers keeping the edges very soft and undefined.

Start to visualize how you would turn the gazes of these new flowers to fit the movement of the background and stems we just added.

Step 37
Mottle the larger 3/4 inch brush with cool Red Violet and touch Quinacridone Violet. Add this to the shadows and cool areas of the yellow blossoms. This color is important because it creates harmony between the roses and the blossoms. Both flowers have this color in the cool areas. Tone the Red Violet with touch Pine Green in deep shadows.

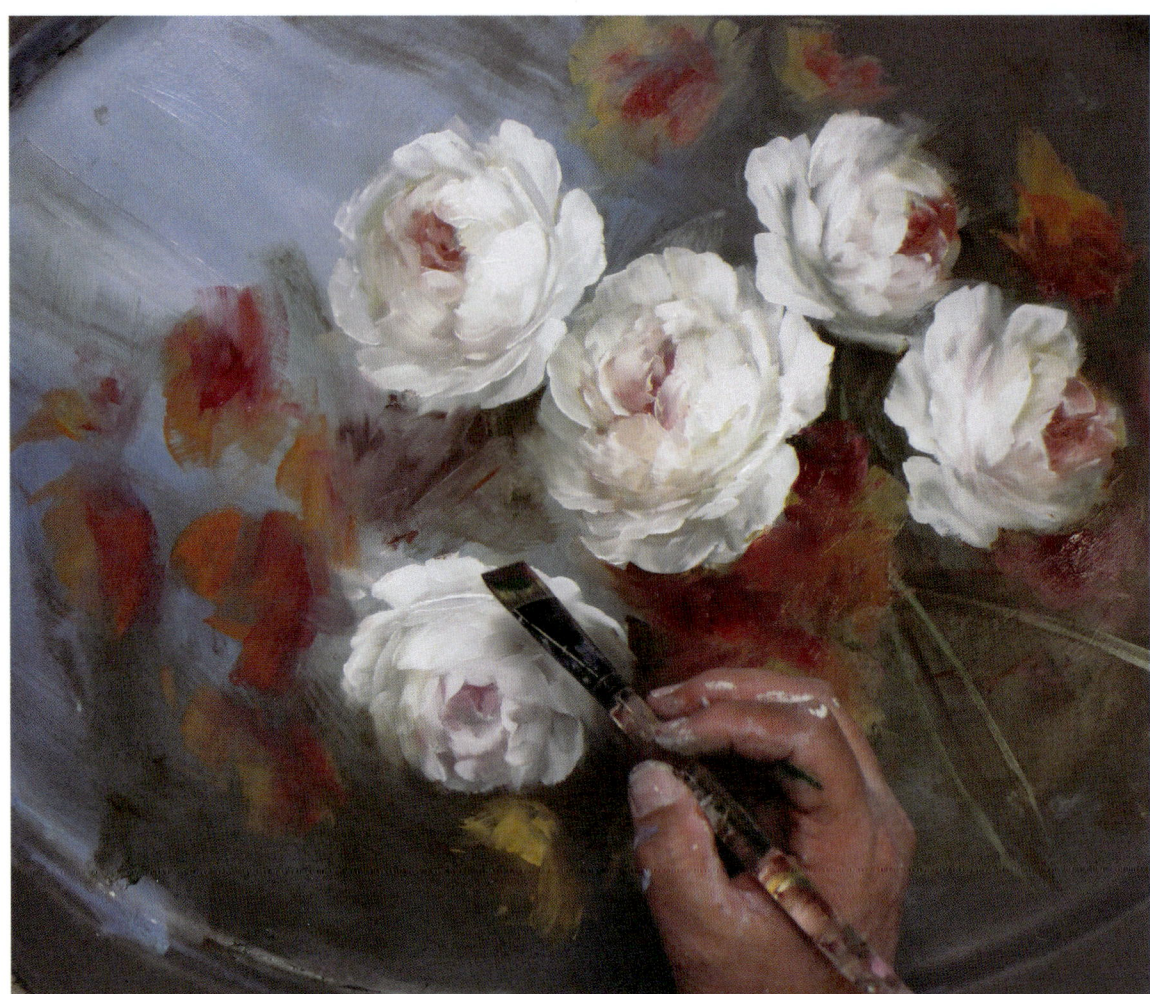

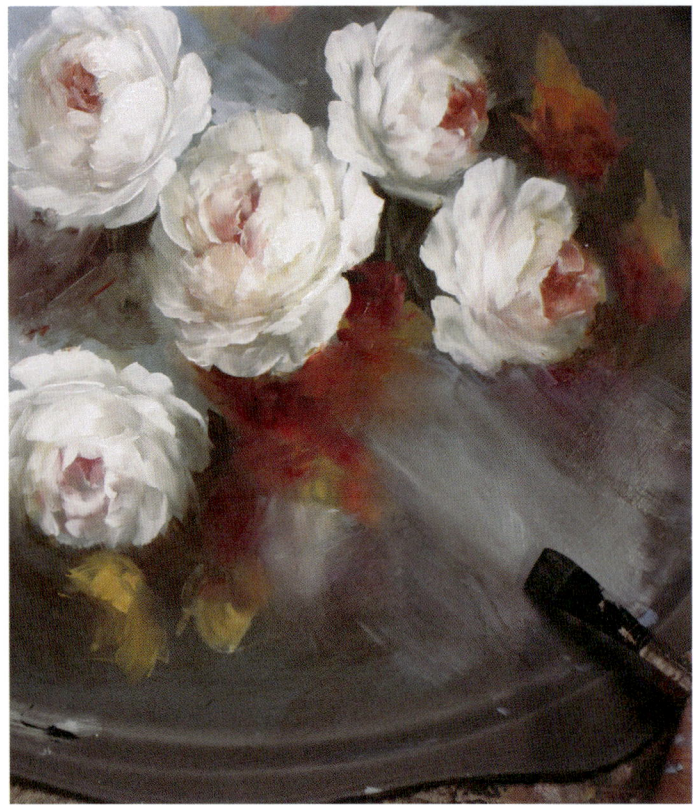

Step 38 Using some of the Phthalo Blue and white from the beginning of the painting, streak down from the roses to increase the movement in the background. Adds lots of interest.

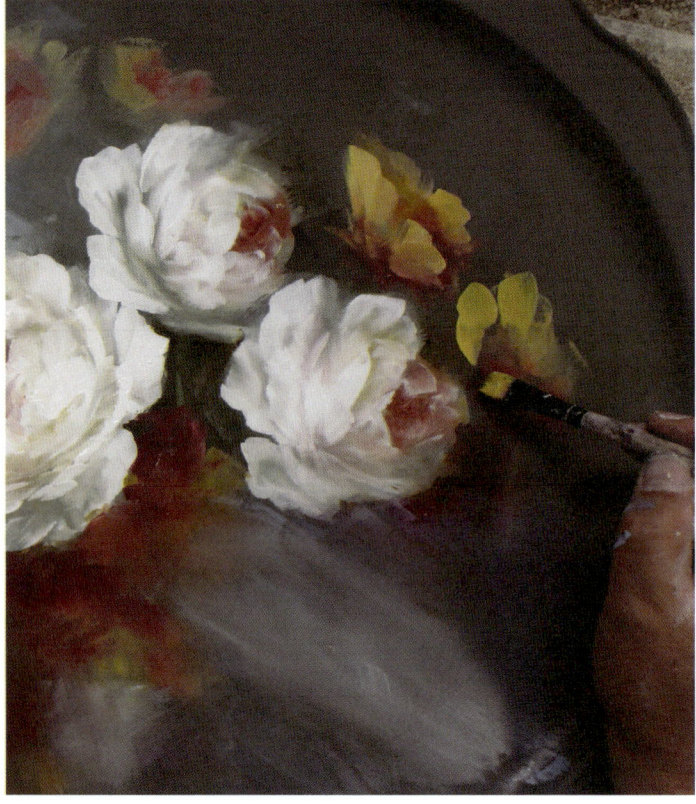

Step 39 Mottle the brush with the brighter Hansa Yellow and touch white. Begin to shape the petals of the blossoms. Let the outside edges stay soft and undefined.

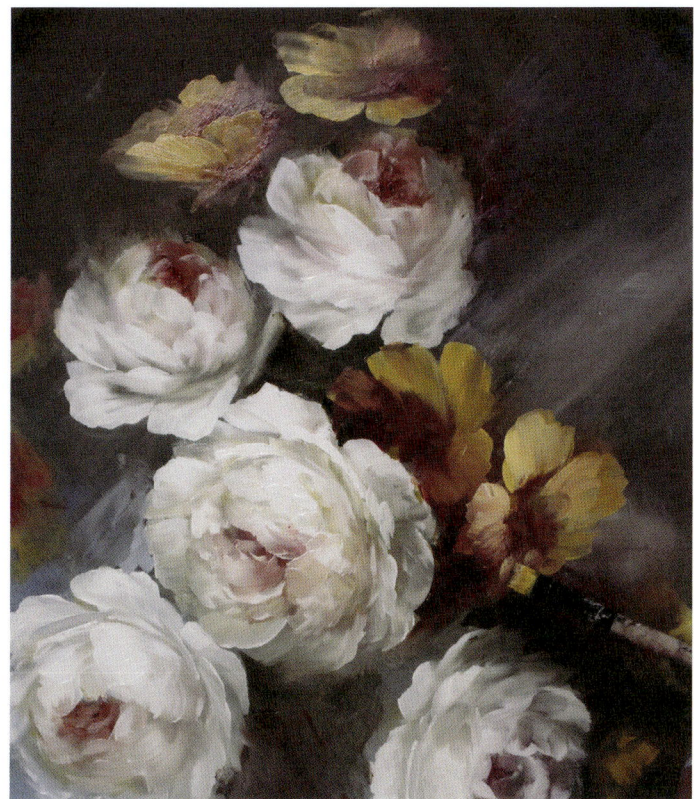

Step 40 Lighten the yellow with more white and add to the blossoms in the center of interest to increase their contrast. No lighter than the queen rose.

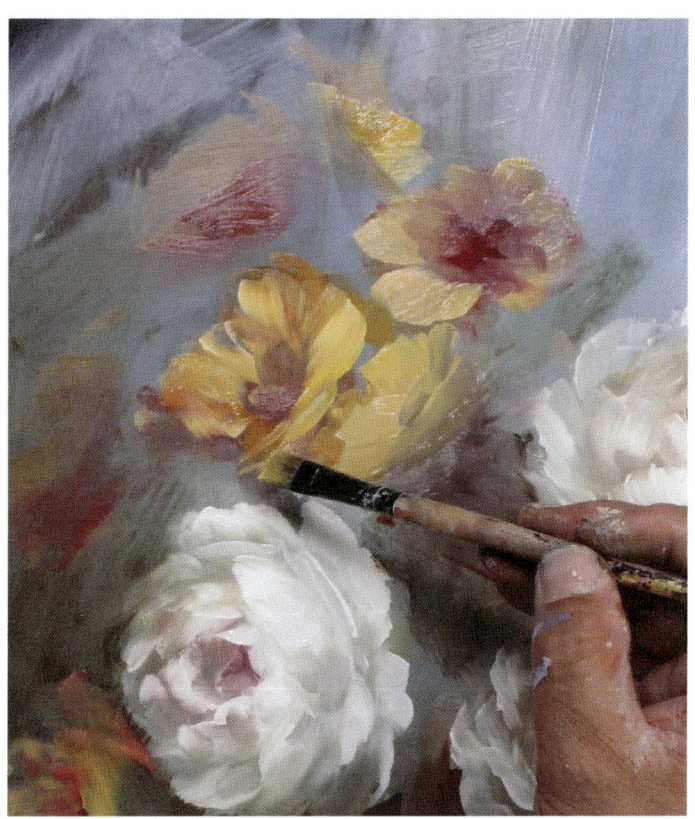

Step 41 Move the color in and out of the blossoms to create petal movement. You can soften the movement with your finger. Shear the edges.

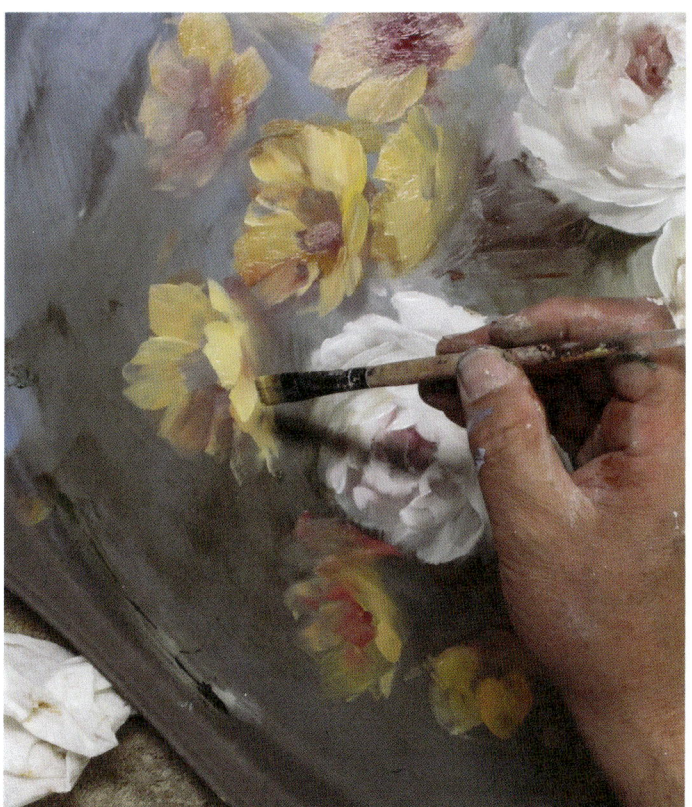

Step 42 Lighten the turned petals on some of the blossoms with more white. Stroke down toward the calyx of the flower. Lift off as you approach the shadows on the blossoms.

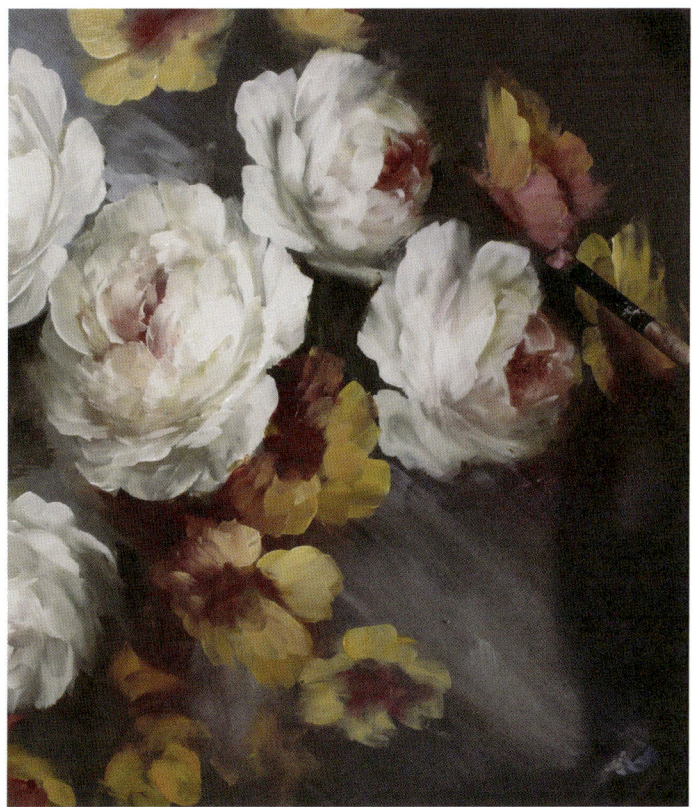

Step 43 Lighten the Red Violet on the blossoms with more white. Add to the light sides of the blossoms and into the transistions of the shadows. Not too light.

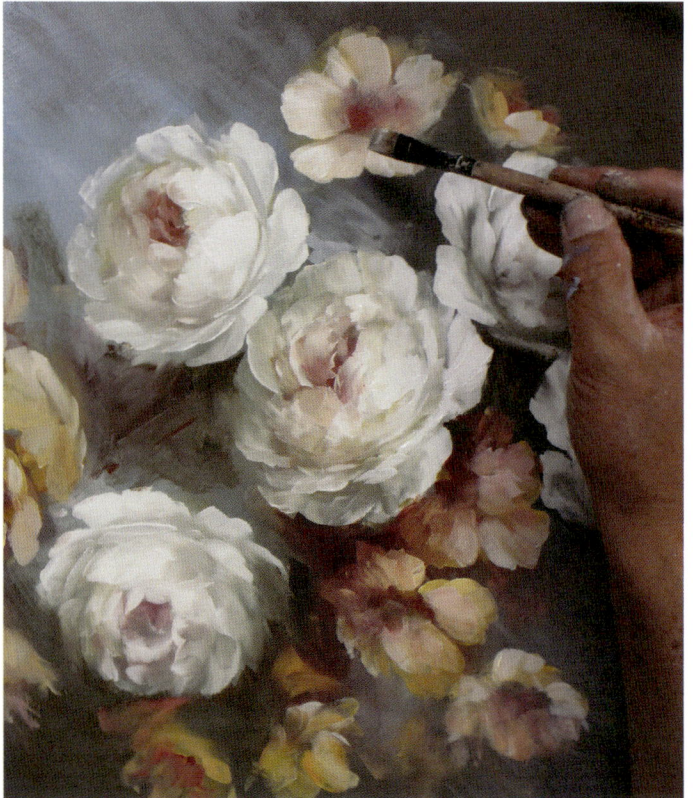

Step 44 Build more white on the blossoms that are closer to the queen rose. This will reinforce the light source. Soften the lights into the darker center of the blossom.

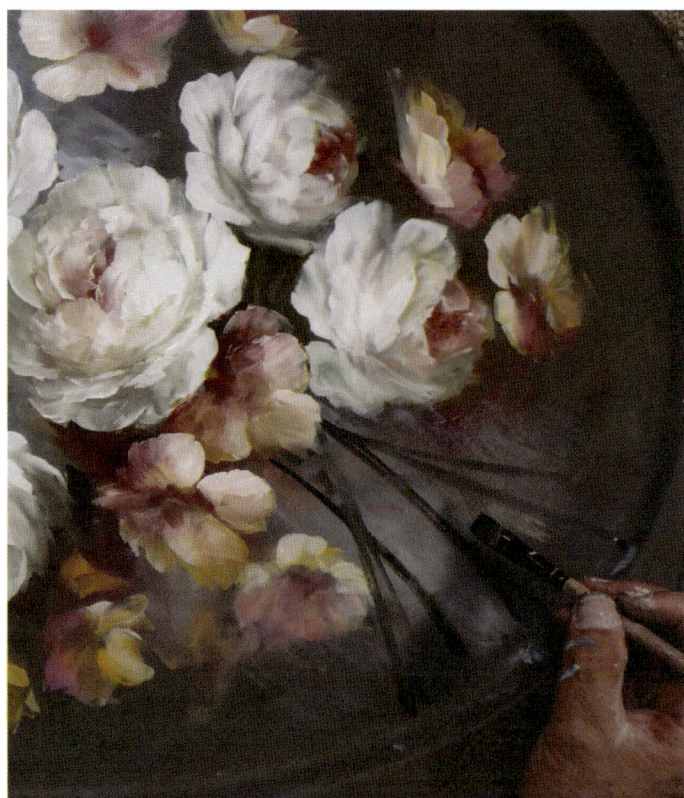

Step 45 Restate the steams of the composition with Pine Green, Burnt Sienna and cooled with Red Violet. Use the chisel of your brush.

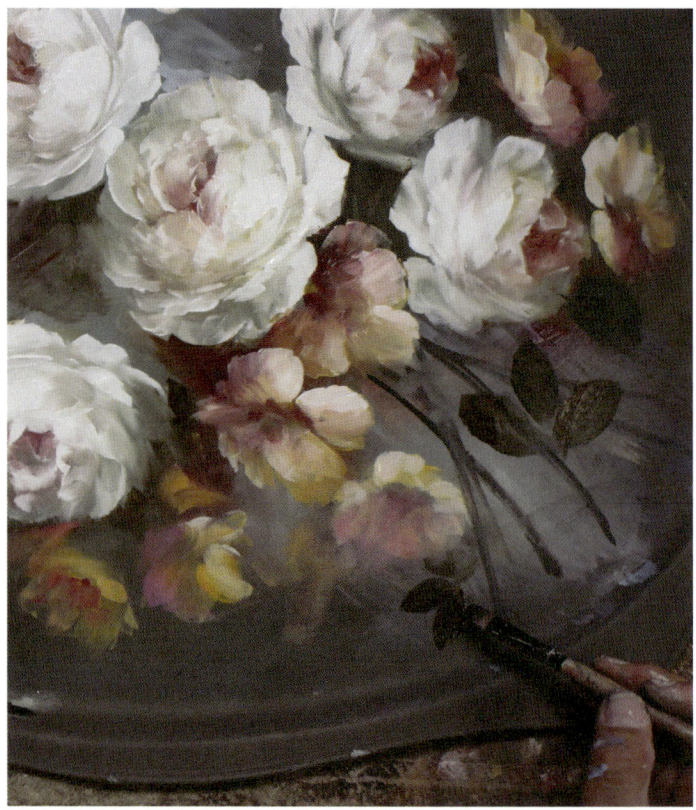

Step 46 Using the same cooler green color, begin to shape some leaves. I used the same leaf technique we did on the earlier lessons. Use 2 to 3 strokes and soften with finger.

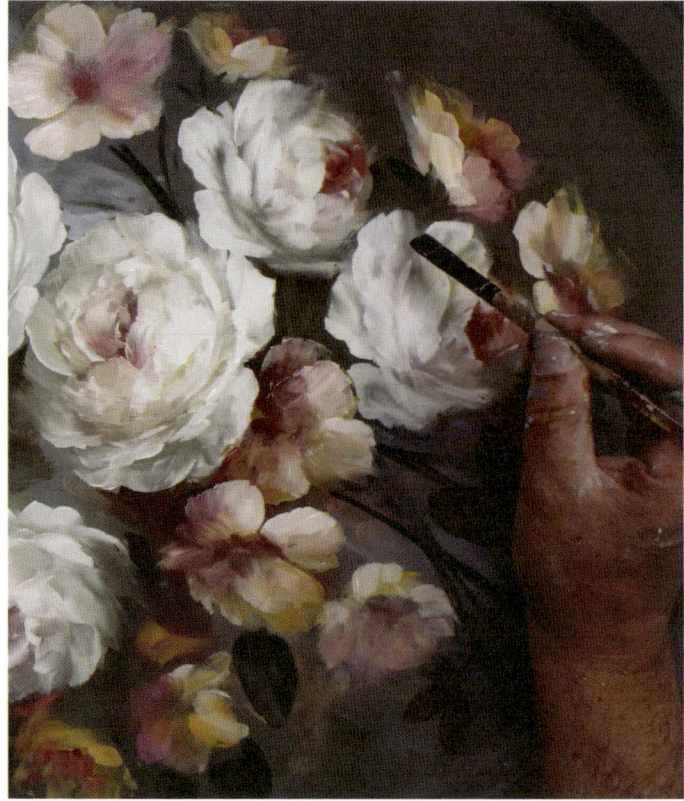

Step 47 Use more of the color to suggest back leaves around the roses and center of interest flowers.

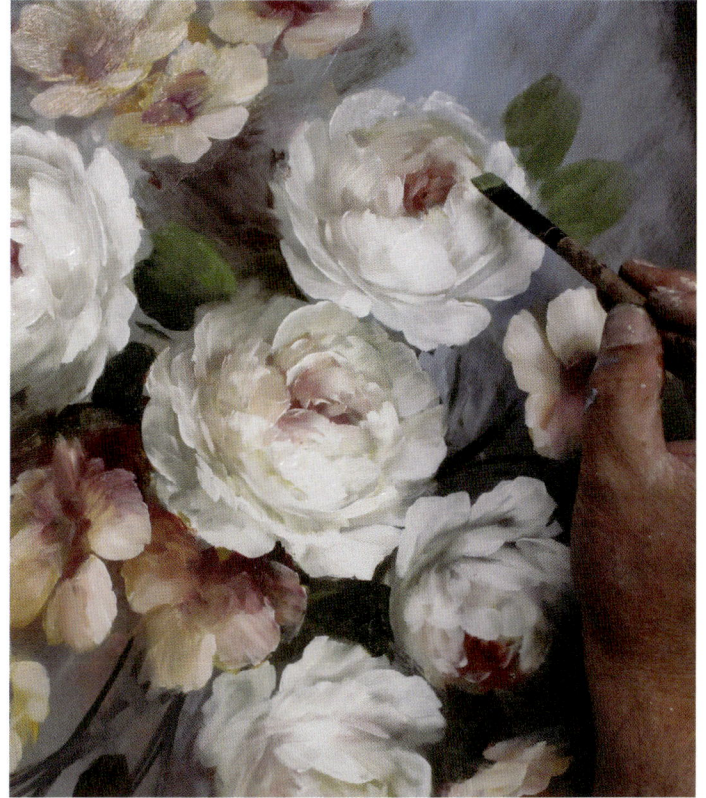

Step 48 Mottle a light green from Hansa and Pine Green. Lighten with touch white. Begin to lighten some of the leaves starting with the center of interest.

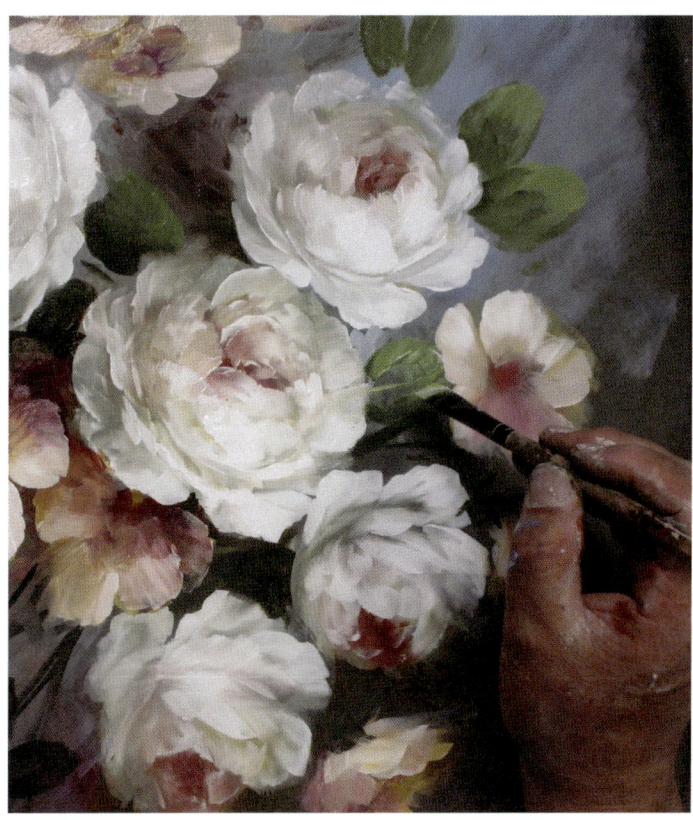

Step 49 Use the chisel of the brush to add vein lines and edges to the leaves in the center. This will give them more details and increase the contrast.

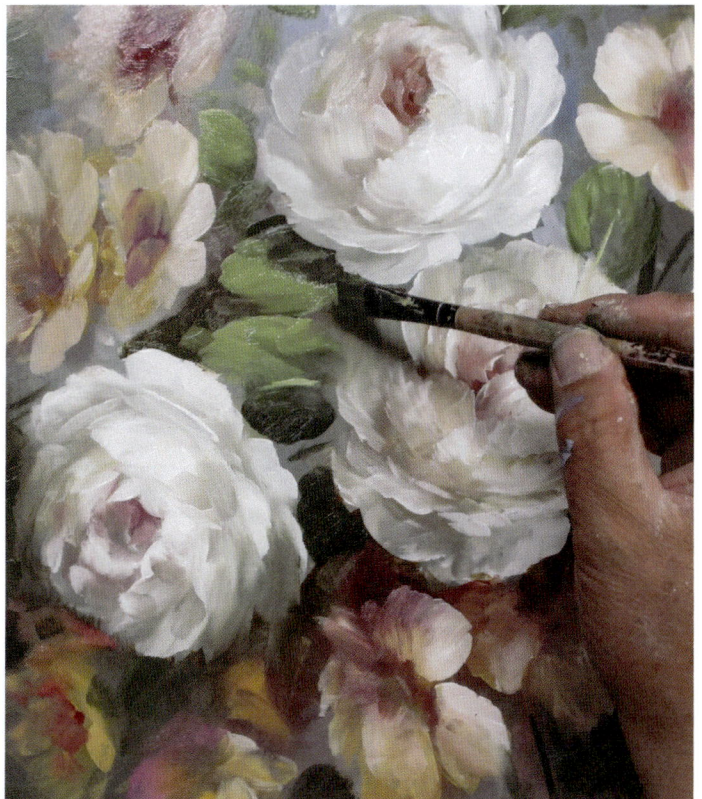

Step 50 Restate some of the shadows around the roses on the leaves with Pine Green cooled and darkened with Red Violet.

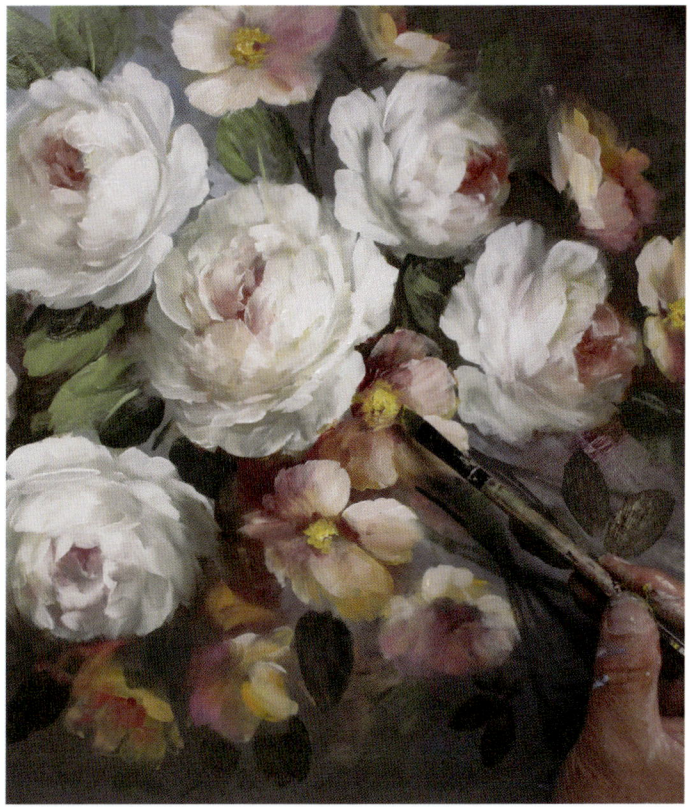

Step 51 Mottle the brush with Yellow Oxide and Hansa Yellow. Lighten with touch white. Tap into the centers of the blossoms letting the color soften as you head towards the petals.

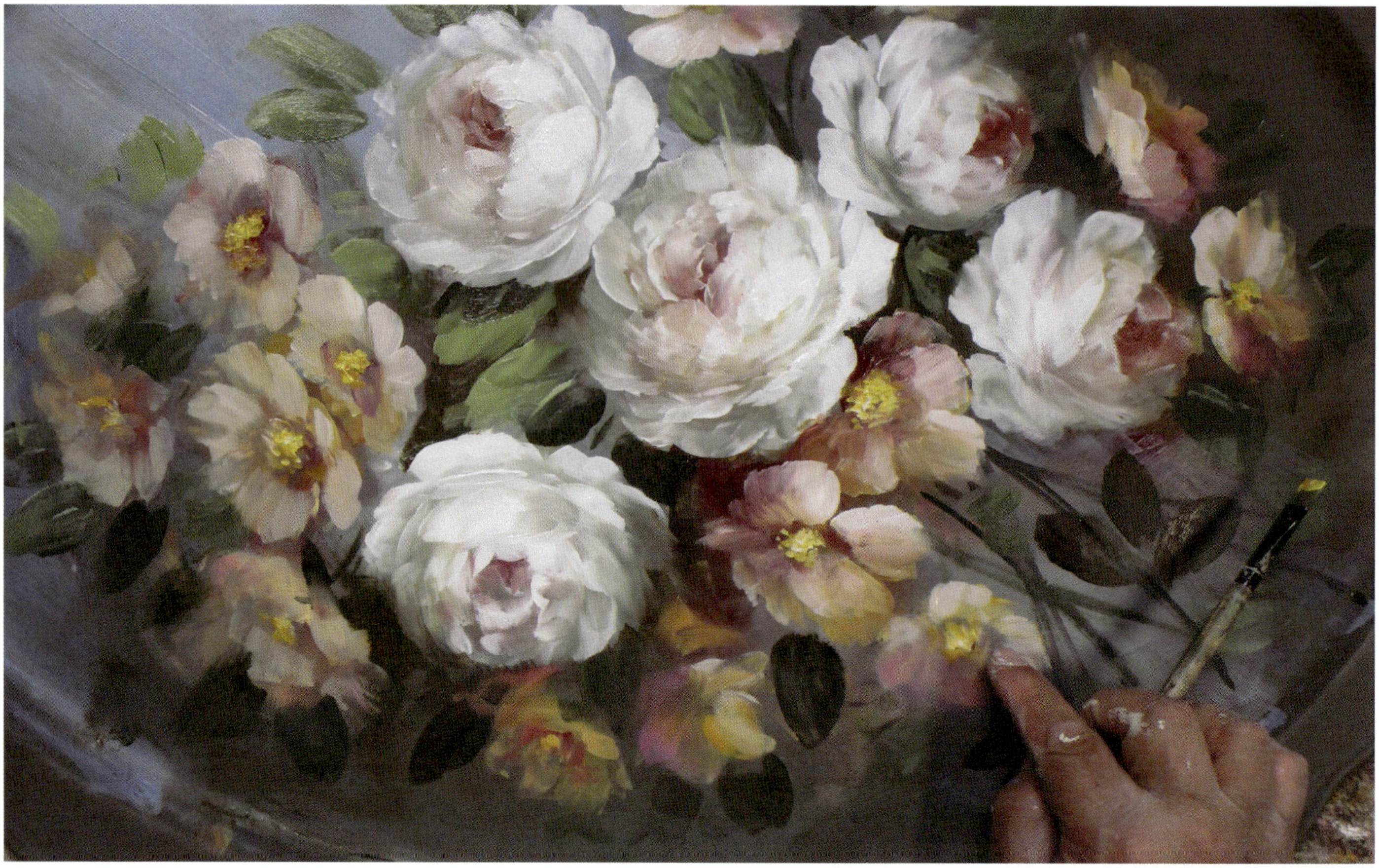

Step 52 Here I am using my finger to soften some of the centers further out on the tray. Keep the contrast on the center blossoms while the ones on the outside blur to keep soft.

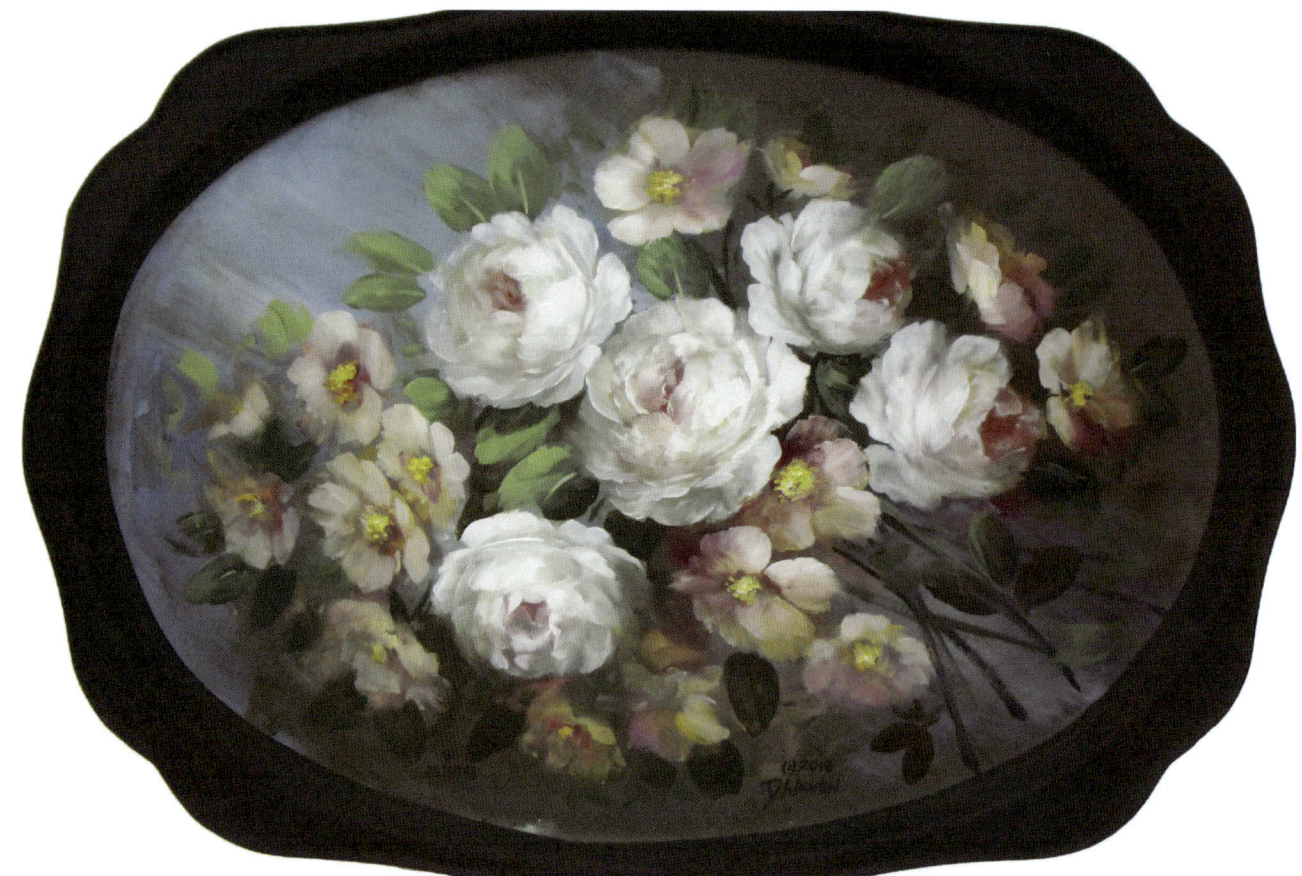

Step 53 I finished the tray with a dark toned blue trim. I felt this framed the tray well and also increased the contrast of the white roses. Love the movement in the background! Enjoy!

Lesson 5
Pattern

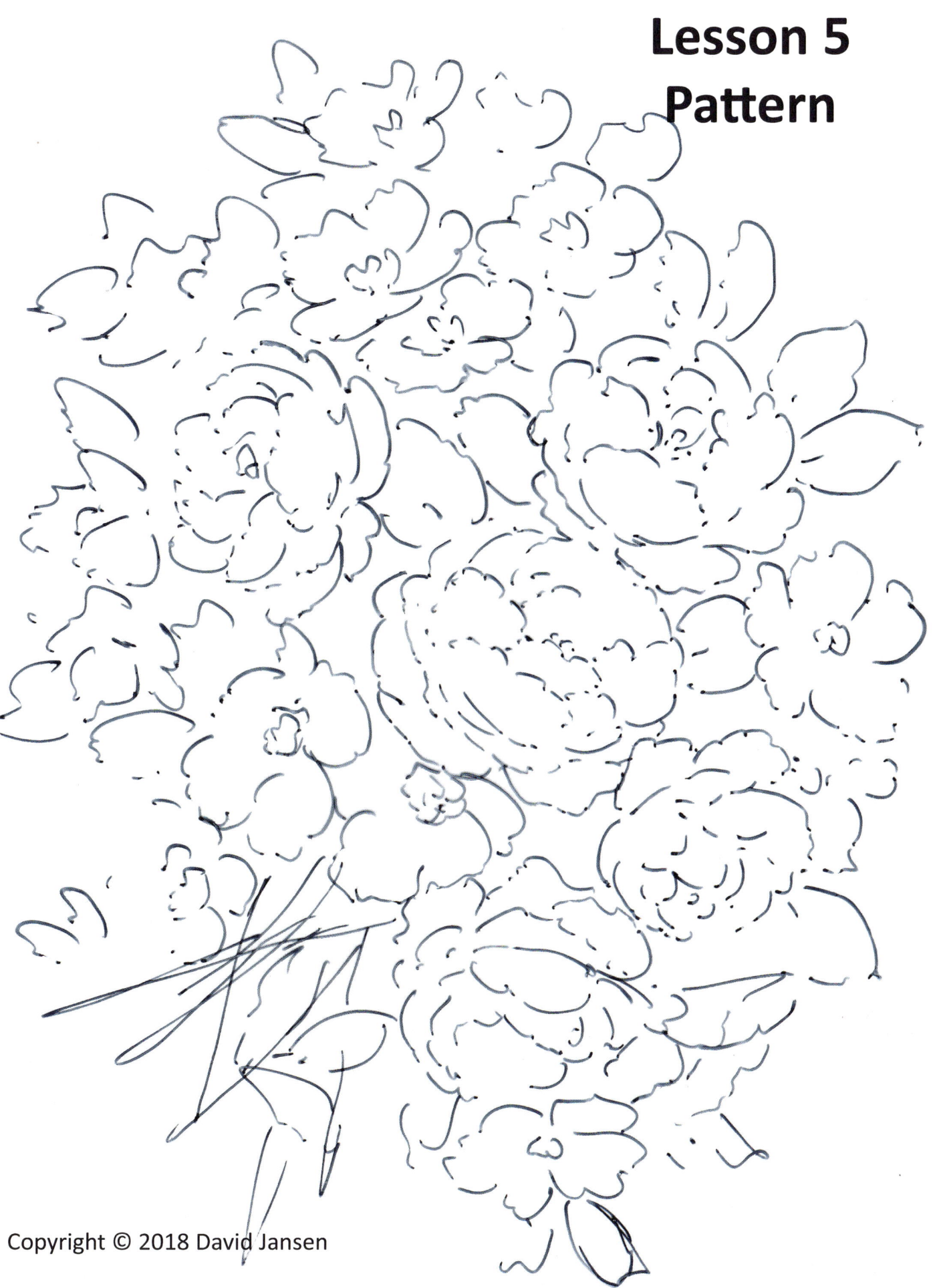

Printed in Great Britain
by Amazon